JAVA

IN A NUTSHELL

Sixth Edition

Benjamin J. Evans and David Flanagan

Beijing · Cambridge · Farnham ·

Java in a Nutshell

by Benjamin J. Evans and David Flanagan

Copyright © 2015 Benjamin J. Evans and David Flanagan. All rights reserved.

Printed in the United States of America.

Published by O'Reilly Media, Inc., 1005 Gravenstein Highway North, Sebastopol, CA 95472.

O'Reilly books may be purchased for educational, business, or sales promotional use. Online editions are also available for most titles (*http://www.safaribooksonline.com*). For more information, contact our corporate/institutional sales department: 800-998-9938 or *corporate@oreilly.com*.

Editors: Mike Loukides and Meghan Blanchette	**Indexer:** Ellen Troutman Zaig
Production Editor: Matthew Hacker	**Interior Designer:** David Futato
Copyeditor: Charles Roumeliotis	**Cover Designer:** Ellie Volckhausen
Proofreader: Jasmine Kwityn	**Illustrator:** Rebecca Demarest

February 1996: First Edition
May 1997: Second Edition
November 1999: Third Edition

March 2002: Fourth Edition
March 2005: Fifth Edition
October 2014: Sixth Edition

Revision History for the Sixth Edition
2014-10-10:   First Release

See *http://oreilly.com/catalog/errata.csp?isbn=9781449370824* for release details.

978-1-449-37082-4

[LSI]

This book is dedicated to all who teach peace and resist violence.

Table of Contents

Foreword. ix

Preface. xi

Part I.   Introducing Java

1. Introduction to the Java Environment. 3
The Language, the JVM, and the Ecosystem   3
A Brief History of Java and the JVM   7
The Lifecycle of a Java Program   9
Java Security   11
Comparing Java to Other Languages   11
Answering Some Criticisms of Java   13

2. Java Syntax from the Ground Up. 17
Java Programs from the Top Down   18
Lexical Structure   18
Primitive Data Types   22
Expressions and Operators   30
Statements   46
Methods   66
Introduction to Classes and Objects   72
Arrays   77
Reference Types   84
Packages and the Java Namespace   88
Java File Structure   93
Defining and Running Java Programs   94
Summary   95

3. Object-Oriented Programming in Java. 97
   Overview of Classes   97
   Fields and Methods   100
   Creating and Initializing Objects   106
   Subclasses and Inheritance   110
   Data Hiding and Encapsulation   121
   Abstract Classes and Methods   128
   Modifier Summary   132

4. The Java Type System. 135
   Interfaces   136
   Java Generics   142
   Enums and Annotations   151
   Nested Types   155
   Lambda Expressions   171
   Conclusion   174

5. Introduction to Object-Oriented Design in Java. 177
   Java Values   177
   Important Methods of java.lang.Object   178
   Aspects of Object-Oriented Design   183
   Exceptions and Exception Handling   193
   Safe Java Programming   195

6. Java's Approach to Memory and Concurrency. 197
   Basic Concepts of Java Memory Management   197
   How the JVM Optimizes Garbage Collection   201
   The HotSpot Heap   203
   Finalization   206
   Java's Support for Concurrency   208
   Working with Threads   218
   Summary   219

Part II.   Working with the Java Platform

7. Programming and Documentation Conventions. 223
   Naming and Capitalization Conventions   223
   Practical Naming   225
   Java Documentation Comments   226
   Conventions for Portable Programs   235

8. **Working with Java Collections.** **239**
    Introduction to Collections API   239
    Lambda Expressions in the Java Collections   258
    Conclusion   266

9. **Handling Common Data Formats.** **267**
    Text   267
    Numbers and Math   275
    Java 8 Date and Time   280
    Conclusion   287

10. **File Handling and I/O.** **289**
    Classic Java I/O   289
    Modern Java I/O   295
    NIO Channels and Buffers   298
    Async I/O   301
    Networking   304

11. **Classloading, Reflection, and Method Handles.** **311**
    Class Files, Class Objects, and Metadata   311
    Phases of Classloading   313
    Secure Programming and Classloading   315
    Applied Classloading   317
    Reflection   320
    Dynamic Proxies   325
    Method Handles   326

12. **Nashorn.** **331**
    Introduction to Nashorn   331
    Executing JavaScript with Nashorn   332
    Nashorn and javax.script   340
    Advanced Nashorn   342
    Conclusion   347

13. **Platform Tools and Profiles.** **349**
    Command-Line Tools   349
    VisualVM   362
    Java 8 Profiles   367
    Conclusion   372

Index. **373**

Foreword

In the winter of 2013–14, the United Kingdom was battered by an extended series of exceptionally violent winter storms. These storms uncovered shipwrecks and some amazing archaeology, especially in my home county of Cornwall. One of the most striking discoveries was a petrified forest, dating back to the end of the last Ice Age, now covered by the sea and sand. Before the sea claimed it again, I was lucky enough to visit it at very low tide and spend some hours exploring it.

Among the remaining roots and tree stumps and beds of organic matter on their way to becoming peat, I could still make out pieces of trunk branch and bark. As I wandered along the shore with the tide coming in, I came across a single hemisphere from a nut—from a tree that no longer grows in these latitudes. Despite being embedded in the organic layer, the shape of the nutshell and its ability to survive over long periods of time was still unmistakable.

In working on this new edition of David's classic text, I hope to have embodied the spirit of that prehistoric tree. If I have preserved the tenacious form and, crucially, the feel of *Java in a Nutshell*, while bringing it to the attention of a new generation of developers, with the important parts emphasized, then I shall be well satisfied.

—Ben Evans, 2014

Preface

This book is a desktop Java reference, designed to sit faithfully by your keyboard while you program. *Part I* of the book is a fast-paced, "no-fluff" introduction to the Java programming language and the core runtime aspects of the Java platform. *Part II* is a reference section that blends elucidation of core concepts with examples of important core APIs. The book covers Java 8, but we recognize that some shops may not have adopted it yet—so where possible we call out if a feature was introduced in Java 8 (and sometimes Java 7). We use Java 8 syntax throughout, including using lambda expressions in code that would previously have used a trivial anonymous nested class.

Changes in the Sixth Edition

The fifth edition of this book covers Java 5, whereas this edition covers Java 8. The language, and the working environment of the programmer, have both changed considerably since the last edition was published nearly a decade ago. This new edition has, accordingly, changed a vast amount as well. One very important aspect is that this book does not attempt to be as complete a description of the core platform APIs as was possible in earlier editions.

For one thing, the sheer size of the core APIs render this utterly impractical for a printed book. A more compelling reason is the continued rise of fast, always-on Internet. The amount of Java programmers who regularly work without Internet access is now vanishingly small. The proper place for detailed reference API docs is online, not printed out.

Accordingly, the reference section, which occupied two-thirds of the fifth edition, is gone. In the space we've recovered, we have tried to update the concept of what it means to be a "Nutshell" guide. The modern Java developer needs to know more than just syntax and APIs. As the Java environment has matured, such topics as concurrency, object-oriented design, memory, and the Java type system have all gained in importance—even among mainstream developers.

In this edition, we have tried to reflect this changed world, and have largely abandoned the historical approach of earlier editions. In particular, the exhaustive attempt to detail exactly which version of Java particular features arrived with has mostly been abandoned—only the most recent versions of Java are likely to be of interest to the majority of Java developers.

Contents of This Book

The first six chapters of this book document the Java language and the Java platform —they should all be considered essential reading. The book is biased toward the Oracle/OpenJDK (Open Java Development Kit) implementation of Java, but not greatly so—developers working with other Java environments will still find plenty to occupy them. *Part I* includes:

Chapter 1, Introduction
> This chapter is an overview of the Java language and the Java platform. It explains the important features and benefits of Java, including the lifecycle of a Java program. We also touch on Java security and answer some criticisms of Java.

Chapter 2, Java Syntax from the Ground Up
> This chapter explains the details of the Java programming language, including the Java 8 language changes. It is a long and detailed chapter that does not assume substantial programming experience. Experienced Java programmers can use it as a language reference. Programmers with substantial experience with languages such as C and C++ should be able to pick up Java syntax quickly by reading this chapter; beginning programmers with only a modest amount of experience should be able to learn Java programming by studying this chapter carefully, although it is best read in conjunction with a second text (such as O'Reilly's *Head First Java* by Bert Bates and Kathy Sierra).

Chapter 3, Object-Oriented Programming in Java
> This chapter describes how the basic Java syntax documented in *Chapter 2* is used to write simple object-oriented programs using classes and objects in Java. The chapter assumes no prior experience with OO programming. It can be used as a tutorial by new programmers or as a reference by experienced Java programmers.

Chapter 4, The Java Type System
> This chapter builds on the basic description of object-oriented programming in Java, and introduces the other aspects of Java's type system, such as generic types, enumerated types, and annotations. With this more complete picture, we can discuss the biggest change in Java 8—the arrival of lambda expressions.

Chapter 5, Introduction to Object-Oriented Design in Java
> This chapter is an overview of some basic techniques used in the design of sound object-oriented programs, and briefly touches on the topic of design patterns and their use in software engineering.

Chapter 6, Java's Approach to Memory and Concurrency

This chapter explains how the Java Virtual Machine manages memory on behalf of the programmer, and how memory and visibility is intimately entwined with Java's support for concurrent programming and threads.

These first six chapters teach you the Java language and get you up and running with the most important concepts of the Java platform. The second part of the book is all about how to get real programming work done in the Java environment. It contains plenty of examples and is designed to complement the cookbook approach found in some other texts. *Part II* includes:

Chapter 7, Programming and Documentation Conventions

This chapter documents important and widely adopted Java programming conventions. It also explains how you can make your Java code self-documenting by including specially formatted documentation comments.

Chapter 8, Working with Java Collections and Arrays

This chapter introduces Java's standard collections libraries. These contain data structures that are vital to the functioning of virtually every Java program—such as List, Map, and Set. The new Stream abstraction and the relationship between lambda expressions and the collections is explained in detail.

Chapter 9, Handling Common Data Formats

This chapter discusses how to use Java to work effectively with very common data formats, such as text, numbers, and temporal (date and time) information.

Chapter 10, File Handling and I/O

This chapter covers several different approaches to file access—from the more classic approach found in older versions of Java, through to more modern and even asynchronous styles. The chapter concludes with a short introduction to networking with the core Java platform APIs.

Chapter 11, Classloading, Reflection, and Method Handles

This chapter introduces the subtle art of metaprogramming in Java—first introducing the concept of metadata about Java types, then turning to the subject of classloading and how Java's security model is linked to the dynamic loading of types. The chapter concludes with some applications of classloading and the relatively new feature of method handles.

Chapter 12, Nashorn

This chapter describes Nashorn, an implementation of JavaScript running atop the Java Virtual Machine. Nashorn ships with Java 8, and provides an alternative to other JavaScript implementations. Toward the end of the chapter, we discuss Avatar.js—a server-side technology compatible with Node.

Chapter 13, Platform Tools and Profiles

Oracle's JDK (as well as OpenJDK) includes a number of useful Java development tools, most notably the Java interpreter and the Java compiler. This chapter documents those tools. The second part of the chapter covers

Compact Profiles—a new feature in Java 8 allowing cut-down Java Runtime Environments (JREs) with a significantly reduced footprint.

Related Books

O'Reilly publishes an entire series of books on Java programming, including several companion books to this one. The companion books are:

Learning Java by Pat Niemeyer and Daniel Leuck

> This book is a comprehensive tutorial introduction to Java, and includes topics such as XML and client-side Java programming.

Java 8 Lambdas by Richard Warburton

> This book documents the new Java 8 feature of lambda expressions in detail, and introduces concepts of functional programming that may be unfamiliar to Java developers coming from earlier versions.

Head First Java by Bert Bates and Kathy Sierra

> This book uses a unique approach to teaching Java. Developers who think visually often find it a great accompaniment to a traditional Java book.

You can find a complete list of Java books from O'Reilly at *http://java.oreilly.com/*.

Examples Online

The examples in this book are available online and can be downloaded from the home page for the book at *http://www.oreilly.com/catalog/javanut6*. You may also want to visit this site for any important notes or errata that have been published there.

Conventions Used in This Book

We use the following formatting conventions in this book:

Italic

> Used for emphasis and to signify the first use of a term. Italic is also used for commands, email addresses, websites, FTP sites, and file and directory names.

Constant Width

> Used for all Java code as well as for anything that you would type literally when programming, including keywords, data types, constants, method names, variables, class names, and interface names.

Constant Width Italic

> Used for the names of function arguments and generally as a placeholder to indicate an item that should be replaced with an actual value in your program.

Sometimes used to refer to a conceptual section or line of code as in *statement*.

 This element signifies a tip or suggestion.

 This element signifies a general note.

 This element indicates a warning or caution.

Request for Comments

You can send comments, fixes and suggestions directly to the authors by using the email address *javanut6@gmail.com*.

Please address comments and questions concerning this book to the publisher:

O'Reilly Media, Inc.
1005 Gravenstein Highway North
Sebastopol, CA 95472
800-998-9938 (in the United States or Canada)
707-829-0515 (international or local)
707-829-0104 (fax)

We have a web page for this book, where we list errata, examples, and any additional information. You can access this page at *http://bit.ly/java_nutshell_6e*.

To comment or ask technical questions about this book, send email to *bookquestions@oreilly.com*.

For more information about our books, courses, conferences, and news, see our website at *http://www.oreilly.com*.

Find us on Facebook: *http://facebook.com/oreilly*

Follow us on Twitter: *http://twitter.com/oreillymedia*

Watch us on YouTube: *http://www.youtube.com/oreillymedia*

Safari® Books Online

 *Safari Books Online* is an on-demand digital library that delivers expert *content* in both book and video form from the world's leading authors in technology and business.

Technology professionals, software developers, web designers, and business and creative professionals use Safari Books Online as their primary resource for research, problem solving, learning, and certification training.

Safari Books Online offers a range of *plans and pricing* for *enterprise, government, education*, and individuals.

Members have access to thousands of books, training videos, and prepublication manuscripts in one fully searchable database from publishers like O'Reilly Media, Prentice Hall Professional, Addison-Wesley Professional, Microsoft Press, Sams, Que, Peachpit Press, Focal Press, Cisco Press, John Wiley & Sons, Syngress, Morgan Kaufmann, IBM Redbooks, Packt, Adobe Press, FT Press, Apress, Manning, New Riders, McGraw-Hill, Jones & Bartlett, Course Technology, and hundreds *more*. For more information about Safari Books Online, please visit us *online*.

Acknowledgments

Meghan Blanchette was the editor of the sixth edition—her attention to detail and cheerful, grounded approach helped provide extra momentum at very useful moments throughout the book's development.

Special thanks are due to Jim Gough, Richard Warburton, John Oliver, Trisha Gee, and Stephen Colebourne.

As always, Martijn Verburg has been a good friend, business partner, sounding board, and font of useful advice.

Ben, in particular, would like to thank everyone who has given him feedback and helped him improve as a writer. Caroline Kvitka, Victor Grazi, Tori Weildt, and Simon Ritter deserve special mention for their helpful suggestions. If he's failed to take all of their excellent advice in this text the blame is, of course, his.

I

Introducing Java

Part I is an introduction to the Java language and the Java platform. These chapters provide enough information for you to get started using Java right away:

Chapter 1, Introduction
Chapter 2, Java Syntax from the Ground Up
Chapter 3, Object-Oriented Programming in Java
Chapter 4, The Java Type System
Chapter 5, Introduction to Object-Oriented Design in Java
Chapter 6, Java's Approach to Memory and Concurrency

Introduction to the Java Environment

Welcome to Java 8. We may be welcoming you back. You may be coming to this eco-system from another language, or maybe this is your first programming language. Whatever road you may have traveled to get here: welcome. We're glad you've arrived.

Java is a powerful, general-purpose programming environment. It is one of the most widely used programming languages in the world, and has been exceptionally successful in business and enterprise computing.

In this chapter, we'll set the scene by describing the Java language (which programmers write their applications in), the Java Virtual Machine (which executes those applications), and the Java ecosystem (which provides a lot of the value of the programming environment to development teams).

We'll briefly cover the history of the Java language and virtual machine, before moving on to discuss the lifecycle of a Java program and clear up some common questions about the differences between Java and other environments.

At the end of the chapter, we'll introduce Java security, and discuss some of the aspects of Java which relate to secure coding.

The Language, the JVM, and the Ecosystem

The Java programming environment has been around since the late 1990s. It comprises the Java language, and the supporting runtime, otherwise known as the Java Virtual Machine (JVM).

At the time that Java was initially developed, this split was considered novel, but recent trends in software development have made it more commonplace. Notably,

Microsoft's .NET environment, announced a few years after Java, adopted a very similar approach to platform architecture.

One important difference between Microsoft's .NET platform and Java is that Java was always conceived as a relatively open ecosystem of multiple vendors. Throughout Java's history, these vendors both cooperated and competed on aspects of Java technology.

One of the main reasons for the success of Java is that this ecosystem is a standardized environment. This means there are specifications for the technologies that comprise the environment. These standards give the developer and consumer confidence that the technology will be compatible with other components, even if they come from a different technology vendor.

The current steward of Java is Oracle Corporation (who acquired Sun Microsystems, the originator of Java). Other corporations, such as Red Hat, IBM, Hewlett-Packard, SAP, Apple, and Fujitsu are also heavily involved in producing implementations of standardized Java technologies.

There is also an open source version of Java, called OpenJDK, which many of these companies collaborate on.

Java actually comprises several different, but related environments and specifications—Java Mobile Edition (Java ME), Java Standard Edition (Java SE), and Java Enterprise Edition (Java EE). In this book, we'll only cover Java SE, version 8.

We will have more to say about standardization later, so let's move on to discuss the Java language and JVM as separate, but related concepts.

What Is the Java Language?

Java programs are written as source code in the Java language. This is a human-readable programming language, which is class based and object oriented. It is considered to be relatively easy to read and write (if occasionally a bit verbose).

Java is intended to be easy to learn and to teach. It builds on industry experience with languages like C++ and tries to remove complex features as well as preserving "what works" from previous programming languages.

Overall, Java is intended to provide a stable, solid base for companies to develop business-critical applications.

As a programming language, it has a relatively conservative design and a slow rate of change. These properties are a conscious attempt to serve the goal of protecting the investment that businesses have made in Java technology.

The language has undergone gradual revision (but no complete rewrites) since its inception in 1996. This does mean that some of Java's original design choices, which were expedient in the late 1990s, are still affecting the language today—see Chapters 2 and 3 for more details.

Java 8 has added the most radical changes seen in the language for almost a decade (some would say since the birth of Java). Features like lambda expressions and the overhaul of the core Collections code will change forever the way that most Java developers write code.

The Java language is governed by the Java Language Specification (JLS), which defines how a conforming implementation must behave.

What Is the JVM?

The JVM is a program that provides the runtime environment necessary for Java programs to execute. Java programs cannot run unless there is a JVM available for the appropriate hardware and OS platform we wish to execute on.

Fortunately, the JVM has been ported to run on a large number of environments—anything from a set-top box or Blu-ray player to a huge mainframe will probably have a JVM available for it.

Java programs are typically started by a command line, such as:

```
java <arguments> <program name>
```

This brings up the JVM as an operating system process that provides the Java runtime environment, and then executes our program in the context of the freshly started (and empty) virtual machine.

It is important to understand that when the JVM takes in a Java program for execution, the program is not provided as Java language source code. Instead, the Java language source must have been converted (or compiled) into a form known as Java bytecode. Java bytecode must be supplied to the JVM in a format called class files—which always have a *.class* extension.

The JVM is an interpreter for the bytecode form of the program—it steps through one bytecode instruction at a time. However, you should also be aware that both the JVM and the user program are capable of spawning additional threads of execution, so that a user program may have many different functions running simultenously.

The design of the JVM built on many years of experience with earlier programming environments, notably C and C++, so we can think of it as having several different goals—which are all intended to make life easier for the programmer:

- Comprise a container for application code to run inside
- Provide a secure execution environment as compared to C/C++
- Take memory management out of the hands of developers
- Provide a cross-platform execution environment

These objectives are often mentioned together when discussing the platform.

We've already mentioned the first of these goals, when we discussed the JVM and its bytecode interpreter—it functions as the container for application code.

We'll discuss the second and third goals in Chapter 6, when we talk about how the Java environment deals with memory management.

The fourth goal, sometimes called "write once, run anywhere" (WORA), is the property that Java class files can be moved from one execution platform to another, and they will run unaltered provided a JVM is available.

This means that a Java program can be developed (and converted to class files) on an Apple Mac machine running OS X, and then the class files can be moved to Linux or Microsoft Windows (or other platforms) and the Java program will run without any further work needed.

 The Java environment has been very widely ported, including to platforms that are very different from mainstream platforms like Linux, Mac, and Windows. In this book, we use the phrase "most implementations" to indicate those platforms that the majority of developers are likely to encounter. Mac, Windows, Linux, Solaris, BSD Unix, AIX, and the like are all considered "mainstream platforms" and count within "most implementations."

In addition to these four primary goals, there is another aspect of the JVM's design that is not always recognized or discussed—it makes use of runtime information to self-manage.

Software research in the 1970s and 1980s revealed that the runtime behavior of programs has a large amount of interesting and useful patterns that cannot be deduced at compile time. The JVM was the first truly mainstream platform to make use of this research.

It collects runtime information to make better decisions about how to execute code. That means that the JVM can monitor and optimize a program running on it in a manner not possible for platforms without this capability.

A key example is the runtime fact that not all parts of a Java program are equally likely to be called during the lifetime of the program—some portions will be called far, far more often than others. The Java platform takes advantage of this fact with a technology called just-in-time (JIT) compilation.

In the HotSpot JVM (which was the JVM that Sun first shipped as part of Java 1.3, and is still in use today), the JVM first identifies which parts of the program are called most often—the "hot methods." Then, the JVM compiles these hot methods directly into machine code—bypassing the JVM interpreter.

The JVM uses the available runtime information to deliver higher performance than was possible from purely interpreted execution. In fact, the optimizations that the JVM uses now in many cases produce performance which surpasses compiled C and C++ code.

The standard that describes how a properly functioning JVM must behave is called the JVM Specification.

What Is the Java Ecosystem?

The Java language is easy to learn and contains relatively few abstractions, compared to other programming languages. The JVM provides a solid, portable, high-performance base for Java (or other languages) to execute on. Taken together, these two connected technologies provide a foundation that businesses can feel confident about when choosing where to base their development efforts.

The benefits of Java do not end there, however. Since Java's inception, an extremely large ecosystem of third-party libraries and components has grown up. This means that a development team can benefit hugely from the existence of connectors and drivers for practically every technology imaginable—both proprietary and open source.

In the modern technology ecosystem it is now rare indeed to find a technology component that does *not* offer a Java connector. From traditional relational databases, to NoSQL, to every type of enterprise monitoring system, to messaging systems —everything integrates with Java.

It is this fact that has been a major driver of adoption of Java technologies by enterprises and larger companies. Development teams have been able to unlock their potential by making use of preexisting libraries and components. This has promoted developer choice and encouraged open, best-of-breed architectures with Java technology cores.

A Brief History of Java and the JVM

Java 1.0 (1996)
> This was the first public version of Java. It contained just 212 classes organized in eight packages. The Java platform has always had an emphasis on backward compatibility, and code written with Java 1.0 will still run today on Java 8 without modification or recompilation.

Java 1.1 (1997)
> This release of Java more than doubled the size of the Java platform. This release introduced "inner classes" and the first version of the Reflection API.

Java 1.2 (1998)
> This was a very significant release of Java; it tripled the size of the Java platform. This release marked the first appearance of the Java Collections API (with sets, maps, and lists). The many new features in the 1.2 release led Sun to rebrand the platform as "the Java 2 Platform." The term "Java 2" was simply a trademark, however, and not an actual version number for the release.

Java 1.3 (2000)

This was primarily a maintenance release, focused on bug fixes, stability, and performance improvements. This release also brought in the HotSpot Java Virtual Machine, which is still in use today (although heavily modified and improved since then).

Java 1.4 (2002)

This was another fairly big release, adding important new functionality such as a higher-performance, low-level I/O API; regular expressions for text handling; XML and XSLT libraries; SSL support; a logging API; and cryptography support.

Java 5 (2004)

This large release of Java introduced a number of changes to the core language itself including generic types, enumerated types (enums), annotations, varargs methods, autoboxing, and a new for loop. These changes were considered significant enough to change the major version number, and to start numbering as major releases. This release included 3,562 classes and interfaces in 166 packages. Notable additions included utilities for concurrent programming, a remote management framework, and classes for the remote management and instrumentation of the Java VM itself.

Java 6 (2006)

This release was also largely a maintenance and performance release. It introduced the Compiler API, expanded the usage and scope of annotations, and provided bindings to allow scripting languages to interoperate with Java. There were also a large number of internal bugfixes and improvements to the JVM and the Swing GUI technology.

Java 7 (2011)

The first release of Java under Oracle's stewardship included a number of major upgrades to the language and platform. The introduction of try-with-resources and the NIO.2 API enabled developers to write much safer and less error-prone code for handling resources and I/O. The Method Handles API provided a simpler and safer alternative to reflection—and opened the door for invokedynamic (the first new bytecode since version 1.0 of Java).

Java 8 (2014)

This latest release of Java introduces potentially the most significant changes to the language since Java 5 (or possibly ever). The introduction of lambda expressions promises the ability to significantly enhance the productivity of developers; the Collections have been updated to make use of lambdas, and the machinery required to achieve this provides a fundamental change in Java's approach to object orientation. Other major updates include an implementation of JavaScript that runs on the JVM (Nashorn), new date and time support, and Java profiles (which provide for different versions of Java that are especially suitable for headless or server deployments).

The Lifecycle of a Java Program

To better understand how Java code is compiled and executed, and the difference between Java and other types of programming environments, consider the pipeline in Figure 1-1.

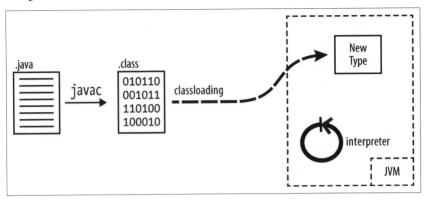

Figure 1-1. How Java code is compiled and loaded

This starts wth Java source, and passes it through the `javac` program to produce class files—which contain the source code compiled to Java bytecode. The class file is the smallest unit of functionality the platform will deal with, and the only way to get new code into a running program.

New class files are onboarded via the classloading mechanism (see Chapter 10 for a lot more detail on how classloading works). This makes the new type available to the interpreter for execution.

Frequently Asked Questions

In this section, we'll discuss some of the most frequently asked questions about Java and the lifecycle of programs written in the Java environment.

What is bytecode?

When developers are first introduced to the JVM, they sometimes think of it as "a computer inside a computer." It's then easy to imagine bytecode as "machine code for the CPU of the internal computer" or "machine code for a made-up processor."

In fact, bytecode is not very similar to machine code that would run on a real hardware processor. Computer scientists would call bytecode a type of "intermediate representation"—a halfway house between source code and machine code.

The whole aim of bytecode is to be a format that can be executed efficiently by the JVM's interpreter.

Is javac a compiler?

Compilers usually produce machine code, but javac produces bytecode, which is not that similar to machine code. However, class files are a bit like object files (like Windows *.dll* files, or Unix *.so* files)—and they are certainly not human readable.

In theoretical computer science terms, javac is most similar to the "front half" of a compiler—it creates the intermediate representation that can then be used to produce (emit) machine code.

However, because creation of class files is a separate build-time step that resembles compilation in C/C++, many developers consider running javac to be compilation. In this book, we will use the terms "source code compiler" or "javac compiler" to mean the production of class files by javac.

We will reserve "compilation" as a standalone term to mean JIT compilation—as it's JIT compilation that actually produces machine code.

Why is it called "bytecode"?

The instruction code (opcode) is just a single byte (some operations also have parameters that follow them in the bytestream)—so there are only 256 possible instructions. In practice, some are unused—about 200 are in use, but some of them aren't emitted by recent versions of javac.

Is bytecode optimized?

In the early days of the platform, javac produced heavily optimized bytecode. This turned out to be a mistake. With the advent of JIT compilation, the important methods are going to be compiled to very fast machine code. It's therefore very important to make the job of the JIT compiler easier—as there are much bigger gains available from JIT compilation than there are from optimizing bytecode, which will still have to be interpreted.

Is bytecode really machine independent? What about things like endianness?

The format of bytecode is always the same, regardless of what type of machine it was created on. This includes the byte ordering (sometimes called "endianness") of the machine. For readers who are interested in the details, bytecode is always big-endian.

Is Java an interpreted language?

The JVM is basically an interpreter (with JIT compilation to give it a big performance boost). However, most interpreted languages (such as PHP, Perl, Ruby, and Python) directly interpret programs from source form (usually by constructing an abstract syntax tree from the input source file). The JVM interpreter, on the other hand, requires class files—which, of course, require a separate source code compilation step with javac.

Can other languages run on the JVM?

Yes. The JVM can run any valid class file, so this means that non-Java languages can run on the JVM in one of two ways. Firstly, they could have a source code compiler (similar to javac) that produces class files, which would run on the JVM just like Java code (this is the approach taken by languages like Scala).

Alternatively, a non-Java language could implement an interpreter and runtime in Java, and then interpret the source form of their language. This second option is the approach taken by languages like JRuby (but JRuby has a very sophisticated runtime that is capable of "secondary JIT compilation" in some circumstances).

Java Security

Java has been designed from the ground up with security in mind; this gives it a great advantage over many other existing systems and platforms. The Java security architecture was designed by security experts and has been studied and probed by many other security experts since the inception of the platform. The consensus is that the architecture itself is strong and robust, without any security holes in the design (at least none that have been discovered yet).

Fundamental to the design of the security model is that bytecode is heavily restricted in what it can express—there is no way, for example, to directly address memory. This cuts out entire classes of security problems that have plagued languages like C and C++. Furthermore, the VM goes through a process known as *bytecode verification* whenever it loads an untrusted class, which removes a further large class of problems (see Chapter 10 for more about bytecode verification).

Despite all this, however, no system can guarantee 100% security, and Java is no exception.

While the design is still theoretically robust, the implementation of the security architecture is another matter, and there is a long history of security flaws being found and patched in particular implementations of Java.

In particular, the release of Java 8 was delayed, at least partly, due to the discovery of a number of security problems that required considerable effort to fix.

In all likelihood, security flaws will continue to be discovered (and patched) in Java VM implementations.

However, it is also worth noting that the majority of Java's recent security issues have been closely linked to Java as a desktop technology. For practical server-side coding, Java remains perhaps the most secure general-purpose platform currently available.

Comparing Java to Other Languages

In this section, we'll briefly highlight some differences between the Java platform and other programming environments you may be familiar with.

Java Compared to C

- Java is object oriented; C is procedural.
- Java is portable as class files; C needs to be recompiled.
- Java provides extensive instrumentation as part of the runtime.
- Java has no pointers and no equivalent of pointer arithmetic.
- Java provides automatic memory management via garbage collection.
- Java has no ability to lay out memory at a low level (no structs).
- Java has no preprocessor.

Java Compared to C++

- Java has a simplified object model compared to C++.
- Java's dispatch is virtual by default.
- Java is always pass-by-value (but one of the possibilities for Java's values are object references).
- Java does not support full multiple inheritance.
- Java's generics are less powerful (but also less dangerous) than C++ templates.
- Java has no operator overloading.

Java Compared to PHP

- Java is statically typed; PHP is dynamically typed.
- Java has a JIT; PHP does not (but might in version 6).
- Java is a general-purpose language; PHP is rarely found outside of websites.
- Java is multithreaded; PHP is not.

Java Compared to JavaScript

- Java is statically typed; JavaScript is dynamically typed.
- Java uses class-based objects; JavaScript is prototype based.
- Java provides good object encapsulation; Javascript does not.
- Java has namespaces; JavaScript does not.
- Java is multithreaded; JavaScript is not.

Answering Some Criticisms of Java

Java has had a long history in the public eye and, as such, has attracted its fair share of criticism over the years. Some of this negative press can be attributed to some technical shortcomings combined with rather overzealous marketing in the first versions of Java.

Some criticisms have, however, entered technical folklore despite no longer being very accurate. In this section, we'll look at some common grumbles and the extent to which they're true for modern versions of the platform.

Overly Verbose

The Java core language has sometimes been criticized as overly verbose. Even simple Java statments such as `Object o = new Object();` seem to be repetitious—the type `Object` appears on both the left and right side of the assignment. Critics point out that this is essentially redundant, that other languages do not need this duplication of type information, and that many support features (e.g., type inference) that remove it.

The counterpoint to this argument is that Java was designed from the start to be easy to read (code is read more often than written) and that many programmers, especially novices, find the extra type information helpful when reading code.

Java is widely used in enterprise environments, which often have separate dev and ops teams. The extra verbosity can often be a blessing when responding to an outage call, or when needing to maintain and patch code that was written by developers who have long since moved on.

In recent versions of Java (7 and later), the language designers have attempted to respond to some of these points, by finding places where the syntax can become less verbose and by making better use of type information. For example:

```
// Files helper methods
byte[] contents =
  Files.readAllBytes(Paths.get("/home/ben/myFile.bin"));

// Diamond syntax for repeated type information
List<String> l = new ArrayList<>();

// Lambda expressions simplify Runnables
ExecutorService threadPool = Executors.newScheduledThreadPool(2);
threadPool.submit(() -> { System.out.println("On Threadpool"); });
```

However, Java's overall philosophy is to make changes to the language only very slowly and carefully, so the pace of these changes may not satsify detractors completely.

Slow to Change

The original Java language is now well over 15 years old, and has not undergone a complete revision in that time. Many other languages (e.g., Microsoft's C#) have released backwards-incompatible versions in the same period—and some developers criticize Java for not doing likewise.

Furthermore, in recent years, the Java language has come under fire for being slow to adopt language features that are now commonplace in other languages.

The conservative approach to language design that Sun (and now Oracle) have displayed is an attempt to avoid imposing the costs and externalities of misfeatures on a very large user base. Many Java shops have made major investments in the technology, and the language designers have taken seriously the responsibility of not affecting the existing user and install base.

Each new language feature needs to be very carefully thought about—not only in isolation, but in terms of how it will interact with all the existing features of the language. New features can sometimes have impacts beyond their immediate scope—and Java is widely used in very large codebases, where there are more potential places for an unexpected interaction to manifest.

It is almost impossible to remove a feature that turns out to be incorrect after it has shipped—Java has a couple of misfeatures (such as the finalization mechanism) and it has never been possible to remove them safely without impacting the install base. The language designers have taken the view that extreme caution is required when evolving the language.

Having said that, the new language features present in Java 8 are a significant step towards addressing the most common complaints about missing features, and should cover many of the idioms that developers have been asking for.

Performance Problems

The Java platform is still sometimes criticized as being slow—but of all the criticisms that are leveled at the platform, this is probably the one that is least justified.

Release 1.3 of Java brought in the HotSpot Virtual Machine and its JIT compiler. Since then, there has been almost 15 years of continual innovation and improvement in the virtual machine and its performance. The Java platform is now blazingly fast, regularly winning performance benchmarks on popular frameworks, and even beating native-compiled C and C++.

Criticism in this area appears to be largely caused by a folk memory that Java used to be slow at some point in the past. Some of the larger and more sprawling architectures that Java has been used within may also have contributed to this impression.

The truth is that any large architecture will require benchmarking, analysis, and performance tuning to get the best out of it—and Java is no exception.

The core of the platform—language and JVM—is and remains one of the fastest general-use environments available to the developer.

Insecure

During 2013 there were a number of security vulnerabilities in the Java platform, which caused the release date of Java 8 to be pushed back. Even before this, some people had criticized Java's record of security vulnerabilities.

Many of these vulnerabilities involved the desktop and GUI components of the Java system, and wouldn't affect websites or other server-side code written in Java.

All programming platforms have security issues at times—and many other languages have a comparable history of security vulnerabilities that have been significantly less well publicized.

Too Corporate

Java is a platform that is extensively used by corporate and enterprise developers. The perception that it is too corporate is therefore an unsurprising one—Java has often been perceived as lacking the "free-wheeling" style of languages that are deemed to be more community oriented.

In truth, Java has always been, and remains, a very widely used language for community and free or open source software development. It is one of the most popular languages for projects hosted on GitHub and other project hosting sites.

Finally, the most widely used implementation of the language itself is based on OpenJDK—which is itself an open source project with a vibrant and growing community.

2

Java Syntax from the Ground Up

This chapter is a terse but comprehensive introduction to Java syntax. It is written primarily for readers who are new to the language but have some previous programming experience. Determined novices with no prior programming experience may also find it useful. If you already know Java, you should find it a useful language reference. The chapter includes some comparisons of Java to C and C++ for the benefit of programmers coming from those languages.

This chapter documents the syntax of Java programs by starting at the very lowest level of Java syntax and building from there, covering increasingly higher orders of structure. It covers:

- The characters used to write Java programs and the encoding of those characters.

- Literal values, identifiers, and other tokens that comprise a Java program.

- The data types that Java can manipulate.

- The operators used in Java to group individual tokens into larger expressions.

- Statements, which group expressions and other statements to form logical chunks of Java code.

- Methods, which are named collections of Java statements that can be invoked by other Java code.

- Classes, which are collections of methods and fields. Classes are the central program element in Java and form the basis for object-oriented programming. Chapter 3 is devoted entirely to a discussion of classes and objects.

- Packages, which are collections of related classes.

- Java programs, which consist of one or more interacting classes that may be drawn from one or more packages.

The syntax of most programming languages is complex, and Java is no exception. In general, it is not possible to document all elements of a language without referring to other elements that have not yet been discussed. For example, it is not really possible to explain in a meaningful way the operators and statements supported by Java without referring to objects. But it is also not possible to document objects thoroughly without referring to the operators and statements of the language. The process of learning Java, or any language, is therefore an iterative one.

Java Programs from the Top Down

Before we begin our bottom-up exploration of Java syntax, let's take a moment for a top-down overview of a Java program. Java programs consist of one or more files, or *compilation units*, of Java source code. Near the end of the chapter, we describe the structure of a Java file and explain how to compile and run a Java program. Each compilation unit begins with an optional package declaration followed by zero or more import declarations. These declarations specify the namespace within which the compilation unit will define names, and the namespaces from which the compilation unit imports names. We'll see package and import again later in this chapter in "Packages and the Java Namespace" on page 88.

The optional package and import declarations are followed by zero or more reference type definitions. We will meet the full variety of possible reference types in Chapters 3 and 4, but for now, we should note that these are most often either class or interface definitions.

Within the definition of a reference type, we will encounter *members* such as *fields*, *methods*, and *constructors*. Methods are the most important kind of member. Methods are blocks of Java code comprised of *statements*.

With these basic terms defined, let's start by approaching a Java program from the bottom up by examining the basic units of syntax—often referred to as *lexical tokens*.

Lexical Structure

This section explains the lexical structure of a Java program. It starts with a discussion of the Unicode character set in which Java programs are written. It then covers the tokens that comprise a Java program, explaining comments, identifiers, reserved words, literals, and so on.

The Unicode Character Set

Java programs are written using Unicode. You can use Unicode characters anywhere in a Java program, including comments and identifiers such as variable names. Unlike the 7-bit ASCII character set, which is useful only for English, and the 8-bit ISO Latin-1 character set, which is useful only for major Western European languages, the Unicode character set can represent virtually every written language in common use on the planet.

If you do not use a Unicode-enabled text editor, or if you do not want to force other programmers who view or edit your code to use a Unicode-enabled editor, you can embed Unicode characters into your Java programs using the special Unicode escape sequence \uxxxx, in other words, a backslash and a lowercase u, followed by four hexadecimal characters. For example, \u0020 is the space character, and \u03c0 is the character π.

Java has invested a large amount of time and engineering effort in ensuring that its Unicode support is first class. If your business application needs to deal with global users, especially in non-Western markets, then the Java platform is a great choice.

Case Sensitivity and Whitespace

Java is a case-sensitive language. Its keywords are written in lowercase and must always be used that way. That is, `While` and `WHILE` are not the same as the `while` keyword. Similarly, if you declare a variable named `i` in your program, you may not refer to it as `I`.

In general, relying on case sensitivity to distinguish identifiers is a terrible idea. Do not use it in your own code, and in particular never give an identifier the same name as a keyword but differently cased.

Java ignores spaces, tabs, newlines, and other whitespace, except when it appears within quoted characters and string literals. Programmers typically use whitespace to format and indent their code for easy readability, and you will see common indentation conventions in the code examples of this book.

Comments

Comments are natural-language text intended for human readers of a program. They are ignored by the Java compiler. Java supports three types of comments. The first type is a single-line comment, which begins with the characters `//` and continues until the end of the current line. For example:

```
int i = 0;    // Initialize the loop variable
```

The second kind of comment is a multiline comment. It begins with the characters `/*` and continues, over any number of lines, until the characters `*/`. Any text between the `/*` and the `*/` is ignored by `javac`. Although this style of comment is typically used for multiline comments, it can also be used for single-line comments.

This type of comment cannot be nested (i.e., one /* */ comment cannot appear within another). When writing multiline comments, programmers often use extra * characters to make the comments stand out. Here is a typical multiline comment:

```
/*
 * First, establish a connection to the server.
 * If the connection attempt fails, quit right away.
 */
```

The third type of comment is a special case of the second. If a comment begins with /**, it is regarded as a special *doc comment*. Like regular multiline comments, doc comments end with */ and cannot be nested. When you write a Java class you expect other programmers to use, use doc comments to embed documentation about the class and each of its methods directly into the source code. A program named javadoc extracts these comments and processes them to create online documentation for your class. A doc comment can contain HTML tags and can use additional syntax understood by javadoc. For example:

```
/**
 * Upload a file to a web server.
 *
 * @param file The file to upload.
 * @return <tt>true</tt> on success,
 *         <tt>false</tt> on failure.
 * @author David Flanagan
 */
```

See Chapter 7 for more information on the doc comment syntax and Chapter 13 for more information on the javadoc program.

Comments may appear between any tokens of a Java program, but may not appear within a token. In particular, comments may not appear within double-quoted string literals. A comment within a string literal simply becomes a literal part of that string.

Reserved Words

The following words are reserved in Java (they are part of the syntax of the language and may not be used to name variables, classes, and so forth):

abstract	const	final	int	public	throw
assert	continue	finally	interface	return	throws
boolean	default	float	long	short	transient
break	do	for	native	static	true
byte	double	goto	new	strictfp	try
case	else	if	null	super	void
catch	enum	implements	package	switch	volatile
char	extends	import	private	synchronized	while
class	false	instanceof	protected	this	

We'll meet each of these reserved words again later in this book. Some of them are the names of primitive types and others are the names of Java statements, both of which are discussed later in this chapter. Still others are used to define classes and their members (see Chapter 3).

Note that `const` and `goto` are reserved but aren't actually used in the language, and that `interface` has an additional variant form—`@interface`, which is used when defining types known as annotations. Some of the reserved words (notably `final` and `default`) have a variety of different meanings depending on context.

Identifiers

An *identifier* is simply a name given to some part of a Java program, such as a class, a method within a class, or a variable declared within a method. Identifiers may be of any length and may contain letters and digits drawn from the entire Unicode character set. An identifier may not begin with a digit. In general, identifiers may not contain punctuation characters. Exceptions include the ASCII underscore (_) and dollar sign ($) as well as other Unicode currency symbols such as £ and ¥.

> Currency symbols are intended for use in automatically generated source code, such as code produced by `javac`. By avoiding the use of currency symbols in your own identifiers, you don't have to worry about collisions with automatically generated identifiers.

Formally, the characters allowed at the beginning of and within an identifier are defined by the methods `isJavaIdentifierStart()` and `isJavaIdentifierPart()` of the class `java.lang.Character`.

The following are examples of legal identifiers:

```
i    x1    theCurrentTime    the_current_time    獺
```

Note in particular the example of a UTF-8 identifier—獺. This is the Kanji character for "otter" and is perfectly legal as a Java identifier. The usage of non-ASCII identifiers is unusual in programs predominantly written by Westerners, but is sometimes seen.

Literals

Literals are values that appear directly in Java source code. They include integer and floating-point numbers, single characters within single quotes, strings of characters within double quotes, and the reserved words `true`, `false`, and `null`. For example, the following are all literals:

```
1    1.0    '1'    "one"    true    false    null
```

The syntax for expressing numeric, character, and string literals is detailed in "Primitive Data Types" on page 22.

Punctuation

Java also uses a number of punctuation characters as tokens. The Java Language Specification divides these characters (somewhat arbitrarily) into two categories, separators and operators. The twelve separators are:

```
(   )   {   }   [   ]

...  @  ::

;   ,   .
```

The operators are:

```
+    -    *    /    %    &    |    ^    <<   >>   >>>
+=   -=   *=   /=   %=   &=   |=   ^=   <<=  >>=  >>>=
=    ==   !=   <    <=   >    >=
!    ~    &&   ||   ++   --   ?    :    ->
```

We'll see separators throughout the book, and will cover each operator individually in "Expressions and Operators" on page 30.

Primitive Data Types

Java supports eight basic data types known as *primitive types* as described in Table 2-1. The primitive types include a Boolean type, a character type, four integer types, and two floating-point types. The four integer types and the two floating-point types differ in the number of bits that represent them and therefore in the range of numbers they can represent.

Table 2-1. Java primitive data types

Type	Contains	Default	Size	Range
boolean	true or false	false	1 bit	NA
char	Unicode character	\u0000	16 bits	\u0000 to \uFFFF
byte	Signed integer	0	8 bits	-128 to 127
short	Signed integer	0	16 bits	-32768 to 32767
int	Signed integer	0	32 bits	-2147483648 to 2147483647
long	Signed integer	0	64 bits	-9223372036854775808 to 9223372036854775807
float	IEEE 754 floating point	0.0	32 bits	1.4E-45 to 3.4028235E+38
double	IEEE 754 floating point	0.0	64 bits	4.9E-324 to 1.7976931348623157E+308

The next section summarizes these primitive data types. In addition to these primitive types, Java supports nonprimitive data types known as reference types, which are introduced in "Reference Types" on page 84.

The boolean Type

The `boolean` type represents truth values. This type has only two possible values, representing the two Boolean states: on or off, yes or no, true or false. Java reserves the words `true` and `false` to represent these two Boolean values.

Programmers coming to Java from other languages (especially JavaScript) should note that Java is much stricter about its Boolean values than other languages—in particular, a `boolean` is neither an integral nor an object type, and incompatible values cannot be used in place of a `boolean`. In other words, you cannot take shortcuts such as the following in Java:

```
Object o = new Object();
int i = 1;

if (o) {
  while(i) {
    //...
  }
}
```

Instead, Java forces you to write cleaner code by explicitly stating the comparisons you want:

```
if (o != null) {
  while(i != 0) {
    // ...
  }
}
```

The char Type

The `char` type represents Unicode characters. Java has a slightly unique approach to representing characters—`javac` accepts identifiers as UTF-8 (a variable-width encoding) in input, but represents chars internally as a fixed-width encoding that is 16 bits wide.

These distinctions do not normally need to concern the developer, however. In most cases, all that is required is to remember the rule that to include a character literal in a Java program, simply place it between single quotes (apostrophes):

```
char c = 'A';
```

You can, of course, use any Unicode character as a character literal, and you can use the \u Unicode escape sequence. In addition, Java supports a number of other escape sequences that make it easy both to represent commonly used nonprinting ASCII characters such as `newline` and to escape certain punctuation characters that have special meaning in Java. For example:

```
char tab = '\t', nul = '\000', aleph = '\u05D0', slash = '\\';
```

Table 2-2 lists the escape characters that can be used in char literals. These characters can also be used in string literals, which are covered in the next section.

Table 2-2. Java escape characters

Escape sequence	Character value
\b	Backspace
\t	Horizontal tab
\n	Newline
\f	Form feed
\r	Carriage return
\"	Double quote
\'	Single quote
\\	Backslash
\ *xxx*	The Latin-1 character with the encoding *xxx*, where *xxx* is an octal (base 8) number between 000 and 377. The forms \ *x* and \ *xx* are also legal, as in \ *0*, but are not recommended because they can cause difficulties in string constants where the escape sequence is followed by a regular digit. This form is generally discouraged in favor of the \uXXXX form.
\u *xxxx*	The Unicode character with encoding *xxxx*, where *xxxx* is four hexadecimal digits. Unicode escapes can appear anywhere in a Java program, not only in character and string literals.

char values can be converted to and from the various integral types, and the char data type is a 16-bit integral type. Unlike byte, short, int, and long, however, char is an unsigned type. The Character class defines a number of useful static methods for working with characters, including isDigit(), isJavaLetter(), isLowerCase(), and toUpperCase().

The Java language and its char type were designed with Unicode in mind. The Unicode standard is evolving, however, and each new version of Java adopts a new version of Unicode. Java 7 uses Unicode 6.0 and Java 8 uses Unicode 6.2.

Recent releases of Unicode include characters whose encodings, or *codepoints*, do not fit in 16 bits. These supplementary characters, which are mostly infrequently used Han (Chinese) ideographs, occupy 21 bits and cannot be represented in a single char value. Instead, you must use an int value to hold the codepoint of a supplementary character, or you must encode it into a so-called "surrogate pair" of two char values.

Unless you commonly write programs that use Asian languages, you are unlikely to encounter any supplementary characters. If you do anticipate having to process characters that do not fit into a char, methods have been added to the Character, String, and related classes for working with text using int codepoints.

String literals

In addition to the char type, Java also has a data type for working with strings of text (usually simply called *strings*). The String type is a class, however, and is not one of the primitive types of the language. Because strings are so commonly used, though, Java does have a syntax for including string values literally in a program. A String literal consists of arbitrary text within double quotes (as opposed to the single quotes for char literals). For example:

```
"Hello, world"
"'This' is a string!"
```

String literals can contain any of the escape sequences that can appear as char literals (see Table 2-2). Use the \" sequence to include a double quote within a String literal. Because String is a reference type, string literals are described in more detail later in this chapter in "Object Literals" on page 74. Chapter 9 contains more details on some of the ways you can work with String objects in Java.

Integer Types

The integer types in Java are byte, short, int, and long. As shown in Table 2-1, these four types differ only in the number of bits and, therefore, in the range of numbers each type can represent. All integral types represent signed numbers; there is no unsigned keyword as there is in C and C++.

Literals for each of these types are written exactly as you would expect: as a string of decimal digits, optionally preceded by a minus sign.[1] Here are some legal integer literals:

```
0
1
123
-42000
```

Integer literals can also be expressed in hexadecimal, binary, or octal notation. A literal that begins with 0x or 0X is taken as a hexadecimal number, using the letters A to F (or a to f) as the additional digits required for base-16 numbers.

---

1 Technically, the minus sign is an operator that operates on the literal, but is not part of the literal itself.

Integer binary literals start with 0b and may, of course, only feature the digits 1 or 0. As binary literals can be very long, underscores are often used as part of a binary literal. The underscore character is ignored whenever it is encountered in any numerical literal—it's allowed purely to help with readability of literals.

Java also supports octal (base-8) integer literals. These literals begin with a leading 0 and cannot include the digits 8 or 9. They are not often used and should be avoided unless needed. Legal hexadecimal, binary, and octal literals include:

```
0xff            // Decimal 255, expressed in hexadecimal
0377            // The same number, expressed in octal (base 8)
0b0010_1111     // Decimal 47, expressed in binary
0xCAFEBABE      // A magic number used to identify Java class files
```

Integer literals are 32-bit int values unless they end with the character L or l, in which case they are 64-bit long values:

```
1234            // An int value
1234L           // A long value
0xffL           // Another long value
```

Integer arithmetic in Java never produces an overflow or an underflow when you exceed the range of a given integer type. Instead, numbers just wrap around. For example:

```
byte b1 = 127, b2 = 1;        // Largest byte is 127
byte sum = (byte)(b1 + b2);   // Sum wraps to -128, the smallest byte
```

Neither the Java compiler nor the Java interpreter warns you in any way when this occurs. When doing integer arithmetic, you simply must ensure that the type you are using has a sufficient range for the purposes you intend. Integer division by zero and modulo by zero are illegal and cause an ArithmeticException to be thrown.

Each integer type has a corresponding wrapper class: Byte, Short, Integer, and Long. Each of these classes defines MIN_VALUE and MAX_VALUE constants that describe the range of the type. The classes also define useful static methods, such as Byte.parseByte() and Integer.parseInt(), for converting strings to integer values.

Floating-Point Types

Real numbers in Java are represented by the float and double data types. As shown in Table 2-1, float is a 32-bit, single-precision floating-point value, and double is a 64-bit, double-precision floating-point value. Both types adhere to the IEEE 754-1985 standard, which specifies both the format of the numbers and the behavior of arithmetic for the numbers.

Floating-point values can be included literally in a Java program as an optional string of digits, followed by a decimal point and another string of digits. Here are some examples:

```
123.45
0.0
.01
```

Floating-point literals can also use exponential, or scientific, notation, in which a number is followed by the letter e or E (for exponent) and another number. This second number represents the power of 10 by which the first number is multiplied. For example:

```
1.2345E02    // 1.2345 * 10^2 or 123.45
1e-6         // 1 * 10^-6 or 0.000001
6.02e23      // Avogadro's Number: 6.02 * 10^23
```

Java Syntax

Floating-point literals are double values by default. To include a float value literally in a program, follow the number with f or F:

```
double d = 6.02E23;
float f = 6.02e23f;
```

Floating-point literals cannot be expressed in hexadecimal, binary, or octal notation.

Floating-Point Representations

Most real numbers, by their very nature, cannot be represented exactly in any finite number of bits. Thus, it is important to remember that float and double values are only approximations of the numbers they are meant to represent. A float is a 32-bit approximation, which results in at least six significant decimal digits, and a double is a 64-bit approximation, which results in at least 15 significant digits. In Chapter 9, we will cover floating-point representations in more detail.

In addition to representing ordinary numbers, the float and double types can also represent four special values: positive and negative infinity, zero, and NaN. The infinity values result when a floating-point computation produces a value that overflows the representable range of a float or double. When a floating-point computation underflows the representable range of a float or a double, a zero value results.

The Java floating-point types make a distinction between positive zero and negative zero, depending on the direction from which the underflow occurred. In practice, positive and negative zero behave pretty much the same. Finally, the last special floating-point value is NaN, which stands for "Not-a-number." The NaN value results when an illegal floating-point operation, such as 0.0/0.0, is performed. Here are examples of statements that result in these special values:

```
double inf = 1.0/0.0;       // Infinity
double neginf = -1.0/0.0;   // Negative Infinity
double negzero = -1.0/inf;  // Negative zero
double NaN = 0.0/0.0;       // Not-a-number
```

Because the Java floating-point types can handle overflow to infinity and underflow to zero and have a special NaN value, floating-point arithmetic never throws exceptions, even when performing illegal operations, like dividing zero by zero or taking the square root of a negative number.

The `float` and `double` primitive types have corresponding classes, named `Float` and `Double`. Each of these classes defines the following useful constants: `MIN_VALUE`, `MAX_VALUE`, `NEGATIVE_INFINITY`, `POSITIVE_INFINITY`, and `NaN`.

The infinite floating-point values behave as you would expect. Adding or subtracting any finite value to or from infinity, for example, yields infinity. Negative zero behaves almost identically to positive zero, and, in fact, the `==` equality operator reports that negative zero is equal to positive zero. One way to distinguish negative zero from positive, or regular, zero is to divide by it: 1.0/0.0 yields positive infinity, but 1.0 divided by negative zero yields negative infinity. Finally, because NaN is Not-a-number, the `==` operator says that it is not equal to any other number, including itself! To check whether a `float` or `double` value is NaN, you must use the `Float.isNaN()` and `Double.isNaN()` methods.

Primitive Type Conversions

Java allows conversions between integer values and floating-point values. In addition, because every character corresponds to a number in the Unicode encoding, `char` values can be converted to and from the integer and floating-point types. In fact, `boolean` is the only primitive type that cannot be converted to or from another primitive type in Java.

There are two basic types of conversions. A *widening conversion* occurs when a value of one type is converted to a wider type—one that has a larger range of legal values. For example, Java performs widening conversions automatically when you assign an `int` literal to a `double` variable or a `char` literal to an `int` variable.

Narrowing conversions are another matter, however. A *narrowing conversion* occurs when a value is converted to a type that is not wider than it is. Narrowing conversions are not always safe: it is reasonable to convert the integer value 13 to a `byte`, for example, but it is not reasonable to convert 13,000 to a `byte`, because `byte` can hold only numbers between -128 and 127. Because you can lose data in a narrowing conversion, the Java compiler complains when you attempt any narrowing conversion, even if the value being converted would in fact fit in the narrower range of the specified type:

```
int i = 13;
byte b = i;    // The compiler does not allow this
```

The one exception to this rule is that you can assign an integer literal (an `int` value) to a `byte` or `short` variable if the literal falls within the range of the variable.

If you need to perform a narrowing conversion and are confident you can do so without losing data or precision, you can force Java to perform the conversion using a language construct known as a *cast*. Perform a cast by placing the name of the desired type in parentheses before the value to be converted. For example:

```
int i = 13;
byte b = (byte) i;    // Force the int to be converted to a byte
i = (int) 13.456;     // Force this double literal to the int 13
```

Casts of primitive types are most often used to convert floating-point values to integers. When you do this, the fractional part of the floating-point value is simply truncated (i.e., the floating-point value is rounded toward zero, not toward the nearest integer). The static methods `Math.round()`, `Math.floor()`, and `Math.ceil()` perform other types of rounding.

The `char` type acts like an integer type in most ways, so a `char` value can be used anywhere an `int` or `long` value is required. Recall, however, that the `char` type is *unsigned*, so it behaves differently than the `short` type, even though both are 16 bits wide:

```
short s = (short) 0xffff; // These bits represent the number -1
char c = '\uffff';        // The same bits, as a Unicode character
int i1 = s;               // Converting the short to an int yields -1
int i2 = c;               // Converting the char to an int yields 65535
```

Table 2-3 shows which primitive types can be converted to which other types and how the conversion is performed. The letter N in the table means that the conversion cannot be performed. The letter Y means that the conversion is a widening conversion and is therefore performed automatically and implicitly by Java. The letter C means that the conversion is a narrowing conversion and requires an explicit cast.

Finally, the notation Y* means that the conversion is an automatic widening conversion, but that some of the least significant digits of the value may be lost in the conversion. This can happen when converting an `int` or `long` to a floating-point type— see the table for details. The floating-point types have a larger range than the integer types, so any `int` or `long` can be represented by a `float` or `double`. However, the floating-point types are approximations of numbers and cannot always hold as many significant digits as the integer types (see Chapter 9 for some more detail about floating-point numbers).

Table 2-3. Java primitive type conversions

	Convert to:							
Convert from:	boolean	byte	short	char	int	long	float	double
boolean	-	N	N	N	N	N	N	N
byte	N	-	Y	C	Y	Y	Y	Y
short	N	C	-	C	Y	Y	Y	Y

Convert from:	Convert to: boolean	byte	short	char	int	long	float	double
char	N	C	C	-	Y	Y	Y	Y
int	N	C	C	C	-	Y	Y*	Y
long	N	C	C	C	C	-	Y*	Y*
float	N	C	C	C	C	C	-	Y
double	N	C	C	C	C	C	C	-

Expressions and Operators

So far in this chapter, we've learned about the primitive types that Java programs can manipulate and seen how to include primitive values as *literals* in a Java program. We've also used *variables* as symbolic names that represent, or hold, values. These literals and variables are the tokens out of which Java programs are built.

An *expression* is the next higher level of structure in a Java program. The Java interpreter *evaluates* an expression to compute its value. The very simplest expressions are called *primary expressions* and consist of literals and variables. So, for example, the following are all expressions:

```
1.7      // A floating-point literal
true     // A Boolean literal
sum      // A variable
```

When the Java interpreter evaluates a literal expression, the resulting value is the literal itself. When the interpreter evaluates a variable expression, the resulting value is the value stored in the variable.

Primary expressions are not very interesting. More complex expressions are made by using *operators* to combine primary expressions. For example, the following expression uses the assignment operator to combine two primary expressions—a variable and a floating-point literal—into an assignment expression:

```
sum = 1.7
```

But operators are used not only with primary expressions; they can also be used with expressions at any level of complexity. The following are all legal expressions:

```
sum = 1 + 2 + 3 * 1.2 + (4 + 8)/3.0
sum/Math.sqrt(3.0 * 1.234)
(int)(sum + 33)
```

Operator Summary

The kinds of expressions you can write in a programming language depend entirely on the set of operators available to you. Java has a wealth of operators, but to work effectively with them, there are two important concepts that need to be understood: *precedence* and *associativity*. These concepts—and the operators themselves—are explained in more detail in the following sections.

Precedence

The P column of Table 2-4 specifies the *precedence* of each operator. Precedence specifies the order in which operations are performed. Operations that have higher precedence are performed before those with lower precedence. For example, consider this expression:

```
a + b * c
```

The multiplication operator has higher precedence than the addition operator, so a is added to the product of b and c, just as we expect from elementary mathematics. Operator precedence can be thought of as a measure of how tightly operators bind to their operands. The higher the number, the more tightly they bind.

Default operator precedence can be overridden through the use of parentheses that explicitly specify the order of operations. The previous expression can be rewritten to specify that the addition should be performed before the multiplication:

```
(a + b) * c
```

The default operator precedence in Java was chosen for compatibility with C; the designers of C chose this precedence so that most expressions can be written naturally without parentheses. There are only a few common Java idioms for which parentheses are required. Examples include:

```
// Class cast combined with member access
((Integer) o).intValue();

// Assignment combined with comparison
while((line = in.readLine()) != null) { ... }

// Bitwise operators combined with comparison
if ((flags & (PUBLIC | PROTECTED)) != 0) { ... }
```

Associativity

Associativity is a property of operators that defines how to evaluate expressions that would otherwise be ambiguous. This is particularly important when an expression involves several operators that have the same precedence.

Most operators are left-to-right associative, which means that the operations are performed from left to right. The assignment and unary operators, however, have right-to-left associativity. The A column of Table 2-4 specifies the associativity of each operator or group of operators. The value L means left to right, and R means right to left.

The additive operators are all left-to-right associative, so the expression a+b-c is evaluated from left to right: (a+b)-c. Unary operators and assignment operators are evaluated from right to left. Consider this complex expression:

```
a = b += c = -~d
```

This is evaluated as follows:

```
a = (b += (c = -(~d)))
```

As with operator precedence, operator associativity establishes a default order of evaluation for an expression. This default order can be overridden through the use of parentheses. However, the default operator associativity in Java has been chosen to yield a natural expression syntax, and you should rarely need to alter it.

Operator summary table

Table 2-4 summarizes the operators available in Java. The P and A columns of the table specify the precedence and associativity of each group of related operators, respectively. You should use this table as a quick reference for operators (especially their precedence) when required.

Table 2-4. Java operators

P	A	Operator	Operand type(s)	Operation performed
16	L	.	object, member	Object member access
		[ ]	array, int	Array element access
		(*args*)	method, arglist	Method invocation
		++, --	variable	Post-increment, post-decrement
15	R	++, --	variable	Pre-increment, pre-decrement
		+, -	number	Unary plus, unary minus
		~	integer	Bitwise complement
		!	boolean	Boolean NOT
14	R	new	class, arglist	Object creation
		(*type*)	type, any	Cast (type conversion)
13	L	*, /, %	number, number	Multiplication, division, remainder
12	L	+, -	number, number	Addition, subtraction

P	A	Operator	Operand type(s)	Operation performed
		+	string, any	String concatenation
11	L	<<	integer, integer	Left shift
		>>	integer, integer	Right shift with sign extension
		>>>	integer, integer	Right shift with zero extension
10	L	<, <=	number, number	Less than, less than or equal
		>, >=	number, number	Greater than, greater than or equal
		instanceof	reference, type	Type comparison
9	L	==	primitive, primitive	Equal (have identical values)
		!=	primitive, primitive	Not equal (have different values)
		==	reference, reference	Equal (refer to same object)
		!=	reference, reference	Not equal (refer to different objects)
8	L	&	integer, integer	Bitwise AND
		&	boolean, boolean	Boolean AND
7	L	^	integer, integer	Bitwise XOR
		^	boolean, boolean	Boolean XOR
6	L	|	integer, integer	Bitwise OR
		|	boolean, boolean	Boolean OR
5	L	&&	boolean, boolean	Conditional AND
4	L	||	boolean, boolean	Conditional OR
3	R	? :	boolean, any	Conditional (ternary) operator
2	R	=	variable, any	Assignment
		*=, /=, %=,	variable, any	Assignment with operation

P	A	Operator	Operand type(s)	Operation performed
		+=, -=, <<=,		
		>>=, >>>=,		
		&=, ^=, |=		
1	R	→	arglist, method body	lambda expression

Operand number and type

The fourth column of Table 2-4 specifies the number and type of the operands expected by each operator. Some operators operate on only one operand; these are called unary operators. For example, the unary minus operator changes the sign of a single number:

```
-n            // The unary minus operator
```

Most operators, however, are binary operators that operate on two operand values. The - operator actually comes in both forms:

```
a - b         // The subtraction operator is a binary operator
```

Java also defines one ternary operator, often called the conditional operator. It is like an if statement inside an expression. Its three operands are separated by a question mark and a colon; the second and third operands must be convertible to the same type:

```
x > y ? x : y  // Ternary expression; evaluates to larger of x and y
```

In addition to expecting a certain number of operands, each operator also expects particular types of operands. The fourth column of the table lists the operand types. Some of the codes used in that column require further explanation:

Number
> An integer, floating-point value, or character (i.e., any primitive type except boolean). Autounboxing (see "Boxing and Unboxing Conversions" on page 87) means that the wrapper classes (such as Character, Integer, and Double) for these types can be used in this context as well.

Integer
> A byte, short, int, long, or char value (long values are not allowed for the array access operator [ ]). With autounboxing, Byte, Short, Integer, Long, and Character values are also allowed.

Reference
> An object or array.

Variable

A variable or anything else, such as an array element, to which a value can be assigned.

Return type

Just as every operator expects its operands to be of specific types, each operator produces a value of a specific type. The arithmetic, increment and decrement, bitwise, and shift operators return a double if at least one of the operands is a double. They return a float if at least one of the operands is a float. They return a long if at least one of the operands is a long. Otherwise, they return an int, even if both operands are byte, short, or char types that are narrower than int.

The comparison, equality, and Boolean operators always return boolean values. Each assignment operator returns whatever value it assigned, which is of a type compatible with the variable on the left side of the expression. The conditional operator returns the value of its second or third argument (which must both be of the same type).

Side effects

Every operator computes a value based on one or more operand values. Some operators, however, have *side effects* in addition to their basic evaluation. If an expression contains side effects, evaluating it changes the state of a Java program in such a way that evaluating the expression again may yield a different result.

For example, the ++ increment operator has the side effect of incrementing a variable. The expression ++a increments the variable a and returns the newly incremented value. If this expression is evaluated again, the value will be different. The various assignment operators also have side effects. For example, the expression a*=2 can also be written as a=a*2. The value of the expression is the value of a multiplied by 2, but the expression has the side effect of storing that value back into a.

The method invocation operator () has side effects if the invoked method has side effects. Some methods, such as Math.sqrt(), simply compute and return a value without side effects of any kind. Typically, however, methods do have side effects. Finally, the new operator has the profound side effect of creating a new object.

Order of evaluation

When the Java interpreter evaluates an expression, it performs the various operations in an order specified by the parentheses in the expression, the precedence of the operators, and the associativity of the operators. Before any operation is performed, however, the interpreter first evaluates the operands of the operator. (The exceptions are the &&, ||, and ?: operators, which do not always evaluate all their operands.) The interpreter always evaluates operands in order from left to right. This matters if any of the operands are expressions that contain side effects. Consider this code, for example:

```
int a = 2;
int v = ++a + ++a * ++a;
```

Although the multiplication is performed before the addition, the operands of the + operator are evaluated first. As the operands of ++ are both a+, these are evaluated to 3 and 4, and so the expression evaluates to 3 + 4 * 5, or 23.

Arithmetic Operators

The arithmetic operators can be used with integers, floating-point numbers, and even characters (i.e., they can be used with any primitive type other than boolean). If either of the operands is a floating-point number, floating-point arithmetic is used; otherwise, integer arithmetic is used. This matters because integer arithmetic and floating-point arithmetic differ in the way division is performed and in the way underflows and overflows are handled, for example. The arithmetic operators are:

Addition (+)

The + operator adds two numbers. As we'll see shortly, the + operator can also be used to concatenate strings. If either operand of + is a string, the other one is converted to a string as well. Be sure to use parentheses when you want to combine addition with concatenation. For example:

```
System.out.println("Total: " + 3 + 4);    // Prints "Total: 34", not 7!
```

Subtraction (-)

When the - operator is used as a binary operator, it subtracts its second operand from its first. For example, 7-3 evaluates to 4. The - operator can also perform unary negation.

Multiplication (*)

The * operator multiplies its two operands. For example, 7*3 evaluates to 21.

Division (/)

The / operator divides its first operand by its second. If both operands are integers, the result is an integer, and any remainder is lost. If either operand is a floating-point value, however, the result is a floating-point value. When dividing two integers, division by zero throws an ArithmeticException. For floating-point calculations, however, division by zero simply yields an infinite result or NaN:

```
7/3        // Evaluates to 2
7/3.0f     // Evaluates to 2.333333f
7/0        // Throws an ArithmeticException
7/0.0      // Evaluates to positive infinity
0.0/0.0    // Evaluates to NaN
```

Modulo (%)

The % operator computes the first operand modulo the second operand (i.e., it returns the remainder when the first operand is divided by the second operand an integral number of times). For example, 7%3 is 1. The sign of the result is the same as the sign of the first operand. While the modulo operator is typically used with integer operands, it also works for floating-point values. For example, 4.3%2.1 evaluates to 0.1. When operating with integers, trying to compute a value modulo zero causes an `ArithmeticException`. When working with floating-point values, anything modulo 0.0 evaluates to NaN, as does infinity modulo anything.

Unary minus (-)

When the - operator is used as a unary operator—that is, before a single operand—it performs unary negation. In other words, it converts a positive value to an equivalently negative value, and vice versa.

String Concatenation Operator

In addition to adding numbers, the + operator (and the related += operator) also concatenates, or joins, strings. If either of the operands to + is a string, the operator converts the other operand to a string. For example:

```
// Prints "Quotient: 2.3333333"
System.out.println("Quotient: " + 7/3.0f);
```

As a result, you must be careful to put any addition expressions in parentheses when combining them with string concatenation. If you do not, the addition operator is interpreted as a concatenation operator.

The Java interpreter has built-in string conversions for all primitive types. An object is converted to a string by invoking its `toString()` method. Some classes define custom `toString()` methods so that objects of that class can easily be converted to strings in this way. An array is converted to a string by invoking the built-in `toString()` method, which, unfortunately, does not return a useful string representation of the array contents.

Increment and Decrement Operators

The ++ operator increments its single operand, which must be a variable, an element of an array, or a field of an object, by 1. The behavior of this operator depends on its position relative to the operand. When used before the operand, where it is known as the *pre-increment* operator, it increments the operand and evaluates to the incremented value of that operand. When used after the operand, where it is known as the *post-increment* operator, it increments its operand, but evaluates to the value of that operand before it was incremented.

For example, the following code sets both i and j to 2:

```
i = 1;
j = ++i;
```

But these lines set i to 2 and j to 1:

```
i = 1;
j = i++;
```

Similarly, the -- operator decrements its single numeric operand, which must be a variable, an element of an array, or a field of an object, by one. Like the ++ operator, the behavior of -- depends on its position relative to the operand. When used before the operand, it decrements the operand and returns the decremented value. When used after the operand, it decrements the operand, but returns the *undecremented* value.

The expressions x++ and x-- are equivalent to x=x+1 and x=x-1, respectively, except that when using the increment and decrement operators, x is only evaluated once. If x is itself an expression with side effects, this makes a big difference. For example, these two expressions are not equivalent:

```
a[i++]++;                   // Increments an element of an array
// Adds 1 to an array element and stores new value in another element
a[i++] = a[i++] + 1;
```

These operators, in both prefix and postfix forms, are most commonly used to increment or decrement the counter that controls a loop.

Comparison Operators

The comparison operators consist of the equality operators that test values for equality or inequality and the relational operators used with ordered types (numbers and characters) to test for greater than and less than relationships. Both types of operators yield a boolean result, so they are typically used with if statements and while and for loops to make branching and looping decisions. For example:

```
if (o != null) ...;         // The not equals operator
while(i < a.length) ...;    // The less than operator
```

Java provides the following equality operators:

Equals (==)

The == operator evaluates to true if its two operands are equal and false otherwise. With primitive operands, it tests whether the operand values themselves are identical. For operands of reference types, however, it tests whether the operands refer to the same object or array. In other words, it does not test the equality of two distinct objects or arrays. In particular, note that you cannot test two distinct strings for equality with this operator.

If == is used to compare two numeric or character operands that are not of the same type, the narrower operand is converted to the type of the wider operand before the comparison is done. For example, when comparing a short to a float, the short is first converted to a float before the comparison is performed. For floating-point numbers, the special negative zero value tests equal to the regular, positive zero value. Also, the special NaN (Not-a-number) value is not equal to any other number, including itself. To test whether a floating-point value is NaN, use the Float.isNan() or Double.isNan() method.

Not equals (!=)

The != operator is exactly the opposite of the == operator. It evaluates to true if its two primitive operands have different values or if its two reference operands refer to different objects or arrays. Otherwise, it evaluates to false.

The relational operators can be used with numbers and characters, but not with boolean values, objects, or arrays because those types are not ordered. Java provides the following relational operators:

Less than (<)

Evaluates to true if the first operand is less than the second.

Less than or equal (<=)

Evaluates to true if the first operand is less than or equal to the second.

Greater than (>)

Evaluates to true if the first operand is greater than the second.

Greater than or equal (>=)

Evaluates to true if the first operand is greater than or equal to the second.

Boolean Operators

As we've just seen, the comparison operators compare their operands and yield a boolean result, which is often used in branching and looping statements. In order to make branching and looping decisions based on conditions more interesting than a single comparison, you can use the Boolean (or logical) operators to combine multiple comparison expressions into a single, more complex expression. The Boolean operators require their operands to be boolean values and they evaluate to boolean values. The operators are:

Conditional AND (&&)

This operator performs a Boolean AND operation on its operands. It evaluates to true if and only if both its operands are true. If either or both operands are false, it evaluates to false. For example:

```
if (x < 10 && y > 3) ... // If both comparisons are true
```

This operator (and all the Boolean operators except the unary ! operator) have a lower precedence than the comparison operators. Thus, it is perfectly legal to write a line of code like the one just shown. However, some programmers prefer to use parentheses to make the order of evaluation explicit:

```
if ((x < 10) && (y > 3)) ...
```

You should use whichever style you find easier to read.

This operator is called a conditional AND because it conditionally evaluates its second operand. If the first operand evaluates to false, the value of the expression is false, regardless of the value of the second operand. Therefore, to increase efficiency, the Java interpreter takes a shortcut and skips the second operand. The second operand is not guaranteed to be evaluated, so you must use caution when using this operator with expressions that have side effects. On the other hand, the conditional nature of this operator allows us to write Java expressions such as the following:

```
if (data != null && i < data.length && data[i] != -1)
    ...
```

The second and third comparisons in this expression would cause errors if the first or second comparisons evaluated to `false`. Fortunately, we don't have to worry about this because of the conditional behavior of the && operator.

Conditional OR (| |)

This operator performs a Boolean OR operation on its two `boolean` operands. It evaluates to `true` if either or both of its operands are `true`. If both operands are `false`, it evaluates to `false`. Like the && operator, | | does not always evaluate its second operand. If the first operand evaluates to `true`, the value of the expression is `true`, regardless of the value of the second operand. Thus, the operator simply skips the second operand in that case.

Boolean NOT (!)

This unary operator changes the `boolean` value of its operand. If applied to a `true` value, it evaluates to `false`, and if applied to a `false` value, it evaluates to `true`. It is useful in expressions like these:

```
if (!found) ...          // found is a boolean declared somewhere
while (!c.isEmpty()) ... // The isEmpty() method returns a boolean
```

Because ! is a unary operator, it has a high precedence and often must be used with parentheses:

```
if (!(x > y && y > z))
```

Boolean AND (&)

When used with `boolean` operands, the & operator behaves like the && operator, except that it always evaluates both operands, regardless of the value of the first operand. This operator is almost always used as a bitwise operator with integer operands, however, and many Java programmers would not even recognize its use with `boolean` operands as legal Java code.

Boolean OR (|)

This operator performs a Boolean OR operation on its two `boolean` operands. It is like the | | operator, except that it always evaluates both operands, even if the first one is `true`. The | operator is almost always used as a bitwise operator on integer operands; its use with `boolean` operands is very rare.

Boolean XOR (^)

When used with `boolean` operands, this operator computes the exclusive OR (XOR) of its operands. It evaluates to `true` if exactly one of the two operands is true. In other words, it evaluates to false if both operands are false or if both operands are true. Unlike the && and || operators, this one must always evaluate both operands. The ^ operator is much more commonly used as a bitwise operator on integer operands. With boolean operands, this operator is equivalent to the != operator.

Bitwise and Shift Operators

Java Syntax

The bitwise and shift operators are low-level operators that manipulate the individual bits that make up an integer value. The bitwise operators are not commonly used in modern Java except for low-level work (e.g., network programming). They are used for testing and setting individual flag bits in a value. In order to understand their behavior, you must understand binary (base-2) numbers and the two's complement format used to represent negative integers.

You cannot use these operators with floating-point, boolean, array, or object operands. When used with boolean operands, the &, |, and \^ operators perform a different operation, as described in the previous section.

If either of the arguments to a bitwise operator is a long, the result is a long. Otherwise, the result is an int. If the left operand of a shift operator is a long, the result is a long; otherwise, the result is an int. The operators are:

Bitwise complement (~)
> The unary ~ operator is known as the bitwise complement, or bitwise NOT, operator. It inverts each bit of its single operand, converting 1s to 0s and 0s to 1s. For example:
> ```
> byte b = ~12;          // ~00001100 =  => 11110011 or -13 decimal
> flags = flags & ~f;    // Clear flag f in a set of flags
> ```

Bitwise AND (&)
> This operator combines its two integer operands by performing a Boolean AND operation on their individual bits. The result has a bit set only if the corresponding bit is set in both operands. For example:
> ```
> 10 & 7                 // 00001010 & 00000111 =  => 00000010 or 2
> if ((flags & f) != 0)  // Test whether flag f is set
> ```
> When used with boolean operands, & is the infrequently used Boolean AND operator described earlier.

Bitwise OR (|)
> This operator combines its two integer operands by performing a Boolean OR operation on their individual bits. The result has a bit set if the corresponding bit is set in either or both of the operands. It has a zero bit only where both corresponding operand bits are zero. For example:
> ```
> 10 | 7                 // 00001010 | 00000111 =  => 00001111 or 15
> flags = flags | f;     // Set flag f
> ```

When used with `boolean` operands, | is the infrequently used Boolean OR operator described earlier.

Bitwise XOR (^)

This operator combines its two integer operands by performing a Boolean XOR (exclusive OR) operation on their individual bits. The result has a bit set if the corresponding bits in the two operands are different. If the corresponding operand bits are both 1s or both 0s, the result bit is a 0. For example:

```
10 ^ 7          // 00001010 ^ 00000111 =  => 00001101 or 13
```

When used with `boolean` operands, ^ is the seldom used Boolean XOR operator.

Left shift (<<)

The << operator shifts the bits of the left operand left by the number of places specified by the right operand. High-order bits of the left operand are lost, and zero bits are shifted in from the right. Shifting an integer left by n places is equivalent to multiplying that number by 2^n. For example:

```
10 << 1    // 00001010 << 1 = 00010100 = 20 = 10*2
7 << 3     // 00000111 << 3 = 00111000 = 56 = 7*8
-1 << 2    // 0xFFFFFFFF << 2 = 0xFFFFFFFC = -4 = -1*4
```

If the left operand is a `long`, the right operand should be between 0 and 63. Otherwise, the left operand is taken to be an `int`, and the right operand should be between 0 and 31.

Signed right shift (>>)

The >> operator shifts the bits of the left operand to the right by the number of places specified by the right operand. The low-order bits of the left operand are shifted away and are lost. The high-order bits shifted in are the same as the original high-order bit of the left operand. In other words, if the left operand is positive, 0s are shifted into the high-order bits. If the left operand is negative, 1s are shifted in instead. This technique is known as *sign extension*; it is used to preserve the sign of the left operand. For example:

```
10 >> 1    // 00001010 >> 1 = 00000101 = 5 = 10/2
27 >> 3    // 00011011 >> 3 = 00000011 = 3 = 27/8
-50 >> 2   // 11001110 >> 2 = 11110011 = -13 != -50/4
```

If the left operand is positive and the right operand is n, the >> operator is the same as integer division by 2^n.

Unsigned right shift (>>>)

This operator is like the >> operator, except that it always shifts zeros into the high-order bits of the result, regardless of the sign of the left-hand operand. This technique is called *zero extension*; it is appropriate when the left operand is being treated as an unsigned value (despite the fact that Java integer types are all signed). These are examples:

```
0xff >>> 4     // 11111111 >>> 4 = 00001111 = 15  = 255/16
-50 >>> 2      // 0xFFFFFFCE >>> 2 = 0x3FFFFFF3 = 1073741811
```

Assignment Operators

The assignment operators store, or assign, a value into some kind of variable. The left operand must evaluate to an appropriate local variable, array element, or object field. The right side can be any value of a type compatible with the variable. An assignment expression evaluates to the value that is assigned to the variable. More importantly, however, the expression has the side effect of actually performing the assignment. Unlike all other binary operators, the assignment operators are right-associative, which means that the assignments in a=b=c are performed right to left, as follows: a=(b=c).

The basic assignment operator is =. Do not confuse it with the equality operator, ==. In order to keep these two operators distinct, we recommend that you read = as "is assigned the value."

In addition to this simple assignment operator, Java also defines 11 other operators that combine assignment with the 5 arithmetic operators and the 6 bitwise and shift operators. For example, the += operator reads the value of the left variable, adds the value of the right operand to it, stores the sum back into the left variable as a side effect, and returns the sum as the value of the expression. Thus, the expression x+=2 is almost the same as x=x+2. The difference between these two expressions is that when you use the += operator, the left operand is evaluated only once. This makes a difference when that operand has a side effect. Consider the following two expressions, which are not equivalent:

```
a[i++] += 2;
a[i++] = a[i++] + 2;
```

The general form of these combination assignment operators is:

```
var op= value
```

This is equivalent (unless there are side effects in var) to:

```
var = var op value
```

The available operators are:

```
+=    -=    *=    /=    %=    // Arithmetic operators plus assignment

&=    |=    ^=                // Bitwise operators plus assignment

<<=   >>=   >>>=              // Shift operators plus assignment
```

The most commonly used operators are += and -=, although &= and |= can also be useful when working with boolean flags. For example:

```
i += 2;         // Increment a loop counter by 2
c -= 5;         // Decrement a counter by 5
```

```
flags |= f;        // Set a flag f in an integer set of flags
flags &= ~f;       // Clear a flag f in an integer set of flags
```

The Conditional Operator

The conditional operator ?: is a somewhat obscure ternary (three-operand) operator inherited from C. It allows you to embed a conditional within an expression. You can think of it as the operator version of the if/else statement. The first and second operands of the conditional operator are separated by a question mark (?) while the second and third operands are separated by a colon (:). The first operand must evaluate to a boolean value. The second and third operands can be of any type, but they must be convertible to the same type.

The conditional operator starts by evaluating its first operand. If it is true, the operator evaluates its second operand and uses that as the value of the expression. On the other hand, if the first operand is false, the conditional operator evaluates and returns its third operand. The conditional operator never evaluates both its second and third operand, so be careful when using expressions with side effects with this operator. Examples of this operator are:

```
int max = (x > y) ? x : y;
String name = (name != null) ? name : "unknown";
```

Note that the ?: operator has lower precedence than all other operators except the assignment operators, so parentheses are not usually necessary around the operands of this operator. Many programmers find conditional expressions easier to read if the first operand is placed within parentheses, however. This is especially true because the conditional if statement always has its conditional expression written within parentheses.

The instanceof Operator

The instanceof operator is intimately bound up with objects and the operation of the Java type system. If this is your first look at Java, it may be preferable to skim this definition and return to this section after you have a decent grasp of Java's objects.

instanceof requires an object or array value as its left operand and the name of a reference type as its right operand. It evaluates to true if the object or array is an *instance* of the specified type; it returns false otherwise. If the left operand is null, instanceof always evaluates to false. If an instanceof expression evaluates to true, it means that you can safely cast and assign the left operand to a variable of the type of the right operand.

The instanceof operator can be used only with reference types and objects, not primitive types and values. Examples of instanceof are:

```
// True: all strings are instances of String
"string" instanceof String
// True: strings are also instances of Object
```

```
"" instanceof Object
// False: null is never an instance of anything
null instanceof String

Object o = new int[] {1,2,3};
o instanceof int[]    // True: the array value is an int array
o instanceof byte[]   // False: the array value is not a byte array
o instanceof Object   // True: all arrays are instances of Object

// Use instanceof to make sure that it is safe to cast an object
if (object instanceof Point) {
    Point p = (Point) object;
}
```

Special Operators

Java has six language constructs that are sometimes considered operators and some-times considered simply part of the basic language syntax. These "operators" were included in Table 2-4 in order to show their precedence relative to the other true operators. The use of these language constructs is detailed elsewhere in this book, but is described briefly here so that you can recognize them in code examples:

Object member access (.)

An *object* is a collection of data and methods that operate on that data; the data fields and methods of an object are called its members. The dot (.) operator accesses these members. If o is an expression that evaluates to an object refer-ence, and f is the name of a field of the object, o.f evaluates to the value con-tained in that field. If m is the name of a method, o.m refers to that method and allows it to be invoked using the ( ) operator shown later.

Array element access ([ ])

An *array* is a numbered list of values. Each element of an array can be referred to by its number, or *index*. The [ ] operator allows you to refer to the individ-ual elements of an array. If a is an array, and i is an expression that evaluates to an int, a[i] refers to one of the elements of a. Unlike other operators that work with integer values, this operator restricts array index values to be of type int or narrower.

Method invocation (( ))

A *method* is a named collection of Java code that can be run, or *invoked*, by fol-lowing the name of the method with zero or more comma-separated expres-sions contained within parentheses. The values of these expressions are the *arguments* to the method. The method processes the arguments and optionally returns a value that becomes the value of the method invocation expression. If o.m is a method that expects no arguments, the method can be invoked with o.m(). If the method expects three arguments, for example, it can be invoked with an expression such as o.m(x,y,z). Before the Java interpreter invokes a method, it evaluates each of the arguments to be passed to the method. These expressions are guaranteed to be evaluated in order from left to right (which matters if any of the arguments have side effects).

Lambda expression (→)
> A *lambda expression* is an anonymous collection of executable Java code, essentially a method body. It consists of a method argument list (zero or more comma-separated expressions contained within parentheses) followed by the lambda *arrow* operator followed by a block of Java code. If the block of code comprises just a single statement, then the usual curly braces to denote block boundaries can be omitted.

Object creation (new)
> In Java, objects (and arrays) are created with the new operator, which is followed by the type of the object to be created and a parenthesized list of arguments to be passed to the object *constructor*. A constructor is a special block of code that initializes a newly created object, so the object creation syntax is similar to the Java method invocation syntax. For example:
>
> ```
> new ArrayList();
> new Point(1,2)
> ```

Type conversion or casting (())
> As we've already seen, parentheses can also be used as an operator to perform narrowing type conversions, or casts. The first operand of this operator is the type to be converted to; it is placed between the parentheses. The second operand is the value to be converted; it follows the parentheses. For example:
>
> ```
> (byte) 28          // An integer literal cast to a byte type
> (int) (x + 3.14f)  // A floating-point sum value cast to an integer
> (String)h.get(k)   // A generic object cast to a string
> ```

Statements

A *statement* is a basic unit of execution in the Java language—it expresses a single piece of intent by the programmer. Unlike expressions, Java statements do not have a value. Statements also typically contain expressions and operators (especially assignment operators) and are frequently executed for the side effects that they cause.

Many of the statements defined by Java are flow-control statements, such as conditionals and loops, that can alter the default, linear order of execution in well-defined ways. Table 2-5 summarizes the statements defined by Java.

Table 2-5. Java statements

Statement	Purpose	Syntax
expression	side effects	*var* = *expr* ; *expr* ++; *method* (); new *Type* ( );
compound	group statements	{ *statements* }
empty	do nothing	;
labeled	name a statement	*label* : *statement*
variable	declare a variable	[final] *type name* [= *value*] [, *name* [= *value*]] ...;
if	conditional	if (*expr*) *statement* [else *statement*]
switch	conditional	switch (*expr*) { [case *expr* : *statements*] ... [default: *statements*] }
while	loop	while (*expr*) *statement*
do	loop	do *statement* while (*expr*);
for	simplified loop	for (*init* ; *test* ; *increment*) *statement*
foreach	collection iteration	for (*variable* : *iterable*) *statement*
break	exit block	break [*label*] ;
continue	restart loop	continue [*label*] ;
return	end method	return [*expr*] ;
synchronized	critical section	synchronized (*expr*) { *statements* }
throw	throw exception	throw *expr* ;
try	handle exception	try { *statements* } [catch (*type name*) { *statements* }] ... [finally { *statements* }]
assert	verify invariant	assert *invariant* [: *error*];

Expression Statements

As we saw earlier in the chapter, certain types of Java expressions have side effects. In other words, they do not simply evaluate to some value; they also change the program state in some way. Any expression with side effects can be used as a statement simply by following it with a semicolon. The legal types of expression statements are assignments, increments and decrements, method calls, and object creation. For example:

```
a = 1;                              // Assignment
x *= 2;                             // Assignment with operation
i++;                                // Post-increment
--c;                                // Pre-decrement
System.out.println("statement");    // Method invocation
```

Compound Statements

A *compound statement* is any number and kind of statements grouped together within curly braces. You can use a compound statement anywhere a statement is required by Java syntax:

```
for(int i = 0; i < 10; i++) {
    a[i]++;            // Body of this loop is a compound statement.
    b[i]--;            // It consists of two expression statements
}                      // within curly braces.
```

The Empty Statement

An *empty statement* in Java is written as a single semicolon. The empty statement doesn't do anything, but the syntax is occasionally useful. For example, you can use it to indicate an empty loop body in a for loop:

```
for(int i = 0; i < 10; a[i++]++)    // Increment array elements
    /* empty */;                    // Loop body is empty statement
```

Labeled Statements

A *labeled statement* is simply a statement that has been given a name by prepending an identifier and a colon to it. Labels are used by the break and continue statements. For example:

```
rowLoop: for(int r = 0; r < rows.length; r++) {        // Labeled loop
    colLoop: for(int c = 0; c < columns.length; c++) { // Another one
        break rowLoop;                                 // Use a label
    }
}
```

Local Variable Declaration Statements

A *local variable*, often simply called a variable, is a symbolic name for a location to store a value that is defined within a method or compound statement. All variables must be declared before they can be used; this is done with a variable declaration statement. Because Java is a statically typed language, a variable declaration specifies the type of the variable, and only values of that type can be stored in the variable.

In its simplest form, a variable declaration specifies a variable's type and name:

```
int counter;
String s;
```

A variable declaration can also include an *initializer*: an expression that specifies an initial value for the variable. For example:

```
int i = 0;
String s = readLine();
int[] data = {x+1, x+2, x+3}; // Array initializers are discussed later
```

The Java compiler does not allow you to use a local variable that has not been initialized, so it is usually convenient to combine variable declaration and initialization into a single statement. The initializer expression need not be a literal value or a constant expression that can be evaluated by the compiler; it can be an arbitrarily complex expression whose value is computed when the program is run.

A single variable declaration statement can declare and initialize more than one variable, but all variables must be of the same type. Variable names and optional initializers are separated from each other with commas:

```
int i, j, k;
float x = 1.0, y = 1.0;
String question = "Really Quit?", response;
```

Variable declaration statements can begin with the `final` keyword. This modifier specifies that once an initial value is specified for the variable, that value is never allowed to change:

```
final String greeting = getLocalLanguageGreeting();
```

We will have more to say about the `final` keyword later on, especially when talking about the immutable style of programming.

C programmers should note that Java variable declaration statements can appear anywhere in Java code; they are not restricted to the beginning of a method or block of code. Local variable declarations can also be integrated with the *initialize* portion of a for loop, as we'll discuss shortly.

Local variables can be used only within the method or block of code in which they are defined. This is called their *scope* or *lexical scope*:

```
void method() {              // A method definition
    int i = 0;               // Declare variable i
    while (i < 10) {         // i is in scope here
        int j = 0;           // Declare j; the scope of j begins here
        i++;                 // i is in scope here; increment it
    }                        // j is no longer in scope;
    System.out.println(i);   // i is still in scope here
}                            // The scope of i ends here
```

The if/else Statement

The if statement is a fundamental control statement that allows Java to make decisions or, more precisely, to execute statements conditionally. The if statement has an associated expression and statement. If the expression evaluates to true, the interpreter executes the statement. If the expression evaluates to false, the interpreter skips the statement.

 Java allows the expression to be of the wrapper type Boolean instead of the primitive type boolean. In this case, the wrapper object is automatically unboxed.

Here is an example if statement:

```
if (username == null)        // If username is null,
    username = "John Doe";   // use a default value
```

Although they look extraneous, the parentheses around the expression are a required part of the syntax for the if statement. As we already saw, a block of statements enclosed in curly braces is itself a statement, so we can write if statements that look like this as well:

```
if ((address == null) || (address.equals(""))) {
    address = "[undefined]";
    System.out.println("WARNING: no address specified.");
}
```

An if statement can include an optional else keyword that is followed by a second statement. In this form of the statement, the expression is evaluated, and, if it is true, the first statement is executed. Otherwise, the second statement is executed. For example:

```
if (username != null)
    System.out.println("Hello " + username);
else {
    username = askQuestion("What is your name?");
    System.out.println("Hello " + username + ". Welcome!");
}
```

When you use nested if/else statements, some caution is required to ensure that the else clause goes with the appropriate if statement. Consider the following lines:

```
if (i == j)
    if (j == k)
        System.out.println("i equals k");
else
    System.out.println("i doesn't equal j");    // WRONG!!
```

In this example, the inner `if` statement forms the single statement allowed by the syntax of the outer `if` statement. Unfortunately, it is not clear (except from the hint given by the indentation) which `if` the `else` goes with. And in this example, the indentation hint is wrong. The rule is that an `else` clause like this is associated with the nearest `if` statement. Properly indented, this code looks like this:

```
if (i == j)
    if (j == k)
        System.out.println("i equals k");
    else
        System.out.println("i doesn't equal j");    // WRONG!!
```

This is legal code, but it is clearly not what the programmer had in mind. When working with nested `if` statements, you should use curly braces to make your code easier to read. Here is a better way to write the code:

```
if (i == j) {
    if (j == k)
        System.out.println("i equals k");
}
else {
    System.out.println("i doesn't equal j");
}
```

The else if clause

The `if/else` statement is useful for testing a condition and choosing between two statements or blocks of code to execute. But what about when you need to choose between several blocks of code? This is typically done with an `else if` clause, which is not really new syntax, but a common idiomatic usage of the standard `if/else` statement. It looks like this:

```
if (n == 1) {
    // Execute code block #1
}
else if (n == 2) {
    // Execute code block #2
}
else if (n == 3) {
    // Execute code block #3
}
else {
    // If all else fails, execute block #4
}
```

There is nothing special about this code. It is just a series of `if` statements, where each `if` is part of the `else` clause of the previous statement. Using the `else if` idiom is preferable to, and more legible than, writing these statements out in their fully nested form:

```
if (n == 1) {
    // Execute code block #1
```

```
    }
    else {
       if (n == 2) {
          // Execute code block #2
       }
       else {
         if (n == 3) {
            // Execute code block #3
         }
         else {
            // If all else fails, execute block #4
         }
       }
    }
}
```

The switch Statement

An if statement causes a branch in the flow of a program's execution. You can use multiple if statements, as shown in the previous section, to perform a multiway branch. This is not always the best solution, however, especially when all of the branches depend on the value of a single variable. In this case, it is inefficient to repeatedly check the value of the same variable in multiple if statements.

A better solution is to use a switch statement, which is inherited from the C programming language. Although the syntax of this statement is not nearly as elegant as other parts of Java, the brute practicality of the construct makes it worthwhile.

 A switch statement starts with an expression whose type is an int, short, char, byte (or their wrapper type), String, or an enum (see Chapter 4 for more on enumerated types).

This expression is followed by a block of code in curly braces that contains various entry points that correspond to possible values for the expression. For example, the following switch statement is equivalent to the repeated if and else/if statements shown in the previous section:

```
switch(n) {
   case 1:                  // Start here if n == 1
      // Execute code block #1
      break;                // Stop here
   case 2:                  // Start here if n == 2
      // Execute code block #2
      break;                // Stop here
   case 3:                  // Start here if n == 3
      // Execute code block #3
      break;                // Stop here
   default:                 // If all else fails...
      // Execute code block #4
```

```
        break;                      // Stop here
    }
```

As you can see from the example, the various entry points into a `switch` statement are labeled either with the keyword `case`, followed by an integer value and a colon, or with the special `default` keyword, followed by a colon. When a `switch` statement executes, the interpreter computes the value of the expression in parentheses and then looks for a `case` label that matches that value. If it finds one, the interpreter starts executing the block of code at the first statement following the `case` label. If it does not find a `case` label with a matching value, the interpreter starts execution at the first statement following a special-case `default:` label. Or, if there is no `default:` label, the interpreter skips the body of the `switch` statement altogether.

Note the use of the `break` keyword at the end of each `case` in the previous code. The `break` statement is described later in this chapter, but, in this case, it causes the interpreter to exit the body of the `switch` statement. The `case` clauses in a `switch` statement specify only the starting point of the desired code. The individual cases are not independent blocks of code, and they do not have any implicit ending point. Therefore, you must explicitly specify the end of each case with a `break` or related statement. In the absence of `break` statements, a `switch` statement begins executing code at the first statement after the matching `case` label and continues executing statements until it reaches the end of the block. On rare occasions, it is useful to write code like this that falls through from one `case` label to the next, but 99% of the time you should be careful to end every `case` and `default` section with a statement that causes the `switch` statement to stop executing. Normally you use a `break` statement, but `return` and `throw` also work.

A `switch` statement can have more than one `case` clause labeling the same statement. Consider the `switch` statement in the following method:

```
boolean parseYesOrNoResponse(char response) {
    switch(response) {
      case 'y':
      case 'Y': return true;
      case 'n':
      case 'N': return false;
      default:
        throw new IllegalArgumentException("Response must be Y or N");
    }
}
```

The `switch` statement and its `case` labels have some important restrictions. First, the expression associated with a `switch` statement must have an appropriate type—either `byte`, `char`, `short`, `int` (or their wrappers), or an enum type or a `String`. The floating-point and `boolean` types are not supported, and neither is `long`, even though `long` is an integer type. Second, the value associated with each `case` label must be a constant value or a constant expression the compiler can evaluate. A `case` label cannot contain a runtime expression involving variables or method calls, for example. Third, the `case` label values must be within the range of the data type used for the switch expression. And finally, it is not legal to have two or more case labels with the same value or more than one default label.

The while Statement

The while statement is a basic statement that allows Java to perform repetitive actions—or, to put it another way, it is one of Java's primary *looping constructs*. It has the following syntax:

```
while (expression)
    statement
```

The while statement works by first evaluating the *expression*, which must result in a boolean or Boolean value. If the value is false, the interpreter skips the *statement* associated with the loop and moves to the next statement in the program. If it is true, however, the *statement* that forms the body of the loop is executed, and the *expression* is reevaluated. Again, if the value of *expression* is false, the interpreter moves on to the next statement in the program; otherwise, it executes the *statement* again. This cycle continues while the *expression* remains true (i.e., until it evaluates to false), at which point the while statement ends, and the interpreter moves on to the next statement. You can create an infinite loop with the syntax while(true).

Here is an example while loop that prints the numbers 0 to 9:

```
int count = 0;
while (count < 10) {
    System.out.println(count);
    count++;
}
```

As you can see, the variable count starts off at 0 in this example and is incremented each time the body of the loop runs. Once the loop has executed 10 times, the expression becomes false (i.e., count is no longer less than 10), the while statement finishes, and the Java interpreter can move to the next statement in the program. Most loops have a counter variable like count. The variable names i, j, and k are commonly used as loop counters, although you should use more descriptive names if it makes your code easier to understand.

The do Statement

A do loop is much like a while loop, except that the loop expression is tested at the bottom of the loop rather than at the top. This means that the body of the loop is always executed at least once. The syntax is:

```
do
    statement
while (expression);
```

Notice a couple of differences between the do loop and the more ordinary while loop. First, the do loop requires both the do keyword to mark the beginning of the loop and the while keyword to mark the end and introduce the loop condition. Also, unlike the while loop, the do loop is terminated with a semicolon. This is because the do loop ends with the loop condition rather than simply ending with a curly brace that marks the end of the loop body. The following do loop prints the same output as the while loop just discussed:

```
int count = 0;
do {
    System.out.println(count);
    count++;
} while(count < 10);
```

The do loop is much less commonly used than its while cousin because, in practice, it is unusual to encounter a situation where you are sure you always want a loop to execute at least once.

The for Statement

The for statement provides a looping construct that is often more convenient than the while and do loops. The for statement takes advantage of a common looping pattern. Most loops have a counter, or state variable of some kind, that is initialized before the loop starts, tested to determine whether to execute the loop body, and then incremented or updated somehow at the end of the loop body before the test expression is evaluated again. The initialization, test, and update steps are the three crucial manipulations of a loop variable, and the for statement makes these three steps an explicit part of the loop syntax:

```
for(initialize; test; update) {
    statement
}
```

This for loop is basically equivalent to the following while loop:

```
initialize;
while (test) {
    statement;
    update;
}
```

Placing the *initialize, test,* and *update* expressions at the top of a for loop makes it especially easy to understand what the loop is doing, and it prevents mistakes such as forgetting to initialize or update the loop variable. The interpreter discards the values of the *initialize* and *update* expressions, so to be useful, these expressions must have side effects. *initialize* is typically an assignment expression while *update* is usually an increment, decrement, or some other assignment.

The following for loop prints the numbers 0 to 9, just as the previous while and do loops have done:

```
int count;
for(count = 0 ; count < 10 ; count++)
    System.out.println(count);
```

Notice how this syntax places all the important information about the loop variable on a single line, making it very clear how the loop executes. Placing the update expression in the for statement itself also simplifies the body of the loop to a single statement; we don't even need to use curly braces to produce a statement block.

The for loop supports some additional syntax that makes it even more convenient to use. Because many loops use their loop variables only within the loop, the for loop allows the *initialize* expression to be a full variable declaration, so that the variable is scoped to the body of the loop and is not visible outside of it. For example:

```
for(int count = 0 ; count < 10 ; count++)
    System.out.println(count);
```

Furthermore, the for loop syntax does not restrict you to writing loops that use only a single variable. Both the *initialize* and *update* expressions of a for loop can use a comma to separate multiple initializations and update expressions. For example:

```
for(int i = 0, j = 10 ; i < 10 ; i++, j--)
    sum += i * j;
```

Even though all the examples so far have counted numbers, for loops are not restricted to loops that count numbers. For example, you might use a for loop to iterate through the elements of a linked list:

```
for(Node n = listHead; n != null; n = n.nextNode())
    process(n);
```

The *initialize, test,* and *update* expressions of a for loop are all optional; only the semicolons that separate the expressions are required. If the *test* expression is omitted, it is assumed to be true. Thus, you can write an infinite loop as for(;;).

The foreach Statement

Java's for loop works well for primitive types, but it is needlessly clunky for handling collections of objects. Instead, an alternative syntax known as a *foreach* loop is used for handling collections of objects that need to be looped over.

The foreach loop uses the keyword for followed by an opening parenthesis, a variable declaration (without initializer), a colon, an expression, a closing parenthesis, and finally the statement (or block) that forms the body of the loop:

```
for( declaration : expression )
    statement
```

Despite its name, the foreach loop does not have a keyword foreach—instead, it is common to read the colon as "in"—as in "foreach name in studentNames."

For the while, do, and for loops, we've shown an example that prints 10 numbers. The foreach loop can do this too, but it needs a collection to iterate over. In order to loop 10 times (to print out 10 numbers), we need an array or other collection with 10 elements. Here's code we can use:

```
// These are the numbers we want to print
int[] primes = new int[] { 2, 3, 5, 7, 11, 13, 17, 19, 23, 29 };
// This is the loop that prints them
for(int n : primes)
    System.out.println(n);
```

What foreach cannot do

Foreach is different from the while, for, or do loops, because it hides the loop counter or Iterator from you. This is a very powerful idea, as we'll see when we discuss lambda expressions, but there are some algorithms that cannot be expressed very naturally with a foreach loop.

For example, suppose you want to print the elements of an array as a comma-separated list. To do this, you need to print a comma after every element of the array except the last, or equivalently, before every element of the array except the first. With a traditional for loop, the code might look like this:

```
for(int i = 0; i < words.length; i++) {
    if (i > 0) System.out.print(", ");
    System.out.print(words[i]);
}
```

This is a very straightforward task, but you simply cannot do it with foreach. The problem is that the foreach loop doesn't give you a loop counter or any other way to tell if you're on the first iteration, the last iteration, or somewhere in between.

 A similar issue exists when using foreach to iterate through the elements of a collection. Just as a foreach loop over an array has no way to obtain the array index of the current element, a foreach loop over a collection has no way to obtain the Iterator object that is being used to itemize the elements of the collection.

Here are some other things you cannot do with a foreach style loop:

- Iterate backward through the elements of an array or List.

- Use a single loop counter to access the same-numbered elements of two distinct arrays.

- Iterate through the elements of a List using calls to its get() method rather than calls to its iterator.

The break Statement

A break statement causes the Java interpreter to skip immediately to the end of a containing statement. We have already seen the break statement used with the switch statement. The break statement is most often written as simply the keyword break followed by a semicolon:

```
break;
```

When used in this form, it causes the Java interpreter to immediately exit the innermost containing while, do, for, or switch statement. For example:

```
for(int i = 0; i < data.length; i++) {
    if (data[i] == target) {  // When we find what we're looking for,
        index = i;            // remember where we found it
        break;                // and stop looking!
    }
}   // The Java interpreter goes here after executing break
```

The break statement can also be followed by the name of a containing labeled statement. When used in this form, break causes the Java interpreter to immediately exit the named block, which can be any kind of statement, not just a loop or switch. For example:

```
TESTFORNULL: if (data != null) {
    for(int row = 0; row < numrows; row++) {
        for(int col = 0; col < numcols; col++) {
            if (data[row][col] == null)
                break TESTFORNULL;          // treat the array as undefined.
        }
    }
}   // Java interpreter goes here after executing break TESTFORNULL
```

The continue Statement

While a break statement exits a loop, a continue statement quits the current iteration of a loop and starts the next one. continue, in both its unlabeled and labeled forms, can be used only within a while, do, or for loop. When used without a label, continue causes the innermost loop to start a new iteration. When used with a label that is the name of a containing loop, it causes the named loop to start a new iteration. For example:

```
for(int i = 0; i < data.length; i++) {  // Loop through data.
    if (data[i] == -1)                   // If a data value is missing,
        continue;                        // skip to the next iteration.
    process(data[i]);                    // Process the data value.
}
```

while, do, and for loops differ slightly in the way that continue starts a new iteration:

- With a while loop, the Java interpreter simply returns to the top of the loop, tests the loop condition again, and, if it evaluates to true, executes the body of the loop again.

- With a do loop, the interpreter jumps to the bottom of the loop, where it tests the loop condition to decide whether to perform another iteration of the loop.

- With a for loop, the interpreter jumps to the top of the loop, where it first evaluates the *update* expression and then evaluates the *test* expression to decide whether to loop again. As you can see from the examples, the behavior of a for loop with a continue statement is different from the behavior of the "basically equivalent" while loop presented earlier; *update* gets evaluated in the for loop but not in the equivalent while loop.

The return Statement

A return statement tells the Java interpreter to stop executing the current method. If the method is declared to return a value, the return statement must be followed by an expression. The value of the expression becomes the return value of the method. For example, the following method computes and returns the square of a number:

```
double square(double x) {    // A method to compute x squared
    return x * x;            // Compute and return a value
}
```

Some methods are declared void to indicate that they do not return any value. The Java interpreter runs methods like this by executing their statements one by one until it reaches the end of the method. After executing the last statement, the interpreter returns implicitly. Sometimes, however, a void method has to return explicitly before reaching the last statement. In this case, it can use the return statement by itself, without any expression. For example, the following method prints, but does not return, the square root of its argument. If the argument is a negative number, it returns without printing anything:

```
// A method to print square root of x
void printSquareRoot(double x) {
    if (x < 0) return;                   // If x is negative, return
    System.out.println(Math.sqrt(x));    // Print the square root of x
}                                        // Method end: return implicitly
```

The synchronized Statement

Java has always provided support for multithreaded programming. We cover this in some detail later on (especially in "Java's Support for Concurrency" on page 208)— but the reader should be aware that concurrency is difficult to get right, and has a number of subtleties.

In particular, when working with multiple threads, you must often take care to prevent multiple threads from modifying an object simultaneously in a way that might corrupt the object's state. Java provides the synchronized statement to help the programmer prevent corruption. The syntax is:

```
synchronized ( expression ) {
    statements
}
```

expression is an expression that must evaluate to an object or an array. *statements* constitute the code of the section that could cause damage and must be enclosed in curly braces.

Before executing the statement block, the Java interpreter first obtains an exclusive lock on the object or array specified by *expression*. It holds the lock until it is finished running the block, then releases it. While a thread holds the lock on an object, no other thread can obtain that lock.

The synchronized keyword is also available as a method modifier in Java, and when applied to a method, the synchronized keyword indicates that the entire method is locked. For a synchronized class method (a static method), Java obtains an exclusive lock on the class before executing the method. For a synchronized instance method, Java obtains an exclusive lock on the class instance. (Class and instance methods are discussed in Chapter 3.)

The throw Statement

An *exception* is a signal that indicates some sort of exceptional condition or error has occurred. To *throw* an exception is to signal an exceptional condition. To *catch* an exception is to handle it—to take whatever actions are necessary to recover from it. In Java, the throw statement is used to throw an exception:

```
throw expression;
```

The *expression* must evaluate to an exception object that describes the exception or error that has occurred. We'll talk more about types of exceptions shortly; for now, all you need to know is that an exception is represented by an object, which has a slightly specialized role. Here is some example code that throws an exception:

```
public static double factorial(int x) {
    if (x < 0)
        throw new IllegalArgumentException("x must be >= 0");
    double fact;
    for(fact=1.0; x > 1; fact *= x, x--)
        /* empty */ ;          // Note use of the empty statement
    return fact;
}
```

When the Java interpreter executes a throw statement, it immediately stops normal program execution and starts looking for an exception handler that can catch, or handle, the exception. Exception handlers are written with the try/catch/finally statement, which is described in the next section. The Java interpreter first looks at the enclosing block of code to see if it has an associated exception handler. If so, it exits that block of code and starts running the exception-handling code associated with the block. After running the exception handler, the interpreter continues execution at the statement immediately following the handler code.

If the enclosing block of code does not have an appropriate exception handler, the interpreter checks the next higher enclosing block of code in the method. This continues until a handler is found. If the method does not contain an exception handler that can handle the exception thrown by the throw statement, the interpreter stops running the current method and returns to the caller. Now the interpreter starts looking for an exception handler in the blocks of code of the calling method. In this way, exceptions propagate up through the lexical structure of Java methods, up the call stack of the Java interpreter. If the exception is never caught, it propagates all the way up to the main() method of the program. If it is not handled in that method, the Java interpreter prints an error message, prints a stack trace to indicate where the exception occurred, and then exits.

The try/catch/finally Statement

Java has two slightly different exception-handling mechanisms. The classic form is the try/catch/finally statement. The try clause of this statement establishes a block of code for exception handling. This try block is followed by zero or more catch clauses, each of which is a block of statements designed to handle specific exceptions. Each catch block can handle more than one different exception—to indicate that a catch block should handle multiple exceptions, we use the | symbol to separate the different exceptions a catch block should handle. The catch clauses are followed by an optional finally block that contains cleanup code guaranteed to be executed regardless of what happens in the try block.

---

try Block Syntax

Both the catch and finally clauses are optional, but every try block must be accompanied by at least one or the other. The try, catch, and finally blocks all begin and end with curly braces. These are a required part of the syntax and cannot be omitted, even if the clause contains only a single statement.

The following code illustrates the syntax and purpose of the try/catch/finally statement:

```
try {
    // Normally this code runs from the top of the block to the bottom
    // without problems. But it can sometimes throw an exception,
    // either directly with a throw statement or indirectly by calling
    // a method that throws an exception.
}
catch (SomeException e1) {
```

```
    // This block contains statements that handle an exception object
    // of type SomeException or a subclass of that type. Statements in
    // this block can refer to that exception object by the name e1.
}
catch (AnotherException | YetAnotherException e2) {
    // This block contains statements that handle an exception of
    // type AnotherException or YetAnotherException, or a subclass of
    // either of those types. Statements in this block refer to the
    // exception object they receive by the name e2.
}
finally {
    // This block contains statements that are always executed
    // after we leave the try clause, regardless of whether we leave it:
    //    1) normally, after reaching the bottom of the block;
    //    2) because of a break, continue, or return statement;
    //    3) with an exception that is handled by a catch clause above;
    //    4) with an uncaught exception that has not been handled.
    // If the try clause calls System.exit(), however, the interpreter
    // exits before the finally clause can be run.
}
```

try

The try clause simply establishes a block of code that either has its exceptions handled or needs special cleanup code to be run when it terminates for any reason. The try clause by itself doesn't do anything interesting; it is the catch and finally clauses that do the exception-handling and cleanup operations.

catch

A try block can be followed by zero or more catch clauses that specify code to handle various types of exceptions. Each catch clause is declared with a single argument that specifies the types of exceptions the clause can handle (possibly using the special | syntax to indicate that the catch block can handle more than one type of exception) and also provides a name the clause can use to refer to the exception object it is currently handling. Any type that a catch block wishes to handle must be some subclass of Throwable.

When an exception is thrown, the Java interpreter looks for a catch clause with an argument that matches the same type as the exception object or a superclass of that type. The interpreter invokes the first such catch clause it finds. The code within a catch block should take whatever action is necessary to cope with the exceptional condition. If the exception is a java.io.FileNotFoundException exception, for example, you might handle it by asking the user to check his spelling and try again.

It is not required to have a catch clause for every possible exception; in some cases, the correct response is to allow the exception to propagate up and be caught by the invoking method. In other cases, such as a programming error signaled by Null PointerException, the correct response is probably not to catch the exception at all, but allow it to propagate and have the Java interpreter exit with a stack trace and an error message.

finally

The finally clause is generally used to clean up after the code in the try clause (e.g., close files and shut down network connections). The finally clause is useful because it is guaranteed to be executed if any portion of the try block is executed, regardless of how the code in the try block completes. In fact, the only way a try clause can exit without allowing the finally clause to be executed is by invoking the System.exit() method, which causes the Java interpreter to stop running.

In the normal case, control reaches the end of the try block and then proceeds to the finally block, which performs any necessary cleanup. If control leaves the try block because of a return, continue, or break statement, the finally block is executed before control transfers to its new destination.

If an exception occurs in the try block and there is an associated catch block to handle the exception, control transfers first to the catch block and then to the finally block. If there is no local catch block to handle the exception, control transfers first to the finally block, and then propagates up to the nearest containing catch clause that can handle the exception.

If a finally block itself transfers control with a return, continue, break, or throw statement or by calling a method that throws an exception, the pending control transfer is abandoned, and this new transfer is processed. For example, if a finally clause throws an exception, that exception replaces any exception that was in the process of being thrown. If a finally clause issues a return statement, the method returns normally, even if an exception has been thrown and has not yet been handled.

try and finally can be used together without exceptions or any catch clauses. In this case, the finally block is simply cleanup code that is guaranteed to be executed, regardless of any break, continue, or return statements within the try clause.

The try-with-resources Statement

The standard form of a try block is very general, but there is a common set of circumstances that require developers to be very careful when writing catch and finally blocks. These circumstances are when operating with resources that need to be cleaned up or closed when no longer needed.

Java (since version 7) provides a very useful mechanism for automatically closing resources that require cleanup. This is known as try-with-resources, or TWR. We discuss TWR in detail in "Classic Java I/O" on page 289—but for completeness, let's introduce the syntax now. The following example shows how to open a file using the `FileInputStream` class (which results in an object which will require cleanup):

```java
try (InputStream is = new FileInputStream("/Users/ben/details.txt")) {
    // ... process the file
}
```

This new form of `try` takes parameters that are all objects that require cleanup.[2] These objects are scoped to this `try` block, and are then cleaned up automatically no matter how this block is exited. The developer does not need to write any `catch` or `finally` blocks—the Java compiler automatically inserts correct cleanup code.

All new code that deals with resources should be written in the TWR style—it is considerably less error prone than manually writing `catch` blocks, and does not suffer from the problems that plague techniques such as finalization (see "Finalization" on page 206 for details).

The assert Statement

An `assert` statement is an attempt to provide a capability to verify design assumptions in Java code. An *assertion* consists of the `assert` keyword followed by a boolean expression that the programmer believes should always evaluate to `true`. By default, assertions are not enabled, and the `assert` statement does not actually do anything.

It is possible to enable assertions as a debugging tool, however; when this is done, the `assert` statement evaluates the expression. If it is indeed `true`, `assert` does nothing. On the other hand, if the expression evaluates to `false`, the assertion fails, and the `assert` statement throws a `java.lang.AssertionError`.

Outside of the core JDK libraries, the `assert` statement is *extremely* rarely used. It turns out to be too inflexible for testing most applications and is not often used by ordinary developers, except sometimes for field-debugging complex multithreaded applications.

The `assert` statement may include an optional second expression, separated from the first by a colon. When assertions are enabled and the first expression evaluates to `false`, the value of the second expression is taken as an error code or error message and is passed to the `AssertionError()` constructor. The full syntax of the statement is:

```java
assert assertion;
```

or:

```java
assert assertion : errorcode;
```

---

2 Technically, they must all implement the `AutoCloseable` interface.

To use assertions effectively, you must also be aware of a couple of fine points. First, remember that your programs will normally run with assertions disabled and only sometimes with assertions enabled. This means that you should be careful not to write assertion expressions that contain side effects.

 You should never throw `AssertionError` from your own code, as it may have unexpected results in future versions of the platform.

If an `AssertionError` is thrown, it indicates that one of the programmer's assumptions has not held up. This means that the code is being used outside of the parameters for which it was designed, and it cannot be expected to work correctly. In short, there is no plausible way to recover from an `AssertionError`, and you should not attempt to catch it (unless you catch it at the top level simply so that you can display the error in a more user-friendly fashion).

Enabling assertions

For efficiency, it does not make sense to test assertions each time code is executed— `assert` statements encode assumptions that should always be true. Thus, by default, assertions are disabled, and `assert` statements have no effect. The assertion code remains compiled in the class files, however, so it can always be enabled for diagnostic or debugging purposes. You can enable assertions, either across the board or selectively, with command-line arguments to the Java interpreter.

To enable assertions in all classes except for system classes, use the `-ea` argument. To enable assertions in system classes, use `-esa`. To enable assertions within a specific class, use `-ea` followed by a colon and the classname:

```
java -ea:com.example.sorters.MergeSort com.example.sorters.Test
```

To enable assertions for all classes in a package and in all of its subpackages, follow the `-ea` argument with a colon, the package name, and three dots:

```
java -ea:com.example.sorters... com.example.sorters.Test
```

You can disable assertions in the same way, using the `-da` argument. For example, to enable assertions throughout a package and then disable them in a specific class or subpackage, use:

```
java -ea:com.example.sorters... -da:com.example.sorters.QuickSort
java -ea:com.example.sorters... -da:com.example.sorters.plugins..
```

Finally, it is possible to control whether or not assertions are enabled or disabled at classloading time. If you use a custom classloader (see Chapter 11 for details on custom classloading) in your program and want to turn on assertions, you may be interested in these methods.

Methods

A *method* is a named sequence of Java statements that can be invoked by other Java code. When a method is invoked, it is passed zero or more values known as *arguments*. The method performs some computations and, optionally, returns a value. As described earlier in "Expressions and Operators" on page 30, a method invocation is an expression that is evaluated by the Java interpreter. Because method invocations can have side effects, however, they can also be used as expression statements. This section does not discuss method invocation, but instead describes how to define methods.

Defining Methods

You already know how to define the body of a method; it is simply an arbitrary sequence of statements enclosed within curly braces. What is more interesting about a method is its *signature*.[3] The signature specifies the following:

- The name of the method
- The number, order, type, and name of the parameters used by the method
- The type of the value returned by the method
- The checked exceptions that the method can throw (the signature may also list unchecked exceptions, but these are not required)
- Various method modifiers that provide additional information about the method

A method signature defines everything you need to know about a method before calling it. It is the method *specification* and defines the API for the method. In order to use the Java platform's online API reference, you need to know how to read a method signature. And, in order to write Java programs, you need to know how to define your own methods, each of which begins with a method signature.

A method signature looks like this:

```
modifiers type name ( paramlist ) [ throws exceptions ]
```

The signature (the method specification) is followed by the method body (the method implementation), which is simply a sequence of Java statements enclosed in curly braces. If the method is *abstract* (see Chapter 3), the implementation is omitted, and the method body is replaced with a single semicolon.

The signature of a method may also include type variable declarations—such methods are known as *generic methods*. Generic methods and type variables are discussed in Chapter 4.

---

3 In the Java Language Specification, the term "signature" has a technical meaning that is slightly different than that used here. This book uses a less formal definition of method signature.

Here are some example method definitions, which begin with the signature and are followed by the method body:

```java
// This method is passed an array of strings and has no return value.
// All Java programs have an entry point with this name and signature.
public static void main(String[] args) {
    if (args.length > 0) System.out.println("Hello " + args[0]);
    else System.out.println("Hello world");
}

// This method is passed two double arguments and returns a double.
static double distanceFromOrigin(double x, double y) {
    return Math.sqrt(x*x + y*y);
}

// This method is abstract which means it has no body.
// Note that it may throw exceptions when invoked.
protected abstract String readText(File f, String encoding)
    throws FileNotFoundException, UnsupportedEncodingException;
```

modifiers is zero or more special modifier keywords, separated from each other by spaces. A method might be declared with the `public` and `static` modifiers, for example. The allowed modifiers and their meanings are described in the next section.

The *type* in a method signature specifies the return type of the method. If the method does not return a value, *type* must be `void`. If a method is declared with a non-`void` return type, it must include a `return` statement that returns a value of (or convertible to) the declared type.

A *constructor* is a block of code, similar to a method, that is used to initialize newly created objects. As we'll see in Chapter 3, constructors are defined in a very similar way to methods, except that their signatures do not include this *type* specification.

The *name* of a method follows the specification of its modifiers and type. Method names, like variable names, are Java identifiers and, like all Java identifiers, may contain letters in any language represented by the Unicode character set. It is legal, and often quite useful, to define more than one method with the same name, as long as each version of the method has a different parameter list. Defining multiple methods with the same name is called *method overloading*.

Unlike some other languages, Java does not have anonymous methods. Instead, Java 8 introduces lambda expressions, which are similar to anonymous methods, but which the Java runtime automatically converts to a suitable named method— see "Lambda Expressions" on page 76 for more details.

For example, the `System.out.println()` method we've seen already is an overloaded method. One method by this name prints a string and other methods by the same name print the values of the various primitive types. The Java compiler decides which method to call based on the type of the argument passed to the method.

When you are defining a method, the name of the method is always followed by the method's parameter list, which must be enclosed in parentheses. The parameter list defines zero or more arguments that are passed to the method. The parameter specifications, if there are any, each consist of a type and a name and are separated from each other by commas (if there are multiple parameters). When a method is invoked, the argument values it is passed must match the number, type, and order of the parameters specified in this method signature line. The values passed need not have exactly the same type as specified in the signature, but they must be convertible to those types without casting.

When a Java method expects no arguments, its parameter list is simply ( ), not (void). Java does not regard void as a type—C and C++ programmers in particular should pay heed.

Java allows the programmer to define and invoke methods that accept a variable number of arguments, using a syntax known colloquially as *varargs*. Varargs are covered in detail later in this chapter.

The final part of a method signature is the throws clause, which is used to list the *checked exceptions* that a method can throw. Checked exceptions are a category of exception classes that must be listed in the throws clauses of methods that can throw them. If a method uses the throw statement to throw a checked exception, or if it calls some other method that throws a checked exception and does not catch or handle that exception, the method must declare that it can throw that exception. If a method can throw one or more checked exceptions, it specifies this by placing the throws keyword after the argument list and following it by the name of the exception class or classes it can throw. If a method does not throw any exceptions, it does not use the throws keyword. If a method throws more than one type of exception, separate the names of the exception classes from each other with commas. More on this in a bit.

Method Modifiers

The modifiers of a method consist of zero or more modifier keywords such as pub lic, static, or abstract. Here is a list of allowed modifiers and their meanings:

abstract

An abstract method is a specification without an implementation. The curly braces and Java statements that would normally comprise the body of the method are replaced with a single semicolon. A class that includes an abstract method must itself be declared abstract. Such a class is incomplete and cannot be instantiated (see Chapter 3).

final

A final method may not be overridden or hidden by a subclass, which makes it amenable to compiler optimizations that are not possible for regular methods. All private methods are implicitly final, as are all methods of any class that is declared final.

native

The native modifier specifies that the method implementation is written in some "native" language such as C and is provided externally to the Java program. Like abstract methods, native methods have no body: the curly braces are replaced with a semicolon.

Implementing native Methods

When Java was first released, native methods were sometimes used for efficiency reasons. That is almost never necessary today. Instead, native methods are used to interface Java code to existing libraries written in C or C++. native methods are implicitly platform-dependent, and the procedure for linking the implementation with the Java class that declares the method is dependent on the implementation of the Java virtual machine. native methods are not covered in this book.

---

public, protected, private

These access modifiers specify whether and where a method can be used outside of the class that defines it. These very important modifiers are explained in Chapter 3.

static

A method declared static is a *class method* associated with the class itself rather than with an instance of the class (we cover this in more detail in Chapter 3).

strictfp

The fp in this awkwardly named, rarely used modifier stands for "floating point." Java normally takes advantage of any extended precision available to the runtime platform's floating-point hardware. The use of this keyword forces Java to strictly obey the standard while running the strictfp method and only perform floating-point arithmetic using 32- or 64-bit floating-point formats, even if this makes the results less accurate.

synchronized

The synchronized modifier makes a method threadsafe. Before a thread can invoke a synchronized method, it must obtain a lock on the method's class (for static methods) or on the relevant instance of the class (for non-static methods). This prevents two threads from executing the method at the same time.

The synchronized modifier is an implementation detail (because methods can make themselves threadsafe in other ways) and is not formally part of the method specification or API. Good documentation specifies explicitly whether a method is threadsafe; you should not rely on the presence or absence of the synchronized keyword when working with multithreaded programs.

 Annotations are an interesting special case (see Chapter 4 for more on annotations)—they can be thought of as a halfway house between a method modifier and additional supplementary type information.

Checked and Unchecked Exceptions

The Java exception-handling scheme distinguishes between two types of exceptions, known as *checked* and *unchecked* exceptions.

The distinction between checked and unchecked exceptions has to do with the circumstances under which the exceptions could be thrown. Checked exceptions arise in specific, well-defined circumstances, and very often are conditions from which the application may be able to partially or fully recover.

For example, consider some code that might find its configuration file in one of several possible directories. If we attempt to open the file from a directory it isn't present in, then a FileNotFoundException will be thrown. In our example, we want to catch this exception and move on to try the next possible location for the file. In other words, although the file not being present is an exceptional condition, it is one from which we can recover, and it is an understood and anticipated failure.

On the other hand, in the Java environment there are a set of failures that cannot easily be predicted or anticipated, due to such things as runtime conditions or abuse of library code. There is no good way to predict an OutOfMemoryError, for example, and any method that uses objects or arrays can throw a NullPointerException if it is passed an invalid null argument.

These are the unchecked exceptions—and practically any method can throw an unchecked exception at essentially any time. They are the Java environment's version of Murphy's law: "Anything that can go wrong, will go wrong." Recovery from an unchecked exception is usually very difficult, if not impossible—simply due to their sheer unpredictability.

To figure out whether an exception is checked or unchecked, remember that exceptions are Throwable objects and that exceptions fall into two main categories, specified by the Error and Exception subclasses. Any exception object that is an Error is unchecked. There is also a subclass of Exception called RuntimeException—and any subclass of RuntimeException is also an unchecked exception. All other exceptions are checked exceptions.

Working with checked exceptions

Java has different rules for working with checked and unchecked exceptions. If you write a method that throws a checked exception, you must use a throws clause to declare the exception in the method signature. The Java compiler checks to make sure you have declared them in method signatures and produces a compilation error if you have not (that's why they're called "checked exceptions").

Even if you never throw a checked exception yourself, sometimes you must use a throws clause to declare a checked exception. If your method calls a method that can throw a checked exception, you must either include exception-handling code to handle that exception or use throws to declare that your method can also throw that exception.

For example, the following method tries to estimate the size of a web page—it uses the standard java.net libraries, and the class URL (we'll meet these in Chapter 10) to contact the web page. It uses methods and constructors that can throw various types of java.io.IOException objects, so it declares this fact with a throws clause:

```
public static estimateHomepageSize(String host) throws IOException {
    URL url = new URL("htp://"+ host +"/");
    try (InputStream in = url.openStream()) {
        return in.available();
    }
}
```

In fact, the preceding code has a bug: we've misspelled the protocol specifier—there's no such protocol as *htp://*. So, the estimateHomepageSize() method will always fail with a MalformedURLException.

How do you know if the method you are calling can throw a checked exception? You can look at its method signature to find out. Or, failing that, the Java compiler will tell you (by reporting a compilation error) if you've called a method whose exceptions you must handle or declare.

Variable-Length Argument Lists

Methods may be declared to accept, and may be invoked with, variable numbers of arguments. Such methods are commonly known as *varargs* methods. The "print formatted" method System.out.printf() as well as the related format() methods of String use varargs, as do a number of important methods from the Reflection API of java.lang.reflect.

A variable-length argument list is declared by following the type of the last argument to the method with an ellipsis (...), indicating that this last argument can be repeated zero or more times. For example:

```
public static int max(int first, int... rest) {
    /* body omitted for now */
}
```

Varargs methods are handled purely by the compiler. They operate by converting the variable number of arguments into an array. To the Java runtime, the `max()` method is indistinguishable from this one:

```
public static int max(int first, int[] rest) {
    /* body omitted for now */
}
```

To convert a varargs signature to the "real" signature, simply replace ... with [ ]. Remember that only one ellipsis can appear in a parameter list, and it may only appear on the last parameter in the list.

Let's flesh out the `max()` example a little:

```
public static int max(int first, int... rest) {
    int max = first;
    for(int i : rest) { // legal because rest is actually an array
        if (i > max) max = i;
    }
    return max;
}
```

This `max()` method is declared with two arguments. The first is just a regular `int` value. The second, however, may be repeated zero or more times. All of the following are legal invocations of `max()`:

```
max(0)
max(1, 2)
max(16, 8, 4, 2, 1)
```

Because varargs methods are compiled into methods that expect an array of arguments, invocations of those methods are compiled to include code that creates and initializes such an array. So the call `max(1,2,3)` is compiled to this:

```
max(1, new int[] { 2, 3 })
```

In fact, if you already have method arguments stored in an array, it is perfectly legal for you to pass them to the method that way, instead of writing them out individually. You can treat any ... argument as if it were declared as an array. The converse is not true, however: you can only use varargs method invocation syntax when the method is actually declared as a varargs method using an ellipsis.

Introduction to Classes and Objects

Now that we have introduced operators, expressions, statements, and methods, we can finally talk about classes. A *class* is a named collection of fields that hold data values and methods that operate on those values. Classes are just one of five reference types supported by Java, but they are the most important type. Classes are thoroughly documented in a chapter of their own (Chapter 3). We introduce them here, however, because they are the next higher level of syntax after methods, and because the rest of this chapter requires a basic familiarity with the concept of a class and the basic syntax for defining a class, instantiating it, and using the resulting *object*.

The most important thing about classes is that they define new data types. For example, you might define a class named `Point` to represent a data point in the two-dimensional Cartesian coordinate system. This class would define fields (each of type `double`) to hold the *x* and *y* coordinates of a point and methods to manipulate and operate on the point. The `Point` class is a new data type.

When discussing data types, it is important to distinguish between the data type itself and the values the data type represents. `char` is a data type: it represents Unicode characters. But a `char` value represents a single specific character. A class is a data type; a class value is called an *object*. We use the name class because each class defines a type (or kind, or species, or class) of objects. The `Point` class is a data type that represents *x,y* points, while a `Point` object represents a single specific *x,y* point. As you might imagine, classes and their objects are closely linked. In the sections that follow, we will discuss both.

Defining a Class

Here is a possible definition of the `Point` class we have been discussing:

```java
/** Represents a Cartesian (x,y) point */
public class Point {
    // The coordinates of the point
    public double x, y;
    public Point(double x, double y) {      // A constructor that
        this.x = x; this.y = y;              // initializes the fields
    }

    public double distanceFromOrigin() {    // A method that operates
        return Math.sqrt(x*x + y*y);         // on the x and y fields
    }
}
```

This class definition is stored in a file named *Point.java* and compiled to a file named *Point.class*, where it is available for use by Java programs and other classes. This class definition is provided here for completeness and to provide context, but don't expect to understand all the details just yet; most of Chapter 3 is devoted to the topic of defining classes.

Keep in mind that you don't have to define every class you want to use in a Java program. The Java platform includes thousands of predefined classes that are guaranteed to be available on every computer that runs Java.

Creating an Object

Now that we have defined the `Point` class as a new data type, we can use the following line to declare a variable that holds a `Point` object:

```java
Point p;
```

Declaring a variable to hold a `Point` object does not create the object itself, however. To actually create an object, you must use the new operator. This keyword is followed by the object's class (i.e., its type) and an optional argument list in parentheses. These arguments are passed to the constructor for the class, which initializes internal fields in the new object:

```
// Create a Point object representing (2,-3.5).
// Declare a variable p and store a reference to the new Point object
Point p = new Point(2.0, -3.5);

// Create some other objects as well
// A Date object that represents the current time
Date d = new Date();
// A HashSet object to hold a set of object
Set words = new HashSet();
```

The new keyword is by far the most common way to create objects in Java. A few other ways are also worth mentioning. First, classes that meet certain criteria are so important that Java defines special literal syntax for creating objects of those types (as we discuss later in this section). Second, Java supports a dynamic loading mechanism that allows programs to load classes and create instances of those classes dynamically. See Chapter 11 for more details. Finally, objects can also be created by deserializing them. An object that has had its state saved, or serialized, usually to a file, can be re-created using the `java.io.ObjectInputStream` class.

Using an Object

Now that we've seen how to define classes and instantiate them by creating objects, we need to look at the Java syntax that allows us to use those objects. Recall that a class defines a collection of fields and methods. Each object has its own copies of those fields and has access to those methods. We use the dot character (.) to access the named fields and methods of an object. For example:

```
Point p = new Point(2, 3);          // Create an object
double x = p.x;                      // Read a field of the object
p.y = p.x * p.x;                     // Set the value of a field
double d = p.distanceFromOrigin();  // Access a method of the object
```

This syntax is very common when programming in object-oriented languages, and Java is no exception, so you'll see it a lot. Note, in particular, p.distanceFromOri gin(). This expression tells the Java compiler to look up a method named distance FromOrigin() (which is defined by the class Point) and use that method to perform a computation on the fields of the object p. We'll cover the details of this operation in Chapter 3.

Object Literals

In our discussion of primitive types, we saw that each primitive type has a literal syntax for including values of the type literally into the text of a program. Java also defines a literal syntax for a few special reference types, as described next.

String literals

The String class represents text as a string of characters. Because programs usually communicate with their users through the written word, the ability to manipulate strings of text is quite important in any programming language. In Java, strings are objects; the data type used to represent text is the String class. Modern Java programs usually use more string data than anything else.

Java Syntax

Accordingly, because strings are such a fundamental data type, Java allows you to include text literally in programs by placing it between double-quote (") characters. For example:

```
String name = "David";
System.out.println("Hello, " + name);
```

Don't confuse the double-quote characters that surround string literals with the single-quote (or apostrophe) characters that surround char literals. String literals can contain any of the escape sequences char literals can (see Table 2-2). Escape sequences are particularly useful for embedding double-quote characters within double-quoted string literals. For example:

```
String story = "\t\"How can you stand it?\" he asked sarcastically.\n";
```

String literals cannot contain comments and may consist of only a single line. Java does not support any kind of continuation-character syntax that allows two separate lines to be treated as a single line. If you need to represent a long string of text that does not fit on a single line, break it into independent string literals and use the + operator to concatenate the literals. For example:

```
// This is illegal; string  literals cannot be broken across lines.
String x = "This is a test of the
            emergency broadcast system";

String s = "This is a test of the " +    // Do this instead
           "emergency broadcast system";
```

This concatenation of literals is done when your program is compiled, not when it is run, so you do not need to worry about any kind of performance penalty.

Type literals

The second type that supports its own special object literal syntax is the class named Class. Instances of the Class class represent a Java data type, and contain metadata about the type that is referred to. To include a Class object literally in a Java program, follow the name of any data type with .class. For example:

```
Class<?> typeInt = int.class;
Class<?> typeIntArray = int[].class;
Class<?> typePoint = Point.class;
```

The null reference

The null keyword is a special literal value that is a reference to nothing, or an absence of a reference. The null value is unique because it is a member of every reference type. You can assign null to variables of any reference type. For example:

```
String s = null;
Point p = null;
```

Lambda Expressions

In Java 8, a major new feature was introduced—*lambda expressions*. These are a very common programming language construct, and in particular are extremely widely used in the family of languages known as *functional programming languages* (e.g., Lisp, Haskell, and OCaml). The power and flexibility of lambdas goes far beyond just functional languages, and they can be found in almost all modern programming languages.

Definition of a Lambda Expression

A lambda expression is essentially a function that does not have a name, and can be treated as a value in the language. As Java does not allow code to run around on its own outside of classes, in Java, this means that a lambda is an anonymous method that is defined on some class (that is possibly unknown to the developer).

The syntax for a lambda expression looks like this:

```
( paramlist ) -> { statements }
```

One simple, very traditional example:

```
Runnable r = () -> System.out.println("Hello World");
```

When a lambda expression is used as a value it is automatically converted to a new object of the correct type for the variable that it is being placed into. This auto-conversion and *type inference* is essential to Java's approach to lambda expressions. Unfortunately, it relies on a proper understanding of Java's type system as a whole. "Lambda Expressions" on page 171 provides a more detailed explanation of lambda expressions—so for now, it suffices to simply recognize the syntax for lambdas.

A slightly more complex example:

```
ActionListener listener = (e) -> {
  System.out.println("Event fired at: "+ e.getWhen());
  System.out.println("Event command: "+ e.getActionCommand());
};
```

Arrays

An *array* is a special kind of object that holds zero or more primitive values or references. These values are held in the *elements* of the array, which are unnamed variables referred to by their position or *index*. The type of an array is characterized by its *element type*, and all elements of the array must be of that type.

Array elements are numbered starting with zero, and valid indexes range from zero to the number of elements minus one. The array element with index 1, for example, is the *second* element in the array. The number of elements in an array is its *length*. The length of an array is specified when the array is created, and it never changes.

The element type of an array may be any valid Java type, including array types. This means that Java supports arrays of arrays, which provide a kind of multidimensional array capability. Java does not support the matrix-style multidimensional arrays found in some languages.

Array Types

Array types are reference types, just as classes are. Instances of arrays are objects, just as the instances of a class are.[4] Unlike classes, array types do not have to be defined. Simply place square brackets after the element type. For example, the following code declares three variables of array type:

```
byte b;                      // byte is a primitive type
byte[] arrayOfBytes;         // byte[] is an array of byte values
byte[][] arrayOfArrayOfBytes; // byte[][] is an array of byte[]
String[] points;             // String[] is an array of strings
```

The length of an array is not part of the array type. It is not possible, for example, to declare a method that expects an array of exactly four `int` values, for example. If a method parameter is of type `int[]`, a caller can pass an array with any number (including zero) of elements.

Array types are not classes, but array instances are objects. This means that arrays inherit the methods of `java.lang.Object`. Arrays implement the `Cloneable` interface and override the `clone()` method to guarantee that an array can always be cloned and that `clone()` never throws a `CloneNotSupportedException`. Arrays also implement `Serializable` so that any array can be serialized if its element type can be serialized. Finally, all arrays have a `public final int` field named `length` that specifies the number of elements in the array.

Array type widening conversions

Because arrays extend `Object` and implement the `Cloneable` and `Serializable` interfaces, any array type can be widened to any of these three types. But certain

---

4 There is a terminology difficulty when discussing arrays. Unlike with classes and their instances, we use the term "array" for both the array type and the array instance. In practice, it is usually clear from context whether a type or a value is being discussed.

array types can also be widened to other array types. If the element type of an array is a reference type T, and T is assignable to a type S, the array type T[] is assignable to the array type S[]. Note that there are no widening conversions of this sort for arrays of a given primitive type. As examples, the following lines of code show legal array widening conversions:

```
String[] arrayOfStrings;      // Created elsewhere
int[][] arrayOfArraysOfInt;   // Created elsewhere
// String is assignable to Object,
// so String[] is assignable to Object[]
Object[] oa = arrayOfStrings;
// String implements Comparable, so a String[] can
// be considered a Comparable[]
Comparable[] ca = arrayOfStrings;
// An int[] is an Object, so int[][] is assignable to Object[]
Object[] oa2 = arrayOfArraysOfInt;
// All arrays are cloneable, serializable Objects
Object o = arrayOfStrings;
Cloneable c = arrayOfArraysOfInt;
Serializable s = arrayOfArraysOfInt[0];
```

This ability to widen an array type to another array type means that the compile-time type of an array is not always the same as its runtime type.

This widening is known as *array covariance*—and as we shall see in "Wildcards" on page 146 it is regarded by modern standards as a historical artifact and a misfeature, because of the mismatch between compile and runtime typing that it exposes.

The compiler must usually insert runtime checks before any operation that stores a reference value into an array element to ensure that the runtime type of the value matches the runtime type of the array element. If the runtime check fails, an ArrayS toreException is thrown.

C compatibility syntax

As we've seen, an array type is written simply by placing brackets after the element type. For compatibility with C and C++, however, Java supports an alternative syntax in variable declarations: brackets may be placed after the name of the variable instead of, or in addition to, the element type. This applies to local variables, fields, and method parameters. For example:

```
// This line declares local variables of type int, int[] and int[][]
int justOne, arrayOfThem[], arrayOfArrays[][];

// These three lines declare fields of the same array type:
public String[][] aas1;   // Preferred Java syntax
public String aas2[][];   // C syntax
public String[] aas3[];   // Confusing hybrid syntax
```

```
// This method signature includes two parameters with the same type
public static double dotProduct(double[] x, double y[]) { ... }
```

 This compatibility syntax is extremely uncommon, and you should not use it.

Creating and Initializing Arrays

To create an array value in Java, you use the new keyword, just as you do to create an object. Array types don't have constructors, but you are required to specify a length whenever you create an array. Specify the desired size of your array as a nonnegative integer between square brackets:

```
// Create a new array to hold 1024 bytes
byte[] buffer = new byte[1024];
// Create an array of 50 references to strings
String[] lines = new String[50];
```

When you create an array with this syntax, each of the array elements is automatically initialized to the same default value that is used for the fields of a class: false for boolean elements, \u0000 for char elements, 0 for integer elements, 0.0 for floating-point elements, and null for elements of reference type.

Array creation expressions can also be used to create and initialize a multidimensional array of arrays. This syntax is somewhat more complicated and is explained later in this section.

Array initializers

To create an array and initialize its elements in a single expression, omit the array length and follow the square brackets with a comma-separated list of expressions within curly braces. The type of each expression must be assignable to the element type of the array, of course. The length of the array that is created is equal to the number of expressions. It is legal, but not necessary, to include a trailing comma following the last expression in the list. For example:

```
String[] greetings = new String[] { "Hello", "Hi", "Howdy" };
int[] smallPrimes = new int[] { 2, 3, 5, 7, 11, 13, 17, 19, };
```

Note that this syntax allows arrays to be created, initialized, and used without ever being assigned to a variable. In a sense, these array creation expressions are anonymous array literals. Here are examples:

```
// Call a method, passing an anonymous array literal that
// contains two strings
String response = askQuestion("Do you want to quit?",
                             new String[] {"Yes", "No"});
```

```
// Call another method with an anonymous array (of anonymous objects)
double d = computeAreaOfTriangle(new Point[] { new Point(1,2),
                                               new Point(3,4),
                                               new Point(3,2) });
```

When an array initializer is part of a variable declaration, you may omit the new keyword and element type and list the desired array elements within curly braces:

```
String[] greetings = { "Hello", "Hi", "Howdy" };
int[] powersOfTwo = {1, 2, 4, 8, 16, 32, 64, 128};
```

Array literals are created and initialized when the program is run, not when the program is compiled. Consider the following array literal:

```
int[] perfectNumbers = {6, 28};
```

This is compiled into Java byte codes that are equivalent to:

```
int[] perfectNumbers = new int[2];
perfectNumbers[0] = 6;
perfectNumbers[1] = 28;
```

The fact that Java does all array initialization at runtime has an important corollary. It means that the expressions in an array initializer may be computed at runtime and need not be compile-time constants. For example:

```
Point[] points = { circle1.getCenterPoint(), circle2.getCenterPoint() };
```

Using Arrays

Once an array has been created, you are ready to start using it. The following sections explain basic access to the elements of an array and cover common idioms of array usage such as iterating through the elements of an array and copying an array or part of an array.

Accessing array elements

The elements of an array are variables. When an array element appears in an expression, it evaluates to the value held in the element. And when an array element appears on the left-hand side of an assignment operator, a new value is stored into that element. Unlike a normal variable, however, an array element has no name, only a number. Array elements are accessed using a square bracket notation. If a is an expression that evaluates to an array reference, you index that array and refer to a specific element with a[i], where i is an integer literal or an expression that evaluates to an int. For example:

```
// Create an array of two strings
String[] responses = new String[2];
responses[0] = "Yes";   // Set the first element of the array
responses[1] = "No";    // Set the second element of the array

// Now read these array elements
```

```
System.out.println(question + " (" + responses[0] + "/" +
                    responses[1] + " ): ");

// Both the array reference and the array index may be more complex
double datum = data.getMatrix()[data.row() * data.numColumns() +
                    data.column()];
```

The array index expression must be of type int, or a type that can be widened to an int: byte, short, or even char. It is obviously not legal to index an array with a boolean, float, or double value. Remember that the length field of an array is an int and that arrays may not have more than Integer.MAX_VALUE elements. Indexing an array with an expression of type long generates a compile-time error, even if the value of that expression at runtime would be within the range of an int.

Array bounds

Remember that the first element of an array a is a[0] , the second element is a[1], and the last is a[a.length-1].

A common bug involving arrays is use of an index that is too small (a negative index) or too large (greater than or equal to the array length). In languages like C or C++, accessing elements before the beginning or after the end of an array yields unpredictable behavior that can vary from invocation to invocation and platform to platform. Such bugs may not always be caught, and if a failure occurs, it may be at some later time. While it is just as easy to write faulty array indexing code in Java, Java guarantees predictable results by checking every array access at runtime. If an array index is too small or too large, Java immediately throws an ArrayIndexOutOf BoundsException.

Iterating arrays

It is common to write loops that iterate through each of the elements of an array in order to perform some operation on it. This is typically done with a for loop. The following code, for example, computes the sum of an array of integers:

```
int[] primes = { 2, 3, 5, 7, 11, 13, 17, 19, 23 };
int sumOfPrimes = 0;
for(int i = 0; i < primes.length; i++)
    sumOfPrimes += primes[i];
```

The structure of this for loop is idiomatic, and you'll see it frequently. Java also has the foreach syntax that we've already met. The summing code could be rewritten succinctly as follows:

```
for(int p : primes) sumOfPrimes += p;
```

Copying arrays

All array types implement the Cloneable interface, and any array can be copied by invoking its clone() method. Note that a cast is required to convert the return value

to the appropriate array type, but that the clone() method of arrays is guaranteed
not to throw CloneNotSupportedException:

```
int[] data = { 1, 2, 3 };
int[] copy = (int[]) data.clone();
```

The clone() method makes a shallow copy. If the element type of the array is a reference type, only the references are copied, not the referenced objects themselves.
Because the copy is shallow, any array can be cloned, even if the element type is not
itself Cloneable.

Sometimes you simply want to copy elements from one existing array to another
existing array. The System.arraycopy() method is designed to do this efficiently,
and you can assume that Java VM implementations perform this method using
high-speed block copy operations on the underlying hardware.

arraycopy() is a straightforward function that is difficult to use only because it has
five arguments to remember. First pass the source array from which elements are to
be copied. Second, pass the index of the start element in that array. Pass the destination array and the destination index as the third and fourth arguments. Finally, as
the fifth argument, specify the number of elements to be copied.

arraycopy() works correctly even for overlapping copies within the same array. For
example, if you've "deleted" the element at index 0 from array a and want to shift the
elements between indexes 1 and n down one so that they occupy indexes 0 through
n-1 you could do this:

```
System.arraycopy(a, 1, a, 0, n);
```

Array utilities

The java.util.Arrays class contains a number of static utility methods for working with arrays. Most of these methods are heavily overloaded, with versions for
arrays of each primitive type and another version for arrays of objects. The sort()
and binarySearch() methods are particularly useful for sorting and searching
arrays. The equals() method allows you to compare the content of two arrays. The
Arrays.toString() method is useful when you want to convert array content to a
string, such as for debugging or logging output.

The Arrays class also includes deepEquals(), deepHashCode(), and deepTo
String() methods that work correctly for multidimensional arrays.

Multidimensional Arrays

As we've seen, an array type is written as the element type followed by a pair of
square brackets. An array of char is char[], and an array of arrays of char is char[]
[]. When the elements of an array are themselves arrays, we say that the array is
multidimensional. In order to work with multidimensional arrays, you need to
understand a few additional details.

Imagine that you want to use a multidimensional array to represent a multiplication table:

```java
int[][] products;      // A multiplication table
```

Each of the pairs of square brackets represents one dimension, so this is a two-dimensional array. To access a single int element of this two-dimensional array, you must specify two index values, one for each dimension. Assuming that this array was actually initialized as a multiplication table, the int value stored at any given element would be the product of the two indexes. That is, products[2][4] would be 8, and products[3][7] would be 21.

To create a new multidimensional array, use the new keyword and specify the size of both dimensions of the array. For example:

```java
int[][] products = new int[10][10];
```

In some languages, an array like this would be created as a single block of 100 int values. Java does not work this way. This line of code does three things:

- Declares a variable named products to hold an array of arrays of int.
- Creates a 10-element array to hold 10 arrays of int.
- Creates 10 more arrays, each of which is a 10-element array of int. It assigns each of these 10 new arrays to the elements of the initial array. The default value of every int element of each of these 10 new arrays is 0.

To put this another way, the previous single line of code is equivalent to the following code:

```java
int[][] products = new int[10][]; // An array to hold 10 int[] values
for(int i = 0; i < 10; i++)       // Loop 10 times...
    products[i] = new int[10];    // ...and create 10 arrays
```

The new keyword performs this additional initialization automatically for you. It works with arrays with more than two dimensions as well:

```java
float[][][] globalTemperatureData = new float[360][180][100];
```

When using new with multidimensional arrays, you do not have to specify a size for all dimensions of the array, only the leftmost dimension or dimensions. For example, the following two lines are legal:

```java
float[][][] globalTemperatureData = new float[360][][];
float[][][] globalTemperatureData = new float[360][180][];
```

The first line creates a single-dimensional array, where each element of the array can hold a float[][]. The second line creates a two-dimensional array, where each element of the array is a float[]. If you specify a size for only some of the dimensions of an array, however, those dimensions must be the leftmost ones. The following lines are not legal:

```
float[][][] globalTemperatureData = new float[360][][100];  // Error!
float[][][] globalTemperatureData = new float[][180][100];  // Error!
```

Like a one-dimensional array, a multidimensional array can be initialized using an array initializer. Simply use nested sets of curly braces to nest arrays within arrays. For example, we can declare, create, and initialize a 5 × 5 multiplication table like this:

```
int[][] products = { {0, 0, 0, 0, 0},
                     {0, 1, 2, 3, 4},
                     {0, 2, 4, 6, 8},
                     {0, 3, 6, 9, 12},
                     {0, 4, 8, 12, 16} };
```

Or, if you want to use a multidimensional array without declaring a variable, you can use the anonymous initializer syntax:

```
boolean response = bilingualQuestion(question, new String[][] {
                                     { "Yes", "No" },
                                     { "Oui", "Non" }});
```

When you create a multidimensional array using the new keyword, it is usually good practice to only use *rectangular* arrays: one in which all the array values for a given dimension have the same size.

Reference Types

Now that we've covered arrays and introduced classes and objects, we can turn to a more general description of *reference types*. Classes and arrays are two of Java's five kinds of reference types. Classes were introduced earlier and are covered in complete detail, along with *interfaces*, in Chapter 3. Enumerated types and annotation types are reference types introduced in Chapter 4.

This section does not cover specific syntax for any particular reference type, but instead explains the general behavior of reference types and illustrates how they differ from Java's primitive types. In this section, the term *object* refers to a value or instance of any reference type, including arrays.

Reference Versus Primitive Types

Reference types and objects differ substantially from primitive types and their primitive values:

- Eight primitive types are defined by the Java language, and the programmer cannot define new primitive types. Reference types are user-defined, so there is an unlimited number of them. For example, a program might define a class named Point and use objects of this newly defined type to store and manipulate x,y points in a Cartesian coordinate system.

- Primitive types represent single values. Reference types are aggregate types that hold zero or more primitive values or objects. Our hypothetical Point class, for example, might hold two double values to represent the x and y coordinates of the points. The char[] and Point[] array types are aggregate types because they hold a sequence of primitive char values or Point objects.

- Primitive types require between one and eight bytes of memory. When a primitive value is stored in a variable or passed to a method, the computer makes a copy of the bytes that hold the value. Objects, on the other hand, may require substantially more memory. Memory to store an object is dynamically allocated on the heap when the object is created and this memory is automatically "garbage collected" when the object is no longer needed.

When an object is assigned to a variable or passed to a method, the memory that represents the object is not copied. Instead, only a reference to that memory is stored in the variable or passed to the method.

References are completely opaque in Java and the representation of a reference is an implementation detail of the Java runtime. If you are a C programmer, however, you can safely imagine a reference as a pointer or a memory address. Remember, though, that Java programs cannot manipulate references in any way.

Unlike pointers in C and C++, references cannot be converted to or from integers, and they cannot be incremented or decremented. C and C++ programmers should also note that Java does not support the & address-of operator or the * and -> dereference operators.

Manipulating Objects and Reference Copies

The following code manipulates a primitive int value:

```
int x = 42;
int y = x;
```

After these lines execute, the variable y contains a copy of the value held in the variable x. Inside the Java VM, there are two independent copies of the 32-bit integer 42.

Now think about what happens if we run the same basic code but use a reference type instead of a primitive type:

```
Point p = new Point(1.0, 2.0);
Point q = p;
```

After this code runs, the variable q holds a copy of the reference held in the variable p. There is still only one copy of the Point object in the VM, but there are now two copies of the reference to that object. This has some important implications. Suppose the two previous lines of code are followed by this code:

```
System.out.println(p.x);  // Print out the x coordinate of p: 1.0
q.x = 13.0;               // Now change the X coordinate of q
System.out.println(p.x);  // Print out p.x again; this time it is 13.0
```

Because the variables p and q hold references to the same object, either variable can be used to make changes to the object, and those changes are visible through the other variable as well. As arrays are a kind of object then the same thing happens with arrays, as illustrated by the following code:

```
// greet holds an array reference
char[] greet = { 'h','e','l','l','o' };
char[] cuss = greet;            // cuss holds the same reference
cuss[4] = '!';                  // Use reference to change an element
System.out.println(greet);      // Prints "hell!"
```

A similar difference in behavior between primitive types and reference types occurs when arguments are passed to methods. Consider the following method:

```
void changePrimitive(int x) {
    while(x > 0) {
        System.out.println(x--);
    }
}
```

When this method is invoked, the method is given a copy of the argument used to invoke the method in the parameter x. The code in the method uses x as a loop counter and decrements it to zero. Because x is a primitive type, the method has its own private copy of this value, so this is a perfectly reasonable thing to do.

On the other hand, consider what happens if we modify the method so that the parameter is a reference type:

```
void changeReference(Point p) {
    while(p.x > 0) {
        System.out.println(p.x--);
    }
}
```

When this method is invoked, it is passed a private copy of a reference to a Point object and can use this reference to change the Point object. For example, consider the following:

```
Point q = new Point(3.0, 4.5);  // A point with an x coordinate of 3
changeReference(q);             // Prints 3,2,1 and modifies the Point
System.out.println(q.x);        // The x coordinate of q is now 0!
```

When the changeReference() method is invoked, it is passed a copy of the reference held in variable q. Now both the variable q and the method parameter p hold references to the same object. The method can use its reference to change the contents of the object. Note, however, that it cannot change the contents of the variable q. In other words, the method can change the Point object beyond recognition, but it cannot change the fact that the variable q refers to that object.

Comparing Objects

We've seen that primitive types and reference types differ significantly in the way they are assigned to variables, passed to methods, and copied. The types also differ in the way they are compared for equality. When used with primitive values, the equality operator (==) simply tests whether two values are identical (i.e., whether they have exactly the same bits). With reference types, however, == compares references, not actual objects. In other words, == tests whether two references refer to the same object; it does not test whether two objects have the same content. Here's an example:

```
String letter = "o";
String s = "hello";            // These two String objects
String t = "hell" + letter;    // contain exactly the same text.
if (s == t) System.out.println("equal"); // But they are not equal!

byte[] a = { 1, 2, 3 };
// A copy with identical content.
byte[] b = (byte[]) a.clone();
if (a == b) System.out.println("equal"); // But they are not equal!
```

When working with reference types, there are two kinds of equality: equality of reference and equality of object. It is important to distinguish between these two kinds of equality. One way to do this is to use the word "identical" when talking about equality of references and the word "equal" when talking about two distinct objects that have the same content. To test two nonidentical objects for equality, pass one of them to the equals() method of the other:

```
String letter = "o";
String s = "hello";            // These two String objects
String t = "hell" + letter;    // contain exactly the same text.
if (s.equals(t)) {             // And the equals() method
    System.out.println("equal"); // tells us so.
}
```

All objects inherit an equals() method (from Object), but the default implementation simply uses == to test for identity of references, not equality of content. A class that wants to allow objects to be compared for equality can define its own version of the equals() method. Our Point class does not do this, but the String class does, as indicated in the code example. You can call the equals() method on an array, but it is the same as using the == operator, because arrays always inherit the default equals() method that compares references rather than array content. You can compare arrays for equality with the convenience method java.util.Arrays.equals().

Boxing and Unboxing Conversions

Primitive types and reference types behave quite differently. It is sometimes useful to treat primitive values as objects, and for this reason, the Java platform includes *wrapper classes* for each of the primitive types. Boolean, Byte, Short, Character, Integer, Long, Float, and Double are immutable, final classes whose instances each hold a single primitive value. These wrapper classes are usually used when you want to store primitive values in collections such as java.util.List:

```
// Create a List collection
List numbers = new ArrayList();
// Store a wrapped primitive
numbers.add(new Integer(-1));
// Extract the primitive value
int i = ((Integer)numbers.get(0)).intValue();
```

Java allows types of conversions known as boxing and unboxing conversions. Boxing conversions convert a primitive value to its corresponding wrapper object and unboxing conversions do the opposite. You may explicitly specify a boxing or unboxing conversion with a cast, but this is unnecessary, as these conversions are automatically performed when you assign a value to a variable or pass a value to a method. Furthermore, unboxing conversions are also automatic if you use a wrapper object when a Java operator or statement expects a primitive value. Because Java performs boxing and unboxing automatically, this language feature is often known as *autoboxing*.

Here are some examples of automatic boxing and unboxing conversions:

```
Integer i = 0;    // int literal 0 boxed to an Integer object
Number n = 0.0f;  // float literal boxed to Float and widened to Number
Integer i = 1;    // this is a boxing conversion
int j = i;        // i is unboxed here
i++;              // i is unboxed, incremented, and then boxed up again
Integer k = i+2;  // i is unboxed and the sum is boxed up again
i = null;
j = i;            // unboxing here throws a NullPointerException
```

Autoboxing makes dealing with collections much easier as well. Let's look at an example that uses Java's *generics* (a language feature we'll meet properly in "Java Generics" on page 142) that allows us to restrict what types can be put into lists and other collections:

```
List<Integer> numbers = new ArrayList<>(); // Create a List of Integer
numbers.add(-1);                           // Box int to Integer
int i = numbers.get(0);                    // Unbox Integer to int
```

Packages and the Java Namespace

A *package* is a named collection of classes, interfaces, and other reference types. Packages serve to group related classes and define a namespace for the classes they contain.

The core classes of the Java platform are in packages whose names begin with java. For example, the most fundamental classes of the language are in the package java.lang. Various utility classes are in java.util. Classes for input and output are in java.io, and classes for networking are in java.net. Some of these packages contain subpackages, such as java.lang.reflect and java.util.regex.

Extensions to the Java platform that have been standardized by Oracle (or originally Sun) typically have package names that begin with `javax`. Some of these extensions, such as `javax.swing` and its myriad subpackages, were later adopted into the core platform itself. Finally, the Java platform also includes several "endorsed standards," which have packages named after the standards body that created them, such as `org.w3c` and `org.omg`.

Every class has both a simple name, which is the name given to it in its definition, and a fully qualified name, which includes the name of the package of which it is a part. The `String` class, for example, is part of the `java.lang` package, so its fully qualified name is `java.lang.String`.

This section explains how to place your own classes and interfaces into a package and how to choose a package name that won't conflict with anyone else's package name. Next, it explains how to selectively import type names or static members into the namespace so that you don't have to type the package name of every class or interface you use.

Package Declaration

To specify the package a class is to be part of, you use a `package` declaration. The `package` keyword, if it appears, must be the first token of Java code (i.e., the first thing other than comments and space) in the Java file. The keyword should be followed by the name of the desired package and a semicolon. Consider a Java file that begins with this directive:

```
package org.apache.commons.net;
```

All classes defined by this file are part of the package `org.apache.commons.net`.

If no `package` directive appears in a Java file, all classes defined in that file are part of an unnamed default package. In this case, the qualified and unqualified names of a class are the same.

The possibility of naming conflicts means that you should not use the default package. As your project grows more complicated, conflicts become almost inevitable—much better to create packages right from the start.

Globally Unique Package Names

One of the important functions of packages is to partition the Java namespace and prevent name collisions between classes. It is only their package names that keep the `java.util.List` and `java.awt.List` classes distinct, for example. In order for this to work, however, package names must themselves be distinct. As the developer of Java, Oracle controls all package names that begin with `java`, `javax`, and `sun`.

One scheme in common use is to use your domain name, with its elements reversed, as the prefix for all your package names. For example, the Apache Project produces a networking library as part of the Apache Commons project. The Commons project can be found at *http://commons.apache.org/* and accordingly, the package name used for the networking library is `org.apache.commons.net`.

Note that these package-naming rules apply primarily to API developers. If other programmers will be using classes that you develop along with unknown other classes, it is important that your package name be globally unique. On the other hand, if you are developing a Java application and will not be releasing any of the classes for reuse by others, you know the complete set of classes that your application will be deployed with and do not have to worry about unforeseen naming conflicts. In this case, you can choose a package naming scheme for your own convenience rather than for global uniqueness. One common approach is to use the application name as the main package name (it may have subpackages beneath it).

Importing Types

When referring to a class or interface in your Java code, you must, by default, use the fully qualified name of the type, including the package name. If you're writing code to manipulate a file and need to use the `File` class of the `java.io` package, you must type `java.io.File`. This rule has three exceptions:

- Types from the package `java.lang` are so important and so commonly used that they can always be referred to by their simple names.

- The code in a type `p.T` may refer to other types defined in the package `p` by their simple names.

- Types that have been *imported* into the namespace with an `import` declaration may be referred to by their simple names.

The first two exceptions are known as "automatic imports." The types from `java.lang` and the current package are "imported" into the namespace so that they can be used without their package name. Typing the package name of commonly used types that are not in `java.lang` or the current package quickly becomes tedious, and so it is also possible to explicitly import types from other packages into the namespace. This is done with the `import` declaration.

`import` declarations must appear at the start of a Java file, immediately after the `package` declaration, if there is one, and before any type definitions. You may use any number of `import` declarations in a file. An `import` declaration applies to all type definitions in the file (but not to any `import` declarations that follow it).

The `import` declaration has two forms. To import a single type into the namespace, follow the `import` keyword with the name of the type and a semicolon:

```
import java.io.File;    // Now we can type File instead of java.io.File
```

This is known as the "single type import" declaration.

The other form of import is the "on-demand type import." In this form, you specify the name of a package followed by the characters .* to indicate that any type from that package may be used without its package name. Thus, if you want to use several other classes from the java.io package in addition to the File class, you can simply import the entire package:

```
import java.io.*;   // Use simple names for all classes in java.io
```

This on-demand import syntax does not apply to subpackages. If I import the java.util package, I must still refer to the java.util.zip.ZipInputStream class by its fully qualified name.

Using an on-demand type import declaration is not the same as explicitly writing out a single type import declaration for every type in the package. It is more like an explicit single type import for every type in the package *that you actually use* in your code. This is the reason it's called "on demand"; types are imported as you use them.

Naming conflicts and shadowing

import declarations are invaluable to Java programming. They do expose us to the possibility of naming conflicts, however. Consider the packages java.util and java.awt. Both contain types named List.

java.util.List is an important and commonly used interface. The java.awt package contains a number of important types that are commonly used in client-side applications, but java.awt.List has been superseded and is not one of these important types. It is illegal to import both java.util.List and java.awt.List in the same Java file. The following single type import declarations produce a compilation error:

```
import java.util.List;
import java.awt.List;
```

Using on-demand type imports for the two packages is legal:

```
import java.util.*;   // For collections and other utilities.
import java.awt.*;    // For fonts, colors, and graphics.
```

Difficulty arises, however, if you actually try to use the type List. This type can be imported "on demand" from either package, and any attempt to use List as an unqualified type name produces a compilation error. The workaround, in this case, is to explicitly specify the package name you want.

Because java.util.List is much more commonly used than java.awt.List, it is useful to combine the two on-demand type import declarations with a single-type import declaration that serves to disambiguate what we mean when we say List:

```
import java.util.*;    // For collections and other utilities.
import java.awt.*;     // For fonts, colors, and graphics.
import java.util.List; // To disambiguate from java.awt.List
```

With these `import` declarations in place, we can use `List` to mean the `java.util.List` interface. If we actually need to use the `java.awt.List` class, we can still do so as long as we include its package name. There are no other naming conflicts between `java.util` and `java.awt`, and their types will be imported "on demand" when we use them without a package name.

Importing Static Members

As well as types, you can import the static members of types using the keywords `import static`. (Static members are explained in Chapter 3. If you are not already familiar with them, you may want to come back to this section later.) Like type import declarations, these static import declarations come in two forms: single static member import and on-demand static member import. Suppose, for example, that you are writing a text-based program that sends a lot of output to `System.out`. In this case, you might use this single static member import to save yourself typing:

```
import static java.lang.System.out;
```

With this import in place, you can then use `out.println()` instead of `System.out.println()`. Or suppose you are writing a program that uses many of the trigonometric and other functions of the `Math` class. In a program that is clearly focused on numerical methods like this, having to repeatedly type the class name "Math" does not add clarity to your code; it just gets in the way. In this case, an on-demand static member import may be appropriate:

```
import static java.lang.Math.*
```

With this import declaration, you are free to write concise expressions like `sqrt(abs(sin(x)))` without having to prefix the name of each static method with the class name `Math`.

Another important use of `import static` declarations is to import the names of constants into your code. This works particularly well with enumerated types (see Chapter 4). Suppose, for example, that you want to use the values of this enumerated type in code you are writing:

```
package climate.temperate;
enum Seasons { WINTER, SPRING, SUMMER, AUTUMN };
```

You could import the type `climate.temperate.Seasons` and then prefix the constants with the type name: `Seasons.SPRING`. For more concise code, you could import the enumerated values themselves:

```
import static climate.temperate.Seasons.*;
```

Using static member import declarations for constants is generally a better technique than implementing an interface that defines the constants.

Static member imports and overloaded methods

A static import declaration imports a *name*, not any one specific member with that name. Because Java allows method overloading and allows a type to have fields and methods with the same name, a single static member import declaration may actually import more than one member. Consider this code:

```
import static java.util.Arrays.sort;
```

This declaration imports the name "sort" into the namespace, not any one of the 19 sort() methods defined by java.util.Arrays. If you use the imported name sort to invoke a method, the compiler will look at the types of the method arguments to determine which method you mean.

It is even legal to import static methods with the same name from two or more different types as long as the methods all have different signatures. Here is one natural example:

```
import static java.util.Arrays.sort;
import static java.util.Collections.sort;
```

You might expect that this code would cause a syntax error. In fact, it does not because the sort() methods defined by the Collections class have different signatures than all of the sort() methods defined by the Arrays class. When you use the name "sort" in your code, the compiler looks at the types of the arguments to determine which of the 21 possible imported methods you mean.

Java File Structure

This chapter has taken us from the smallest to the largest elements of Java syntax, from individual characters and tokens to operators, expressions, statements, and methods, and on up to classes and packages. From a practical standpoint, the unit of Java program structure you will be dealing with most often is the Java file. A Java file is the smallest unit of Java code that can be compiled by the Java compiler. A Java file consists of:

- An optional package directive
- Zero or more import or import static directives
- One or more type definitions

These elements can be interspersed with comments, of course, but they must appear in this order. This is all there is to a Java file. All Java statements (except the package and import directives, which are not true statements) must appear within methods, and all methods must appear within a type definition.

Java files have a couple of other important restrictions. First, each file can contain at most one top-level class that is declared public. A public class is one that is designed for use by other classes in other packages. A class can contain any number of nested or inner classes that are public. We'll see more about the public modifier and nested classes in Chapter 3.

The second restriction concerns the filename of a Java file. If a Java file contains a public class, the name of the file must be the same as the name of the class, with the extension *.java* appended. Therefore, if Point is defined as a public class, its source code must appear in a file named *Point.java*. Regardless of whether your classes are public or not, it is good programming practice to define only one per file and to give the file the same name as the class.

When a Java file is compiled, each of the classes it defines is compiled into a separate *class* file that contains Java byte codes to be interpreted by the Java Virtual Machine. A class file has the same name as the class it defines, with the extension *.class* appended. Thus, if the file *Point.java* defines a class named Point, a Java compiler compiles it to a file named *Point.class*. On most systems, class files are stored in directories that correspond to their package names. The class com.davidflana gan.examples.Point is thus defined by the class file *com/davidflanagan/examples/ Point.class*.

The Java interpreter knows where the class files for the standard system classes are located and can load them as needed. When the interpreter runs a program that wants to use a class named com.davidflanagan.examples.Point, it knows that the code for that class is located in a directory named *com/davidflanagan/examples/* and, by default, it "looks" in the current directory for a subdirectory of that name. In order to tell the interpreter to look in locations other than the current directory, you must use the -classpath option when invoking the interpreter or set the CLASS PATH environment variable. For details, see the documentation for the Java interpreter, *java*, in Chapter 8.

Defining and Running Java Programs

A Java program consists of a set of interacting class definitions. But not every Java class or Java file defines a program. To create a program, you must define a class that has a special method with the following signature:

```
public static void main(String[] args)
```

This main() method is the main entry point for your program. It is where the Java interpreter starts running. This method is passed an array of strings and returns no value. When main() returns, the Java interpreter exits (unless main() has created separate threads, in which case the interpreter waits for all those threads to exit).

To run a Java program, you run the Java interpreter, *java*, specifying the fully qualified name of the class that contains the main() method. Note that you specify the name of the class, *not* the name of the class file that contains the class. Any additional arguments you specify on the command line are passed to the main() method as its String[] parameter. You may also need to specify the -classpath option (or

-cp) to tell the interpreter where to look for the classes needed by the program. Consider the following command:

```
java -classpath /opt/Jude com.davidflanagan.jude.Jude datafile.jude
```

java is the command to run the Java interpreter. -classpath /usr/local/Jude tells the interpreter where to look for .class files. com.davidflanagan.jude.Jude is the name of the program to run (i.e., the name of the class that defines the main() method). Finally, *datafile.jude* is a string that is passed to that main() method as the single element of an array of String objects.

There is an easier way to run programs. If a program and all its auxiliary classes (except those that are part of the Java platform) have been properly bundled in a Java archive (JAR) file, you can run the program simply by specifying the name of the JAR file. In the next example, we show how to start up the Censum garbage collection log analyzer:

```
java -jar /usr/local/Censum/censum.jar
```

Some operating systems make JAR files automatically executable. On those systems, you can simply say:

```
% /usr/local/Censum/censum.jar
```

See Chapter 13 for more details on how to execute Java programs.

Summary

In this chapter, we've introduced the basic syntax of the Java language. Due to the interlocking nature of the syntax of programming languages, it is perfectly fine if you don't feel at this point that you have completely grasped all of the syntax of the language. It is by practice that we acquire proficiency in any language, human or computer.

It is also worth observing that some parts of syntax are far more regularly used than others. For example, the strictfp and assert keywords are almost never used. Rather than trying to grasp every aspect of Java's syntax, it is far better to begin to acquire facility in the core aspects of Java and then return to any details of syntax that may still be troubling you. With this in mind, let's move to the next chapter and begin to discuss the classes and objects that are so central to Java and the basics of Java's approach to object-oriented programming.

3

Object-Oriented Programming in Java

Now that we've covered fundamental Java syntax, we are ready to begin object-oriented programming in Java. All Java programs use objects, and the type of an object is defined by its *class* or *interface*. Every Java program is defined as a class, and nontrivial programs include a number of classes and interface definitions. This chapter explains how to define new classes and how to do object-oriented programming with them. We also introduce the concept of an interface, but a full discussion of interfaces and Java's type system is deferred until Chapter 4.

If you have experience with OO programming, however, be careful. The term "object-oriented" has different meanings in different languages. Don't assume that Java works the same way as your favorite OO language. (This is particularly true for C++ or Python programmers).

This is a fairly lengthy chapter, so let's begin with an overview and some definitions.

Overview of Classes

Classes are the most fundamental structural element of all Java programs. You cannot write Java code without defining a class. All Java statements appear within classes, and all methods are implemented within classes.

Basic OO Definitions

Here are a couple important definitions:

Class

A *class* is a collection of data fields that hold values and methods that operate on those values. A class defines a new reference type, such as the `Point` type defined in Chapter 2.

The `Point` class defines a type that is the set of all possible two-dimensional points.

Object

An *object* is an *instance* of a class.

A `Point` object is a value of that type: it represents a single two-dimensional point.

Objects are often created by *instantiating* a class with the `new` keyword and a constructor invocation, as shown here:

```
Point p = new Point(1.0, 2.0);
```

Constructors are covered later in this chapter in "Creating and Initializing Objects" on page 106.

A class definition consists of a *signature* and a *body*. The class signature defines the name of the class and may also specify other important information. The body of a class is a set of *members* enclosed in curly braces. The members of a class usually include fields and methods, and may also include constructors, initializers, and nested types.

Members can be *static* or nonstatic. A static member belongs to the class itself while a nonstatic member is associated with the instances of a class (see "Fields and Methods" on page 100).

There are four very common kinds of members—class fields, class methods, instance fields, and instance methods. The majority of work done with Java involves interacting with these kinds of members.

The signature of a class may declare that the class *extends* another class. The extended class is known as the *superclass* and the extension is known as the *subclass*. A subclass *inherits* the members of its superclass and may declare new members or *override* inherited methods with new implementations.

The members of a class may have *access modifiers* `public`, `protected`, or `private`.[1] These modifiers specify their visibility and accessibility to clients and to subclasses. This allows classes to control access to members that are not part of their public API. This ability to hide members enables an object-oriented design technique known as *data encapsulation*, which we discuss in "Data Hiding and Encapsulation" on page 121.

---

1 There is also the default, aka package, visibility that we will meet later.

Other Reference Types

The signature of a class may also declare that the class *implements* one or more interfaces. An *interface* is a reference type similar to a class that defines method signatures but does not usually include method bodies to implement the methods.

However, from Java 8 onward, interfaces may use the keyword `default` to indicate that a method specified in the interface is optional. If a method is optional, the interface file must include a default implementation (hence the choice of keyword) which will be used by all implementing classes that do not provide an implementation of the optional method.

A class that implements an interface is required to provide bodies for the interface's nondefault methods. Instances of a class that implement an interface are also instances of the interface type.

Classes and interfaces are the most important of the five fundamental reference types defined by Java. Arrays, enumerated types (or "enums"), and annotation types (usually just called "annotations") are the other three. Arrays are covered in Chapter 2. Enums are a specialized kind of class and annotations are a specialized kind of interface—both are discussed later in Chapter 4, along with a full discussion of interfaces.

Class Definition Syntax

At its simplest level, a class definition consists of the keyword `class` followed by the name of the class and a set of class members within curly braces. The `class` keyword may be preceded by modifier keywords and annotations. If the class extends another class, the class name is followed by the `extends` keyword and the name of the class being extended. If the class implements one or more interfaces, then the class name or the `extends` clause is followed by the `implements` keyword and a comma-separated list of interface names. For example:

```
public class Integer extends Number implements Serializable, Comparable {
    // class members go here
}
```

A generic class may also have type parameters and wildcards as part of its definition (see Chapter 4).

Class declarations may include modifier keywords. In addition to the access control modifiers (`public`, `protected`, etc.), these include:

abstract
: An `abstract` class is one whose implementation is incomplete and cannot be instantiated. Any class with one or more `abstract` methods must be declared `abstract`. Abstract classes are discussed in "Abstract Classes and Methods" on page 128.

final

The final modifier specifies that the class may not be extended. A class cannot be declared to be both abstract and final.

strictfp

If a class is declared strictfp, all its methods behave as if they were declared strictfp. This modifier is extremely rarely used.

Fields and Methods

A class can be viewed as a collection of data (also referred to as state) and code to operate on that state. The data is stored in fields, and the code is organized into methods.

This section covers fields and methods, the two most important kinds of class members. Fields and methods come in two distinct types: class members (also known as static members) are associated with the class itself, while instance members are associated with individual instances of the class (i.e., with objects). This gives us four kinds of members:

- Class fields
- Class methods
- Instance fields
- Instance methods

The simple class definition for the class Circle, shown in Example 3-1, contains all four types of members.

Example 3-1. A simple class and its members

```
public class Circle {
  // A class field
  public static final double PI= 3.14159;      // A useful constant

  // A class method: just compute a value based on the arguments
  public static double radiansToDegrees(double radians) {
    return radians * 180 / PI;
  }

  // An instance field
  public double r;                             // The radius of the circle

  // Two instance methods: they operate on the instance fields of an object
  public double area() {                       // Compute the area of the circle
    return PI * r * r;
  }
```

```
public double circumference() {    // Compute the circumference
                                   // of the circle
    return 2 * PI * r;
  }
}
```

 It is not normally good practice to have a public field r—instead, it would be much more usual to have a private field r and a method radius() to provide access to it. The reason for this will be explained later, in "Data Hiding and Encapsulation" on page 121. For now, we use a public field simply to give examples of how to work with instance fields.

The following sections explain all four common kinds of members. First, we cover the declaration syntax for fields. (The syntax for declaring methods is covered later in this chapter in "Data Hiding and Encapsulation" on page 121.)

Field Declaration Syntax

Field declaration syntax is much like the syntax for declaring local variables (see Chapter 2) except that field definitions may also include modifiers. The simplest field declaration consists of the field type followed by the field name. The type may be preceded by zero or more modifier keywords or annotations, and the name may be followed by an equals sign and initializer expression that provides the initial value of the field. If two or more fields share the same type and modifiers, the type may be followed by a comma-separated list of field names and initializers. Here are some valid field declarations:

```
int x = 1;
private String name;
public static final int DAYS_PER_WEEK = 7;
String[] daynames = new String[DAYS_PER_WEEK];
private int a = 17, b = 37, c = 53;
```

Field modifiers are comprised of zero or more of the following keywords:

public, protected, private
> These access modifiers specify whether and where a field can be used outside of the class that defines it.

static
> If present, this modifier specifies that the field is associated with the defining class itself rather than with each instance of the class.

final
> This modifier specifies that once the field has been initialized, its value may never be changed. Fields that are both static and final are compile-time

constants that javac may inline. `final` fields can also be used to create classes whose instances are immutable.

`transient`

This modifier specifies that a field is not part of the persistent state of an object and that it need not be serialized along with the rest of the object.

`volatile`

This modifier indicates that the field has extra semantics for concurrent use by two or more threads. The `volatile` modifier says that the value of a field must always be read from and flushed to main memory, and that it may not be cached by a thread (in a register or CPU cache). See Chapter 6 for more details.

Class Fields

A *class field* is associated with the class in which it is defined rather than with an instance of the class. The following line declares a class field:

```
public static final double PI = 3.14159;
```

This line declares a field of type `double` named `PI` and assigns it a value of 3.14159.

The `static` modifier says that the field is a class field. Class fields are sometimes called static fields because of this `static` modifier. The `final` modifier says that the value of the field does not change. Because the field `PI` represents a constant, we declare it `final` so that it cannot be changed. It is a convention in Java (and many other languages) that constants are named with capital letters, which is why our field is named `PI`, not `pi`. Defining constants like this is a common use for class fields, meaning that the `static` and `final` modifiers are often used together. Not all class fields are constants, however. In other words, a field can be declared `static` without being declared `final`.

 The use of public static fields that are not `final` is almost never a good practice—as multiple threads could update the field and cause behavior that is extremely hard to debug.

A public static field is essentially a global variable. The names of class fields are qualified by the unique names of the classes that contain them, however. Thus, Java does not suffer from the name collisions that can affect other languages when different modules of code define global variables with the same name.

The key point to understand about a static field is that there is only a single copy of it. This field is associated with the class itself, not with instances of the class. If you look at the various methods of the `Circle` class, you'll see that they use this field. From inside the `Circle` class, the field can be referred to simply as `PI`. Outside the class, however, both class and field names are required to uniquely specify the field. Methods that are not part of `Circle` access this field as `Circle.PI`.

Class Methods

As with class fields, *class methods* are declared with the `static` modifier:

```
public static double radiansToDegrees(double rads) {
  return rads * 180 / PI;
}
```

This line declares a class method named `radiansToDegrees()`. It has a single parameter of type `double` and returns a `double` value.

Like class fields, class methods are associated with a class, rather than with an object. When invoking a class method from code that exists outside the class, you must specify both the name of the class and the method. For example:

```
// How many degrees is 2.0 radians?
double d = Circle.radiansToDegrees(2.0);
```

If you want to invoke a class method from inside the class in which it is defined, you don't have to specify the class name. You can also shorten the amount of typing required via the use of a static import (as discussed in Chapter 2).

Note that the body of our `Circle.radiansToDegrees( )` method uses the class field `PI`. A class method can use any class fields and class methods of its own class (or of any other class).

A class method cannot use any instance fields or instance methods because class methods are not associated with an instance of the class. In other words, although the `radiansToDegrees()` method is defined in the `Circle` class, it cannot use the instance part of any `Circle` objects.

One way to think about this is that in any instance, we always have a `this` reference to the current object. But class methods are not associated with a specific instance, so have no `this` reference, and no access to instance fields.

As we discussed earlier, a class field is essentially a global variable. In a similar way, a class method is a global method, or global function. Although `radiansToDegrees()` does not operate on `Circle` objects, it is defined within the `Circle` class because it is a utility method that is sometimes useful when working with circles, and so it makes sense to package it along with the other functionality of the `Circle` class.

Instance Fields

Any field declared without the `static` modifier is an *instance field*:

```
public double r;     // The radius of the circle
```

Instance fields are associated with instances of the class, so every `Circle` object we create has its own copy of the `double` field `r`. In our example, `r` represents the radius of a specific circle. Each Circle object can have a radius independent of all other Circle objects.

Inside a class definition, instance fields are referred to by name alone. You can see an example of this if you look at the method body of the circumference() instance method. In code outside the class, the name of an instance method must be prefixed with a reference to the object that contains it. For example, if the variable c holds a reference to a Circle object, we use the expression c.r to refer to the radius of that circle:

```
Circle c = new Circle(); // Create a Circle object; store a ref in c
c.r = 2.0;               // Assign a value to its instance field r
Circle d = new Circle(); // Create a different Circle object
d.r = c.r * 2;           // Make this one twice as big
```

Instance fields are key to object-oriented programming. Instance fields hold the state of an object; the values of those fields make one object distinct from another.

Instance Methods

An *instance method* operates on a specific instance of a class (an object), and any method not declared with the static keyword is automatically an instance method.

Instance methods are the feature that makes object-oriented programming start to get interesting. The Circle class defined in Example 3-1 contains two instance methods, area() and circumference(), that compute and return the area and circumference of the circle represented by a given Circle object.

To use an instance method from outside the class in which it is defined, we must prefix it with a reference to the instance that is to be operated on. For example:

```
// Create a Circle object; store in variable c
Circle c = new Circle();
c.r = 2.0;               // Set an instance field of the object
double a = c.area();     // Invoke an instance method of the object
```

This is why it is called object-oriented programming; the object is the focus here, not the function call.

From within an instance method, we naturally have access to all the instance fields that belong to the object the method was called on. Recall that an object is often best considered to be a bundle containing state (represented as the fields of the object), and behavior (the methods to act on that state).

All instance methods are implemented using an implicit parameter not shown in the method signature. The implicit argument is named this; it holds a reference to the object through which the method is invoked. In our example, that object is a Circle.

 The bodies of the area() and circumference() methods both use the class field PI. We saw earlier that class methods can use only class fields and class methods, not instance fields or methods. Instance methods are not restricted in this way: they can use any member of a class, whether it is declared static or not.

How the this Reference Works

The implicit this parameter is not shown in method signatures because it is usually not needed; whenever a Java method accesses the instance fields in its class, it is implicit that it is accessing fields in the object referred to by the this parameter. The same is true when an instance method invokes another instance method in the same class—it's taken that this means "call the instance method on the current object."

However, you can use the this keyword explicitly when you want to make it clear that a method is accessing its own fields and/or methods. For example, we can rewrite the area() method to use this explicitly to refer to instance fields:

```
public double area() { return Circle.PI * this.r * this.r; }
```

This code also uses the class name explicitly to refer to class field PI. In a method this simple, it is not normally necessary to be quite so explicit. In more complicated cases, however, you may sometimes find that it increases the clarity of your code to use an explicit this where it is not strictly required.

In some cases, the this keyword *is* required, however. For example, when a method parameter or local variable in a method has the same name as one of the fields of the class, you must use this to refer to the field, because the field name used alone refers to the method parameter or local variable.

For example, we can add the following method to the Circle class:

```
public void setRadius(double r) {
    this.r = r;      // Assign the argument (r) to the field (this.r)
                     // Note that we cannot just say r = r
}
```

Some developers will deliberately choose the names of their method arguments in such a way that they don't clash with field names, so the use of this can largely be avoided.

Finally, note that while instance methods can use the this keyword, class methods cannot. This is because class methods are not associated with individual objects.

Creating and Initializing Objects

Now that we've covered fields and methods, let's move on to other important members of a class. In particular, we'll look at constructors—these are class members whose job is to initialize the fields of a class as new instances of the class are created.

Take another look at how we've been creating Circle objects:

```
Circle c = new Circle();
```

This can easily be read as the creation of a new instance of Circle, by calling something that looks a bit like a method. In fact, Circle() is an example of a *constructor*. This is a member of a class that has the same name as the class, and has a body, like a method.

Here's how a constructor works. The new operator indicates that we need to create a new instance of the class. First of all, memory is allocated to hold the new object instance. Then, the constructor body is called, with any arguments that have been specified. The constructor uses these arguments to do whatever initialization of the new object is necessary.

Every class in Java has at least one *constructor*, and their purpose is to perform any necessary initialization for a new object. Because we didn't explicitly define a constructor for our Circle class in Example 3-1, the javac compiler automatically gave us a constructor (called the default constructor) that takes no arguments and performs no special initialization.

Defining a Constructor

There is some obvious initialization we could do for our circle objects, so let's define a constructor. Example 3-2 shows a new definition for Circle that contains a constructor that lets us specify the radius of a new Circle object. We've also taken the opportunity to make the field r protected (to prevent access to it from arbitrary objects).

Example 3-2. A constructor for the Circle class

```
public class Circle {
    public static final double PI = 3.14159;  // A constant
    // An instance field that holds the radius of the circle
    protected double r;

    // The constructor: initialize the radius field
    public Circle(double r) { this.r = r; }

    // The instance methods: compute values based on the radius
    public double circumference() { return 2 * PI * r; }
    public double area() { return PI * r*r; }
    public double radius() { return r; }
}
```

When we relied on the default constructor supplied by the compiler, we had to write code like this to initialize the radius explicitly:

```
Circle c = new Circle();
c.r = 0.25;
```

With the new constructor, the initialization becomes part of the object creation step:

```
Circle c = new Circle(0.25);
```

Here are some basic facts regarding naming, declaring, and writing constructors:

- The constructor name is always the same as the class name.
- A constructor is declared without a return type, not even void.
- The body of a constructor is initializing the object. You can think of this as setting up the contents of the this reference
- A constructor may not return this or any other value.

Defining Multiple Constructors

Sometimes you want to initialize an object in a number of different ways, depending on what is most convenient in a particular circumstance. For example, we might want to initialize the radius of a circle to a specified value or a reasonable default value. Here's how we can define two constructors for Circle:

```
public Circle() { r = 1.0; }
public Circle(double r) { this.r = r; }
```

Because our Circle class has only a single instance field, we can't initialize it too many ways, of course. But in more complex classes, it is often convenient to define a variety of constructors.

It is perfectly legal to define multiple constructors for a class, as long as each constructor has a different parameter list. The compiler determines which constructor you wish to use based on the number and type of arguments you supply. This ability to define multiple constructors is analogous to method overloading.

Invoking One Constructor from Another

A specialized use of the this keyword arises when a class has multiple constructors; it can be used from a constructor to invoke one of the other constructors of the same class. In other words, we can rewrite the two previous Circle constructors as follows:

```
// This is the basic constructor: initialize the radius
public Circle(double r) { this.r = r; }
// This constructor uses this() to invoke the constructor above
public Circle() { this(1.0); }
```

This is a useful technique when a number of constructors share a significant amount of initialization code, as it avoids repetition of that code. In more complex cases, where the constructors do a lot more initialization, this can be a very useful technique.

There is an important restriction on using this(): it can appear only as the first statement in a constructor—but the call may be followed by any additional initialization a particular constructor needs to perform. The reason for this restriction involves the automatic invocation of superclass constructors, which we'll explore later in this chapter.

Field Defaults and Initializers

The fields of a class do not necessarily require initialization. If their initial values are not specified, the fields are automatically initialized to the default value false, \u0000, 0, 0.0, or null, depending on their type (see Table 2-1 for more details). These default values are specified by the Java language specification and apply to both instance fields and class fields.

If the default field value is not appropriate for your field, you can instead explicitly provide a different initial value. For example:

```
public static final double PI = 3.14159;
public double r = 1.0;
```

 Field declarations are not part of any method. Instead, the Java compiler generates initialization code for the field automatically and puts it into all the constructors for the class. The initialization code is inserted into a constructor in the order in which it appears in the source code, which means that a field initializer can use the initial values of any fields declared before it.

Consider the following code excerpt, which shows a constructor and two instance fields of a hypothetical class:

```
public class SampleClass {
  public int len = 10;
  public int[] table = new int[len];

  public SampleClass() {
    for(int i = 0; i < len; i++) table[i] = i;
  }

  // The rest of the class is omitted...
}
```

In this case, the code generated by javac for the constructor is actually equivalent to the following:

```
public SampleClass() {
  len = 10;
  table = new int[len];
  for(int i = 0; i < len; i++) table[i] = i;
}
```

If a constructor begins with a this() call to another constructor, the field initialization code does not appear in the first constructor. Instead, the initialization is handled in the constructor invoked by the this() call.

So, if instance fields are initialized in constructor, where are class fields initialized? These fields are associated with the class, even if no instances of the class are ever created. This means they need to be initialized even before a constructor is called.

To support this, javac generates a class initialization method automatically for every class. Class fields are initialized in the body of this method, which is invoked exactly once before the class is first used (often when the class is first loaded by the Java VM.)

As with instance field initialization, class field initialization expressions are inserted into the class initialization method in the order in which they appear in the source code. This means that the initialization expression for a class field can use the class fields declared before it. The class initialization method is an internal method that is hidden from Java programmers. In the class file, it bears the name <clinit> (and this method could be seen by, for example, examining the class file with javap—see Chapter 13 for more details on how to use javap to do this).

Initializer blocks

So far, we've seen that objects can be initialized through the initialization expressions for their fields and by arbitrary code in their constructors. A class has a class initialization method, which is like a constructor, but we cannot explicitly define the body of this method as we can for a constructor. Java does allow us to write arbitrary code for the initialization of class fields, however, with a construct known as a *static initializer*. A static initializer is simply the keyword static followed by a block of code in curly braces. A static initializer can appear in a class definition anywhere a field or method definition can appear. For example, consider the following code that performs some nontrivial initialization for two class fields:

```
// We can draw the outline of a circle using trigonometric functions
// Trigonometry is slow, though, so we precompute a bunch of values
public class TrigCircle {
  // Here are our static lookup tables and their own initializers
  private static final int NUMPTS = 500;
  private static double sines[] = new double[NUMPTS];
  private static double cosines[] = new double[NUMPTS];

  // Here's a static initializer that fills in the arrays
  static {
    double x = 0.0;
```

```
      double delta_x = (Circle.PI/2)/(NUMPTS-1);
      for(int i = 0, x = 0.0; i < NUMPTS; i++, x += delta_x) {
        sines[i] = Math.sin(x);
        cosines[i] = Math.cos(x);
      }
    }
    // The rest of the class is omitted...
  }
```

A class can have any number of static initializers. The body of each initializer block is incorporated into the class initialization method, along with any static field initialization expressions. A static initializer is like a class method in that it cannot use the this keyword or any instance fields or instance methods of the class.

Classes are also allowed to have *instance initializers*. An instance initializer is like a static initializer, except that it initializes an object, not a class. A class can have any number of instance initializers, and they can appear anywhere a field or method definition can appear. The body of each instance initializer is inserted at the beginning of every constructor for the class, along with any field initialization expressions. An instance initializer looks just like a static initializer, except that it doesn't use the static keyword. In other words, an instance initializer is just a block of arbitrary Java code that appears within curly braces.

Instance initializers can initialize arrays or other fields that require complex initialization. They are sometimes useful because they locate the initialization code right next to the field, instead of separating into a constructor. For example:

```
private static final int NUMPTS = 100;
private int[] data = new int[NUMPTS];
{ for(int i = 0; i < NUMPTS; i++) data[i] = i; }
```

In practice, however, this use of instance initializers is fairly rare.

Subclasses and Inheritance

The Circle defined earlier is a simple class that distinguishes circle objects only by their radii. Suppose, instead, that we want to represent circles that have both a size and a position. For example, a circle of radius 1.0 centered at point 0,0 in the Cartesian plane is different from the circle of radius 1.0 centered at point 1,2. To do this, we need a new class, which we'll call PlaneCircle.

We'd like to add the ability to represent the position of a circle without losing any of the existing functionality of the Circle class. This is done by defining PlaneCircle as a subclass of Circle so that PlaneCircle inherits the fields and methods of its superclass, Circle. The ability to add functionality to a class by subclassing, or extending, is central to the object-oriented programming paradigm.

Extending a Class

In Example 3-3, we show how we can implement `PlaneCircle` as a subclass of the `Circle` class.

Example 3-3. Extending the Circle class

```java
public class PlaneCircle extends Circle {
  // We automatically inherit the fields and methods of Circle,
  // so we only have to put the new stuff here.
  // New instance fields that store the center point of the circle
  private final double cx, cy;

  // A new constructor to initialize the new fields
  // It uses a special syntax to invoke the Circle() constructor
  public PlaneCircle(double r, double x, double y) {
    super(r);        // Invoke the constructor of the superclass, Circle()
    this.cx = x;     // Initialize the instance field cx
    this.cy = y;     // Initialize the instance field cy
  }

  public double getCentreX() {
    return cx;
  }

  public double getCentreY() {
    return cy;
  }

  // The area() and circumference() methods are inherited from Circle
  // A new instance method that checks whether a point is inside the circle
  // Note that it uses the inherited instance field r
  public boolean isInside(double x, double y) {
    double dx = x - cx, dy = y - cy;            // Distance from center
    double distance = Math.sqrt(dx*dx + dy*dy); // Pythagorean theorem
    return (distance < r);                      // Returns true or false
  }
}
```

Note the use of the keyword `extends` in the first line of Example 3-3. This keyword tells Java that `PlaneCircle` extends, or subclasses, `Circle`, meaning that it inherits the fields and methods of that class.

 There are several different ways to express the idea that our new object type has the characteristics of a `Circle` as well as having a position. This is probably the simplest, but is not always the most suitable, especially in larger systems.

The definition of the isInside() method shows field inheritance; this method uses the field r (defined by the Circle class) as if it were defined right in PlaneCircle itself. PlaneCircle also inherits the methods of Circle. Therefore, if we have a PlaneCircle object referenced by variable pc, we can say:

```
double ratio = pc.circumference() / pc.area();
```

This works just as if the area() and circumference() methods were defined in PlaneCircle itself.

Another feature of subclassing is that every PlaneCircle object is also a perfectly legal Circle object. If pc refers to a PlaneCircle object, we can assign it to a Circle variable and forget all about its extra positioning capabilities:

```
// Unit circle at the origin
PlaneCircle pc = new PlaneCircle(1.0, 0.0, 0.0);
Circle c = pc;      // Assigned to a Circle variable without casting
```

This assignment of a PlaneCircle object to a Circle variable can be done without a cast. As we discussed in Chapter 2 a conversion like this is always legal. The value held in the Circle variable c is still a valid PlaneCircle object, but the compiler cannot know this for sure, so it doesn't allow us to do the opposite (narrowing) conversion without a cast:

```
// Narrowing conversions require a cast (and a runtime check by the VM)
PlaneCircle pc2 = (PlaneCircle) c;
boolean origininside = ((PlaneCircle) c).isInside(0.0, 0.0);
```

This distinction is covered in more detail in "Lambda Expressions" on page 171, where we talk about the distinction between the compile and runtime type of an object.

Final classes

When a class is declared with the final modifier, it means that it cannot be extended or subclassed. java.lang.String is an example of a final class. Declaring a class final prevents unwanted extensions to the class: if you invoke a method on a String object, you know that the method is the one defined by the String class itself, even if the String is passed to you from some unknown outside source.

Superclasses, Object, and the Class Hierarchy

In our example, PlaneCircle is a subclass of Circle. We can also say that Circle is the superclass of PlaneCircle. The superclass of a class is specified in its extends clause:

```
public class PlaneCircle extends Circle { ... }
```

Every class you define has a superclass. If you do not specify the superclass with an extends clause, the superclass is the class java.lang.Object. The Object class is special for a couple of reasons:

- It is the only class in Java that does not have a superclass.
- All Java classes inherit the methods of Object.

Because every class (except Object) has a superclass, classes in Java form a class hierarchy, which can be represented as a tree with Object at its root.

 Object has no superclass, but every other class has exactly one superclass. A subclass cannot extend more than one superclass. See Chapter 4 for more information on how to achieve a similar result.

Figure 3-1 shows a partial class hierarchy diagram that includes our Circle and PlaneCircle classes, as well as some of the standard classes from the Java API.

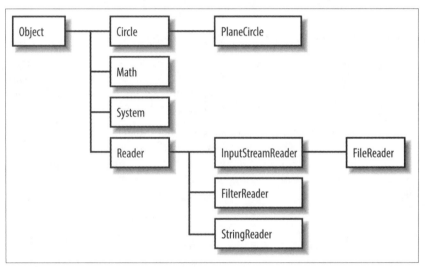

Figure 3-1. A class hierarchy diagram

Subclass Constructors

Look again at the PlaneCircle() constructor from Example 3-3:

```
public PlaneCircle(double r, double x, double y) {
    super(r);        // Invoke the constructor of the superclass, Circle()
    this.cx = x;     // Initialize the instance field cx
    this.cy = y;     // Initialize the instance field cy
}
```

Although this constructor explicitly initializes the cx and cy fields newly defined by PlaneCircle, it relies on the superclass Circle() constructor to initialize the inherited fields of the class. To invoke the superclass constructor, our constructor calls super().

super is a reserved word in Java. One of its uses is to invoke the constructor of a superclass from within a subclass constructor. This use is analogous to the use of this() to invoke one constructor of a class from within another constructor of the same class. Invoking a constructor using super() is subject to the same restrictions as is using this():

- super() can be used in this way only within a constructor.
- The call to the superclass constructor must appear as the first statement within the constructor, even before local variable declarations.

The arguments passed to super() must match the parameters of the superclass constructor. If the superclass defines more than one constructor, super() can be used to invoke any one of them, depending on the arguments passed.

Constructor Chaining and the Default Constructor

Java guarantees that the constructor of a class is called whenever an instance of that class is created. It also guarantees that the constructor is called whenever an instance of any subclass is created. In order to guarantee this second point, Java must ensure that every constructor calls its superclass constructor.

Thus, if the first statement in a constructor does not explicitly invoke another constructor with this() or super(), the javac compiler inserts the call super() (i.e., it calls the superclass constructor with no arguments). If the superclass does not have a visible constructor that takes no arguments, this implicit invocation causes a compilation error.

Consider what happens when we create a new instance of the PlaneCircle class.

- First, the PlaneCircle constructor is invoked.
- This constructor explicitly calls super(r) to invoke a Circle constructor.
- That Circle() constructor implicitly calls super() to invoke the constructor of its superclass, Object (Object only has one constructor).
- At this point, we've reached the top of the hierarchy and constructors start to run.
- The body of the Object constructor runs first.
- When it returns, the body of the Circle() constructor runs.
- Finally, when the call to super(r) returns, the remaining statements of the PlaneCircle() constructor are executed.

What all this means is that constructor calls are chained; any time an object is created, a sequence of constructors is invoked, from subclass to superclass on up to

Object at the root of the class hierarchy. Because a superclass constructor is always invoked as the first statement of its subclass constructor, the body of the Object constructor always runs first, followed by the constructor of its subclass and on down the class hierarchy to the class that is being instantiated.

Whenever a constructor is invoked, it can count on the fields of its superclass to be initialized by the time the constructor starts to run.

The default constructor

There is one missing piece in the previous description of constructor chaining. If a constructor does not invoke a superclass constructor, Java does so implicitly. But what if a class is declared without a constructor? In this case, Java implicitly adds a constructor to the class. This default constructor does nothing but invoke the super-class constructor.

For example, if we don't declare a constructor for the PlaneCircle class, Java implicitly inserts this constructor:

```
public PlaneCircle() { super(); }
```

If the superclass, Circle, doesn't declare a no-argument constructor, the super() call in this automatically inserted default constructor for PlaneCircle() causes a compilation error. In general, if a class does not define a no-argument constructor, all its subclasses must define constructors that explicitly invoke the superclass con-structor with the necessary arguments.

If a class does not declare any constructors, it is given a no-argument constructor by default. Classes declared public are given public constructors. All other classes are given a default constructor that is declared without any visibility modifier: such a constructor has default visibility. (The notion of visibility is explained later in this chapter.)

If you are creating a public class that should not be publicly instantiated, you should declare at least one non-public constructor to prevent the insertion of a default public constructor. Classes that should never be instantiated (such as java.lang.Math or java.lang.System) should define a private constructor. Such a constructor can never be invoked from outside of the class, but it prevents the automatic insertion of the default constructor.

Hiding Superclass Fields

For the sake of example, imagine that our PlaneCircle class needs to know the dis-tance between the center of the circle and the origin (0,0). We can add another instance field to hold this value:

```
public double r;
```

Adding the following line to the constructor computes the value of the field:

```
this.r = Math.sqrt(cx*cx + cy*cy);  // Pythagorean theorem
```

But wait; this new field r has the same name as the radius field r in the Circle superclass. When this happens, we say that the field r of PlaneCircle *hides* the field r of Circle. (This is a contrived example, of course: the new field should really be called distanceFromOrigin).

In code that you write, you should avoid declaring fields with names that hide superclass fields. It is almost always a sign of bad code.

With this new definition of PlaneCircle, the expressions r and this.r both refer to the field of PlaneCircle. How, then, can we refer to the field r of Circle that holds the radius of the circle? A special syntax for this uses the super keyword:

```
r          // Refers to the PlaneCircle field
this.r     // Refers to the PlaneCircle field
super.r    // Refers to the Circle field
```

Another way to refer to a hidden field is to cast this (or any instance of the class) to the appropriate superclass and then access the field:

```
((Circle) this).r    // Refers to field r of the Circle class
```

This casting technique is particularly useful when you need to refer to a hidden field defined in a class that is not the immediate superclass. Suppose, for example, that classes A, B, and C all define a field named x and that C is a subclass of B, which is a subclass of A. Then, in the methods of class C, you can refer to these different fields as follows:

```
x                // Field x in class C
this.x           // Field x in class C
super.x          // Field x in class B
((B)this).x      // Field x in class B
((A)this).x      // Field x in class A
super.super.x    // Illegal; does not refer to x in class A
```

You cannot refer to a hidden field x in the superclass of a superclass with super.super.x. This is not legal syntax.

Similarly, if you have an instance c of class C, you can refer to the three fields named x like this:

```
c.x            // Field x of class C
((B)c).x       // Field x of class B
((A)c).x       // Field x of class A
```

So far, we've been discussing instance fields. Class fields can also be hidden. You can use the same super syntax to refer to the hidden value of the field, but this is never necessary, as you can always refer to a class field by prepending the name of the desired class. Suppose, for example, that the implementer of PlaneCircle decides that the Circle.PI field does not express to enough decimal places. She can define her own class field PI:

```
public static final double PI = 3.14159265358979323846;
```

Now code in PlaneCircle can use this more accurate value with the expressions PI or PlaneCircle.PI. It can also refer to the old, less accurate value with the expressions super.PI and Circle.PI. However, the area() and circumference() methods inherited by PlaneCircle are defined in the Circle class, so they use the value Circle.PI, even though that value is hidden now by PlaneCircle.PI.

Overriding Superclass Methods

When a class defines an instance method using the same name, return type, and parameters as a method in its superclass, that method *overrides* the method of the superclass. When the method is invoked for an object of the class, it is the new definition of the method that is called, not the old definition from the superclass.

The return type of the overriding method may be a subclass of the return type of the original method (instead of being exactly the same type). This is known as a *covariant return*.

Method overriding is an important and useful technique in object-oriented programming. PlaneCircle does not override either of the methods defined by Circle, but suppose we define another subclass of Circle, named Ellipse.

It is important for Ellipse to override the area() and circumference() methods of Circle in this case, because the formulas used to compute the area and circumference of a circle do not work for ellipses.

The upcoming discussion of method overriding considers only instance methods. Class methods behave quite differently, and they cannot be overridden. Just like fields, class methods can be hidden by a subclass but not overridden. As noted earlier in this chapter, it is good programming style to always prefix a class method invocation with the name of the class in which it is defined. If you consider the class name part of the class method name, the two methods have different names, so nothing is actually hidden at all.

Before we go any further with the discussion of method overriding, you should understand the difference between method overriding and method overloading. As we discussed in Chapter 2, method overloading refers to the practice of defining multiple methods (in the same class) that have the same name but different parameter lists. This is very different from method overriding, so don't get them confused.

Overriding is not hiding

Although Java treats the fields and methods of a class analogously in many ways, method overriding is not like field hiding at all. You can refer to hidden fields simply by casting an object to an instance of the appropriate superclass, but you cannot invoke overridden instance methods with this technique. The following code illustrates this crucial difference:

```
class A {                              // Define a class named A
  int i = 1;                           // An instance field
  int f() { return i; }                // An instance method
  static char g() { return 'A'; }      // A class method
}

class B extends A {                    // Define a subclass of A
  int i = 2;                           // Hides field i in class A
  int f() { return -i; }               // Overrides method f in class A
  static char g() { return 'B'; }      // Hides class method g() in class A
}

public class OverrideTest {
  public static void main(String args[]) {
    B b = new B();                     // Creates a new object of type B
    System.out.println(b.i);           // Refers to B.i; prints 2
    System.out.println(b.f());         // Refers to B.f(); prints -2
    System.out.println(b.g());         // Refers to B.g(); prints B
    System.out.println(B.g());         // A better way to invoke B.g()

    A a = (A) b;                       // Casts b to an instance of class A
    System.out.println(a.i);           // Now refers to A.i; prints 1
    System.out.println(a.f());         // Still refers to B.f(); prints -2
    System.out.println(a.g());         // Refers to A.g(); prints A
    System.out.println(A.g());         // A better way to invoke A.g()
  }
}
```

While this difference between method overriding and field hiding may seem surprising at first, a little thought makes the purpose clear.

Suppose we are manipulating a bunch of Circle and Ellipse objects. To keep track of the circles and ellipses, we store them in an array of type Circle[]. We can do this because Ellipse is a subclass of Circle, so all Ellipse objects are legal Circle objects.

When we loop through the elements of this array, we don't have to know or care whether the element is actually a `Circle` or an `Ellipse`. What we do care about very much, however, is that the correct value is computed when we invoke the `area()` method of any element of the array. In other words, we don't want to use the formula for the area of a circle when the object is actually an ellipse!

All we really want is for the objects we're computing the areas of to "do the right thing"—the `Circle` objects to use their definition of how to compute their own area, and the `Ellipse` objects to use the definition that is correct for them.

Seen in this context, it is not surprising at all that method overriding is handled differently by Java than is field hiding.

Virtual method lookup

If we have a `Circle[]` array that holds `Circle` and `Ellipse` objects, how does the compiler know whether to call the `area()` method of the `Circle` class or the `Ellipse` class for any given item in the array? In fact, the source code compiler cannot know this at compilation time.

Instead, `javac` creates bytecode that uses *virtual* method lookup at runtime. When the interpreter runs the code, it looks up the appropriate `area()` method to call for each of the objects in the array. That is, when the interpreter interprets the expression `o.area()`, it checks the actual runtime type of the object referred to by the variable o and then finds the `area()` method that is appropriate for that type.

 Some other languages (such as C# or C++) do not do virtual lookup by default and instead have a `virtual` keyword that programmers must explicitly use if they want to allow subclasses to be able to override a method.

The JVM does not simply use the `area()` method that is associated with the static type of the variable o, as that would not allow method overriding to work in the way detailed earlier. Virtual method lookup is the default for Java instance methods. See Chapter 4 for more details about compile-time and runtime type and how this affects virtual method lookup.

Invoking an overridden method

We've seen the important differences between method overriding and field hiding. Nevertheless, the Java syntax for invoking an overridden method is quite similar to the syntax for accessing a hidden field: both use the `super` keyword. The following code illustrates:

```java
class A {
    int i = 1;             // An instance field hidden by subclass B
    int f() { return i; }  // An instance method overridden by subclass B
}
```

```
class B extends A {
   int i;                      // This field hides i in A
   int f() {                   // This method overrides f() in A
      i = super.i + 1;         // It can retrieve A.i like this
      return super.f() + i;    // It can invoke A.f() like this
   }
}
```

Recall that when you use super to refer to a hidden field, it is the same as casting this to the superclass type and accessing the field through that. Using super to invoke an overridden method, however, is not the same as casting the this reference. In other words, in the previous code, the expression super.f() is not the same as ((A)this).f().

When the interpreter invokes an instance method with the super syntax, a modified form of virtual method lookup is performed. The first step, as in regular virtual method lookup, is to determine the actual class of the object through which the method is invoked. Normally, the runtime search for an appropriate method definition would begin with this class. When a method is invoked with the super syntax, however, the search begins at the superclass of the class. If the superclass implements the method directly, that version of the method is invoked. If the superclass inherits the method, the inherited version of the method is invoked.

Note that the super keyword invokes the most immediately overridden version of a method. Suppose class A has a subclass B that has a subclass C and that all three classes define the same method f(). The method C.f() can invoke the method B.f(), which it overrides directly, with super.f(). But there is no way for C.f() to invoke A.f() directly: super.super.f() is not legal Java syntax. Of course, if C.f() invokes B.f(), it is reasonable to suppose that B.f() might also invoke A.f().

This kind of chaining is relatively common when working with overridden methods: it is a way of augmenting the behavior of a method without replacing the method entirely.

Don't confuse the use of super to invoke an overridden method with the super() method call used in a constructor to invoke a superclass constructor. Although they both use the same keyword, these are two entirely different syntaxes. In particular, you can use super to invoke an overridden method anywhere in the overriding class while you can use super() only to invoke a superclass constructor as the very first statement of a constructor.

It is also important to remember that super can be used only to invoke an overridden method from within the class that overrides it. Given a reference to an Ellipse object e, there is no way for a program that uses e to invoke the area() method defined by the Circle class on e.

Data Hiding and Encapsulation

We started this chapter by describing a class as a collection of data and methods. One of the most important object-oriented techniques we haven't discussed so far is hiding the data within the class and making it available only through the methods. This technique is known as *encapsulation* because it seals the data (and internal methods) safely inside the "capsule" of the class, where it can be accessed only by trusted users (i.e., the methods of the class).

Why would you want to do this? The most important reason is to hide the internal implementation details of your class. If you prevent programmers from relying on those details, you can safely modify the implementation without worrying that you will break existing code that uses the class.

You should always encapsulate your code. It is almost always impossible to reason through and ensure the correctness of code that hasn't been well-encapsulated, especially in multithreaded environments (and essentially all Java programs are multithreaded).

Another reason for encapsulation is to protect your class against accidental or willful stupidity. A class often contains a number of interdependent fields that must be in a consistent state. If you allow a programmer (including yourself) to manipulate those fields directly, he may change one field without changing important related fields, leaving the class in an inconsistent state. If instead he has to call a method to change the field, that method can be sure to do everything necessary to keep the state consistent. Similarly, if a class defines certain methods for internal use only, hiding these methods prevents users of the class from calling them.

Here's another way to think about encapsulation: when all the data for a class is hidden, the methods define the only possible operations that can be performed on objects of that class.

Once you have carefully tested and debugged your methods, you can be confident that the class will work as expected. On the other hand, if all the fields of the class can be directly manipulated, the number of possibilities you have to test becomes unmanageable.

This idea can be carried to a very powerful conclusion, as we will see in "Safe Java Programming" on page 195 when we discuss the *safety* of Java programs (which differs from the concept of *type safety* of the Java programming language).

Other, secondary, reasons to hide fields and methods of a class include:

- Internal fields and methods that are visible outside the class just clutter up the API. Keeping visible fields to a minimum keeps your class tidy and therefore easier to use and understand.

- If a method is visible to the users of your class, you have to document it. Save yourself time and effort by hiding it instead.

Access Control

Java defines access control rules that can restrict members of a class from being used outside the class. In a number of examples in this chapter, you've seen the `public` modifier used in field and method declarations. This `public` keyword, along with `protected` and `private` (and one other, special one) are *access control modifiers*; they specify the access rules for the field or method.

Access to packages

Access control on a per-package basis is not directly part of the Java language. Instead, access control is usually done at the level of classes and members of classes.

A package that has been loaded is always accessible to code defined within the same package. Whether it is accessible to code from other packages depends on the way the package is deployed on the host system. When the class files that comprise a package are stored in a directory, for example, a user must have read access to the directory and the files within it in order to have access to the package.

Access to classes

By default, top-level classes are accessible within the package in which they are defined. However, if a top-level class is declared `public`, it is accessible everywhere.

In Chapter 4, we'll meet nested classes. These are classes that can be defined as members of other classes. Because these inner classes are members of a class, they also obey the member access-control rules.

Access to members

The members of a class are always accessible within the body of the class. By default, members are also accessible throughout the package in which the class is defined. This default level of access is often called *package access*. It is only one of four possible levels of access. The other three levels are defined by the `public`, `protected`, and `private` modifiers. Here is some example code that uses these modifiers:

```
public class Laundromat {     // People can use this class.
   private Laundry[] dirty;    // They cannot use this internal field,
   public void wash() { ... } // but they can use these public methods
   public void dry() { ... }  // to manipulate the internal field.
   // A subclass might want to tweak this field
   protected int temperature;
}
```

These access rules apply to members of a class:

- All the fields and methods of a class can always be used within the body of the class itself.

- If a member of a class is declared with the public modifier, it means that the member is accessible anywhere the containing class is accessible. This is the least restrictive type of access control.

- If a member of a class is declared private, the member is never accessible, except within the class itself. This is the most restrictive type of access control.

- If a member of a class is declared protected, it is accessible to all classes within the package (the same as the default package accessibility) and also accessible within the body of any subclass of the class, regardless of the package in which that subclass is defined.

- If a member of a class is not declared with any of these modifiers, it has *default* access (sometimes called *package* access) and it is accessible to code within all classes that are defined in the same package but inaccessible outside of the package.

Default access is *more* restrictive than protected—as default access does not allow access by subclasses outside the package.

protected access requires more elaboration. Suppose class A declares a protected field x and is extended by a class B, which is defined in a different package (this last point is important). Class B inherits the protected field x, and its code can access that field in the current instance of B or in any other instances of B that the code can refer to. This does not mean, however, that the code of class B can start reading the protected fields of arbitrary instances of A.

Let's look at this language detail in code. Here's the definition for A:

```
package javanut6.ch03;

public class A {
    protected final String name;
```

```
    public A(String named) {
        name = named;
    }

    public String getName() {
        return name;
    }
}
```

Here's the definition for B:

```
package javanut6.ch03.different;

import javanut6.ch03.A;

public class B extends A {

    public B(String named) {
        super(named);
    }

    @Override
    public String getName() {
        return "B: " + name;
    }
}
```

 Java packages do not "nest," so javanut6.ch03.different is just a different package than javanut6.ch03; it is not contained inside it or related to it in any way.

However, if we try to add this new method to B, we will get a compilation error, because instances of B do not have access to arbitrary instances of A:

```
    public String examine(A a) {
        return "B sees: " + a.name;
    }
```

If we change the method to this:

```
    public String examine(B b) {
        return "B sees another B: " + b.name;
    }
```

then the compiler is happy, because instances of the same exact type can always see each other's protected fields. Of course, if B was in the same package as A then any instance of B could read any protected field of any instance of A because protected fields are visible to every class in the same package.

Access control and inheritance

The Java specification states that:

- A subclass inherits all the instance fields and instance methods of its superclass accessible to it.
- If the subclass is defined in the same package as the superclass, it inherits all non-private instance fields and methods.
- If the subclass is defined in a different package, it inherits all protected and public instance fields and methods.
- private fields and methods are never inherited; neither are class fields or class methods.
- Constructors are not inherited (instead, they are chained, as described earlier in this chapter).

However, some programmers are confused by the statement that a subclass does not inherit the inaccessible fields and methods of its superclass. It could be taken to imply that when you create an instance of a subclass, no memory is allocated for any private fields defined by the superclass. This is not the intent of the statement, however.

Every instance of a subclass does, in fact, include a complete instance of the superclass within it, including all inaccessible fields and methods.

This existence of potentially inaccessible members seems to be in conflict with the statement that the members of a class are always accessible within the body of the class. To clear up this confusion, we define "inherited members" to mean those superclass members that are accessible.

Then the correct statement about member accessibility is: "All inherited members and all members defined in this class are accessible." An alternative way of saying this is:

- A class inherits *all* instance fields and instance methods (but not constructors) of its superclass.
- The body of a class can always access all the fields and methods it declares itself. It can also access the *accessible* fields and members it inherits from its superclass.

Member access summary

We summarize the member access rules in Table 3-1.

Table 3-1. Class member accessibility

| Accessible to | Member visibility | | | |
	Public	Protected	Default	Private
Defining class	Yes	Yes	Yes	Yes
Class in same package	Yes	Yes	Yes	No
Subclass in different package	Yes	Yes	No	No
Nonsubclass different package	Yes	No	No	No

Here are some simple rules of thumb for using visibility modifiers:

- Use public only for methods and constants that form part of the public API of the class. The only acceptable usage of public fields is for constants or immutable objects, and they must be also declared final.

- Use protected for fields and methods that aren't required by most programmers using the class but that may be of interest to anyone creating a subclass as part of a different package.

> protected members are technically part of the exported API of a class. They must be documented and cannot be changed without potentially breaking code that relies on them.

- Use the default package visibility for fields and methods that are internal implementation details but are used by cooperating classes in the same package.

- Use private for fields and methods that are used only inside the class and should be hidden everywhere else.

If you are not sure whether to use protected, package, or private accessibility, start with private. If this is overly restrictive, you can always relax the access restrictions slightly (or provide accessor methods, in the case of fields).

This is especially important when designing APIs because increasing access restrictions is not a backward-compatible change and can break code that relies on access to those members.

Data Accessor Methods

In the Circle example, we declared the circle radius to be a public field. The Circle class is one in which it may well be reasonable to keep that field publicly accessible; it is a simple enough class, with no dependencies between its fields. On the other hand, our current implementation of the class allows a Circle object to have a negative radius, and circles with negative radii should simply not exist. As long as the radius is stored in a public field, however, any programmer can set the field to any value she wants, no matter how unreasonable. The only solution is to restrict the programmer's direct access to the field and define public methods that provide indirect access to the field. Providing public methods to read and write a field is not the same as making the field itself public. The crucial difference is that methods can perform error checking.

We might, for example, want to prevent Circle objects with negative radii—these are obviously not sensible, but our current implementation does not prohibit this. In Example 3-4, we show how we might change the definition of Circle to prevent this.

This version of Circle declares the r field to be protected and defines accessor methods named getRadius() and setRadius() to read and write the field value while enforcing the restriction on negative radius values. Because the r field is protected, it is directly (and more efficiently) accessible to subclasses.

Example 3-4. The Circle class using data hiding and encapsulation

```
package shapes;         // Specify a package for the class

public class Circle {    // The class is still public
  // This is a generally useful constant, so we keep it public
  public static final double PI = 3.14159;

  protected double r;    // Radius is hidden but visible to subclasses

  // A method to enforce the restriction on the radius
  // This is an implementation detail that may be of interest to subclasses
  protected void checkRadius(double radius) {
    if (radius < 0.0)
      throw new IllegalArgumentException("radius may not be negative.");
  }

  // The non-default constructor
  public Circle(double r) {
    checkRadius(r);
    this.r = r;
  }

  // Public data accessor methods
  public double getRadius() { return r; }
  public void setRadius(double r) {
    checkRadius(r);
    this.r = r;
  }
```

```
// Methods to operate on the instance field
public double area() { return PI * r * r; }
public double circumference() { return 2 * PI * r; }
}
```

We have defined the Circle class within a package named shapes. Because r is pro
tected, any other classes in the shapes package have direct access to that field and
can set it however they like. The assumption here is that all classes within the
shapes package were written by the same author or a closely cooperating group of
authors and that the classes all trust each other not to abuse their privileged level of
access to each other's implementation details.

Finally, the code that enforces the restriction against negative radius values is itself
placed within a protected method, checkRadius(). Although users of the Circle
class cannot call this method, subclasses of the class can call it and even override it if
they want to change the restrictions on the radius.

It is a common convention in Java that data accessor methods
begin with the prefixes "get" and "set." But if the field being
accessed is of type boolean, the get() method may be
replaced with an equivalent method that begins with "is." For
example, the accessor method for a boolean field named read
able is typically called isReadable() instead of
getReadable().

Abstract Classes and Methods

In Example 3-4, we declared our Circle class to be part of a package named shapes.
Suppose we plan to implement a number of shape classes: Rectangle, Square,
Ellipse, Triangle, and so on. We can give these shape classes our two basic area()
and circumference() methods. Now, to make it easy to work with an array of
shapes, it would be helpful if all our shape classes had a common superclass, Shape.
If we structure our class hierarchy this way, every shape object, regardless of the
actual type of shape it represents, can be assigned to variables, fields, or array elements of type Shape. We want the Shape class to encapsulate whatever features all
our shapes have in common (e.g., the area() and circumference() methods). But
our generic Shape class doesn't represent any real kind of shape, so it cannot define
useful implementations of the methods. Java handles this situation with *abstract
methods*.

Java lets us define a method without implementing it by declaring the method with
the abstract modifier. An abstract method has no body; it simply has a signature

definition followed by a semicolon.[2] Here are the rules about `abstract` methods and the `abstract` classes that contain them:

- Any class with an `abstract` method is automatically `abstract` itself and must be declared as such. To fail to do so is a compilation error.

- An `abstract` class cannot be instantiated.

- A subclass of an `abstract` class can be instantiated only if it overrides each of the `abstract` methods of its superclass and provides an implementation (i.e., a method body) for all of them. Such a class is often called a *concrete* subclass, to emphasize the fact that it is not `abstract`.

- If a subclass of an `abstract` class does not implement all the `abstract` methods it inherits, that subclass is itself `abstract` and must be declared as such.

- `static`, `private`, and `final` methods cannot be `abstract`, because these types of methods cannot be overridden by a subclass. Similarly, a `final` class cannot contain any `abstract` methods.

- A class can be declared `abstract` even if it does not actually have any `abstract` methods. Declaring such a class `abstract` indicates that the implementation is somehow incomplete and is meant to serve as a superclass for one or more subclasses that complete the implementation. Such a class cannot be instantiated.

The `Classloader` class that we will meet in Chapter 11 is a good example of an abstract class that does not have any abstract methods.

Let's look at an example of how these rules work. If we define the `Shape` class to have abstract `area()` and `circumference()` methods, any subclass of `Shape` is required to provide implementations of these methods so that it can be instantiated. In other words, every `Shape` object is guaranteed to have implementations of these methods defined. Example 3-5 shows how this might work. It defines an `abstract` `Shape` class and two concrete subclasses of it.

Example 3-5. An abstract class and concrete subclasses

```
public abstract class Shape {
    public abstract double area();            // Abstract methods: note
    public abstract double circumference();   // semicolon instead of body.
```

---

2 An `abstract` method in Java is something like a pure virtual function in C++ (i.e., a virtual function that is declared = 0). In C++, a class that contains a pure virtual function is called an abstract class and cannot be instantiated. The same is true of Java classes that contain `abstract` methods.

```
}
class Circle extends Shape {
  public static final double PI = 3.14159265358979323846;
  protected double r;                             // Instance data
  public Circle(double r) { this.r = r; }         // Constructor
  public double getRadius() { return r; }         // Accessor
  public double area() { return PI*r*r; }         // Implementations of
  public double circumference() { return 2*PI*r; } // abstract methods.
}

class Rectangle extends Shape {
  protected double w, h;                          // Instance data
  public Rectangle(double w, double h) {          // Constructor
    this.w = w;   this.h = h;
  }
  public double getWidth() { return w; }          // Accessor method
  public double getHeight() { return h; }         // Another accessor
  public double area() { return w*h; }            // Implementation of
  public double circumference() { return 2*(w + h); } // abstract methods
}
```

Each abstract method in Shape has a semicolon right after its parentheses. They have no curly braces, and no method body is defined. Using the classes defined in Example 3-5, we can now write code such as:

```
Shape[] shapes = new Shape[3];        // Create an array to hold shapes
shapes[0] = new Circle(2.0);          // Fill in the array
shapes[1] = new Rectangle(1.0, 3.0);
shapes[2] = new Rectangle(4.0, 2.0);

double totalArea = 0;
for(int i = 0; i < shapes.length; i++)
    totalArea += shapes[i].area();    // Compute the area of the shapes
```

Notice two important points here:

- Subclasses of Shape can be assigned to elements of an array of Shape. No cast is necessary. This is another example of a widening reference type conversion (discussed in Chapter 2).

- You can invoke the area() and circumference() methods for any Shape object, even though the Shape class does not define a body for these methods. When you do this, the method to be invoked is found using virtual method lookup, which means that the area of a circle is computed using the method defined by Circle, and the area of a rectangle is computed using the method defined by Rectangle.

Reference Type Conversions

Objects can be converted between different reference types. As with primitive types, reference type conversions can be widening conversions (allowed automatically by the compiler) or narrowing conversions that require a cast (and possibly a runtime check). In order to understand reference type conversions, you need to understand that reference types form a hierarchy, usually called the *class hierarchy*.

Every Java reference type *extends* some other type, known as its *superclass*. A type inherits the fields and methods of its superclass and then defines its own additional fields and methods. A special class named Object serves as the root of the class hierarchy in Java. All Java classes extend Object directly or indirectly. The Object class defines a number of special methods that are inherited (or overridden) by all objects.

The predefined String class and the Point class we discussed earlier in this chapter both extend Object. Thus, we can say that all String objects are also Object objects. We can also say that all Point objects are Object objects. The opposite is not true, however. We cannot say that every Object is a String because, as we've just seen, some Object objects are Point objects.

With this simple understanding of the class hierarchy, we can define the rules of reference type conversion:

- An object cannot be converted to an unrelated type. The Java compiler does not allow you to convert a String to a Point, for example, even if you use a cast operator.

- An object can be converted to the type of its superclass or of any ancestor class. This is a widening conversion, so no cast is required. For example, a String value can be assigned to a variable of type Object or passed to a method where an Object parameter is expected.

 No conversion is actually performed; the object is simply treated as if it were an instance of the superclass. This is sometimes referred to as the Liskov substitution principle, after Barbara Liskov, the computer scientist who first explicitly formulated it.

- An object can be converted to the type of a subclass, but this is a narrowing conversion and requires a cast. The Java compiler provisionally allows this kind of conversion, but the Java interpreter checks at runtime to make sure it is valid. Only cast an object to the type of a subclass if you are sure, based on the logic of your program, that the object is actually an instance of the subclass. If it is not, the interpreter throws a ClassCastException. For example, if we assign a String object to a variable of type Object, we can later cast the value of that variable back to type String:

```
Object o = "string";     // Widening conversion from String
                         // to Object Later in the program...
String s = (String) o;   // Narrowing conversion from Object
                         // to String
```

Arrays are objects and follow some conversion rules of their own. First, any array can be converted to an Object value through a widening conversion. A narrowing conversion with a cast can convert such an object value back to an array. Here's an example:

```
// Widening conversion from array to Object
Object o = new int[] {1,2,3};
// Later in the program...

int[] a = (int[]) o;      // Narrowing conversion back to array type
```

In addition to converting an array to an object, an array can be converted to another type of array if the "base types" of the two arrays are reference types that can themselves be converted. For example:

```
// Here is an array of strings.
String[] strings = new String[] { "hi", "there" };
// A widening conversion to CharSequence[] is allowed because String
// can be widened to CharSequence
CharSequence[] sequences = strings;
// The narrowing conversion back to String[] requires a cast.
strings = (String[]) sequences;
// This is an array of arrays of strings
String[][] s = new String[][] { strings };
// It cannot be converted to CharSequence[] because String[] cannot be
// converted to CharSequence: the number of dimensions don't match

sequences = s;  // This line will not compile
// s can be converted to Object or Object[], because all array types
// (including String[] and String[][]) can be converted to Object.
Object[] objects = s;
```

Note that these array conversion rules apply only to arrays of objects and arrays of arrays. An array of primitive type cannot be converted to any other array type, even if the primitive base types can be converted:

```
// Can't convert int[] to double[] even though
// int can be widened to double
// This line causes a compilation error
double[] data = new int[] {1,2,3};
// This line is legal, however, because int[] can be converted to Object
Object[] objects = new int[][] {{1,2},{3,4}};
```

Modifier Summary

As we've seen, classes, interfaces, and their members can be declared with one or more *modifiers*—keywords such as public, static, and final. Let's conclude this

---

chapter by listing the Java modifiers, explaining what types of Java constructs they can modify, and explaining what they do. Table 3-2 has the details; you can also refer back to "Overview of Classes" on page 97 and "Field Declaration Syntax" on page 101 as well as "Method Modifiers" on page 68.

Table 3-2. Java modifiers

Modifier	Used on	Meaning
abstract	Class	The class cannot be instantiated and may contain unimplemented methods.
	Interface	All interfaces are abstract. The modifier is optional in interface declarations.
	Method	No body is provided for the method; it is provided by a subclass. The signature is followed by a semicolon. The enclosing class must also be abstract.
default	Method	Implementation of this interface method is optional. The interface provides a default implementation for classes that elect not to implement it. See Chapter 4 for more details.
final	Class	The class cannot be subclassed.
	Method	The method cannot be overridden.
	Field	The field cannot have its value changed. static final fields are compile-time constants.
	Variable	A local variable, method parameter, or exception parameter cannot have its value changed.
native	Method	The method is implemented in some platform-dependent way (often in C). No body is provided; the signature is followed by a semicolon.
<None> (package)	Class	A non-public class is accessible only in its package.
	Interface	A non-public interface is accessible only in its package.
	Member	A member that is not private, protected, or public has package visibility and is accessible only within its package.
private	Member	The member is accessible only within the class that defines it.
protected	Member	The member is accessible only within the package in which it is defined and within subclasses.
public	Class	The class is accessible anywhere its package is.

Modifier	Used on	Meaning
	Interface	The interface is accessible anywhere its package is.
	Member	The member is accessible anywhere its class is.
strictfp	Class	All methods of the class are implicitly strictfp.
	Method	All floating-point computation done by the method must be performed in a way that strictly conforms to the IEEE 754 standard. In particular, all values, including intermediate results, must be expressed as IEEE float or double values and cannot take advantage of any extra precision or range offered by native platform floating-point formats or hardware. This modifier is extremely rarely used.
static	Class	An inner class declared static is a top-level class, not associated with a member of the containing class. See Chapter 4 for more details.
	Method	A static method is a class method. It is not passed an implicit this object reference. It can be invoked through the class name.
	Field	A static field is a class field. There is only one instance of the field, regardless of the number of class instances created. It can be accessed through the class name.
	Initializer	The initializer is run when the class is loaded rather than when an instance is created.
synchronized	Method	The method makes nonatomic modifications to the class or instance, so care must be taken to ensure that two threads cannot modify the class or instance at the same time. For a static method, a lock for the class is acquired before executing the method. For a non-static method, a lock for the specific object instance is acquired. See Chapter 5 for more details.
transient	Field	The field is not part of the persistent state of the object and should not be serialized with the object. Used with object serialization; see java.io.ObjectOutputStream.
volatile	Field	The field can be accessed by unsynchronized threads, so certain optimizations must not be performed on it. This modifier can sometimes be used as an alternative to synchronized. See Chapter 5 for more details.

4

The Java Type System

In this chapter, we move beyond basic object-oriented programming with classes and into the additional concepts required to work effectively with Java's static type system.

A *statically typed* language is one in which variables have definite types, and where it is a compile-time error to assign a value of an incompatible type to a variable. Java is an example of a statically typed language. Languages that only check type compatibility at runtime are called *dynamically typed*—JavaScript is an example of a dynamically typed language.

Java's type system involves not only classes and primitive types, but also other kinds of reference type that are related to the basic concept of a class, but which differ in some way, and are usually treated in a special way by javac or the JVM.

We have already met arrays and classes, two of Java's most widely used kinds of reference type. This chapter starts by discussing another very important kind of reference type—*interfaces*. We then move on to discuss Java's *generics*, which have a major role to play in Java's type system. With these topics under our belts, we can discuss the differences between compile-time and runtime types in Java.

To complete the full picture of Java's reference types, we look at specialized kinds of classes and interfaces—known as *enums* and *annotations*. We conclude the chapter by looking at *nested types* and finally the new *lambda expressions* functionality introduced in Java 8.

Let's get started by taking a look at interfaces—probably the most important of Java's reference types after classes, and a key building block for the whole of Java's type system.

Interfaces

In Chapter 3, we met the idea of inheritance. We also saw that a Java class can only inherit from a single class. This is quite a big restriction on the kinds of object-oriented programs that we want to make. The designers of Java knew this, but they also wanted to ensure that Java's approach to object-oriented programming was less complex than, for example, that of C++.

The solution that they chose was to create the concept of an interface. Like a class, an *interface* defines a new reference type. As its name implies, an interface is intended to represent only an API—so it provides a description of a type, and the methods (and signatures) that classes that *implement* that API should provide.

In general, a Java interface does not provide any implementation code for the methods that it describes. These methods are considered *mandatory*—any class that wishes to implement the interface must provide an implementation of these methods.

However, an interface may wish to mark that some API methods are optional, and that implementing classes do not need to implement them if they choose not to. This is done with the `default` keyword—and the interface must provide a *default* implementation of these optional methods, which will be used by any implementation that elects not to implement them.

 The ability to have optional methods in interfaces is new in Java 8. It is not available in any earlier version. See "Default Methods" on page 140 for a full description of how optional (also called default) methods work.

It is not possible to directly instantiate an interface and create a member of the interface type. Instead, a class must *implement* the interface to provide the necessary method bodies.

Any instances of that class are members of both the type defined by the class and the type defined by the interface. Objects that do not share the same class or superclass may still be members of the same type by virtue of implementing the same interface.

Defining an Interface

An interface definition is much like a class definition in which all the (nondefault) methods are abstract and the keyword `class` has been replaced with `interface`. For example, the following code shows the definition of an interface named `Centered`. A `Shape` class, such as those defined in Chapter 3, might implement this interface if it wants to allow the coordinates of its center to be set and queried:

```
interface Centered {
    void setCenter(double x, double y);
```

```
    double getCenterX();
    double getCenterY();
}
```

A number of restrictions apply to the members of an interface:

- All mandatory methods of an interface are implicitly `abstract` and must have a semicolon in place of a method body. The `abstract` modifier is allowed, but by convention is usually omitted.

- An interface defines a public API. All members of an interface are implicitly `public`, and it is conventional to omit the unnecessary `public` modifier. It is a compile-time error to try to define a `protected` or `private` method in an interface.

- An interface may not define any instance fields. Fields are an implementation detail, and an interface is a specification not an implementation. The only fields allowed in an interface definition are constants that are declared both `static` and `final`.

- An interface cannot be instantiated, so it does not define a constructor.

- Interfaces may contain nested types. Any such types are implicitly `public` and `static`. See "Nested Types" on page 155 for a full description of nested types.

- As of Java 8, an interface may contain static methods. Previous versions of Java did not allow this, and this is widely believed to have been a flaw in the design of the Java language.

Extending Interfaces

Interfaces may extend other interfaces, and, like a class definition, an interface definition may include an `extends` clause. When one interface extends another, it inherits all the methods and constants of its superinterface and can define new methods and constants. Unlike classes, however, the `extends` clause of an interface definition may include more than one superinterface. For example, here are some interfaces that extend other interfaces:

```
interface Positionable extends Centered {
    void setUpperRightCorner(double x, double y);
    double getUpperRightX();
    double getUpperRightY();
}
interface Transformable extends Scalable, Translatable, Rotatable {}
interface SuperShape extends Positionable, Transformable {}
```

An interface that extends more than one interface inherits all the methods and constants from each of those interfaces and can define its own additional methods and constants. A class that implements such an interface must implement the abstract methods defined directly by the interface, as well as all the abstract methods inherited from all the superinterfaces.

Implementing an Interface

Just as a class uses extends to specify its superclass, it can use implements to name one or more interfaces it supports. implements is a Java keyword that can appear in a class declaration following the extends clause. implements should be followed by a comma-separated list of interfaces that the class implements.

When a class declares an interface in its implements clause, it is saying that it provides an implementation (i.e., a body) for each mandatory method of that interface. If a class implements an interface but does not provide an implementation for every mandatory interface method, it inherits those unimplemented abstract methods from the interface and must itself be declared abstract. If a class implements more than one interface, it must implement every mandatory method of each interface it implements (or be declared abstract).

The following code shows how we can define a CenteredRectangle class that extends the Rectangle class from Chapter 3 and implements our Centered interface:

```java
public class CenteredRectangle extends Rectangle implements Centered {
    // New instance fields
    private double cx, cy;

    // A constructor
    public CenteredRectangle(double cx, double cy, double w, double h) {
        super(w, h);
        this.cx = cx;
        this.cy = cy;
    }

    // We inherit all the methods of Rectangle but must
    // provide implementations of all the Centered methods.
    public void setCenter(double x, double y) { cx = x; cy = y; }
    public double getCenterX() { return cx; }
    public double getCenterY() { return cy; }
}
```

Suppose we implement CenteredCircle and CenteredSquare just as we have implemented this CenteredRectangle class. Each class extends Shape, so instances of the classes can be treated as instances of the Shape class, as we saw earlier. Because each class implements the Centered interface, instances can also be treated as instances of that type. The following code demonstrates how objects can be members of both a class type and an interface type:

```java
Shape[] shapes = new Shape[3];      // Create an array to hold shapes

// Create some centered shapes, and store them in the Shape[]
// No cast necessary: these are all widening conversions
shapes[0] = new CenteredCircle(1.0, 1.0, 1.0);
shapes[1] = new CenteredSquare(2.5, 2, 3);
shapes[2] = new CenteredRectangle(2.3, 4.5, 3, 4);
```

```
// Compute average area of the shapes and
// average distance from the origin
double totalArea = 0;
double totalDistance = 0;
for(int i = 0; i < shapes.length; i++) {
  totalArea += shapes[i].area();   // Compute the area of the shapes

  // Be careful—in general, the use of instanceof to determine the
  // runtime type of an object is quite often an indication of a
  // problem with the design
  if (shapes[i] instanceof Centered) { // The shape is a Centered shape
    // Note the required cast from Shape to Centered (no cast would
    // be required to go from CenteredSquare to Centered, however).
    Centered c = (Centered) shapes[i];

    double cx = c.getCenterX();    // Get coordinates of the center
    double cy = c.getCenterY();    // Compute distance from origin
    totalDistance += Math.sqrt(cx*cx + cy*cy);
  }
}
System.out.println("Average area: " + totalArea/shapes.length);
System.out.println("Average distance: " + totalDistance/shapes.length);
```

Interfaces are data types in Java, just like classes. When a class implements an interface, instances of that class can be assigned to variables of the interface type.

Don't interpret this example to imply that you must assign a CenteredRectangle object to a Centered variable before you can invoke the setCenter() method or to a Shape variable before you can invoke the area() method. CenteredRectangle defines setCenter() and inherits area() from its Rectangle superclass, so you can always invoke these methods.

Implementing Multiple Interfaces

Suppose we want shape objects that can be positioned in terms of not only their center points but also their upper-right corners. And suppose we also want shapes that can be scaled larger and smaller. Remember that although a class can extend only a single superclass, it can implement any number of interfaces. Assuming we have defined appropriate UpperRightCornered and Scalable interfaces, we can declare a class as follows:

```
public class SuperDuperSquare extends Shape
  implements Centered, UpperRightCornered, Scalable {
  // Class members omitted here
}
```

When a class implements more than one interface, it simply means that it must provide implementations for all abstract (aka mandatory) methods in all its interfaces.

Default Methods

With the advent of Java 8, it is possible to include methods in interfaces that include an implementation. In this section, we'll discuss these methods, which represent optional methods in the API the interfaces represents—they're usually called *default methods*. Let's start by looking at the reasons why we need the default mechanism in the first place.

Backward compatibility

The Java platform has always been very concerned with backwards compatibility. This means that code that was written (or even compiled) for an earlier version of the platform must continue to keep working with later releases of the platform. This principle allows development groups to have a high degree of confidence that an upgrade of their JDK or JRE will not break currently working applications.

Backward compatibility is a great strength of the Java platform, but in order to achieve it, some constraints are placed on the platform. One of them is that interfaces may not have new mandatory methods added to them in a new release of the interface.

For example, let's suppose that we want to update the `Positionable` interface with the ability to add a bottom-left bounding point as well:

```
public interface Positionable extends Centered {
  void setUpperRightCorner(double x, double y);
  double getUpperRightX();
  double getUpperRightY();
  void setLowerLeftCorner(double x, double y);
  double getLowerLeftX();
  double getLowerLeftY();
}
```

With this new definition, if we try to use this new interface with code developed for the old then it just won't work, as the existing code is missing the mandatory methods `setLowerLeftCorner()`, `getLowerLeftX()`, and `getLowerLeftY()`.

You can see this effect quite easily in your own code. Compile a class file that depends on an interface. Then add a new mandatory method to the interface, and try to run the program with the new version of the interface, together with your old class file. You should see the program crash with a `NoClassDefError`.

This limitation was a concern for the designers of Java 8—as one of their goals was to be able to upgrade the core Java Collections libraries, and introduce methods that made use of lambda expressions.

To solve this problem, a new mechanism was needed, essentially to allow interfaces to evolve by allowing new, optional methods to be added to interfaces without breaking backward compatibility.

Implementation of default methods

To add new methods to an interface without breaking backward compatability requires that some implementation must be provided for the older implementations of the interface so that they can continue to work. This mechanism is a `default` method, and it was first added to the platform in JDK 8.

 A default method (sometimes called an optional method) can be added to any interface. This must include an implementation, called the *default implementation*, which is written inline in the interface definition.

The basic behavior of default methods is:

- An implementing class may (but is not required to) implement the default method.
- If an implementing class implements the default method, then the implementation in the class is used.
- If no other implementation can be found, then the default implementation is used.

An example default method is the sort() method. It's been added to the interface java.util.List in JDK 8, and is defined as:

```
// The <E> syntax is Java's way of writing a generic type—see
// the next section for full details. If you aren't familiar with
// generics, just ignore that syntax for now.
interface List<E> {
  // Other members omitted

  public default void sort(Comparator<? super E> c) {
    Collections.<E>sort(this, c);
  }
}
```

Thus, from Java 8 upward, any object that implements List has an instance method sort() that can be used to sort the list using a suitable Comparator. As the return type is void, we might expect that this is an in-place sort, and this is indeed the case.

Marker Interfaces

Sometimes it is useful to define an interface that is entirely empty. A class can implement this interface simply by naming it in its implements clause without having to implement any methods. In this case, any instances of the class become valid instances of the interface. Java code can check whether an object is an instance of the interface using the instanceof operator, so this technique is a useful way to provide additional information about an object.

The java.io.Serializable interface is a marker interface of this sort. A class implements the Serializable interface to tell ObjectOutputStream that its instances may safely be serialized. java.util.RandomAccess is another example: java.util.List implementations implement this interface to advertise that they provide fast random access to the elements of the list. For example, ArrayList implements RandomAccess, while LinkedList does not. Algorithms that care about the performance of random-access operations can test for RandomAccess like this:

```
// Before sorting the elements of a long arbitrary list, we may want
// to make sure that the list allows fast random access.  If not,
// it may be quicker make a random-access copy of the list before
// sorting it. Note that this is not necessary when using
// java.util.Collections.sort().
List l = ...;  // Some arbitrary list we're given
if (l.size() > 2 && !(l instanceof RandomAccess))  l = new ArrayList(l);
sortListInPlace(l);
```

As we will see later, Java's type system is very tightly connected to the names that types have—an approach called *nominal typing*. A marker interface is a great example of this—it has nothing at all *except* a name.

Java Generics

One of the great strengths of the Java platform is the standard library that it ships. It provides a great deal of useful functionality—and in particular robust implementations of common data structures. These implementations are relatively simple to develop with and are well documented. The libraries are known as the Java Collections, and we will spend a big chunk of Chapter 8 discussing them. For a far more complete treatment, see the book *Java Generics and Collections* by Maurice Naftalin and Philip Wadler (O'Reilly).

Although they were still very useful, the earliest versions of the collections had a fairly major limitation, however. This limitation was that the data structure (often called the *container*) essentially hid the type of the data being stored in it.

Data hiding and encapsulation is a great principle of object-oriented programming, but in this case, the opaque nature of the container caused a lot of problems for the developer.

Let's kick off the section by demonstrating the problem, and showing how the introduction of *generic types* can solve it, and make life much easier for Java developers.

Introduction to Generics

If we want to build a collection of Shape instances, we can use a List to hold them, like this:

```
List shapes = new ArrayList();    // Create a List to hold shapes

// Create some centered shapes, and store them in the list
shapes.add(new CenteredCircle(1.0, 1.0, 1.0));
// This is legal Java—but is a very bad design choice
shapes.add(new CenteredSquare(2.5, 2, 3));

// List::get() returns Object, so to get back a
// CenteredCircle we must cast
CenteredCircle c = (CentredCircle)shapes.get(0);

// Next line causes a runtime failure
CenteredCircle c = (CentredCircle)shapes.get(1);
```

A problem with this code stems from the requirement to perform a cast to get the shape objects back out in a usable form—the List doesn't know what type of objects it contains. Not only that, but it's actually possible to put different types of objects into the same container—and everything will work fine until an illegal cast is used, and the program crashes.

What we really want is a form of List that understands what type it contains. Then, javac could detect when an illegal argument was passed to the methods of List and cause a compilation error, rather than deferring the issue to runtime.

Java provides syntax to cater for this—to indicate that a type is a container that holds instances of another reference type we enclose the *payload* type that the container holds within angle brackets:

```
// Create a List-of-CenteredCircle
List<CenteredCircle> shapes = new ArrayList<CenteredCircle>();

// Create some centered shapes, and store them in the list
shapes.add(new CenteredCircle(1.0, 1.0, 1.0));

// Next line will cause a compilation error
shapes.add(new CenteredSquare(2.5, 2, 3));

// List<CenteredCircle>::get() returns a CenteredCircle, no cast needed
CenteredCircle c = shapes.get(0);
```

This syntax ensures that a large class of unsafe code is caught by the compiler, before it gets anywhere near runtime. This is, of course, the whole point of static type systems—to use compile-time knowledge to help eliminate whole swathes of runtime problems.

Container types are usually called *generic types*—and they are declared like this:

```
interface Box<T> {
  void box(T t);
  T unbox();
}
```

This indicates that the Box interface is a general construct, which can hold any type of payload. It isn't really a complete interface by itself—it's more like a general description of a whole family of interfaces, one for each type that can be used in place of T.

Generic Types and Type Parameters

We've seen how to use a generic type, to provide enhanced program safety, by using compile-time knowledge to prevent simple type errors. In this section, let's dig deeper into the properties of generic types.

The syntax <T> has a special name—it's called a *type parameter*, and another name for a generic type is a *parameterized type*. This should convey the sense that the container type (e.g., List) is parameterized by another type (the payload type). When we write a type like Map<String, Integer>, we are assigning concrete values to the type parameters.

When we define a type that has parameters, we need to do so in a way that does not make assumptions about the type parameters. So the List type is declared in a generic way as List<E>, and the type parameter E is used all the way through to stand as a placeholder for the actual type that the programmer will use for the payload when she makes use of the List data structure.

 Type parameters always stand in for reference types. It is not possible to use a primitive type as a value for a type parameter.

The type parameter can be used in the signatures and bodies of methods as though it is a real type, for example:

```
interface List<E> extends Collection<E> {
  boolean add(E e);
  E get(int index);
  // other methods omitted
}
```

Note how the type parameter E can be used as a parameter for both return types and method arguments. We don't assume that the payload type has any specific properties, and only make the basic assumption of consistency—that the type we put in is the sane type that we will later get back out.

Diamond Syntax

When creating an instance of a generic type, the right-hand side of the assignment statement repeats the value of the type parameter. This is usually unnecessary, as the compiler can infer the values of the type parameters. In modern versions of Java, we can leave out the repeated type values in what is called *diamond syntax*.

Let's look at an example of how to use diamond syntax, by rewriting one of our earlier examples:

```
// Create a List-of-CenteredCircle using diamond syntax
List<CenteredCircle> shapes = new ArrayList<>();
```

This is a small improvement in the verbosity of the assignment statement—we've managed to save a few characters of typing. We'll return to the topic of type inference when we discuss lambda expressions towards the end of this chapter.

Type Erasure

In "Default Methods" on page 140, we discussed the Java platform's strong preference for backwards compatibility. The addition of generics in Java 5 was another example of where backwards compatibility was an issue for a new language feature.

The central question was how to make a type system that allowed older, nongeneric collection classes to be used along with newer, generic collections. The design decision was to achieve this by the use of casts:

```
List someThings = getSomeThings();
// Unsafe cast, but we know that the
// contents of someThings are really strings
List<String> myStrings = (List<String>)someThings;
```

This means that List and List<String> are compatible as types, at least at some level. Java achieves this compatibility by *type erasure*. This means that generic type parameters are only visible at compile time—they are stripped out by javac and are not reflected in the bytecode.[1]

 The nongeneric type List is usually called a *raw type*. It is still perfectly legal Java to work with the raw form of types—even for types that are now generic. This is almost always a sign of poor quality code, however.

The mechanism of type erasure gives rise to a difference in the type system seen by javac and that seen by the JVM—we will discuss this fully in "Compile and Runtime Typing" on page 150.

---

1 Some small traces of generics remain, which can be seen at runtime via reflection.

Type erasure also prohibits some other definitions, which would otherwise seem legal. In this code, we want to count the orders as represented in two slightly different data structures:

```java
// Won't compile
interface OrderCounter {
  // Name maps to list of order numbers
  int totalOrders(Map<String, List<String>> orders);

  // Name maps to total orders made so far
  int totalOrders(Map<String, Integer> orders);
}
```

This seems like perfectly legal Java code—but it will not compile. The issue is that although the two methods seem like normal overloads, after type erasure, the signature of both methods becomes:

```java
int totalOrders(Map);
```

All that is left after type erasure is the raw type of the container—in this case, Map. The runtime would be unable to distinguish between the methods by signature, and so the language specification makes this syntax illegal.

Wildcards

A parameterized type, such as ArrayList<T>, is not *instantiable*—we cannot create instances of them. This is because <T> is just a type parameter—merely a placeholder for a genuine type. It is only when we provide a concrete value for the type parameter, (e.g., ArrayList<String>), that the type becomes fully formed and we can create objects of that type.

This poses a problem if the type that we want to work with is unknown at compile time. Fortunately, the Java type system is able to accommodate this concept. It does so by having an explicit concept of the *unknown type*—which is represented as <?>. This is the simplest example of Java's *wildcard types*.

We can write expressions that involve the unknown type:

```java
ArrayList<?> mysteryList = unknownList();
Object o = mysteryList.get(0);
```

This is perfectly valid Java—ArrayList<?> is a complete type that a variable can have, unlike ArrayList<T>. We don't know anything about the payload type of mysteryList, but that may not be a problem for our code. When working with the unknown type, there are some limitations on its use in user code. For example, this code will not compile:

```java
// Won't compile
mysteryList.add(new Object());
```

The reason for this is simple—we don't know what the payload type of mysteryList is! For example, if mysteryList was really a instance of ArrayList<String>, then we wouldn't expect to be able to put an Object into it.

The only value that we know we can always insert into a container is null—as we know that null is a possible value for any reference type. This isn't that useful, and for this reason, the Java language spec also rules out instantiating a container object with the unknown type as payload, for example:

```
// Won't compile
List<?> unknowns = new ArrayList<?>();
```

A very important use for the unknown type stems from the question, "Is List<String> a subtype of List<Object>?" That is, can we write this?

```
// Is this legal?
List<Object> objects = new ArrayList<String>();
```

At first glance, this seems entirely reasonable—String is a subclass of Object, so we know that any String element in our collection is also a valid Object. However, consider the following code:

```
// Is this legal?
List<Object> objects = new ArrayList<String>();

// If so, what do we do about this?
objects.add(new Object());
```

As the type of objects was declared to be List<Object>, then it should be legal to add an Object instance to it. However, as the actual instance holds strings, then trying to add an Object would not be compatible, and so this would fail at runtime.

The resolution for this is to realize that although this is legal (because String inherits from Object):

```
Object o = new String("X");
```

that does not mean that the corresponding statement for generic container types is also true:

```
// Won't compile
List<Object> objects = new ArrayList<String>();
```

Another way of saying this is that List<String> is *not* a subtype of List<Object>. If we want to have a subtyping relationship for containers, then we need to use the unknown type:

```
// Perfectly legal
List<?> objects = new ArrayList<String>();
```

This means that List<String> *is* a subtype of List<?>—although when we use an assignment like the preceding one, we have lost some type information. For example, the return type of get() is now effectively Object. You should also note that List<?> is not a subtype of any List<T>, for any value of T.

The unknown type sometimes confuses developers—provoking questions like, "Why wouldn't you just use Object instead of the unknown type?" However, as we've seen, the need to have subtyping relationships between generic types essentially requires us to have a notion of the unknown type.

Bounded wildcards

In fact, Java's wildcard types extend beyond just the unknown type, with the concept of *bounded wildcards*, also called *type parameter constraints*. This is the ability to restrict the types that can be used as the value of a type parameter.

They are used to describe the inheritance hierarchy of a mostly unknown type— effectively making statements like, for example, "I don't know anything about this type, except that it must implement List." This would be written as ? extends List in the type parameter. This provides a useful lifeline to the programmer— instead of being restricted to the totally unknown type, she knows that at least the capabilities of the type bound are available.

 The extends keyword is always used, regardless of whether the constraining type is a class or interface type.

This is an example of a concept called *type variance*, which is the general theory of how inheritance between container types relates to the inheritance of their payload types.

Type covariance
   This means that the container types have the same relationship to each other as the payload types do. This is expressed using the extends keyword.

Type contravariance
   This means that the container types have the inverse relationship to each other as the payload types. This is expressed using the super keyword.

These principles tend to appear when discussing container types that act as producers or consumers of types. For example, if Cat extends Pet, then List<Cat> is a subtype of List<? extends Pet>. The List is acting as a *producer* of Cat objects and the appropriate keyword is extends.

For a container type that is acting purely as a *consumer* of instances of a type, we would use the super keyword.

This is codified in the *Producer Extends, Consumer Super* (PECS) principle coined by Joshua Bloch.

As we will see in Chapter 8, we see both covariance and contravariance throughout the Java Collections. They largely exist to ensure that the generics just "do the right thing" and behave in a manner that should not surprise the developer.

Array Covariance

In the earliest versions of Java, before the collections libraries were even introduced, the problem of type variance in container types was still present for Java's arrays. Without type variance, even simple methods like this `sort()` would have been very difficult to write in a useful way:

```
Arrays.sort(Object[] a);
```

For this reason, arrays in Java are covariant—this was seen as a necessary evil in the very early days of the platform, despite the hole in the static type system that it exposes:

```
// This is completely legal
String[] words = {"Hello World!"};
Object[] objects = words;

// Oh, dear, runtime error
objects[0] = new Integer(42);
```

More recent research on modern open source codebases indicates that array covariance is extremely rarely used and is almost certainly a language misfeature.[2] It should be avoided when writing new code.

Generic Methods

A *generic method* is a method that is able to take instances of any reference type.

For example, this method emulates the behavior of the `,` (comma) operator from the C language, which is usually used to combine expressions with side effects together:

```
// Note that this class is not generic
public class Utils
  public static <T> T comma(T a, T b) {
    return a;
```

---

2 Raoul-Gabriel Urma and Janina Voigt, "Using the OpenJDK to Investigate Covariance in Java," *Java Magazine* (May/June 2012):44–47.

```
    }
}
```

Even though a type parameter is used in the definition of the method, the class it is defined in need not be generic—instead, the syntax is used to indicate that the method can be used freely, and that the return type is the same as the argument.

Using and Designing Generic Types

When working with Java's generics, it can sometimes be helpful to think in terms of two different levels of understanding:

Practitioner
> A practitioner needs to use existing generic libraries, and to build some fairly simple generic classes. At this level, the developer should also understand the basics of type erasure, as several Java syntax features are confusing without at least an awareness of the runtime handling of generics.

Designer
> The designer of new libraries that use generics needs to understand much more of the capabilities of generics. There are some nastier parts of the spec—including a full understanding of wildcards, and advanced topics such as "capture-of" error messages.

Java generics are one of the most complex parts of the language specification with a lot of potential corner cases, which not every developer needs to fully understand, at least on a first encounter with this part of Java's type system.

Compile and Runtime Typing

Consider an example piee>ce of code:

```
List<String> l = new ArrayList<>();
System.out.println(l);
```

We can ask the following question: what is the type of l? The answer to that question depends on whether we consider l at compile time (i.e., the type seen by javac) or at runtime (as seen by the JVM).

javac will see the type of l as List-of-String, and will use that type information to carefully check for syntax errors, such as an attempted add() of an illegal type.

Conversely, the JVM will see l as an object of type ArrayList—as we can see from the println() statement. The runtime type of l is a raw type due to type erasure.

The compile-time and runtime types are therefore slightly different to each other. The slightly strange thing is that in some ways, the runtime type is both more *and* less specific than the compile-time type.

The runtime type is less specific than the compile-time type, because the type information about the payload type is gone—it has been erased, and the resulting runtime type is just a raw type.

The compile-time type is less specific than the runtime type, because we don't know exactly what concrete type l will be—all we know is that it will be of a type compatible with List.

Enums and Annotations

Java has specialized forms of classes and interfaces that are used to fulfill specific roles in the type system. They are known as *enumerated types* and *annotation types,* normally just called *enums* and *annotations.*

Enums

Enums are a variation of classes that have limited functionality and that have only a small number of possible values that the type permits.

For example, suppose we want to define a type to represent the primary colors of red, green, and blue, and we want these to be the only possible values of the type. We can do this by making use of the enum keyword:

```
public enum PrimaryColor {
  // The ; is not required at the end of the list of instances
  RED, GREEN, BLUE
}
```

Instances of the type PrimaryColor can then be referenced as though they were static fields: PrimaryColor.RED, PrimaryColor.GREEN, and PrimaryColor.BLUE.

 In other languages, such as C++, this role is usually fulfilled by using constant integers, but Java's approach provides better type safety, and more flexiblity. For example, as enums are specialized classes, enums can have member fields and methods. If they do have a body (consisting of fields or methods) then the semicolon at the end of the list of instances is required.

For example, suppose that we want to have an enum that encompasses the first few regular polygons (shapes with all sides and all angles equal), and we want them to have some behavior (in the form of methods). We could achieve this by using an enum that takes a value as a parameter, like this:

```
public enum RegularPolygon {
  // The ; is mandatory for enums that have parameters
  TRIANGLE(3), SQUARE(4), PENTAGON(5), HEXAGON(6);

  private Shape shape;
```

```
public Shape getShape() {
  return shape;
}

private RegularPolygon(int sides) {
  switch (sides) {
    case 3:
      // We assume that we have some general constructors
      // for shapes that take the side length and
      // angles in degrees as parameters
      shape = new Triangle(1,1,1,60,60,60);
      break;
    case 4:
      shape = new Rectangle(1,1);
      break;
    case 5:
      shape = new Pentagon(1,1,1,1,1,108,108,108,108,108);
      break;
    case 6:
      shape = new Hexagon(1,1,1,1,1,1,120,120,120,120,120,120);
      break;
  }
}
}
```

These parameters (only one of them in this example) are passed to the constructor to create the individual enum instances. As the enum instances are created by the Java runtime, and can't be instantiated from outside, the constructor is declared as private.

Enums have some special properties:

- All (implicitly) extend java.lang.Enum
- May not be generic
- May implement interfaces
- Cannot be extended
- May only have abstract methods if all enum values provide an implementation body
- May only have a private (or default access) constructor

Annotations

Annotations are a specialized kind of interface that, as the name suggests, annotate some part of a Java program.

For example, consider the @Override annotation. You may have seen it on some methods in some of the earlier examples, and may have asked the following question: what does it do?

The short, and perhaps surprising, answer is that it does nothing at all.

The less short (and flippant) answer is that, like all annotations, it has no direct effect, but instead acts as additional information about the method that it annotates —in this case, it denotes that a method overrides a superclass method.

This acts as a useful hint to compilers and integrated development environments (IDEs)—if a developer has misspelled the name of a method that she intended to be an override of a superclass method, then the presence of the `@Override` annotation on the misspelled method (which does not override anything) alerts the compiler to the fact that something is not right.

Annotations are not allowed to alter program semantics—instead, they provide optional metadata. In its strictest sense, this means that they should not affect program execution and instead can only provide information for compilers and other pre-execution phases.

The platform defines a small number of basic annotations in `java.lang`. The original set were `@Override`, `@Deprecated`, and `@SuppressWarnings`—which were used to indicate that a method was overriden, deprecated, or that it generated some compiler warnings that should be suppressed.

These were augmented by `@SafeVarargs` in Java 7 (which provides extended warning suppression for varargs methods) and `@FunctionalInterface` in Java 8. This last annotation indicates an interface can be used as a target for a lambda expression —it is a useful marker annotation although not mandatory, as we will see.

Annotations have some special properties, compared to regular interfaces:

- All (implicitly) extend `java.lang.annotation.Annotation`
- May not be generic
- May not extend any other interface
- May only define zero-arg methods
- May not define methods that throw exceptions
- Have restrictions on the return types of methods
- Can have a default return value for methods

Defining Custom Annotations

Defining custom annotation types for use in your own code is not that hard. The `@interface` keyword allows the developer to define a new annotation type, in much the same way that `class` or `interface` are used.

The key to writing custom annotations is the use of "meta-annotations." These are special annotations, which appear as annotations on the definition of new (custom) annotation types.

The meta-annotations are defined in `java.lang.annotation` and allow the developer to specify policy for where the new annotation type is to be used, and how it will be treated by the compiler and runtime.

There are two primary meta-annotations that are both essentially required when creating a new annotation type—`@Target` and `@Retention`. These both take values that are represented as enums.

The `@Target` meta-annotation indicates where the new custom annotation can be legally placed within Java source code. The enum `ElementType` has the following possible values: `TYPE`, `FIELD`, `METHOD`, `PARAMETER`, `CONSTRUCTOR`, `LOCAL_VARIABLE`, `ANNOTATION_TYPE`, `PACKAGE`, `TYPE_PARAMETER`, and `TYPE_USE`.

The other meta-annotation is `@Retention`, which indicates how `javac` and the Java runtime should process the custom annotation type. It can have one of three values, which are represented by the enum `RetentionPolicy`:

SOURCE

> Annotations with this retention policy are discarded by `javac` during compilation.

CLASS

> This means that the annotation will be present in the class file, but will not necessarily be accessible at runtime by the JVM. This is rarely used, but is sometimes seen in tools that do offline analysis of JVM bytecode.

RUNTIME

> This indicates that the annotation will be available for user code to access at runtime (by using reflection).

Let's take a look at an example, a simple annotation called `@Nickname`, which allows the developer to define a nickname for a method, which can then be used to find the method reflectively at runtime:

```
@Target(ElementType.METHOD)
@Retention(RetentionPolicy.RUNTIME)
public @interface Nickname {
    String[] value() default {};
}
```

This is all that's required to define the annotation—a syntax element where the annotation can appear, a retention policy, and the name of the element. As we need to be able to state the nickname we're assigning to the method, we also need to

---

define a method on the annotation. Despite this, defining new custom annotations is a remarkably compact undertaking.

In addition to the two primary meta-annotations, there are also the @Inherited and @Documented meta-annotations. These are much less frequently encountered in practice, and details on them can be found in the platform documentation.

Type Annotations

With the release of Java 8, two new values for ElementType were added—TYPE_PARAMETER and TYPE_USE. These new values allow the use of annotations in places where they were previously not legal, such as at any site where a type is used. This enables the developer to write code such as:

```
@NotNull String safeString = getMyString();
```

The extra type information conveyed by the @NotNull can then be used by a special type checker to detect problems (a possible NullPointerException, in this example) and to perform additional static analysis. The basic Java 8 distribution ships with some basic pluggable type checkers, but also provides a framework for allowing developers and library authors to create their own.

In this section, we've met Java's enum and annotation types. Let's move on, to consider the next important part of Java's type system: nested types.

Nested Types

The classes, interfaces, and enum types we have seen so far in this book have all been defined as *top-level types*. This means that they are direct members of packages, defined independently of other types. However, type definitions can also be nested within other type definitions. These *nested types*, commonly known as "inner classes," are a powerful feature of the Java language.

Nested types are used for two separate purposes, both related to encapsulation:

- A type may be nested because it needs especially intimate access to the internals of another type—by being a member type, it has access in the same way that member variables and methods do, and can bend the rules of encapsulation.

- A type may be only required for a very specific reason, and in a very small section of code. It should be tightly localized, as it is really part of the implementation detail and should be encapsulated away from the rest of the system.

Another way of thinking of nested types is that they are types that are somehow tied together with another type—they don't really have a completely independent existence as an entity. Types can be nested within another type in four different ways:

Static member types

> A static member type is any type defined as a `static` member of another type. Nested interfaces, enums, and annotations are always static (even if you don't use the keyword).

Nonstatic member classes

> A "nonstatic member type" is simply a member type that is not declared `static`. Only classes can be nonstatic member types.

Local classes

> A local class is a class that is defined and only visible within a block of Java code. Interfaces, enums, and annotations may not be defined locally.

Anonymous classes

> An anonymous class is a kind of local class that has no meaningful name in the Java language. Interfaces, enums, and annotations cannot be defined anonymously.

The term "nested types," while a correct and precise usage, is not widely used by developers. Instead, most Java prorammers user the much vaguer term "inner class." Depending on the situation, this can refer to a nonstatic member class, local class, or anonymous class, but not a static member type, with no real way to distinguish between them.

Fortunately, although the terminology for describing nested types is not always clear, the syntax for working with them is, and it is usually clear from context which kind of nested type is being discussed.

Let's move on to describe each of the four kinds of nested types in greater detail. Each section describes the features of the nested type, the restrictions on its use, and any special Java syntax used with the type. These four sections are followed by an implementation note that explains how nested types work under the hood.

Static Member Types

A *static member type* is much like a regular top-level type. For convenience, however, it is nested within the namespace of another type. Static member types have the following basic properties:

- A static member type is like the other static members of a class: static fields and static methods.

- A static member type is not associated with any instance of the containing class (i.e., there is no `this` object).

- A static member type can access (only) the `static` members of the class that contains it.

- A static member type has access to all the `static` members (including any other static member types) of its containing type.

- Nested interfaces, enums, and annotations are implicitly static, whether or not the static keyword appears.

- Any type nested within an interface or annotation is also implicitly static.

- Static member types may be defined within top-level types or nested to any depth within other static member types.

- A static member type may not be defined within any other kind of nested type.

Let's look at a quick example of the syntax for static member types. Example 4-1 shows a helper interface defined as a static member of a containing class. The example also shows how this interface is used both within the class that contains it and by external classes. Note the use of its hierarchical name in the external class.

Example 4-1. Defining and using a static member interface

```
// A class that implements a stack as a linked list
public class LinkedStack {

    // This static member interface defines how objects are linked
    // The static keyword is optional: all nested interfaces are static
    static interface Linkable {
        public Linkable getNext();
        public void setNext(Linkable node);
    }

    // The head of the list is a Linkable object
    Linkable head;

    // Method bodies omitted
    public void push(Linkable node) { ... }

    public Object pop() { ... }
}

// This class implements the static member interface
class LinkableInteger implements LinkedStack.Linkable {
    // Here's the node's data and constructor
    int i;
    public LinkableInteger(int i) { this.i = i; }

    // Here are the data and methods required to implement the interface
    LinkedStack.Linkable next;

    public LinkedStack.Linkable getNext() { return next; }

    public void setNext(LinkedStack.Linkable node) { next = node; }
}
```

Features of static member types

A static member type has access to all static members of its containing type, including `private` members. The reverse is true as well: the methods of the containing type have access to all members of a static member type, including the `private` members. A static member type even has access to all the members of any other static member types, including the `private` members of those types. A static member type can use any other static member without qualifying its name with the name of the containing type.

 A static member type cannot have the same name as any of its enclosing classes. In addition, static member types can be defined only within top-level types and other static member types. This is actually part of a larger prohibition against `static` members of any sort within member, local, and anonymous classes.

Top-level types can be declared as either `public` or package-private (if they're declared without the `public` keyword). But declaring top-level types as `private` and `protected` wouldn't make a great deal of sense—`protected` would just mean the same as package-private and a `private` top-level class would be unable to be accessed by any other type.

Static member types, on the other hand, are members and so can use any access control modifiers that other members of the containing type can. These modifiers have the same meanings for static member types as they do for other members of a type. Recall that all members of interfaces (and annotations) are implicitly `public`, so static member types nested within interfaces or annotation types cannot be `protected` or `private`.

For example, in Example 4-1, the `Linkable` interface is declared `public`, so it can be implemented by any class that is interested in being stored on a `LinkedStack`.

In code outside the containing class, a static member type is named by combining the name of the outer type with the name of the inner type (e.g., `LinkedStack.Linkable`).

Under most circumstances, this syntax provides a helpful reminder that the inner class is interconnected with its containing type. However, the Java language does permit you to use the `import` directive to directly import a static member type:

```
import pkg.LinkedStack.Linkable;  // Import a specific nested type
// Import all nested types of LinkedStack
import pkg.LinkedStack.*;
```

The nested type can then be referenced without including the name of its enclosing type (e.g., just as `Linkable`).

You can also use the import static directive to import a static member type. See "Packages and the Java Namespace" on page 88 in Chapter 2 for details on import and import static.

However, importing a nested type obscures the fact that that type is closely associated with its containing type—which is usually important information—and as a result it is not commonly done.

Nonstatic Member Classes

A *nonstatic member class* is a class that is declared as a member of a containing class or enumerated type without the static keyword:

- If a static member type is analogous to a class field or class method, a nonstatic member class is analogous to an instance field or instance method.
- Only classes can be nonstatic member types.
- An instance of a nonstatic member class is always associated with an instance of the enclosing type.
- The code of a nonstatic member class has access to all the fields and methods (both static and non-static) of its enclosing type.
- Several features of Java syntax exist specifically to work with the enclosing instance of a nonstatic member class.

Example 4-2 shows how a member class can be defined and used. This example extends the previous LinkedStack example to allow enumeration of the elements on the stack by defining an iterator() method that returns an implementation of the java.util.Iterator interface. The implementation of this interface is defined as a member class.

Example 4-2. An iterator implemented as a member class

```
import java.util.Iterator;

public class LinkedStack {

    // Our static member interface
    public interface Linkable {
        public Linkable getNext();
        public void setNext(Linkable node);
    }

    // The head of the list
    private Linkable head;

    // Method bodies omitted here
```

```
public void push(Linkable node) { ... }
public Linkable pop() { ... }

// This method returns an Iterator object for this LinkedStack
public Iterator<Linkable> iterator() { return new LinkedIterator(); }

// Here is the implementation of the Iterator interface,
// defined as a nonstatic member class.
protected class LinkedIterator implements Iterator<Linkable> {
    Linkable current;

    // The constructor uses a private field of the containing class
    public LinkedIterator() { current = head; }

    // The following 3 methods are defined by the Iterator interface
    public boolean hasNext() {  return current != null; }

    public Linkable next() {
        if (current == null)
          throw new java.util.NoSuchElementException();
        Linkable value = current;
        current = current.getNext();
        return value;
    }

    public void remove() { throw new UnsupportedOperationException(); }
  }
}
```

Notice how the LinkedIterator class is nested within the LinkedStack class. Because LinkedIterator is a helper class used only within LinkedStack, having it defined so close to where it is used by the containing class makes for a clean design, just as we discussed when we introduced nested types.

Features of member classes

Like instance fields and instance methods, every instance of a nonstatic member class is associated with an instance of the class in which it is defined. This means that the code of a member class has access to all the instance fields and instance methods (as well as the static members) of the containing instance, including any that are declared private.

This crucial feature was already illustrated in Example 4-2. Here is the Linked Stack.LinkedIterator() constructor again:

```
public LinkedIterator() { current = head; }
```

This single line of code sets the current field of the inner class to the value of the head field of the containing class. The code works as shown, even though head is declared as a private field in the containing class.

A nonstatic member class, like any member of a class, can be assigned one of the standard access control modifiers. In Example 4-2, the LinkedIterator class is declared protected, so it is inaccessible to code (in a different package) that uses the LinkedStack class but is accessible to any class that subclasses LinkedStack.

Restrictions on member classes

Member classes have two important restrictions:

- A nonstatic member class cannot have the same name as any containing class or package. This is an important rule, one that is *not* shared by fields and methods.

- Nonstatic member classes cannot contain any static fields, methods, or types, except for constant fields declared both static and final.

static members are top-level constructs not associated with any particular object while every nonstatic member class is associated with an instance of its enclosing class. Defining a static top-level member within a member class that is not at the top level would cause confusion, so it is not allowed.

Syntax for member classes

The most important feature of a member class is that it can access the instance fields and methods in its containing object. We saw this in the LinkedStack.Linked Iterator() constructor of Example 3-8:

```
public LinkedIterator() { current = head; }
```

In this example, head is a field of the enclosing LinkedStack class, and we assign it to the current field of the LinkedIterator class (which is a member of the non-static member class).

If we want to use explicit references, and make use of this, then we have to use a special syntax for explicitly referring to the containing instance of the this object. For example, if we want to be explicit in our constructor, we can use the following syntax:

```
public LinkedIterator() { this.current = LinkedStack.this.head; }
```

The general syntax is *classname*.this, where *classname* is the name of a containing class. Note that member classes can themselves contain member classes, nested to any depth. However, because no member class can have the same name as any containing class, the use of the enclosing class name prepended to this is a perfectly general way to refer to any containing instance.

This special syntax is needed only when referring to a member of a containing class that is hidden by a member of the same name in the member class.

Scope versus inheritance

We notice that a top-level class can extend a member class. With the introduction of nonstatic member classes, two separate hierarchies must be considered for any class. The first is the *inheritance hierarchy*, from superclass to subclass, that defines the fields and methods a member class inherits. The second is the *containment hierarchy*, from containing class to contained class, that defines a set of fields and methods that are in the scope of (and are therefore accessible to) the member class.

It is important to be familiar with the properties and rules of thumb that the two hierarchies have:

- The two hierarchies are entirely distinct from each other; it is important that you do not confuse them.

- Refrain from creating naming conflicts, where a field or method in a superclass has the same name as a field or method in a containing class.

- If such a naming conflict does arise, the inherited field or method takes precedence over the field or method of the same name in the containing class.

- Inherited fields and methods are in the scope of the class that inherits them and take precedence over fields and methods by the same name in enclosing scopes.

- To prevent confusion between the class hierarchy and the containment hierarchy, avoid deep containment hierarchies.

- If a class is nested more than two levels deep, it is probably going to cause more confusion than it is worth.

- If a class has a deep class hierarchy (i.e., it has many ancestors), consider defining it as a top-level class rather than as a nonstatic member class.

Local Classes

A *local class* is declared locally within a block of Java code rather than as a member of a class. Only classes may be defined locally: interfaces, enumerated types, and annotation types must be top-level or static member types. Typically, a local class is defined within a method, but it can also be defined within a static initializer or instance initializer of a class.

Just as all blocks of Java code appear within class definitions, all local classes are nested within containing blocks. For this reason, local classes share many of the features of member classes. It is usually more appropriate to think of them as an entirely separate kind of nested type.

 See Chapter 5 for details as to when it's appropriate to choose a local class versus a lambda expression.

The defining characteristic of a local class is that it is local to a block of code. Like a local variable, a local class is valid only within the scope defined by its enclosing block. Example 4-3 shows how we can modify the iterator() method of the LinkedStack class so it defines LinkedIterator as a local class instead of a member class.

By doing this, we move the definition of the class even closer to where it is used and hopefully improve the clarity of the code even further. For brevity, Example 4-3 shows only the iterator() method, not the entire LinkedStack class that contains it.

Type System

Example 4-3. Defining and using a local class

```java
// This method returns an Iterator object for this LinkedStack
public Iterator<Linkable> Iterator() {
    // Here's the definition of LinkedIterator as a local class
    class LinkedIterator implements Iterator<Linkable> {
        Linkable current;

        // The constructor uses a private field of the containing class
        public LinkedIterator() { current = head; }

        // The following 3 methods are defined by the Iterator interface
        public boolean hasNext() { return current != null; }

        public Linkable next() {
            if (current == null)
              throw new java.util.NoSuchElementException();
            Linkable value = current;
            current = current.getNext();
            return value;
        }

        public void remove() { throw new UnsupportedOperationException(); }
    }

    // Create and return an instance of the class we just defined
    return new LinkedIterator();
}
```

Features of local classes

Local classes have the following interesting features:

- Like member classes, local classes are associated with a containing instance and can access any members, including `private` members, of the containing class.
- In addition to accessing fields defined by the containing class, local classes can access any local variables, method parameters, or exception parameters that are in the scope of the local method definition and are declared `final`.

Restrictions on local classes

Local classes are subject to the following restrictions:

- The name of a local class is defined only within the block that defines it; it can never be used outside that block. (Note, however, that instances of a local class created within the scope of the class can continue to exist outside of that scope. This situation is described in more detail later in this section.)
- Local classes cannot be declared `public`, `protected`, `private`, or `static`.
- Like member classes, and for the same reasons, local classes cannot contain `static` fields, methods, or classes. The only exception is for constants that are declared both `static` and `final`.
- Interfaces, enumerated types, and annotation types cannot be defined locally.
- A local class, like a member class, cannot have the same name as any of its enclosing classes.
- As noted earlier, a local class can use the local variables, method parameters, and even exception parameters that are in its scope but only if those variables or parameters are declared `final`. This is because the lifetime of an instance of a local class can be much longer than the execution of the method in which the class is defined.

A local class has a private internal copy of all local variables it uses (these copies are automatically generated by `javac`). The only way to ensure that the local variable and the private copy are always the same is to insist that the local variable is `final`.

Scope of a local class

In discussing nonstatic member classes, we saw that a member class can access any members inherited from superclasses and any members defined by its containing classes. The same is true for local classes, but local classes can also access `final` local variables and parameters. Example 4-4 illustrates the different kinds of fields and variables that may be accessible to a local class:

Example 4-4. Fields and variables available to a local class

```java
class A { protected char a = 'a'; }
class B { protected char b = 'b'; }

public class C extends A {
  private char c = 'c';             // Private fields visible to local class
  public static char d = 'd';
  public void createLocalObject(final char e)
  {
    final char f = 'f';
    int i = 0;                      // i not final; not usable by local class
    class Local extends B
    {
      char g = 'g';
      public void printVars()
      {
        // All of these fields and variables are accessible to this class
        System.out.println(g);  // (this.g) g is a field of this class
        System.out.println(f);  // f is a final local variable
        System.out.println(e);  // e is a final local parameter
        System.out.println(d);  // (C.this.d) d field of containing class
        System.out.println(c);  // (C.this.c) c field of containing class
        System.out.println(b);  // b is inherited by this class
        System.out.println(a);  // a is inherited by the containing class
      }
    }
    Local l = new Local();      // Create an instance of the local class
    l.printVars();              // and call its printVars() method.
  }
}
```

Lexical Scoping and Local Variables

A local variable is defined within a block of code that defines its *scope*, and outside of that scope, a local variable cannot be accessed and ceases to exist. Any code within the curly braces that define the boundaries of a block can use local variables defined in that block.

This type of scoping, which is known as *lexical scoping*, just defines a section of source code within which a variable can be used. It is common for programmers to think of such a scope as *temporal* instead—that is, to think of a local variable as existing from the time the JVM begins executing the block until the time control exits the block. This is usually a reasonable way to think about local variables and their scope.

The introduction of local classes confuses the picture, however. To see why, notice that instances of a local class can have a lifetime that extends past the time that the JVM exits the block where the local class is defined.

In other words, if you create an instance of a local class, that instance does not automatically go away when the JVM finishes executing the block that defines the class. So, even though the definition of the class was local, instances of that class can escape out of the place they were defined.

This can cause effects that some developers initially find surprising. This is because local classes can use local variables, and so they can contain copies of values from lexical scopes that no longer exist. This can been seen in the following code:

```
public class Weird {
    // A static member interface used below
    public static interface IntHolder { public int getValue(); }

    public static void main(String[] args) {
        IntHolder[] holders = new IntHolder[10];
        for(int i = 0; i < 10; i++) {
            final int fi = i;

            // A local class
            class MyIntHolder implements IntHolder {
                // Use the final variable
                public int getValue() { return fi; }
            }
            holders[i] = new MyIntHolder();
        }

        // The local class is now out of scope, so we can't use it. But we
        // have 10 valid instances of that class in our array. The local
        // variable fi is not in our scope here, but it is still in scope
        // for the getValue() method of each of those 10 objects. So call
        // getValue() for each object and print it out. This prints the
        // digits 0 to 9.
        for(int i = 0; i < 10; i++) {
            System.out.println(holders[i].getValue());
        }
    }
}
```

To make sense of this code, remember that the lexical scope of the methods of a local class has nothing to do with when the interpreter enters and exits the block of code that defines the local class.

Each instance of a local class has an automatically created private copy of each of the final local variables it uses, so, in effect, it has its own private copy of the scope that existed when it was created.

The local class MyIntHolder is sometimes called a *closure*. In more general Java terms, a closure is an object that saves the state of a scope and makes that scope available later.

Closures are useful in some styles of programming, and different programming languages define and implement closures in different ways. Java implements closures as local classes, anonymous classes, and lambda expressions.

Anonymous Classes

An *anonymous class* is a local class without a name. It is defined and instantiated in a single succinct expression using the new operator. While a local class definition is a statement in a block of Java code, an anonymous class definition is an expression, which means that it can be included as part of a larger expression, such as a method call.

For the sake of completeness, we cover anonymous classes here, but for most use cases in Java 8 and later, lambda expressions (see "Conclusion" on page 174) have replaced anonymous classes.

Consider Example 4-5, which shows the LinkedIterator class implemented as an anonymous class within the iterator() method of the LinkedStack class. Compare it with Example 4-4, which shows the same class implemented as a local class.

Example 4-5. An enumeration implemented with an anonymous class

```java
public Iterator<Linkable> iterator() {
    // The anonymous class is defined as part of the return statement
    return new Iterator<Linkable>() {
        Linkable current;
        // Replace constructor with an instance initializer
        { current = head; }

        // The following 3 methods are defined by the Iterator interface
        public boolean hasNext() {  return current != null; }
        public Linkable next() {
            if (current == null)
                throw new java.util.NoSuchElementException();
            Linkable value = current;
            current = current.getNext();
            return value;
        }
        public void remove() { throw new UnsupportedOperationException(); }
    };  // Note the required semicolon. It terminates the return statement
}
```

As you can see, the syntax for defining an anonymous class and creating an instance of that class uses the new keyword, followed by the name of a class and a class body definition in curly braces. If the name following the new keyword is the name of a class, the anonymous class is a subclass of the named class. If the name following new specifies an interface, as in the two previous examples, the anonymous class implements that interface and extends Object.

 The syntax for anonymous classes does not include any way to specify an extends clause, an implements clause, or a name for the class.

Because an anonymous class has no name, it is not possible to define a constructor for it within the class body. This is one of the basic restrictions on anonymous classes. Any arguments you specify between the parentheses following the super-class name in an anonymous class definition are implicitly passed to the superclass constructor. Anonymous classes are commonly used to subclass simple classes that do not take any constructor arguments, so the parentheses in the anonymous class definition syntax are often empty. In the previous examples, each anonymous class implemented an interface and extended Object. Because the Object() constructor takes no arguments, the parentheses were empty in those examples.

Restrictions on anonymous classes

Because an anonymous class is just a type of local class, anonymous classes and local classes share the same restrictions. An anonymous class cannot define any static fields, methods, or classes, except for static final constants. Interfaces, enumerated types, and annotation types cannot be defined anonymously. Also, like local classes, anonymous classes cannot be public, private, protected, or static.

The syntax for defining an anonymous class combines definition with instantiation. Using an anonymous class instead of a local class is not appropriate if you need to create more than a single instance of the class each time the containing block is executed.

Because an anonymous class has no name, it is not possible to define a constructor for an anonymous class. If your class requires a constructor, you must use a local class instead. However, you can often use an instance initializer as a substitute for a constructor.

Although they are not limited to use with anonymous classes, instance initializers (described earlier in "Field Defaults and Initializers" on page 108), were introduced into the language for this purpose. An anonymous class cannot define a constructor, so it only has a default constructor. By using an instance initializer, you can get around the fact that you cannot define a constructor for an anonymous class.

How Nested Types Work

The preceding sections explained the features and behavior of the four kinds of nested types. That should be all you need to know about nested types, especially if all you want to do is use them. You may find it easier to understand nested types if you understand how they are implemented, however.

 The introduction of nested types did not change the Java Virtual Machine or the Java class file format. As far as the Java interpreter is concerned, there is no such thing as a nested type: all classes are normal top-level classes.

In order to make a nested type behave as if it is actually defined inside another class, the Java compiler ends up inserting hidden fields, methods, and constructor arguments into the classes it generates. These hidden fields and methods are often referred to as *synthetic*.

You may want to use the `javap` disassembler to disassemble some of the class files for nested types so you can see what tricks the compiler has used to make the nested types work. (See Chapter 13 for information on `javap`.)

The implementation of nested types works by having `javac` compile each nested type into a separate class file, which is actually a top-level class. The compiled class files have a special naming convention, and have names that would not ordinarily be created from user code.

Recall our first `LinkedStack` example (Example 4-1), which defined a static member interface named `Linkable`. When you compile this `LinkedStack` class, the compiler generates two class files. The first one is *LinkedStack.class*, as expected.

The second class file, however, is called *LinkedStack$Linkable.class*. The $ in this name is automatically inserted by `javac`. This second class file contains the implementation of the static member interface defined in the exercise.

Because the nested type is compiled into an ordinary top-level class, there is no way it can directly access the privileged members of its container. Therefore, if a static member type uses a `private` (or other privileged) member of its containing type, the compiler generates synthetic access methods (with the default package access) and converts the expressions that access the `private` members into expressions that invoke these specially generated methods.

The naming conventions for the four kinds of nested type are:

(Static or nonstatic) member types
> Member types are named according to the `EnclosingType$Member.class` pattern.

Anonymous classes

Because anonymous classes have no names, the names of the class files that represent them are an implementation detail. The Oracle/OpenJDK `javac` uses numbers to provide anonymous class names (e.g., `EnclosingType$1.class`).

Local classes

A local class is named according to a combination (e.g., `EnclosingType$1Mem ber.class`).

Let's also take a quick look at some implementation details of how `javac` provides synthetic access for some of the specific cases that nested types need.

Nonstatic member class implementation

Each instance of a nonstatic member class is associated with an instance of the enclosing class. The compiler enforces this association by defining a synthetic field named `this$0` in each member class. This field is used to hold a reference to the enclosing instance.

Every nonstatic member class constructor is given an extra parameter that initializes this field. Every time a member class constructor is invoked, the compiler automatically passes a reference to the enclosing class for this extra parameter.

Local and anonymous class implementation

A local class is able to refer to fields and methods in its containing class for exactly the same reason that a nonstatic member class can; it is passed a hidden reference to the containing class in its constructor and saves that reference away in a `private` synthetic field added by the compiler. Like nonstatic member classes, local classes can use `private` fields and methods of their containing class because the compiler inserts any required accessor methods.

What makes local classes different from member classes is that they have the ability to refer to local variables in the scope that defines them. The crucial restriction on this ability, however, is that local classes can reference only local variables and parameters that are declared `final`. The reason for this restriction becomes apparent in the implementation.

A local class can use local variables because `javac` automatically gives the class a `private` instance field to hold a copy of each local variable the class uses.

The compiler also adds hidden parameters to each local class constructor to initialize these automatically created `private` fields. A local class does not actually access local variables but merely its own private copies of them. This could cause inconsistencies if the local variables could alter outside of the local class.[3]

---

[3] We will have more to say on this subject when we discuss memory and mutable state in Chapter 6.

Lambda Expressions

One of the most eagerly anticated features of Java 8 was the introduction of lambda expressions. These allow small bits of code to be written inline as literals in a program and facilitate a more functional style of programming Java.

In truth, many of these techniques had always been possible using nested types, via patterns like callbacks and handlers, but the syntax was always quite cumbersome, especially given the need to explicitly define a completely new type even when only needing to express a single line of code in the callback.

As we saw in Chapter 2, the syntax for a lambda expression is to take a list of parameters (the types of which are typically inferred), and to attach that to a method body, like this:

```
(p, q) -> { /* method body */ }
```

This can provide a very compact way to represent simple methods, and can largely obviate the need to use anonymous classes.

 A lambda expression has almost all of the component parts of a method, with the obvious exception that a lambda doesn't have a name. In fact, some developers like to think of lambdas as "anonymous methods."

For example, consider the `list()` method of the `java.io.File` class. This method lists the files in a directory. Before it returns the list, though, it passes the name of each file to a `FilenameFilter` object you must supply. This `FilenameFilter` object accepts or rejects each file.

Here's how you can define a `FilenameFilter` class to list only those files whose names end with *.java*, using an anonymous class:

```
File dir = new File("/src");      // The directory to list

// Now call the list() method with a single anonymous implemenation of
// FilenameFilter as the argument
String[] filelist = dir.list(new FilenameFilter() {
  public boolean accept(File f, String s) {
    return s.endsWith(".java");
  }
});
```

With lambda expressions, this can be simplified:

```
File dir = new File("/src");      // The directory to list

String[] filelist = dir.list((f,s) -> { return s.endsWith(".java"); });
```

For each file in the list, the block of code in the lambda expression is evaluated. If the method returns `true` (which happens if the filename ends in *.java*) then the file is included in the output—which ends up in the array `filelist`.

This pattern, where a block of code is used to test if an element of a container matches a condition, and to only return the elements that pass the condition, is called a *filter idiom*—and is one of the standard techniques of functional programming, which we will discuss in more depth presently.

Lambda Expression Conversion

When `javac` encounters a lambda expression, it interprets it as the body of a method with a specific signature—but which method?

To resolve this question, `javac` looks at the surrounding code. To be legal Java code, the lambda expression must satisfy the following:

- The lambda must appear where an instance of an interface type is expected.
- The expected interface type should have exactly one mandatory method.
- The expected interface method should have a signature that exactly matches that of the lambda expression.

If this is the case, then an instance is created of a type that implements the expected interface, and uses the lambda body as the implementation for the mandatory method.

This slightly complex explanation comes from the decision to keep Java's type system as purely nominative (based on names). The lambda expression is said to be *converted* to an instance of the correct interface type.

Some developers also like to use the term *single abstract method* (or SAM) type to refer to the interface type that the lambda is converted into. This draws attention to the fact that to be usable by the lambda expression mechanism, an interface must have only a single nondefault method.

 Despite the parallels between lambda expressions and anonymous classes, lambdas are *not* simply syntactic sugar over anonymous classes. In fact, lambdas are implemented using method handles (which we will meet in Chapter 11) and a new, special JVM bytecode called `invokedynamic`.

From this discussion, we can see that although Java 8 has added lambda expressions, they have been specifically designed to fit into Java's existing type system—which has a very strong emphasis on nominal typing.

Method References

Recall that we can think of lambda expressions as methods that don't have names. Now, consider this lambda expression:

```
// In real code this would probably be shorter because of type inference
(MyObject myObj) -> myObj.toString()
```

This will be autoconverted to an implementation of a @FunctionalInterface that has a single nondefault method that takes a single MyObject and returns String. However, this seems like excessive boilerplate, and so Java 8 provides a syntax for making this easier to read and write:

```
MyObject::toString
```

This is a shorthand, known as a *method reference*, that uses an existing method as a lambda expression. It can be thought of as using an existing method, but ignoring the name of the method, so it can be can used as a lambda, and autoconverted in the usual way.

Functional Programming

Java is fundamentally an object-oriented lanaguage. However, with the arrival of lambda expressions, it becomes much easier to write code that is closer to the functional approach.

There's no single definition of exactly what constitutes a *functional language*—but there is at least a consensus that it should at least contain the ability to represent a function as a value that can be put into a variable.

Java has always (since version 1.1) been able to represent functions via inner classes, but the syntax was complex and lacking in clarity. Lambda expressions greatly simplify that syntax, and so it is only natural that more developers will be seeking to use aspects of functional programming in their Java code, now that it is considerably easier to do so.

The first taste of functional programming that Java developers are likely to encounter are three basic idioms that are remarkably useful:

map()
: The map idiom is used with lists, and list-like containers. The idea is that a function is passed in that is applied to each element in the collection, and a new collection is created—consisting of the results of applying the function to each element in turn. This means that a map idiom converts a collection of one type to a collection of potentially a different type.

```
filter()
```
We have already met an example of the filter idiom, when we discussed how to replace an anonymous implementation of `FilenameFilter` with a lambda. The filter idiom is used for producing a new subset of a collection, based on some criteria. Note that in functional programming, it is normal to produce a new collection, rather than modifying an existing one in-place.

```
reduce()
```
The reduce idiom has several different guises. It is an aggregation operation, which can be called *fold* or *accumulate* or *aggregate* as well as reduce. The basic idea is to take an initial value, and an aggregation (or reduction) function, and apply the reduction function to each element in turn, building up a final result for the whole collection by making a series of intermediate results—similar to a "running total"—as the reduce operation traverses the collection.

Java has full support for these key functional idioms (and several others). The implementation is explained in some depth in Chapter 8, where we discuss Java's data structures and collections, and in particular the *stream* abstraction, that makes all of this possible.

Let's conclude this introduction with some words of caution. It's worth noting that Java is best regarded as having support for "slightly functional programming." It is not an especially functional language, nor does it try to be. Some particular aspects of Java that mitigate against any claims to being a functional language include the following:

- Java has no structural types, which means no "true" function types. Every lambda is automatically converted to the appropriate nominal type.

- Type erasure causes problems for functional programming—type safety can be lost for higher-order functions.

- Java is inherently mutable (as we'll discuss in Chapter 6)—mutability is often regarded as highly undesirable for functional languages.

Despite this, easy access to the basics of functional programing—and especially idioms such as map, filter, and reduce—is a huge step forward for the Java community. These idioms are so useful that a large majority of Java developers will never need or miss the more advanced capabilities provided by languages with a more thorough-bred functional pedigree.

Conclusion

By examining Java's type system, we have been able to build up a clear picture of the worldview that the Java platform has about data types. Java's type system can be characterized as:

Nominal
> The name of a Java type is of paramount importance. Java does not permit structural types in the way some other languages do.

Static
> All Java variables have types that are known at compile time.

Object/imperative
> Java code is object-oriented, and all code must live inside methods, which must live inside classes. However, Java's primitive types prevent adoption of the "everything is an object" worldview.

Slightly functional
> Java provides support for some of the more common functional idioms, but more as a convenience to programmers than anything else.

Modestly type-inferred
> Java is optimized for readability (even by novice progammers) and prefers to be explicit, even at the cost of repetition of information.

Strongly backward compatible
> Java is primarily a business-focused language, and backward compatibility and protection of existing codebases is a very high priority.

Type erased
> Java permits parameterized types, but this information is not available at runtime.

Java's type system has evolved (albeit slowly and cautiously) over the years—and with the addition of lambda expressions, is now on a par with the type systems of other mainstream programming languages. Lambdas, along with default methods, represent the greatest transformation since the advent of Java 5, and the introduction of generics, annotations, and related innovations.

Default methods represent a major shift in Java's approach to object-oriented programming—perhaps the biggest since the language's inception. From Java 8 onward, interfaces can contain implementation code. This fundamentally changes Java's nature—previously a single-inherited language, Java is now multiply inherited (but only for behavior—there is still no multiple inheritance of state).

Despite all of these innovations, Java's type system is not (and is not intended to be) equipped with the power of the type systems of languages such as Scala or Haskell. Instead, Java's type system is strongly biased in favor of simplicity, readability, and a simple learning curve for newcomers.

Java has also benefited enormously from the approaches to types developed in other languages over the last 10 years. Scala's example of a statically typed language that nevertheless achieves much of the feel of a dynamically typed language by the use of type inference has been a good source of ideas for features to add to Java, even though the languages have quite different design philosophies.

Despite the long wait for lambda expressions in Java, the argument has been settled, and Java is a better language for them. Whether the majority of ordinary Java programmers require the added power—and attendant complexity—that comes from an advanced (and much less nominal) type system such as Scala's, or whether the "slightly functional programming" of Java 8 (e.g., *map, filter, reduce,* and their peers) will suffice for most developers' needs, remains to be seen in the months and years ahead. It should be an interesting journey.

5

Introduction to Object-Oriented Design in Java

In this chapter, we'll look at how to work with Java's objects, covering the key methods of Object, aspects of object-oriented design, and implementing exception handling schemes. Throughout the chapter, we will be introducing some *design patterns* —essentially best practices for solving some very common situations that arise in software design. Towards the end of the chapter, we'll also consider the design of *safe* programs—those that are designed so as not to become inconsistent over time. We'll get started by considering the subject of Java's calling and passing conventions and the nature of Java values.

Java Values

Java's values, and their relationship to the type system, are quite straightforward. Java has two types of values—primitives and object references.

Some books refer to primitives as "value types"—this makes it confusing to think of object references as a value in Java. For this reason, we stick to the term *primitive* when discussing any of Java's eight nonreference types.

These two kinds of values are the only things that can be put into variables. In fact, that's one way to define a value: "a thing that can be put into a variable or passed to a method." For C++ and C programmers, note that object contents cannot be put into variables—so there is no equivalent of a dereference operator or a struct.

The key difference between primitive values and references is that primitive values cannot be altered—the value 2 is always the same value. By contrast, the contents of object references can usually be changed—often referred to as *mutation* of object contents.

Java tries to simplify a concept that often confused C++ programmers—the difference between "contents of an object" and "reference to an object." Unfortunately, it's not possible to completely hide the difference, and so it is necessary for the programmer to understand how reference values work in the platform.

Is Java "Pass by Reference"?

Java handles objects "by reference," but we must not confuse this with the phrase "pass by reference." "Pass by reference" is a term used to describe the method-calling conventions of some programming languages. In a pass-by-reference language, values—even primitive values—are not passed directly to methods. Instead, methods are always passed references to values. Thus, if the method modifies its parameters, those modifications are visible when the method returns, even for primitive types.

Java does *not* do this; it is a "pass-by-value" language. However, when a reference type is involved, the value that is passed is a copy of the reference (as a value). But this is not the same as pass by reference. If Java were a pass-by-reference language, when a reference type is passed to a method, it would be passed as a reference to the reference.

The fact that Java is pass by value can be demonstrated very simply. The following code shows that even after the call to `manipulate()`, the value contained in variable c is unaltered—it is still holding a reference to a `Circle` object of radius 2. If Java was a pass-by-reference language, it would instead be holding a reference to a radius 3 `Circle`:

```
public void manipulate(Circle circle) {
    circle = new Circle(3);
}

Circle c = new Circle(2);
manipulate(c);
System.out.println("Radius: "+ c.getRadius());
```

If we're scrupulously careful about the distinction, and about referring to object references as one of Java's possible kinds of values, then some otherwise surprising features of Java become obvious. Be careful—some older texts are ambiguous on this point. We will meet this concept of Java's values again when we discuss memory and garbage collection in Chapter 6.

Important Methods of java.lang.Object

As we've noted, all classes extend, directly or indirectly, `java.lang.Object`. This class defines a number of useful methods that were designed to be overridden by classes you write. Example 5-1 shows a class that overrides these methods. The

---

sections that follow this example document the default implementation of each method and explain why you might want to override it.

The example uses a lot of the extended features of the type system that we met last chapter. First, it implements a parameterized, or generic, version of the Comparable interface. Second, the example uses the @Override annotation to emphasize (and have the compiler verify) that certain methods override Object.

Example 5-1. A class that overrides important Object methods

```java
// This class represents a circle with immutable position and radius.
public class Circle implements Comparable<Circle> {
    // These fields hold the coordinates of the center and the radius.
    // They are private for data encapsulation and final for immutability
    private final int x, y, r;

    // The basic constructor: initialize the fields to specified values
    public Circle(int x, int y, int r) {
        if (r < 0) throw new IllegalArgumentException("negative radius");
        this.x = x; this.y = y; this.r = r;
    }

    // This is a "copy constructor"--a useful alternative to clone()
    public Circle(Circle original) {
        x = original.x;    // Just copy the fields from the original
        y = original.y;
        r = original.r;
    }

    // Public accessor methods for the private fields.
    // These are part of data encapsulation.
    public int getX() { return x; }
    public int getY() { return y; }
    public int getR() { return r; }

    // Return a string representation
    @Override public String toString() {
        return String.format("center=(%d,%d); radius=%d", x, y, r);
    }

    // Test for equality with another object
    @Override public boolean equals(Object o) {
        // Identical references?
        if (o == this) return true;
        // Correct type and non-null?
        if (!(o instanceof Circle)) return false;
        Circle that = (Circle) o;                  // Cast to our type
        if (this.x == that.x && this.y == that.y && this.r == that.r)
            return true;                           // If all fields match
        else
            return false;                          // If fields differ
```

```
    }

    // A hash code allows an object to be used in a hash table.
    // Equal objects must have equal hash codes.  Unequal objects are
    // allowed to have equal hash codes as well, but we try to avoid that.
    // We must override this method because we also override equals().
    @Override public int hashCode() {
        int result = 17;          // This hash code algorithm from the book
        result = 37*result + x;   // _Effective Java_, by Joshua Bloch
        result = 37*result + y;
        result = 37*result + r;
        return result;
    }

    // This method is defined by the Comparable interface. Compare
    // this Circle to that Circle.  Return a value < 0 if this < that
    // Return 0 if this == that. Return a value > 0 if this > that.
    // Circles are ordered top to bottom, left to right, and then by radius
    public int compareTo(Circle that) {
        // Smaller circles have bigger y
        long result = (long)that.y - this.y;
        // If same compare l-to-r
        if (result==0) result = (long)this.x - that.x;
        // If same compare radius
        if (result==0) result = (long)this.r - that.r;

        // We have to use a long value for subtraction because the
        // differences between a large positive and large negative
        // value could overflow an int. But we can't return the long,
        // so return its sign as an int.
        return Long.signum(result);
    }
}
```

toString()

The purpose of the toString() method is to return a textual representation of an object. The method is invoked automatically on objects during string concatenation and by methods such as System.out.println(). Giving objects a textual representation can be quite helpful for debugging or logging output, and a well-crafted toString() method can even help with tasks such as report generation.

The version of toString() inherited from Object returns a string that includes the name of the class of the object as well as a hexadecimal representation of the hash Code() value of the object (discussed later in this chapter). This default implementation provides basic type and identity information for an object but is not usually very useful. The toString() method in Example 5-1 instead returns a human-readable string that includes the value of each of the fields of the Circle class.

equals()

The == operator tests two references to see if they refer to the same object. If you want to test whether two distinct objects are equal to one another, you must use the equals() method instead. Any class can define its own notion of equality by overriding equals(). The Object.equals() method simply uses the == operator: this default method considers two objects equal only if they are actually the very same object.

The equals() method in Example 5-1 considers two distinct Circle objects to be equal if their fields are all equal. Note that it first does a quick identity test with == as an optimization and then checks the type of the other object with instanceof: a Circle can be equal only to another Circle, and it is not acceptable for an equals() method to throw a ClassCastException. Note that the instanceof test also rules out null arguments: instanceof always evaluates to false if its left-hand operand is null.

hashCode()

Whenever you override equals(), you must also override hashCode(). This method returns an integer for use by hash table data structures. It is critical that two objects have the same hash code if they are equal according to the equals() method. It is important (for efficient operation of hash tables) but not required that unequal objects have unequal hash codes, or at least that unequal objects are unlikely to share a hash code. This second criterion can lead to hashCode() methods that involve mildly tricky arithmetic or bit manipulation.

The Object.hashCode() method works with the Object.equals() method and returns a hash code based on object identity rather than object equality. (If you ever need an identity-based hash code, you can access the functionality of Object.hash Code() through the static method System.identityHashCode().)

> When you override equals(), you must always override hash Code() to guarantee that equal objects have equal hash codes. Failing to do this can cause subtle bugs in your programs.

Because the equals() method in Example 5-1 bases object equality on the values of the three fields, the hashCode() method computes its hash code based on these three fields as well. It is clear from the code that if two Circle objects have the same field values, they will have the same hash code.

Note that the hashCode() method in Example 5-1 does not simply add the three fields and return their sum. Such an implementation would be legal but not efficient because two circles with the same radius but whose x and y coordinates were reversed would then have the same hash code. The repeated multiplication and addition steps "spread out" the range of hash codes and dramatically reduce the likelihood that two unequal Circle objects have the same code. *Effective Java* by Joshua Bloch (Addison Wesley) includes a helpful recipe for constructing efficient hashCode() methods like this one.

Comparable::compareTo()

Example 5-1 includes a compareTo() method. This method is defined by the java.lang.Comparable interface rather than by Object, but it is such a common method to implement that we include it in this section. The purpose of Comparable and its compareTo() method is to allow instances of a class to be compared to each other in the way that the <, <=, >, and >= operators compare numbers. If a class implements Comparable, we can say that one instance is less than, greater than, or equal to another instance. This also means that instances of a Comparable class can be sorted.

Because compareTo() is not declared by the Object class, it is up to each individual class to determine whether and how its instances should be ordered and to include a compareTo() method that implements that ordering. The ordering defined by Example 5-1 compares Circle objects as if they were words on a page. Circles are first ordered from top to bottom: circles with larger *y* coordinates are less than circles with smaller *y* coordinates. If two circles have the same *y* coordinate, they are ordered from left to right. A circle with a smaller *x* coordinate is less than a circle with a larger *x* coordinate. Finally, if two circles have the same *x* and *y* coordinates, they are compared by radius. The circle with the smaller radius is smaller. Notice that under this ordering, two circles are equal only if all three of their fields are equal. This means that the ordering defined by compareTo() is consistent with the equality defined by equals(). This is very desirable (but not strictly required).

The compareTo() method returns an int value that requires further explanation. compareTo() should return a negative number if the this object is less than the object passed to it. It should return 0 if the two objects are equal. And compareTo() should return a positive number if this is greater than the method argument.

clone()

Object defines a method named clone() whose purpose is to return an object with fields set identically to those of the current object. This is an unusual method for two reasons. First, it works only if the class implements the java.lang.Cloneable interface. Cloneable does not define any methods (it is a marker interface) so implementing it is simply a matter of listing it in the implements clause of the class signature. The other unusual feature of clone() is that it is declared protected. Therefore, if you want your object to be cloneable by other classes, you must implement Cloneable and override the clone() method, making it public.

The Circle class of Example 5-1 does not implement Cloneable; instead it provides a *copy constructor* for making copies of Circle objects:

```
Circle original = new Circle(1, 2, 3);  // regular constructor
Circle copy = new Circle(original);     // copy constructor
```

It can be difficult to implement clone() correctly, and it is usually easier and safer to provide a copy constructor. To make the Circle class cloneable, you would add Cloneable to the implements clause and add the following method to the class body:

```
@Override public Object clone() {
  try { return super.clone(); }
  catch(CloneNotSupportedException e) { throw new AssertionError(e); }
}
```

Aspects of Object-Oriented Design

In this section, we will consider several techniques relevant to object-oriented design in Java. This is a very incomplete treatment and merely intended to showcase some examples—the reader is encouraged to consult additional resources, such as the aforementioned *Effective Java* by Joshua Bloch.

We start by considering good practices for defining constants in Java, before moving on to discuss different approaches to using Java's object-oriented capabilities for modeling and domain object design. At the end of the section, we conclude by covering the implementation of some common design patterns in Java.

Constants

As noted earlier, constants can appear in an interface definition. Any class that implements an interface inherits the constants it defines and can use them as if they were defined directly in the class itself. Importantly, there is no need to prefix the constants with the name of the interface or provide any kind of implementation of the constants.

When a set of constants is used by more than one class, it is tempting to define the constants once in an interface and then have any classes that require the constants implement the interface. This situation might arise, for example, when client and server classes implement a network protocol whose details (such as the port number to connect to and listen on) are captured in a set of symbolic constants. As a concrete example, consider the java.io.ObjectStreamConstants interface, which defines constants for the object serialization protocol and is implemented by both ObjectInputStream and ObjectOutputStream.

The primary benefit of inheriting constant definitions from an interface is that it saves typing: you don't need to specify the type that defines the constants. Despite its use with ObjectStreamConstants, this is not a recommended technique. The use of constants is an implementation detail that is not appropriate to declare in the implements clause of a class signature.

A better approach is to define constants in a class and use the constants by typing the full class name and the constant name. You can save typing by importing the constants from their defining class with the import static declaration. See "Packages and the Java Namespace" on page 88 for details.

Interfaces Versus Abstract Classes

The advent of Java 8 has fundamentally changed Java's object-oriented programming model. Before Java 8, interfaces were pure API specification and contained no implementation. This could often lead to duplication of code if the interface had many implementations.

In response, a coding pattern developed. This pattern takes advantage of the fact that an abstract class does not need to be entirely abstract; it can contain a partial implementation that subclasses can take advantage of. In some cases, numerous subclasses can rely on method implementations provided by an abstract superclass.

The pattern consists of an interface that contains the API spec for the basic methods, paired with a primary implementation as an abstract class. A good example would be java.util.List, which is paired with java.util.AbstractList. Two of the main implementations of List that ship with the JDK (ArrayList and Linked List) are subclasses of AbstractList. As another example:

```java
// Here is a basic interface. It represents a shape that fits inside
// of a rectangular bounding box. Any class that wants to serve as a
// RectangularShape can implement these methods from scratch.
public interface RectangularShape {
    void setSize(double width, double height);
    void setPosition(double x, double y);
    void translate(double dx, double dy);
    double area();
    boolean isInside();
}

// Here is a partial implementation of that interface. Many
// implementations may find this a useful starting point.
public abstract class AbstractRectangularShape
                    implements RectangularShape {
    // The position and size of the shape
    protected double x, y, w, h;

    // Default implementations of some of the interface methods
    public void setSize(double width, double height) {
    w = width; h = height;
    }
    public void setPosition(double x, double y) {
    this.x = x; this.y = y;
    }
    public void translate (double dx, double dy) { x += dx; y += dy; }
}
```

The arrival of default methods in Java 8 changes this picture considerably. Interfaces can now contain implementation code, as we saw in "Default Methods" on page 140.

This means that when defining an abstract type (e.g., Shape) that you expect to have many subtypes (e.g., Circle, Rectangle, Square), you are faced with a choice between interfaces and abstract classes. Because they now have very similar features, it is not always clear which to use.

Remember that a class that extends an abstract class cannot extend any other class, and that interfaces still cannot contain any nonconstant fields. This means that there are still some restrictions on how we can use object orientation in our Java programs.

Another important difference between interfaces and abstract classes has to do with compatibility. If you define an interface as part of a public API and then later add a new mandatory method to the interface, you break any classes that implemented the previous version of the interface—in other words, any new interface methods must be declared as default and an implementation provided. If you use an abstract class, however, you can safely add nonabstract methods to that class without requiring modifications to existing classes that extend the abstract class.

 In both cases, adding new methods can cause a clash with subclass methods of the same name and signature—with the subclass methods always winning. For this reason, think carefully when adding new methods—especially when the method names are "obvious" for this type, or where the method could have several possible meanings.

OO Design

In general, the suggested approach is to prefer interfaces when an API specification is needed. The mandatory methods of the interface are nondefault, as they represent the part of the API that must be present for an implementation to be considered valid. Default methods should be used only if a method is truly optional, or if they are really only intended to have a single possible implementation. This latter example is the case for the functional composition present in java.util.function.Function—functions will only ever be composed in the standard way, and it is highly implausible that any sane override of the default compose() method could exist.

Finally, the older technique of merely documenting which methods of an interface are considered "optional" and just throwing a java.lang.UnsupportedOperationException if the programmer does not want to implement them is fraught with problems, and should not be used in new code.

Instance Methods or Class Methods?

Instance methods are one of the key features of object-oriented programming. That doesn't mean, however, that you should shun class methods. In many cases, it is perfectly reasonable to define class methods.

Remember that in Java, class methods are declared with the static keyword, and the terms static method and class method are used interchangeably.

For example, when working with the Circle class you might find that you often want to compute the area of a circle with a given radius but don't want to bother creating a Circle object to represent that circle. In this case, a class method is more convenient:

```java
public static double area(double r) { return PI * r * r; }
```

It is perfectly legal for a class to define more than one method with the same name, as long as the methods have different parameters. This version of the area() method is a class method, so it does not have an implicit this parameter and must have a parameter that specifies the radius of the circle. This parameter keeps it distinct from the instance method of the same name.

As another example of the choice between instance methods and class methods, consider defining a method named bigger() that examines two Circle objects and returns whichever has the larger radius. We can write bigger() as an instance method as follows:

```java
// Compare the implicit "this" circle to the "that" circle passed
// explicitly as an argument and return the bigger one.
public Circle bigger(Circle that) {
  if (this.r > that.r) return this;
  else return that;
}
```

We can also implement bigger() as a class method as follows:

```java
// Compare circles a and b and return the one with the larger radius
public static Circle bigger(Circle a, Circle b) {
  if (a.r > b.r) return a;
  else return b;
}
```

Given two Circle objects, x and y, we can use either the instance method or the class method to determine which is bigger. The invocation syntax differs significantly for the two methods, however:

```java
// Instance method: also y.bigger(x)
Circle biggest = x.bigger(y);
Circle biggest = Circle.bigger(x, y);  // Static method
```

Both methods work well, and, from an object-oriented design standpoint, neither of these methods is "more correct" than the other. The instance method is more formally object oriented, but its invocation syntax suffers from a kind of asymmetry. In a case like this, the choice between an instance method and a class method is simply a design decision. Depending on the circumstances, one or the other will likely be the more natural choice.

A word about System.out.println()

We've frequently encountered the method `System.out.println()`—it's used to display output to the terminal window or console. We've never explained why this method has such a long, awkward name or what those two periods are doing in it. Now that you understand class and instance fields and class and instance methods, it is easier to understand what is going on: `System` is a class. It has a public class field named out. This field is an object of type `java.io.PrintStream`, and it has an instance method named `println()`.

We can use static imports to make this a bit shorter with `import static java.lang.System.out;`—this will enable us to refer to the printing method as `out.println()` but as this is an instance method, we cannot shorten it any further.

Composition Versus Inheritance

Inheritance is not the only technique at our disposal in object-oriented design. Objects can contain references to other objects, so a larger conceptual unit can be aggregated out of smaller component parts—this is known as *composition*. One important related technique is *delegation*, where an object of a particular type holds a reference to a secondary object of a compatible type, and forwards all operations to the secondary object. This is frequently done using interface types, as shown in this example where we model the employment structure of software companies:

```
public interface Employee {
  void work();
}

public class Programmer implements Employee {
  public void work() { /* program computer */ }
}

public class Manager implements Employee {
  private Employee report;

  public Manager(Employee staff) {
    report = staff;
  }

  public Employee setReport(Employee staff) {
    report = staff;
  }

  public void work() {
    report.work();
  }
}
```

The Manager class is said to *delegate* the work() operation to their direct report, and no actual work is performed by the Manager object. Variations of this pattern involve some work being done in the delegating class, with only some calls being forwarded to the delegate object.

Another useful, related technique is called the *decorator pattern*—this provides the capability to extend objects with new functionality, including at runtime. The slight overhead is some extra work needed at design time. Let's look at an example of the decorator pattern as applied to modeling burritos for sale at a taqueria. To keep things simple, we've only modeled a single aspect to be decorated—the price of the burrito:

```java
// The basic interface for our burritos
interface Burrito {
  double getPrice();
}

// Concrete implementation–standard size burrito
public class StandardBurrito implements Burrito {
  private static final double BASE_PRICE = 5.99;

  public double getPrice() {
    return BASE_PRICE;
  }
}

// Larger, super-size burrito
public class SuperBurrito implements Burrito {
  private static final double BASE_PRICE = 6.99;

  public double getPrice() {
    return BASE_PRICE;
  }
}
```

These cover the basic burritos that can be offered—two different sizes, at different prices. Let's enhance this by adding some optional extras—jalapeño chilies and guacamole. The key design point here is to use an abstract base class that all of the optional decorating components will subclass:

```java
/*
 * This class is the Decorator for Burrito–it represents optional
 * extras that the burrito may or may not have.
 */
public abstract class BurritoOptionalExtra implements Burrito {
    private final Burrito burrito;
    private final double price;

    // This constructor is protected to protect against the default
    // constructor and to prevent rogue client code from directly
    // instantiating the base class.
    protected BurritoOptionalExtra(Burrito toDecorate,
```

```
            double myPrice) {
        burrito = toDecorate;
        price = myPrice;
    }

    public final double getPrice() {
        return (burrito.getPrice() + price);
    }
}
```

 The combination of an abstract base, BurritoOptional
Extra, and a protected constructor means that the only valid
way to get a BurritoOptionalExtra is to construct an
instance of one of the subclasses, as they have public constructors (which also hide the setup of the price of the component
from client code).

Let's test the implementation out:

```
Burrito lunch = new Jalapeno(new Guacamole(new SuperBurrito()));
// The overall cost of the burrito is the expected $8.09.
System.out.println("Lunch cost: "+ lunch.getPrice());
```

The decorator pattern is very widely used—not least in the JDK utility classes.
When we discuss Java I/O in Chapter 10, we will see more examples of decorators in
the wild.

Field Inheritance and Accessors

Java offers multiple potential approaches to the design issue of the inheritance of
state. The programmer can choose to mark fields as protected and allow them to
be accessed directly by subclasses (including writing to them). Alternatively, we can
provide *accessor methods* to read (and write, if desired) the actual object fields, while
retaining encapsulation, and leaving the fields as private.

Let's revisit our earlier PlaneCircle example from the end of Chapter 9 and explicitly show the field inheritance:

```
public class Circle {
    // This is a generally useful constant, so we keep it public
    public static final double PI = 3.14159;

    protected double r;      // State inheritance via a protected field

    // A method to enforce the restriction on the radius
    protected void checkRadius(double radius) {
        if (radius < 0.0)
            throw new IllegalArgumentException("radius may not < 0");
    }

    // The non-default constructor
```

```
  public Circle(double r) {
    checkRadius(r);
    this.r = r;
  }

  // Public data accessor methods
  public double getRadius() { return r; }
  public void setRadius(double r) {
    checkRadius(r);
    this.r = r;
  }

  // Methods to operate on the instance field
  public double area() { return PI * r * r; }
  public double circumference() { return 2 * PI * r; }
}

public class PlaneCircle extends Circle {
  // We automatically inherit the fields and methods of Circle,
  // so we only have to put the new stuff here.
  // New instance fields that store the center point of the circle
  private final double cx, cy;

  // A new constructor to initialize the new fields
  // It uses a special syntax to invoke the Circle() constructor
  public PlaneCircle(double r, double x, double y) {
    super(r);        // Invoke the constructor of the superclass
    this.cx = x;     // Initialize the instance field cx
    this.cy = y;     // Initialize the instance field cy
  }

  public double getCentreX() {
    return cx;
  }

  public double getCentreY() {
    return cy;
  }

  // The area() and circumference() methods are inherited from Circle
  // A new instance method that checks whether a point is inside the
  // circle Note that it uses the inherited instance field r
  public boolean isInside(double x, double y) {
    double dx = x - cx, dy = y - cy;
    // Pythagorean theorem
    double distance = Math.sqrt(dx*dx + dy*dy);
    return (distance < r);                     // Returns true or false
  }
}
```

Instead of the preceding code, we can rewrite PlaneCircle using accessor methods, like this:

```
public class PlaneCircle extends Circle {
  // Rest of class is the same as above The field r in
  // the superclass Circle can be made private because
  // we no longer access it directly here

  // Note that we now use the accessor method getRadius()
  public boolean isInside(double x, double y) {
    double dx = x - cx, dy = y - cy;           // Distance from center
    double distance = Math.sqrt(dx*dx + dy*dy); // Pythagorean theorem
    return (distance < getRadius());
  }
}
```

Both approaches are legal Java, but they have some differences. As we discussed in "Data Hiding and Encapsulation" on page 121, fields that are writable outside of the class are usually not a correct way to model object state. In fact, as we will see in "Safe Java Programming" on page 195 and again in "Java's Support for Concurrency" on page 208, they can damage the running state of a program irreparably.

It is therefore unfortunate that the protected keyword in Java allows access to fields (and methods) from both subclasses *and* classes in the same packages as the declaring class. This, combined with the ability for anyone to write a class that belongs to any given package (except system packages), means that protected inheritance of state is potentially flawed in Java.

 Java does not provide a mechanism for a member to be visible only in the declaring class and its subclasses.

OO Design

For all of these reasons, it is usually better to use accessor methods (either public or protected) to provide access to state for subclasses—unless the inherited state is declared final, in which case protected inheritance of state is perfectly permissible.

Singleton

The *singleton pattern* is another well-known design pattern. It is intended to solve the design issue where only a single instance of a class is required or desired. Java provides a number of different possible ways to implement the singleton pattern. In our discussion, we will use a slightly more verbose form, that has the benefit of being very explicit in what needs to happen for a safe singleton:

```
public class Singleton {
  private final static Singleton instance = new Singleton();
  private static boolean initialized = false;

  // Constructor
  private Singleton() {
    super();
```

```
    }

    private void init() {
      /* Do initialization */
    }

    // This method should be the only way to get a reference
    // to the instance
    public static synchronized Singleton getInstance() {
      if (initialized) return instance;
      instance.init();
      initialized = true;
      return instance;
    }
  }
```

The crucial point is that for the singleton pattern to be effective, it must be impossible to create more than one of them, and it must be impossible to get a reference to the object in an uninitialized state (see later in this chapter for more on this important point). To achieve this, we require a `private` constructor, which is only called once. In our version of `Singleton`, we only call the constructor when we initialize the private static variable `instance`. We also separate out the creation of the only `Singleton` object from its initialization—which occurs in the private method `init()`.

With this mechanism in place, the only way to get a reference to the lone instance of `Singleton` is via the static helper method, `getInstance()`. This method checks the flag `initialized` to see if the object is already in an active state. If it is, then a reference to the singleton object is returned. If not, then `getInstance()` calls `init()` to activate the object, and flicks the flag to `true`, so that next time a reference to the `Singleton` is requested, further initialization will not occur.

Finally, we also note that `getInstance()` is a `synchronized` method. See Chapter 6 for full details of what this means, and why it is necessary, but for now, know that it is present to guard against unintended consequences if `Singleton` is used in a multithreaded program.

 Singleton, being one of the simplest patterns, is often overused. When used correctly, it can be a useful technique, but too many singleton classes in a program is a classic sign of badly engineered code.

The singleton pattern has some drawbacks—in particular, it can be hard to test and to separate out from other classes. It also requires care when used in mulithreaded code. Nevertheless, it is important that developers are familiar with, and do not accidentally reinvent it. The singleton pattern is often used in configuration management, but modern code will typically use a framework (often a *dependency*

injection) to provide the programmer with singletons automatically, rather than via an explicit Singleton (or equivalent) class.

Exceptions and Exception Handling

We met checked and unchecked exceptions in "Checked and Unchecked Exceptions" on page 70. In this section, we discuss some additional aspects of the design of exceptions, and how to use them in your own code.

Recall that an exception in Java is an object. The type of this object is java.lang.Throwable, or more commonly, some subclass of Throwable that more specifically describes the type of exception that occurred. Throwable has two standard subclasses: java.lang.Error and java.lang.Exception. Exceptions that are subclasses of Error generally indicate unrecoverable problems: the virtual machine has run out of memory, or a class file is corrupted and cannot be read, for example. Exceptions of this sort can be caught and handled, but it is rare to do so—these are the unchecked exceptions previously mentioned.

Exceptions that are subclasses of Exception, on the other hand, indicate less severe conditions. These exceptions can be reasonably caught and handled. They include such exceptions as java.io.EOFException, which signals the end of a file, and java.lang.ArrayIndexOutOfBoundsException, which indicates that a program has tried to read past the end of an array. These are the checked exceptions from Chapter 2 (except for subclasses of RuntimeException, which are also a form of unchecked exception). In this book, we use the term "exception" to refer to any exception object, regardless of whether the type of that exception is Exception or Error.

Because an exception is an object, it can contain data, and its class can define methods that operate on that data. The Throwable class and all its subclasses include a String field that stores a human-readable error message that describes the exceptional condition. It's set when the exception object is created and can be read from the exception with the getMessage() method. Most exceptions contain only this single message, but a few add other data. The java.io.InterruptedIOException, for example, adds a field named bytesTransferred that specifies how much input or output was completed before the exceptional condition interrupted it.

When designing your own exceptions, you should consider what other additional modeling information is relevant to the exception object. This is usually situation-specific information about the aborted operation, and the exceptional circumstance that was encountered (as we saw with java.io.InterruptedIOException).

There are some trade-offs in the use of exceptions in application design. Using checked exceptions means that the compiler can enforce the handling (or propagation up the call stack) of known conditions that have the potential of recovery or retry. It also means that it's more difficult to forget to actually handle errors—thus reducing the risk that a forgotten error condition causes a system to fail in production.

On the other hand, some applications will not be able to recover from certain conditions—even conditions that are theoretically modelled by checked exceptions. For example, if an application requires a config file to be placed at a specific place in the filesystem and is unable to locate it at startup, there may be very little it can do except print an error message and exit—despite the fact that `java.io.FileNotFoun dException` is a checked exception. Forcing exceptions that cannot be recovered from to be either handled or propagated is, in these circumstances, bordering on perverse.

When designing exception schemes, there are some good practices that you should follow:

- Consider what additional state needs to be placed on the exception—remember that it's also an object like any other.

- `Exception` has four public constructors—under normal circumstances, custom exception classes should implement all of them—to initialize the additional state, or to customize messages.

- Don't create many fine-grained custom exception classes in your APIs—the Java I/O and reflection APIs both suffer from this and it needlessly complicates working with those packages.

- Don't overburden a single exception type with describing too many conditions —for example, the Nashorn JavaScript implementation (new with Java 8) originally had overly coarse-grained exceptions, although this was fixed before release.

Finally, two exception handling antipatterns that you should avoid:

```
// Never just swallow an exception
try {
  someMethodThatMightThrow();
} catch(Exception e){
}

// Never catch, log and rethrow an exception
try {
  someMethodThatMightThrow();
} catch(SpecificException e){
  log(e);
  throw e;
}
```

The former of these two just ignores a condition that almost certainly required some action (even if just a notification in a log). This increases the likelihood of failure elsewhere in the system—potentially far from the original, real source.

The second one just creates noise—we're logging a message but not actually doing anything about the issue—we still require some other code higher up in the system to actually deal with the problem.

Safe Java Programming

Programming languages are sometimes described as being *type safe*—however, this term is used rather loosely by working programmers. There are a number of different viewpoints and definitions when discussing type safety, not all of which are mutually compatible. The most useful view for our purposes is that *type safety* is the property of a programming language that prevents the type of data being incorrectly identified at runtime. This should be thought of as a sliding scale—it is more helpful to think of languages as being more (or less) type safe than each other, rather than a simple binary property of safe / unsafe.

In Java, the static nature of the type system helps prevent a large class of possible errors, by producing compilation errors if, for example, the programmer attempts to assign an incompatible value to a variable. However, Java is not perfectly type safe, as we can perform a cast between any two reference types—this will fail at runtime with a `ClassCastException` if the value is not compatible.

In this book, we prefer to think of safety as inseparable from the broader topic of correctness. This means that we should think in terms of programs, rather than languages. This emphasizes the point that safe code is not guaranteed by any widely used language, and instead considerable programmer effort (and adherence to rigorous coding discipline) must be employed if the end result is to be truly safe and correct.

We approach our view of safe programs by working with the state model abstraction as shown in Figure 5-1. A *safe* program is one in which:

- All objects start off in a legal state after creation
- Externally accessible methods transition objects between legal states
- Externally accessible methods must not return with object in an inconsistent state
- Externally accessible methods must reset object to a legal state before throwing

In this context, "externally accessible" means `public`, package-private, or `pro tected`. This defines a reasonable model for safety of programs, and as it is bound up with defining our abstract types in such a way that their methods ensure consistency of state, it's reasonable to refer to a program satisfying these requirements as a "safe program," regardless of the language in which such a program is implemented.

 Private methods do not have to start or end with object in a legal state, as they cannot be called by an external piece of code.

As you might imagine, actually engineering a substantial piece of code so that we can be sure that the state model and methods respect these properties, can be quite an undertaking. In languages such as Java, in which programmers have direct control over the creation of preemptively multitasked execution threads, this problem is a great deal worse.

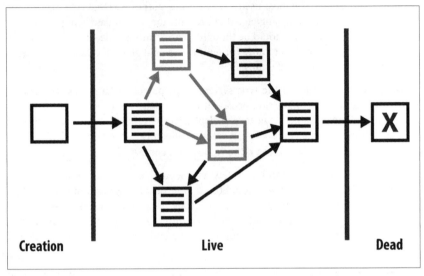

Figure 5-1. Program state transitions

Moving on from our introduction of object-oriented design, there is one final aspect of the Java language and platform that needs to be understood for a sound grounding. That is the nature of memory and concurrency—one of the most complex of the platform, but also one that rewards careful study with large dividends. It is the subject of our next chapter and concludes the first part of this book.

6

Java's Approach to Memory and Concurrency

This chapter is an introduction to the handling of concurrency (multithreading) and memory in the Java platform. These topics are inherently intertwined, so it makes sense to treat them together. We will cover:

- Introduction to Java's memory management
- The basic mark and sweep Garbage Collection (GC) algorithm
- How the HotSpot JVM optimizes GC according to the lifetime of the object
- Java's concurrency primitives
- Data visibility and mutability

Basic Concepts of Java Memory Management

In Java, the memory occupied by an object is automatically reclaimed when the object is no longer needed. This is done through a process known as *garbage collection* (or automatic memory management). Garbage collection is a technique that has been around for years in languages such as Lisp. It takes some getting used to for programmers accustomed to languages such as C and C++, in which you must call the `free()` function or the `delete` operator to reclaim memory.

The fact that you don't need to remember to destroy every object you create is one of the features that makes Java a pleasant language to work with. It is also one of the features that makes programs written in Java less prone to bugs than those written in languages that don't support automatic garbage collection.

Different VM implementations handle garbage collection in different ways, and the specifications do not impose very stringent restrictions on how GC must be implemented. Later in this chapter, we will discuss the HotSpot JVM (which is the basis of both the Oracle and OpenJDK implementations of Java). Although this is not the only JVM that you may encounter, it is the most common among server-side deployments, and provides a good example of a modern production JVM.

Memory Leaks in Java

The fact that Java supports garbage collection dramatically reduces the incidence of *memory leaks*. A memory leak occurs when memory is allocated and never reclaimed. At first glance, it might seem that garbage collection prevents all memory leaks because it reclaims all unused objects.

A memory leak can still occur in Java, however, if a valid (but unused) reference to an unused object is left hanging around. For example, when a method runs for a long time (or forever), the local variables in that method can retain object references much longer than they are actually required. The following code illustrates:

```
public static void main(String args[]) {
    int bigArray[] = new int[100000];

    // Do some computations with bigArray and get a result.
    int result = compute(bigArray);

    // We no longer need bigArray. It will get garbage collected when
    // there are no more references to it. Because bigArray is a local
    // variable, it refers to the array until this method returns. But
    // this method doesn't return. So we've got to explicitly get rid
    // of the referenceourselves, so the garbage collector knows it can
    // reclaim the array.
    bigArray = null;

    // Loop forever, handling the user's input
    for(;;) handle_input(result);
}
```

Memory leaks can also occur when you use a HashMap or similar data structure to associate one object with another. Even when neither object is required anymore, the association remains in the hash table, preventing the objects from being reclaimed until the hash table itself is reclaimed. If the hash table has a substantially longer lifetime than the objects it holds, this can cause memory leaks.

Introducing Mark and Sweep

The JVM knows exactly what objects and arrays it has allocated. They'll be stored in some sort of internal data structure, which we will refer to as the *allocation table*. The JVM can also figure out which local variables in each stack frame refer to which objects and arrays in the heap. Finally, by following references held by objects and arrays in the heap, the JVM can trace through and find all objects and arrays are still referred to, no matter how indirectly.

Thus, the runtime is able to determine when an allocated object is no longer referred to by any other active object or variable. When the interpreter finds such an object, it knows it can safely reclaim the object's memory and does so. Note that the garbage collector can also detect and reclaim cycles of objects that refer to each other, but are not referenced by any other active objects.

We define a *reachable object* to be an object that can be reached by starting from some local variable in one of the methods in the stack trace of some application thread, and following references until we reach the object. Objects of this type are also said to be *live*.[1]

There are a couple of other possibilities of where the chain of references can start apart from local variables. The general name for the root of a reference chain leading to a reachable object is a *GC root*.

With these simple definitions, let's look at a simple method for performing garbage collection based on these principles.

The Basic Mark and Sweep Algorithm

The usual (and simplest) algorithm for the collection process is called *mark and sweep*. This occurs in three phases:

1. Iterate through the allocation table, marking each object as *dead*.

2. Starting from the local variables that point into the heap, follow all references from all objects we reach. Every time we reach an object or array we haven't seen yet, mark it as *live*. Keep going until we've fully explored all references we can reach from the local variables.

3. Sweep across the allocation table again. For each object not marked as live, reclaim the memory in heap and place it back on the free memory list. Remove the object from the allocation table.

---

1 The process whereby we exhaustively explore from the GC roots produces what is known as the *transitive closure* of live objects—a term that is borrowed from the abstract mathematics of graph theory.

The form of mark and sweep just outlined is the usual simplest theoretical form of the algorithm. As we will see in the following sections, real garbage collectors do more work than this. Instead, this description is grounded in basic theory and is designed for easy understanding.

As all objects are allocated from the allocation table, GC will trigger before the heap gets full. In this description of mark and sweep, GC requires exclusive access to the entire heap. This is because application code is constantly running, creating, and changing objects, which could corrupt the results.

In Figure 6-1, we show the effects of trying to garbage collect objects while application threads are running.

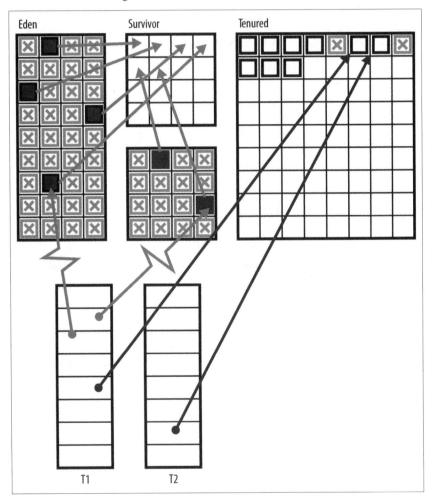

Figure 6-1. Heap mutation

To avoid this, a simple GC like the one just shown will cause a stop-the-world (STW) pause when it runs—because all application threads are stopped, then GC occurs, and finally application threads are started up again. The runtime takes care of this by halting application threads as they reach a *safepoint*—for example the start of a loop or when about to call a method. At these execution points, the runtime knows that it can stop an application thread without a problem.

These pauses sometimes worry developers, but for most mainstream usages, Java is running on top of an operating system that is constantly swapping processes on and off processor cores, so this slight additional stoppage is usually not a concern. In the HotSpot case, a large amount of work has been done to optimize GC and to reduce STW times, for those cases where it is important to an application's workload. We will discuss some of those optimizations in the next section.

How the JVM Optimizes Garbage Collection

The *weak generational hypothesis* (WGH) is a great example of one of the runtime facts about software that we introduced in Chapter 1. Simply put, it is that objects tend to have one of a small number of possible life expectancies (referred to as *generations*).

Usually objects are alive for a very short amount of time (sometimes called transient objects), and then become eligible for garbage collection. However, some small fraction of objects live for longer, and are destined to become part of the longer-term state of the program (sometimes referred to as the *working set* of the program). This can be seen in Figure 6-2 where we see Volume of memory plotted against expected lifetime.

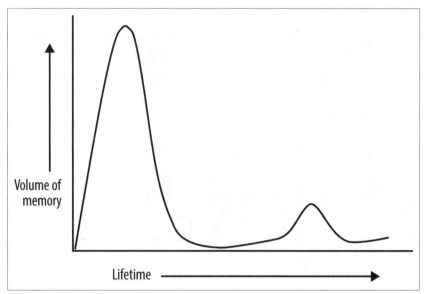

Figure 6-2. Weak generational hypothesis

This fact is not deducible from static analysis, and yet when we measure the runtime behavior of software, we see that it is broadly true across a wide range of workloads.

The HotSpot JVM has a garbage collection subsystem that is designed specifically to take advantage of the weak generational hypothesis, and in this section, we will discuss how these techniques apply to short-lived objects (which is the majority case). This discussion is directly applicable to HotSpot, but other server-class JVMs often employ similar or related techniques.

In its simplest form, a *generational garbage collector* is simply one that takes notice of the WGH. They take the position that some extra bookkeeping to monitor memory will be more than paid for by gains obtained by being friendly to the WGH. In the simplest forms of generational collector, there are usually just two generations—usually referred to as young and old generation.

Evacuation

In our original formulation of mark and sweep, during the cleanup phase, we reclaimed individual objects, and returned their space to the free list. However, if the WGH is true, and on any given GC cycle most objects are dead, then it may make sense to use an alternative approach to reclaiming space.

This works by dividing the heap up into separate memory spaces. Then, on each GC run, we locate only the live objects and move them to a different space, in a process called *evacuation*. Collectors that do this are referred to as *evacuating collectors*—and they have property that the entire memory space can be wiped at the end of the collection, to be reused again and again. Figure 6-3 shows an evacuating collector in action.

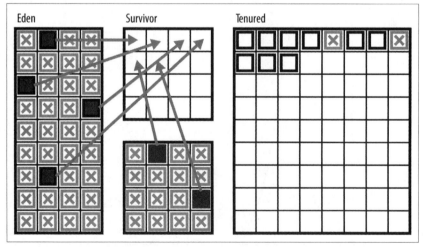

Figure 6-3. Evacuating collectors

This is potentially much more efficient than the naive collection approach, because the dead objects are never touched. GC cycle length is proportional to the number of live objects, rather than the number of allocated objects. The only downside is slightly more bookkeeping—we have to pay the cost of copying the live objects, but this is almost always a very small price compared to the huge gains realized by evacuation strategies.

 HotSpot manages the JVM heap itself, completely in user space, and does not need to perform system calls to allocate or free memory. The area where objects are initially created is usually called Eden or the Nursery, and most production JVMs (at least in the SE/EE space) will use an evacuating strategy when collecting Eden.

The use of an evacuating collector also allows the use of per-thread allocation. This means that each application thread can be given a contiguous chunk of memory (called a *thread-local allocation buffer*) for its exclusive use when allocating new objects. When new objects are allocated, this only involves bumping a pointer in the allocation buffer, an extremely cheap operation.

If an object is created just before a collection starts, then it will not have time to fulfill its purpose and die before the GC cycle starts. In a collector with only two generations, this short-lived object will be moved into the long-lived region, almost immediately die, and then stay there until the next full collection. As these are a lot less frequent (and typically a lot more expensive), this seems rather wasteful.

To mitigate this, HotSpot has a concept of a *survivor space*—this is an area that is used to house objects that have survived from previous collections of young objects. A surviving object is copied by the evacuating collector between survivor spaces until a *tenuring threshold* is reached, when the object will be *promoted* to the old generation.

A full discussion of survivor spaces and how to tune GC is outside the scope of this book—for production applications, specialist material should be consulted.

The HotSpot Heap

The HotSpot JVM is a relatively complex piece of code, made up of an interpreter and a just-in-time compiler, as well as a user-space memory management subsystem. It is comprised of a mixture of C, C++, and a fairly large amount of platform-specific assembly code.

At this point, let's summarize our description of the HotSpot heap, and recap its basic features. The Java heap is a contiguous block of memory, which is reserved at JVM startup, but only some of the heap is initially allocated to the various memory pools. As the application runs, memory pools are resized as needed. These resizes are performed by the GC subsystem.

Objects in the Heap

Objects are created in Eden by application threads, and are removed by a nondeterministic garbage collection cycle. The GC cycle runs when necessary (i.e., when memory is getting low). The heap is divided into two generations, young and old. The young generation comprises three spaces, Eden and two survivor spaces, whereas the old generation has just one memory space

After surviving several GC cycles, objects get promoted to the old generation. Collections that only collect the young generation are usually very cheap (in terms of computation required). HotSpot uses a more advanced form of mark and sweep than we have seen so far, and is prepared to do extra bookkeeping to improve GC performance. In the next section, let's move on to discuss the old generation and how HotSpot handles longer-lived objects.

Collecting the Old Generation

When discussing garbage collectors, there is one other important piece of terminology that developers should know:

Parallel collector
  A garbage collector that uses multiple threads to perform collection

Concurrent collector
  A garbage collector that can run at the same time as application threads are still running

All the collectors we have met up until now are parallel, but not concurrent, collectors. By default, the collector for the old generation is also a parallel (but not concurrent) mark and sweep collector, but HotSpot allows different collectors to be plugged in. For example, later on in this section we'll meet CMS, which is a parallel and mostly concurrent collector that ships with HotSpot.

Returning to the default collector, it seems at first glance to be similar to the collector used for the young generation. However, it differs in one very important respect —it is *not* an evacuating collector. Instead, the old generation is *compacted* when collection occurs. This is important so that the memory space does not become fragmented over the course of time.

Other Collectors

This section is completely HotSpot-specific, and a detailed treatment is outside the scope of the book, but it is worth knowing about the existence of alternate collectors. For non-HotSpot users, you should consult your JVM's documentation to see what options may be available for you.

Concurrent Mark and Sweep

The most widely used alternate collector in HotSpot is Concurrent Mark and Sweep (CMS). This collector is only used to collect the old generation—it is used in conjunction with a parallel collector that has responsibility for cleaning up the young generation.

 CMS is designed for use *only* in low-pause applications, those that cannot deal with a stop-the-world pause of more than a few milliseconds. This is a surprisingly small class—very few applications outside of financial trading have a genuine need for this requirement.

CMS is a complex collector, and often difficult to tune effectively. It can be a very useful tool in the developer's armory, but should not be deployed lightly or blindly. It has these basic properties that you should be aware of, but a full discussion of CMS is beyond the scope of this book. Interested readers should consult specialist blogs and mailing lists (e.g., the "Friends of jClarity" mailing list quite often deals with performance-related questions related to GC):

- CMS only collects the old generation.
- CMS runs alongside application threads for most of the GC cycle, reducing pauses.
- Application threads don't have to stop for as long.
- Has six phases, all designed to minimize STW pause times.
- Replaces main STW pause with two (usually very short) STW pauses.
- Uses considerably more bookkeeping and lots more CPU time.
- GC cycles overall take much longer.
- By default, half of CPUs are used for GC when running concurrently.
- Should not be used except for low-pause applications.
- Definitely should not be used for applications with high-throughput requirements.
- Does not compact, and in cases of high fragmentation will fall back to the default (parallel) collector.

G1

The Garbage First collector (known as G1) is a new garbage collector that was developed during the life of Java 7 (with some preliminary work done in Java 6). It is designed to take over from CMS as the low-pause collector, and allows the user to specify *pause goals* in terms of how long and how often to pause for when doing

GC. Unlike CMS, it is intended to be usable in workloads that have higher through-put requirements.

G1 uses a coarse-grained approach to memory, called regions, and focuses its atten-tion on regions that are mostly garbage, as they have the best free memory recovery. It is an evacuating collector, and does incremental compaction when evacuating individual regions.

The development of a new production-grade collector that is suitable for general-purpose use is not a quick process. Accordingly, although G1 has been in develop-ment for some years, as of early 2014, G1 is still less efficient than CMS on most benchmarks. Having said that, the gap has been steadily closing and G1 is now ahead on some workloads. It is entirely plausible that G1 will become the most com-mon low-pause collector in the coming months and years.

Finally, HotSpot also has a Serial (and SerialOld collector) and a collector known as "Incremental CMS." These collectors are all considered deprecated and should not be used.

Finalization

There is one old technique for resource management known as *finalization* that the developer should be aware of. However, this technique is extremely heavily depre-cated and the vast majority of Java developers should not directly use it under any circumstances.

 Finalization has only a very small number of legitimate use cases, and only a minority of Java developers will encounter them. If in any doubt, do not use finalization—try-with-resources is usually the correct alternative.

The finalization mechanism was intended to automatically release resources once they are no longer needed. Garbage collection automatically frees up the memory resources used by objects, but objects can hold other kinds of resources, such as open files and network connections. The garbage collector cannot free these addi-tional resources for you, so the finalization mechanism was intended to allow the developer to perform cleanup tasks as closing files, terminating network connec-tions, deleting temporary files, and so on.

The finalization mechanism works as follows: if an object has a finalize() method (usually called a *finalizer*), this is invoked sometime after the object becomes unused (or unreachable) but before the garbage collector reclaims the space allocated to the object. The finalizer is used to perform resource cleanup for an object.

In Oracle/OpenJDK the technique used is as follows:

1. When a finalizable object is no longer reachable, a reference to it is placed on an internal *finalization queue* and the object is marked, and considered live for the purposes of the GC run.

2. One by one, objects on the finalization queue are removed and their `finalize()` methods are invoked.

3. After a finalizer is invoked, the object is not freed right away. This is because a finalizer method could resurrect the object by storing the this reference somewhere (for example, in a public static field on some class) so that the object once again has references.

4. Therefore, after `finalize()` has been called, the garbage collection subsytem must redetermine that the object is unreachable before it can be garbage collected.

5. However, even if an object is resurrected, the finalizer method is never invoked more than once.

6. All of this means that objects with a `finalize()` will usually survive for (at least) one extra GC cycle (and if they're long-lived, that means one extra full GC).

The central problem with finalization is that Java makes no guarantees about when garbage collection will occur or in what order objects will be collected. Therefore, the platform can make no guarantees about when (or even whether) a finalizer will be invoked or in what order finalizers will be invoked.

This means that as an automatic cleanup mechanism for protecting scarce resources (such as filehandles), this mechanism is broken by design. We cannot guarantee that finalization will happen fast enough to prevent us from running out of resources.

The only real use case for a finalizer is the case of a class with native methods, holding open some non-Java resource. Even here, the block-structured approach of try-with-resources is preferable, but it can make sense to also declare a `public native finalize()` (which would be called by the `close()` method)—this would release native resources, including off-heap memory that is not under the control of the Java garbage collector.

Finalization Details

For the few use cases where finalization is appropriate, we include some additional details and caveats that occur when using the mechanism:

- The JVM can exit without garbage collecting all outstanding objects, so some finalizers may never be invoked. In this case, resources such as network connections are closed and reclaimed by the operating system. Note, however, that if a finalizer that deletes a file does not run, that file will not be deleted by the operating system.

- To ensure that certain actions are taken before the VM exits, Java provides `Run time::addShutdownHook`—it can safely execute arbitrary code before the JVM exits.

- The `finalize()` method is an instance method, and finalizers act on instances. There is no equivalent mechanism for finalizing a class.

- A finalizer is an instance method that takes no arguments and returns no value. There can be only one finalizer per class, and it must be named `finalize()`.

- A finalizer can throw any kind of exception or error, but when a finalizer is automatically invoked by the garbage collection subsystem, any exception or error it throws is ignored and serves only to cause the finalizer method to return.

Java's Support for Concurrency

The idea of a *thread* is that of a lightweight unit of execution—smaller than a process, but still capable of executing arbitrary Java code. The usual way that this is implemented is for each thread to be a fully fledged unit of execution to the operating system but to belong to a process, with the address space of the process being shared between all threads comprising that process. This means that each thread can be scheduled independently and has its own stack and program counter but shares memory and objects with other threads in the same process.

The Java platform has had support for multithreaded programming from the very first version. The platform exposes the ability to create new threads of execution to the developer. This is usually as simple as:

```
Thread t = new Thread(() -> {System.out.println("Hello Thread");});
t.start();
```

This small piece of code creates and starts a new thread, which executes the body of the lambda expression and then executes. For programmers coming from older versions of Java, the lambda is effectively being converted to an instance of the `Runna ble` interface before being passed to the `Thread` constructor.

The threading mechanism allows new threads to execute concurrently with the original application thread and the threads that the JVM itself starts up for various purposes.

 For most implementations of the Java platform, application threads have their access to the CPU controlled by the operating system *scheduler*—a built-in part of the OS that is responsible for managing timeslices of processor time (and that will not allow an application thread to exceed its allocated time).

In more recent versions of Java, an increasing trend towards *runtime-managed concurrency* has appeared. This is the idea that for many purposes explicit management of threads by developers is not desirable. Instead, the runtime should provide "fire and forget" capabilities, whereby the program specifies what needs to be done, but the low-level details of how this is to be accomplished are left to the runtime.

This viewpoint can be seen in the concurrency toolkit contained in `java.util.con current`, a full discussion of which is outside the scope of this book. The interested reader should refer to *Java Concurrency in Practice* by Brian Goetz et al. (Addison-Wesley).

For the remainder of this chapter, we will introduce the low-level concurrency mechanisms that the Java platform provides, and that every Java developer should be aware of.

Thread Lifecycle

Let's start by looking at the lifecycle of an application thread. Every operating system has a view of threads that can differ in the details (but in most cases is broadly similar at a high level). Java tries hard to abstract these details away, and has an enum called `Thread.State`—which wrappers over the operating system's view of the thread's state. The values of `Thread.State` provide an overview of the lifecycle of a thread:

NEW

> The thread has been created but its `start()` method has not yet been called. All threads start in this state.

RUNNABLE

> The thread is running or is available to run when the operating system schedules it.

BLOCKED

> The thread is not running because it is waiting to acquire a lock so that it can enter a `synchronized` method or block. We'll see more about `synchronized` methods and blocks later in this section.

WAITING

> The thread is not running because it has called `Object.wait()` or `Thread.join()`.

TIMED_WAITING

> The thread is not running because it has called `Thread.sleep()` or has called `Object.wait()` or `Thread.join()` with a timeout value.

TERMINATED

> The thread has completed execution. Its `run()` method has exited normally or by throwing an exception.

These states represent the view of a thread that is common (at least across mainstream operating systems), leading to a view like that in Figure 6-4.

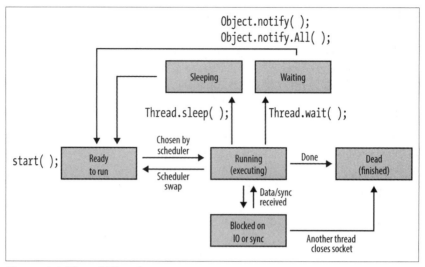

Figure 6-4. Thread lifecycle

Threads can also be made to sleep, by using the `Thread.sleep()` method. This takes an argument in milliseconds, which indicates how long the thread would like to sleep for, like this:

```
try {
    Thread.sleep(2000);
} catch (InterruptedException e) {
    e.printStackTrace();
}
```

 The argument to sleep is a request to the operating system, not a demand. For example, it is possible to sleep for longer than requested, depending on load and other factors specific to the runtime environment.

We will discuss the other methods of `Thread` later in this chapter, but first we need to cover some important theory that deals with how threads access memory, and that is fundamental to understanding why multithreaded programming is hard and can cause developers a lot of problems.

Visibility and Mutability

In Java, this essentially equates to all Java application threads in a process having their own stacks (and local variables) but sharing a single heap. This makes it very easy to share objects between threads, as all that is required is to pass a reference from one thread to another. This is illustrated in Figure 6-5.

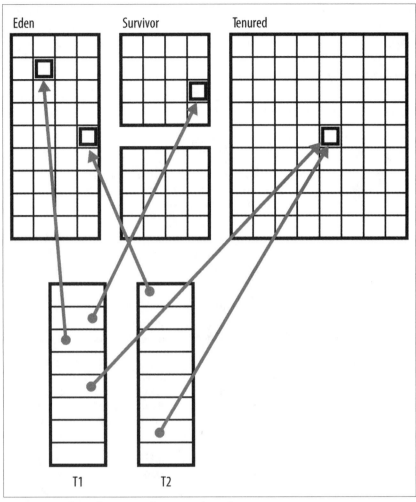

Figure 6-5. Shared memory between threads

This leads to a general design principle of Java—that objects are *visible by default*. If I have a reference to an object, I can copy it and hand it off to another thread with no restrictions. A Java reference is essentially a typed pointer to a location in memory—and threads share the same address space, so visible by default is a natural model.

In addition to visible by default, Java has another property that is important to fully understand concurrency, which is that objects are *mutable*—the contents of an object instance's fields can usually be changed. We can make individual variables or references constant, by using the final keyword, but this does not apply to the contents of the object.

As we will see throughout the rest of this chapter, the combination of these two properties—visibility across threads and object mutability—gives rise to a great many complexities when trying to reason about concurrent Java programs.

Concurrent Safety

If we're to write correct multithreaded code, then we want our programs to satisfy a certain important property. What we want is this:

A *safe multithreaded program* is one in which it is impossible for any object to be seen in an illegal or inconsistent state by any another object, no matter what methods are called, and no matter how the application threads are scheduled by the operating system.

In Chapter 5, we defined a safe object-oriented program to be one where objects are moved from legal state to legal state by calling their accessible methods. This definition works well for single-threaded code. However, there is a particular difficulty that comes about when trying to extend it to concurrent programs.

For most mainstream cases, the operating system will schedule threads to run on particular processor cores at various times, depending on load and what else is running in the system. If load is high, then there may be other processes that also need to run.

The operating system will forcibly remove a Java thread from a CPU core if it needs to. The thread is suspended immediately, no matter what it's doing—including being partway through a method. However, as we discussed in Chapter 5, a method can temporarily put an object into an illegal state while it is working on it, providing it corrects it before the method exits.

This means that if a thread is swapped off before it has completed a long-running method, it may leave an object in an inconsistent state, *even if the program follows the safety rules*. Another way of saying this is that even data types that have been correctly modeled for the single-threaded case still need to protect against the effects of concurrency. Code that adds on this additional layer of protection is called *concurrently safe*.

In the next section, we'll discuss the primary means of achieving this safety, and at the end of the chapter, we'll meet some other mechanisms that can also be useful under some circumstances.

Exclusion and Protecting State

Any code that modifies *or reads* state that can become inconsistent must be protected. To achieve this, the Java platform provides only one mechanism: *exclusion*.

Consider a method that contains a sequence of operations that, if interrupted part-way through, could leave an object in an inconsistent or illegal state. If this illegal state was visible to another object, incorrect code behavior could occur.

For example, consider an ATM or other cash-dispensing machine:

```java
public class Account {
    private double balance = 0.0; // Must be >= 0
    // Assume the existence of other field (e.g. name) and methods
    // such as deposit(), checkBalance() and dispenseNotes()

    public Account(double openingBal) {
        balance = openingBal;
    }

    public boolean withdraw(double amount) {
        if (balance >= amount) {
            try {
                Thread.sleep(2000); // Simulate risk checks
            } catch (InterruptedException e) {
                return false;
            }
            balance = balance - amount;
            dispenseNotes(amount);
            return true;
        }
        return false;
    }
}
```

The sequence of operations that happens inside withdraw() can leave the object in an inconsistent state. In particular, after we've checked the balance, a second thread could come in while the first was sleeping in simulated risk checks, and the account could be overdrawn, in violation of the constraint that balance >= 0.

This is an example of a system where the operations on the objects are single-threaded safe (because the objects cannot reach an illegal state (balance < 0) if called from a single thread), but not concurrently safe.

To allow the developer to make code like this concurrently safe, Java provides the synchronized keyword. This keyword can be applied to a block or to a method, and when it is used, the platform uses it to restrict access to the code inside the block or method.

 Because synchronized surrounds code, many developers are led to the conclusion that concurrency in Java is about code. Some texts even refer to the code that is inside the synchronized block or method as a *critical section* and consider that to be the crucial aspect of concurrency. This is not the case; instead, it is the inconsistency of data that we must guard against, as we will see.

The Java platform keeps track of a special token, called a *monitor*, for every object that it ever creates. These monitors (also called *locks*) are used by `synchronized` to indicate that the following code could temporarily render the object inconsistent. The sequence of events for a synchronized block or method is:

1. Thread needs to modify an object and may make it briefly inconsistent as an intermediate step

2. Thread acquires the monitor, indicating it requires temporary exclusive access to the object

3. Thread modifies the object, leaving it in a consistent, legal state when done

4. Thread releases the monitor

If another thread attempts to acquire the lock while the object is being modified, then the attempt to acquire the lock blocks, until the holding thread releases the lock.

Note that you do not have to use the `synchronized` statement unless your program creates multiple threads that share data. If only one thread ever accesses a data structure, there is no need to protect it with `synchronized`.

One point which is of critical importance—acquiring the monitor does *not* prevent access to the object. It only prevents any other thread from claiming the lock. Correct concurrently safe code requires developers to ensure that all accesses that might modify *or read* potentially inconsistent state acquire the object monitor before operating on, or reading that state.

Put another way, if a `synchronized` method is working on an object and has placed it into an illegal state, and another method (which is not synchronized) reads from the object, it can still see the inconsistent state.

> Synchronization is a cooperative mechanism for protecting state and it is very fragile as a result. A single bug (such as missing a single `synchronized` keyword from a method it's required on) can have catastrophic results for the safety of the system as a whole.

The reason we use the word `synchronized` as the keyword for "requires temporary exclusive access" is that in addition to acquiring the monitor, the JVM also rereads the current state of the object from main memory when the block is entered. Similarly, when the `synchronized` block or method is exited, the JVM flushes any modified state of the object back to main memory.

Without synchronization, different CPU cores in the system may not see the same view of memory, and memory inconsistencies can damage the state of a running program, as we saw in our ATM example.

volatile

Java provides another keyword for dealing with concurrent access to data. This is the `volatile` keyword, and it indicates that before being used by application code, the value of the field or variable must be reread from main memory. Equally, after a volatile value has been modified, then as soon as the write to the variable has completed, it must be written back to main memory.

One common usage of the `volatile` keyword is in the "run-until-shutdown" pattern. This is used in multithreaded programming where an external user or system needs to signal to a processing thread that it should finish the current job being worked on and then shut down gracefully. This is sometimes called the "Graceful Completion" pattern. Let's look at a typical example, supposing that this code for our processing thread is in a class that implements `Runnable`:

```
private volatile boolean shutdown = false;

public void shutdown() {
    shutdown = true;
}

public void run() {
    while (!shutdown) {
        // ... process another task
    }
}
```

All the time that the `shutdown()` method is not called by another thread, the processing thread continues to sequentially process tasks (this is often combined very usefully with a `BlockingQueue` to deliver work). Once `shutdown()` is called by another thread, then the processing thread immediately sees the `shutdown` flag change to `true`. This does not affect the running job, but once the task finishes, the processing thread will not accept another task and instead will shut down gracefully.

Useful Methods of Thread

When creating new application threads, the `Thread` class has a number of methods on it to make the programmer's life easier. This is not an exhaustive list—there are many other methods on `Thread`, but this is a description of some of the more common methods.

getId()

This method returns the ID number of the thread, as a `long`. This ID will stay the same for the lifetime of the thread.

getPriority() and setPriority()

These methods are used to control the priority of threads. The scheduler decides how to handle thread priorities—for example, one strategy could be to not have any low-priority threads run while there are high-priority threads waiting. In most cases, there is no way to influence how the scheduler will interpret priorities. Thread priorities are represented as an integer between 1 and 10.

setName() and getName()

Allows the developer to set or retrieve a name for an individual thread. Naming threads is good practice, as it can make debugging much easier, especially when using a tool such as jvisualvm, which we will discuss in "VisualVM" on page 362.

getState()

Returns a Thread.State object that indicates which state this thread is in, as per the values defined in "Thread Lifecycle" on page 209.

isAlive()

Used to test whether a thread is still alive.

start()

This method is used to create a new application thread, and to schedule it, with the run() method being the entry point for execution. A thread terminates normally when it reaches the end of its run() method or when it executes a return statement in that method.

interrupt()

If a thread is blocked in a sleep(), wait(), or join() call, then calling interrupt() on the Thread object that represents the thread will cause the thread to be sent an InterruptedException (and to wake up). If the thread was involved in interruptible I/O then the I/O will be terminated and the thread will receive a ClosedByInterrup tException. The interrupt status of the thread will be set to true, even if the thread was not engaged in any activity that could be interrupted.

join()

The current thread waits until the thread corresponding to the Thread object has died. It can be thought of as an instruction not to proceed until the other thread has completed.

setDaemon()

A *user thread* is a thread that will prevent the process from exiting if it is still alive—this is the default for threads. Sometimes, programmers want threads that will not prevent an exit from occurring—these are called *daemon threads*. The status of a thread as a daemon or user thread can be controlled by the setDaemon() method.

---

setUncaughtExceptionHandler()

When a thread exits by throwing an exception, the default behavior is to print the name of the thread, the type of the exception, the exception message, and a stack trace. If this isn't sufficient, you can install a custom handler for uncaught exceptions in a thread. For example:

```
// This thread just throws an exception
Thread handledThread =
  new Thread(() -> { throw new UnsupportedOperationException(); });

// Giving threads a name helps with debugging
handledThread.setName("My Broken Thread");

// Here's a handler for the error.
handledThread.setUncaughtExceptionHandler((t, e) -> {
    System.err.printf("Exception in thread %d '%s':" +
        "%s at line %d of %s%n",
        t.getId(),     // Thread id
        t.getName(),   // Thread name
        e.toString(),  // Exception name and message
        e.getStackTrace()[0].getLineNumber(),
        e.getStackTrace()[0].getFileName()); });
handledThread.start();
```

This can be useful in some situations, for example, if one thread is supervising a group of other worker threads, then this pattern can be used to restart any threads that die.

Deprecated Methods of Thread

In addition to the useful methods of Thread, there are a number of unsafe methods that the developer should not use. These methods form part of the original Java thread API, but were quickly found to be not suitable for developer use. Unfortunately, due to Java's backward compatibility requirements, it has not been possible to remove them from the API. The developer simply needs to be aware of them, and to avoid using them under *all* circumstances.

stop()

Thread.stop() is almost impossible to use correctly without violating concurrent safety, as stop() kills the thread immediately, without giving it any opportunity to recover objects to legal states. This is in direct opposition to principles such as concurrent safety, and so should never be used.

suspend(), resume(), and countStackFrames()

The suspend() mechanism does not release any monitors it holds when it suspends, so any other thread that attempts to accesses those monitors will deadlock. In practice, this mechanism produces race conditions between these deadlocks and resume(), that render this group of methods unusable.

destroy()

This method was never implemented—it would have suffered from the same race condition issues as suspend() if it had been.

All of these deprecated methods should always be avoided. Instead, a set of safe alternative patterns that achieve the same intended aims as the preceding methods have been developed. A good example of one of these patterns is the run-until-shutdown pattern that we have already met.

Working with Threads

In order to work effectively with multithreaded code, it's important to have the basic facts about monitors and locks at your command. This checklist contains the main facts that you should know:

- Synchronization is about protecting object state and memory, not code.
- Synchronization is a cooperative mechanism between threads. One bug can break the cooperative model and have far-reaching consequences.
- Acquiring a monitor only prevents other threads from acquiring the monitor—it does not protect the object.
- Unsynchronized methods can see (and modify) inconsistent state, even while the object's monitor is locked.
- Locking an Object[ ] doesn't lock the individual objects.
- Primitives are not mutable, so they can't (and don't need to) be locked.
- synchronized can't appear on a method declaration in an interface.
- Inner classes are just syntactic sugar, so locks on inner classes have no effect on the enclosing class (and vice versa).
- Java's locks are *reentrant*. This means that if a thread holding a monitor encounters a synchronized block for the same monitor, it can enter the block.[2]

We've also seen that threads can be asked to sleep for a period of time. It is also useful to go to sleep for an unspecified amount of time, and wait until a condition is met. In Java, this is handled by the wait() and notify() methods, that are present on Object.

Just as every Java object has a lock associated with it, every object maintains a list of waiting threads. When a thread calls the wait() method of an object, any locks the thread holds are temporarily released, and the thread is added to the list of waiting

---

2 Outside of Java, not all implementations of locks have this property.

threads for that object and stops running. When another thread calls the `noti`
`fyAll()` method of the same object, the object wakes up the waiting threads and
allows them to continue running.

For example, let's look at a simplified version of a queue that is safe for multithreaded use:

```
/*
 * One thread calls push() to put an object on the queue.
 * Another calls pop() to get an object off the queue. If there is no
 * data, pop() waits until there is some, using wait()/notify().
 */
public class WaitingQueue<E> {
    LinkedList<E> q = new LinkedList<E>(); // storage
    public synchronized void push(E o) {
        q.add(o);           // Append the object to the end of the list
        this.notifyAll(); // Tell waiting threads that data is ready
    }
    public synchronized E pop() {
        while(q.size() == 0) {
            try { this.wait(); }
            catch (InterruptedException ignore) {}
        }
        return q.remove();
    }
}
```

This class uses a `wait()` on the instance of `WaitingQueue` if the queue is empty
(which would make the `pop()` fail). The waiting thread temporarily releases its
monitor, allowing another thread to claim it—a thread that might `push()` something new onto the queue. When the original thread is woken up again, it is restar-
ted where it originally began to wait—and it will have reacquired its monitor.

`wait()` and `notify()` must be used inside a synchronized
method or block, because of the temporary relinquishing of
locks that is required for them to work properly.

In general, most developers shouldn't roll their own classes like the one in this
example—instead, make use of the libraries and components that the Java platform
provides for you.

Summary

In this chapter, we've discussed Java's view of memory and concurrency, and seen
how these topics are intrinsically linked. As processors develop more and more
cores, we will need to use concurrent programming techniques to make effective
use of those cores. Concurrency is key to the future of well-performing applications.

Java's threading model is based on three fundamental concepts:

Shared, visible-by-default mutable state
> This means that objects are easily shared between different threads in a process, and that they can be changed ("mutated") by any thread holding a reference to them.

Preemptive thread scheduling
> The OS thread scheduler can swap threads on and off cores at more or less any time.

Object state can only be protected by locks
> Locks can be hard to use correctly, and state is quite vulnerable—even in unexpected places such as read operations.

Taken together, these three aspects of Java's approach to concurrency explain why multithreaded programming can cause so many headaches for developers.

Working with the Java Platform

Part II is an introduction to some of the core libraries that ship with Java and some programming techniques that are common to intermediate and advanced Java programs.

Chapter 7, Programming and Documentation Conventions
Chapter 8, Working with Java Collections and Arrays
Chapter 9, Handling Common Data Formats
Chapter 10, File handling and I/O
Chapter 11, Classloading, Reflection and Method Handles
Chapter 12, Nashorn
Chapter 13, Platform Tools and Profiles

7

Programming and
Documentation Conventions

This chapter explains a number of important and useful Java programming and documentation conventions. It covers:

- General naming and capitalization conventions
- Portability tips and conventions
- javadoc documentation comment syntax and conventions

Naming and Capitalization Conventions

The following widely adopted naming conventions apply to packages, reference types, methods, fields, and constants in Java. Because these conventions are almost universally followed and because they affect the public API of the classes you define, they should be followed carefully:

Packages

It is customary to try to ensure that your publicly visible package names are unique. One very common way of doing this is by prefixing them with the inverted name of an Internet domain that you own (e.g., com.oreilly.javanut shell). All package names should be lowercase.

Packages of code used internally by applications distributed in self-contained JAR files are not publicly visible and need not follow this convention. It is common in this case to use the application name as the package name or as a package prefix.

Reference types

A type name should begin with a capital letter and be written in mixed case (e.g., String). If a class name consists of more than one word, each word should begin with a capital letter (e.g., StringBuffer). If a type name, or one of the words of a type name, is an acronym, the acronym can be written in all capital letters (e.g., URL, HTMLParser).

Because classes and enumerated types are designed to represent objects, you should choose class names that are nouns (e.g., Thread, Teapot, Format Converter).

When an interface is used to provide additional information about the classes that implement it, it is common to choose an interface name that is an adjective (e.g., Runnable, Cloneable, Serializable). Annotation types are also commonly named in this way.

When an interface is intended to work more like an abstract superclass, use a name that is a noun (e.g., Document, FileNameMap, Collection).

Methods

A method name always begins with a lowercase letter. If the name contains more than one word, every word after the first begins with a capital letter (e.g., insert(), insertObject(), insertObjectAt()). This is usually referred to as "Camel-Case."

Method names are typically chosen so that the first word is a verb. Method names can be as long as is necessary to make their purpose clear, but choose succinct names where possible. Avoid overly general method names, such as performAction(), go(), or the dreadful doIt().

Fields and constants

Nonconstant field names follow the same capitalization conventions as method names. If a field is a static final constant, it should be written in uppercase. If the name of a constant includes more than one word, the words should be separated with underscores (e.g., MAX_VALUE). A field name should be chosen to best describe the purpose of the field or the value it holds. The constants defined by enum types are also typically written in all capital letters.

Parameters

Method parameters follow the same capitalization conventions as nonconstant fields. The names of method parameters appear in the documentation for a method, so you should choose names that make the purpose of the parameters as clear as possible. Try to keep parameter names to a single word and use them consistently. For example, if a WidgetProcessor class defines many methods that accept a Widget object as the first parameter, name this parameter widget or even w in each method.

Local variables

Local variable names are an implementation detail and never visible outside your class. Nevertheless, choosing good names makes your code easier to read, understand, and maintain. Variables are typically named following the same conventions as methods and fields.

In addition to the conventions for specific types of names, there are conventions regarding the characters you should use in your names. Java allows the $ character in any identifier, but, by convention, its use is reserved for synthetic names generated by source-code processors. For example, it is used by the Java compiler to make inner classes work. You should not use the $ character in any name that you create.

Java allows names to use any alphanumeric characters from the entire Unicode character set. While this can be convenient for non-English-speaking programmers, this has never really taken off and this usage is extremely rare.

Practical Naming

The names we give to our constructs matter—a lot. Naming is a key part of the process that conveys our abstract designs to our peers. The process of transferring a software design from one human mind to another is hard—harder, in many cases, than the process of transferring our design from our mind to the machines that will execute it.

We must, therefore, do everything we can to ensure that this process is eased. Names are a keystone of this. When reviewing code (and all code should be reviewed), the reviewer should pay particular attention to the names that have been chosen:

- Do the names of the types reflect the purpose of those types?
- Does each method do exactly what its name suggests? Ideally, no more, and no less?
- Are the names descriptive enough? Could a more specific name be used instead?
- Are the names well-suited for the domain they describe?
- Are the names consistent across the domain?
- Do the names mix metaphors?
- Does the name reuse a common term of software engineering?

Mixed metaphors are common in software, especially after several releases of an application. A system that starts off perfectly reasonably with components called Receptionist (for handling incoming connections), Scribe (for persisting orders), and Auditor (for checking and reconciling orders) can quite easily end up in a later release with a class called `Watchdog` for restarting processes. This isn't terrible, but it breaks the established pattern of people's job titles that previously existed.

It is also incredibly important to realize that software changes a lot over time. A perfectly apposite name on release 1 can become highly misleading by release 4. Care should be taken that as the system focus and intent shifts, the names are refactored along with the code. Modern IDEs have no problem with global search and replace of symbols, so there is no need to cling to outdated metaphors once they are no longer useful.

One final note of caution—an overly strict interpretation of these guidelines can lead the developer to some very odd naming constructs. There are a number of excellent descriptions of some of the absurdities that can result by taking these conventions to their extremes.

In other words, none of the conventions described here are mandatory. Following them will, in the vast majority of cases, make your code easier to read and maintain. However, you should recall George Orwell's maxim of style—"Break any of these rules rather than say anything outright barbarous"—and not be afraid to deviate from these guidelines if it makes your code easier to read.

Above all, you should have a sense of the expected lifetime of the code you are writing. A risk calculation system in a bank may have a lifetime of a decade or more, whereas a prototype for a startup may only be relevant for a few weeks. Document accordingly—the longer the code is likely to be live, the better its documentation needs to be.

Java Documentation Comments

Most ordinary comments within Java code explain the implementation details of that code. By contrast, the Java language specification defines a special type of comment known as a *doc comment* that serves to document the API of your code.

A doc comment is an ordinary multiline comment that begins with `/**` (instead of the usual `/*`) and ends with `*/`. A doc comment appears immediately before a type or member definition and contains documentation for that type or member. The documentation can include simple HTML formatting tags and other special keywords that provide additional information. Doc comments are ignored by the compiler, but they can be extracted and automatically turned into online HTML documentation by the `javadoc` program. (See Chapter 13 for more information about `javadoc`.) Here is an example class that contains appropriate doc comments:

```
/**
 * This immutable class represents <i>complex numbers</i>.
 *
 * @author David Flanagan
 * @version 1.0
 */
public class Complex {
    /**
```

```
    * Holds the real part of this complex number.
    * @see #y
    */
   protected double x;

   /**
    * Holds the imaginary part of this complex number.
    * @see #x
    */
   protected double y;

   /**
    * Creates a new Complex object that represents the complex number
    * x+yi. @param x The real part of the complex number.
    * @param y The imaginary part of the complex number.
    */
   public Complex(double x, double y) {
       this.x = x;
       this.y = y;
   }

   /**
    * Adds two Complex objects and produces a third object that
    * represents their sum.
    * @param c1 A Complex object
    * @param c2 Another Complex object
    * @return  A new Complex object that represents the sum of
    *              <code>c1</code> and <code>c2</code>.
    * @exception java.lang.NullPointerException
    *              If either argument is <code>null</code>.
    */
   public static Complex add(Complex c1, Complex c2) {
       return new Complex(c1.x + c2.x, c1.y + c2.y);
   }
}
```

Structure of a Doc Comment

The body of a doc comment should begin with a one-sentence summary of the type or member being documented. This sentence may be displayed by itself as summary documentation, so it should be written to stand on its own. The initial sentence may be followed by any number of other sentences and paragraphs that describe the class, interface, method, or field in full detail.

After the descriptive paragraphs, a doc comment can contain any number of other paragraphs, each of which begins with a special doc-comment tag, such as @author, @param, or @returns. These tagged paragraphs provide specific information about the class, interface, method, or field that the javadoc program displays in a standard way. The full set of doc-comment tags is listed in the next section.

The descriptive material in a doc comment can contain simple HTML markup tags, such as `<i>` for emphasis, `<code>` for class, method, and field names, and `<pre>` for multiline code examples. It can also contain `<p>` tags to break the description into separate paragraphs and `<ul>`, `<li>`, and related tags to display bulleted lists and similar structures. Remember, however, that the material you write is embedded within a larger, more complex HTML document. For this reason, doc comments should not contain major structural HTML tags, such as `<h2>` or `<hr>`, that might interfere with the structure of the larger document.

Avoid the use of the `<a>` tag to include hyperlinks or cross-references in your doc comments. Instead, use the special `{@link}` doc-comment tag, which, unlike the other doc-comment tags, can appear anywhere within a doc comment. As described in the next section, the `{@link}` tag allows you to specify hyperlinks to other classes, interfaces, methods, and fields without knowing the HTML-structuring conventions and filenames used by `javadoc`.

If you want to include an image in a doc comment, place the image file in a *doc-files* subdirectory of the source code directory. Give the image the same name as the class, with an integer suffix. For example, the second image that appears in the doc comment for a class named `Circle` can be included with this HTML tag:

```
<img src="doc-files/Circle-2.gif">
```

Because the lines of a doc comment are embedded within a Java comment, any leading spaces and asterisks (*) are stripped from each line of the comment before processing. Thus, you don't need to worry about the asterisks appearing in the generated documentation or about the indentation of the comment affecting the indentation of code examples included within the comment with a `<pre>` tag.

Doc-Comment Tags

The `javadoc` program recognizes a number of special tags, each of which begins with an @ character. These doc-comment tags allow you to encode specific information into your comments in a standardized way, and they allow `javadoc` to choose the appropriate output format for that information. For example, the `@param` tag lets you specify the name and meaning of a single parameter for a method. `javadoc` can extract this information and display it using an HTML `<dl>` list, an HTML `<table>`, or however it sees fit.

The following doc-comment tags are recognized by `javadoc`; a doc comment should typically use these tags in the order listed here:

`@author name`
> Adds an "Author:" entry that contains the specified name. This tag should be used for every class or interface definition but must not be used for individual methods and fields. If a class has multiple authors, use multiple `@author` tags on adjacent lines. For example:

```
@author Ben Evans
@author David Flanagan
```

List the authors in chronological order, with the original author first. If the author is unknown, you can use "unascribed." javadoc does not output authorship information unless the -author command-line argument is specified.

@version *text*

Inserts a "Version:" entry that contains the specified text. For example:

```
@version 1.32, 08/26/04
```

This tag should be included in every class and interface doc comment but cannot be used for individual methods and fields. This tag is often used in conjunction with the automated version-numbering capabilities of a version control system, such as git, Perforce, or SVN. javadoc does not output version information in its generated documentation unless the -version command-line argument is specified.

@param *parameter-name description*

Adds the specified parameter and its description to the "Parameters:" section of the current method. The doc comment for a method or constructor must contain one @param tag for each parameter the method expects. These tags should appear in the same order as the parameters specified by the method. The tag can be used only in doc comments for methods and constructors.

You are encouraged to use phrases and sentence fragments where possible to keep the descriptions brief. However, if a parameter requires detailed documentation, the description can wrap onto multiple lines and include as much text as necessary. For readability in source-code form, consider using spaces to align the descriptions with each other. For example:

```
@param o      the object to insert
@param index  the position to insert it at
```

@return *description*

Inserts a "Returns:" section that contains the specified description. This tag should appear in every doc comment for a method, unless the method returns void or is a constructor. The description can be as long as necessary, but consider using a sentence fragment to keep it short. For example:

```
@return <code>true</code> if the insertion is successful, or
        <code>false</code> if the list already contains the object.
```

@exception *full-classname description*

Adds a "Throws:" entry that contains the specified exception name and description. A doc comment for a method or constructor should contain an @exception tag for every checked exception that appears in its throws clause. For example:

```
@exception java.io.FileNotFoundException
         If the specified file could not be found
```

The @exception tag can optionally be used to document unchecked exceptions (i.e., subclasses of RuntimeException) the method may throw, when these are exceptions that a user of the method may reasonably want to catch. If a method can throw more than one exception, use multiple @exception tags on adjacent lines and list the exceptions in alphabetical order. The description can be as short or as long as necessary to describe the significance of the exception. This tag can be used only for method and constructor comments. The @throws tag is a synonym for @exception.

@throws *full-classname description*

This tag is a synonym for @exception.

@see *reference*

Adds a "See Also:" entry that contains the specified reference. This tag can appear in any kind of doc comment. The syntax for the *reference* is explained later in this chapter in "Cross-References in Doc Comments" on page 233.

@deprecated *explanation*

This tag specifies that the following type or member has been deprecated and that its use should be avoided. javadoc adds a prominent "Deprecated" entry to the documentation and includes the specified *explanation* text. This text should specify when the class or member was deprecated and, if possible, suggest a replacement class or member and include a link to it. For example:

```
@deprecated As of Version 3.0, this method is replaced
         by {@link #setColor}.
```

The @deprecated tag is an exception to the general rule that javac ignores all comments. When this tag appears, the compiler notes the deprecation in the class file it produces. This allows it to issue warnings for other classes that rely on the deprecated feature.

@since *version*

Specifies when the type or member was added to the API. This tag should be followed by a version number or other version specification. For example:

```
@since JNUT 3.0
```

Every doc comment for a type should include an @since tag, and any members added after the initial release of the type should have @since tags in their doc comments.

@serial *description*

Technically, the way a class is serialized is part of its public API. If you write a class that you expect to be serialized, you should document its serialization format using @serial and the related tags listed next. @serial should appear in the doc comment for any field that is part of the serialized state of a `Serializa ble` class.

For classes that use the default serialization mechanism, this means all fields that are not declared `transient`, including fields declared `private`. The `description` should be a brief description of the field and of its purpose within a serialized object.

You can also use the `@serial` tag at the class and package level to specify whether a "serialized form page" should be generated for the class or package. The syntax is:

```
@serial include
@serial exclude
```

@serialField *name type description*
> A `Serializable` class can define its serialized format by declaring an array of `ObjectStreamField` objects in a field named `serialPersistentFields`. For such a class, the doc comment for `serialPersistentFields` should include an `@serialField` tag for each element of the array. Each tag specifies the name, type, and description for a particular field in the serialized state of the class.

@serialData *description*
> A `Serializable` class can define a `writeObject()` method to write data other than that written by the default serialization mechanism. An `Externalizable` class defines a `writeExternal()` method responsible for writing the complete state of an object to the serialization stream. The `@serialData` tag should be used in the doc comments for these `writeObject()` and `writeExternal()` methods, and the `description` should document the serialization format used by the method.

Inline Doc-Comment Tags

In addition to the preceding tags, javadoc also supports several *inline tags* that may appear anywhere that HTML text appears in a doc comment. Because these tags appear directly within the flow of HTML text, they require the use of curly braces as delimiters to separate the tagged text from the HTML text. Supported inline tags include the following:

{@link *reference* }
> The {@link} tag is like the @see tag except that instead of placing a link to the specified *reference* in a special "See Also:" section, it inserts the link inline. An {@link} tag can appear anywhere that HTML text appears in a doc comment. In other words, it can appear in the initial description of the class, interface, method, or field and in the descriptions associated with the @param, @returns, @exception, and @deprecated tags. The *reference* for the {@link} tag uses the syntax described next in "Cross-References in Doc Comments" on page 233. For example:

```
@param regexp The regular expression to search for. This string
              argument must follow the syntax rules described for
              {@link java.util.regex.Pattern}.
```

{@linkplain *reference* **}**

The {@linkplain} tag is just like the {@link} tag, except that the text of the
link is formatted using the normal font rather than the code font used by the
{@link} tag. This is most useful when *reference* contains both a *feature* to
link to and a *label* that specifies alternate text to be displayed in the link. See
"Cross-References in Doc Comments" on page 233 for a discussion of the *fea
ture* and *label* portions of the *reference* argument.

{@inheritDoc}

When a method overrides a method in a superclass or implements a method in
an interface, you can omit a doc comment, and javadoc automatically inherits
the documentation from the overridden or implemented method. The {@inher
itDoc} tag allows you to inherit the text of individual tags. This tag also allows
you to inherit and augment the descriptive text of the comment. To inherit
individual tags, use it like this:

```
@param index @{inheritDoc}
@return @{inheritDoc}
```

{@docRoot}

This inline tag takes no parameters and is replaced with a reference to the root
directory of the generated documentation. It is useful in hyperlinks that refer to
an external file, such as an image or a copyright statement:

```
<img src="{@docroot}/images/logo.gif">
This is <a href="{@docRoot}/legal.html">Copyrighted</a> material.
```

{@literal *text* **}**

This inline tag displays *text* literally, escaping any HTML in it and ignoring
any javadoc tags it may contain. It does not retain whitespace formatting but is
useful when used within a <pre> tag.

{@code *text* **}**

This tag is like the {@literal} tag, but displays the literal *text* in code font.
Equivalent to:

```
&lt;code&gt;{@literal <replaceable>text</replaceable>}&lt;/code&gt;
```

{@value}

The {@value} tag, with no arguments, is used inline in doc comments for
static final fields and is replaced with the constant value of that field.

{@value *reference* **}**

This variant of the {@value} tag includes a *reference* to a static final field
and is replaced with the constant value of that field.

Cross-References in Doc Comments

The @see tag and the inline tags {@link}, {@linkplain}, and {@value} all encode a cross-reference to some other source of documentation, typically to the documentation comment for some other type or member.

reference can take three different forms. If it begins with a quote character, it is taken to be the name of a book or some other printed resource and is displayed as is. If *reference* begins with a < character, it is taken to be an arbitrary HTML hyperlink that uses the <a> tag and the hyperlink is inserted into the output documentation as is. This form of the @see tag can insert links to other online documents, such as a programmer's guide or user's manual.

If *reference* is not a quoted string or a hyperlink, it is expected to have the following form:

```
feature [label]
```

In this case, javadoc outputs the text specified by *label* and encodes it as a hyperlink to the specified *feature*. If *label* is omitted (as it usually is), javadoc uses the name of the specified *feature* instead.

feature can refer to a package, type, or type member, using one of the following forms:

pkgname
>   A reference to the named package. For example:
>
> ```
> @see java.lang.reflect
> ```

pkgname.typename
>   A reference to a class, interface, enumerated type, or annotation type specified with its full package name. For example:
>
> ```
> @see java.util.List
> ```

typename
>   A reference to a type specified without its package name. For example:
>
> ```
> @see List
> ```
>
>   javadoc resolves this reference by searching the current package and the list of imported classes for a class with this name.

typename # methodname
>   A reference to a named method or constructor within the specified type. For example:
>
> ```
> @see java.io.InputStream#reset
> @see InputStream#close
> ```

If the type is specified without its package name, it is resolved as described for *typename*. This syntax is ambiguous if the method is overloaded or the class defines a field by the same name.

typename # *methodname* (*paramtypes*)

A reference to a method or constructor with the type of its parameters explicitly specified. This is useful when cross-referencing an overloaded method. For example:

```
@see InputStream#read(byte[], int, int)
```

methodname

A reference to a nonoverloaded method or constructor in the current class or interface or one of the containing classes, superclasses, or superinterfaces of the current class or interface. Use this concise form to refer to other methods in the same class. For example:

```
@see #setBackgroundColor
```

methodname (*paramtypes*)

A reference to a method or constructor in the current class or interface or one of its superclasses or containing classes. This form works with overloaded methods because it lists the types of the method parameters explicitly. For example:

```
@see #setPosition(int, int)
```

typename # *fieldname*

A reference to a named field within the specified class. For example:

```
@see java.io.BufferedInputStream#buf
```

If the type is specified without its package name, it is resolved as described for *typename*.

fieldname

A reference to a field in the current type or one of the containing classes, superclasses, or superinterfaces of the current type. For example:

```
@see #x
```

Doc Comments for Packages

Documentation comments for classes, interfaces, methods, constructors, and fields appear in Java source code immediately before the definitions of the features they document. javadoc can also read and display summary documentation for packages. Because a package is defined in a directory, not in a single file of source code, javadoc looks for the package documentation in a file named *package.html* in the directory that contains the source code for the classes of the package.

The *package.html* file should contain simple HTML documentation for the package. It can also contain @see, @link, @deprecated, and @since tags. Because *package.html* is not a file of Java source code, the documentation it contains should be HTML and should *not* be a Java comment (i.e., it should not be enclosed within /** and */ characters). Finally, any @see and @link tags that appear in *package.html* must use fully qualified class names.

In addition to defining a *package.html* file for each package, you can also provide high-level documentation for a group of packages by defining an *overview.html* file in the source tree for those packages. When javadoc is run over that source tree, it uses *overview.html* as the highest level overview it displays.

Conventions for Portable Programs

One of the earliest slogans for Java was "write once, run anywhere." This emphasizes that Java makes it easy to write portable programs, but it is still possible to write Java programs that do not automatically run successfully on any Java platform. The following tips help to avoid portability problems.

Native methods
> Portable Java code can use any methods in the core Java APIs, including methods implemented as native methods. However, portable code must not define its own native methods. By their very nature, native methods must be ported to each new platform, so they directly subvert the "write once, run anywhere" promise of Java.

The Runtime.exec() method
> Calling the Runtime.exec() method to spawn a process and execute an external command on the native system is rarely allowed in portable code. This is because the native OS command to be executed is never guaranteed to exist or behave the same way on all platforms. The only time it is legal to use Runtime.exec() in portable code is when the user is allowed to specify the command to run, either by typing the command at runtime or by specifying the command in a configuration file or preferences dialog box.

The System.getenv() method
> Using System.getenv() is inherently nonportable.

Undocumented classes
> Portable Java code must use only classes and interfaces that are a documented part of the Java platform. Most Java implementations ship with additional undocumented public classes that are part of the implementation but not part of the Java platform specification. Nothing prevents a program from using and relying on these undocumented classes, but doing so is not portable because the classes are not guaranteed to exist in all Java implementations or on all platforms.

> Of particular note is the sun.misc.Unsafe class, which provides access to a number of "unsafe" methods, which can allow developers to circumvent a

number of key restrictions of the Java platform. Developers should not make direct use of the Unsafe class under any circumstances.

The java.awt.peer package

The interfaces in the java.awt.peer package are part of the Java platform but are documented for use by AWT implementors only. Applications that use these interfaces directly are not portable.

Implementation-specific features

Portable code must not rely on features specific to a single implementation. For example, Microsoft distributed a version of the Java runtime system that included a number of additional methods that were not part of the Java platform as defined by the specifications. Any program that depends on such extensions is obviously not portable to other platforms.

Implementation-specific bugs

Just as portable code must not depend on implementation-specific features, it must not depend on implementation-specific bugs. If a class or method behaves differently than the specification says it should, a portable program cannot rely on this behavior, which may be different on different platforms, and ultimately may be fixed.

Implementation-specific behavior

Sometimes different platforms and different implementations present different behaviors, all of which are legal according to the Java specification. Portable code must not depend on any one specific behavior. For example, the Java specification does not indicate whether threads of equal priority share the CPU or if one long-running thread can starve another thread at the same priority. If an application assumes one behavior or the other, it may not run properly on all platforms.

Standard extensions

Portable code can rely on standard extensions to the Java platform, but, if it does so, it should clearly specify which extensions it uses and exit cleanly with an appropriate error message when run on a system that does not have the extensions installed.

Complete programs

Any portable Java program must be complete and self-contained: it must supply all the classes it uses, except core platform and standard extension classes.

Defining system classes

Portable Java code never defines classes in any of the system or standard extension packages. Doing so violates the protection boundaries of those packages and exposes package-visible implementation details.

Hardcoded filenames

A portable program contains no hardcoded file or directory names. This is because different platforms have significantly different filesystem organizations

---

and use different directory separator characters. If you need to work with a file or directory, have the user specify the filename, or at least the base directory beneath which the file can be found. This specification can be done at runtime, in a configuration file, or as a command-line argument to the program. When concatenating a file or directory name to a directory name, use the File() constructor or the File.separator constant.

Line separators

Different systems use different characters or sequences of characters as line separators. Do not hardcode \n, \r, or \r\n as the line separator in your program. Instead, use the println() method of PrintStream or PrintWriter, which automatically terminates a line with the line separator appropriate for the platform, or use the value of the line.separator system property. You can also use the "%n" format string to printf() and format() methods of java.util.Formatter and related classes.

8

Working with Java Collections

This chapter introduces Java's interpretation of fundamental data structures, known as the Java Collections. These abstractions are core to many (if not most) programming types, and form an essential part of any programmers basic toolkit. Accordingly, this is one of the most important chapters of the entire book, and provides a toolkit that is essential to virtually all Java programmers.

In this chapter, we will introduce the fundamental interfaces and the type hierarchy, show how to use them, and discuss aspects of their overall design. Both the "classic" approach to handling the Collections and the newer approach (using the Streams API and the lambda expressions functionality introduced in Java 8) will be covered.

Introduction to Collections API

The Java Collections are a set of generic interfaces that describe the most common forms of data structure. Java ships with several implementations of each of the classic data structures, and because the types are represented as interfaces, it is very possible for development teams to develop their own, specialized implementations of the interfaces for use in their own projects.

The Java Collections define two fundamental types of data structures. A `Collection` is a grouping of objects, while a `Map` is a set of mappings, or associations, between objects. The basic layout of the Java Collections is shown in Figure 8-1.

Within this basic description, a `Set` is a type of `Collection` with no duplicates, and a `List` is a `Collection` in which the elements are ordered (but may contain duplicates).

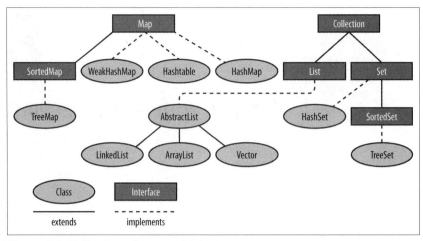

Figure 8-1. Collections classes and inheritance

SortedSet and SortedMap are specialized sets and maps that maintain their elements in a sorted order.

Collection, Set, List, Map, SortedSet, and SortedMap are all interfaces, but the java.util package also defines various concrete implementations, such as lists based on arrays and linked lists, and maps and sets based on hash tables or binary trees. Other important interfaces are Iterator and Iterable, which allow you to loop through the objects in a collection, as we will see later on.

The Collection Interface

Collection<E> is a parameterized interface that represents a generalized grouping of objects of type E. Methods are defined for adding and removing objects from the group, testing an object for membership in the group, and iterating through all elements in the group. Additional methods return the elements of the group as an array and return the size of the collection.

> The grouping within a Collection may or may not allow duplicate elements and may or may not impose an ordering on the elements.

The Java Collections Framework provides Collection because it defines the features common to all common forms of data structure. The JDK ships Set, List, and Queue as subinterfaces of Collection. The following code illustrates the operations you can perform on Collection objects:

```
// Create some collections to work with.
Collection<String> c = new HashSet<>();  // An empty set
```

```
// We'll see these utility methods later Be aware that there are
// some subtleties to watch out for when using them
Collection<String> d = Arrays.asList("one", "two");
Collection<String> e = Collections.singleton("three");

// Add elements to a collection. These methods return true
// if the collection changes, which is useful with Sets that
// don't allow duplicates.
c.add("zero");          // Add a single element
c.addAll(d);            // Add all of the elements in d

// Copy a collection: most implementations have a copy constructor
Collection<String> copy = new ArrayList<String>(c);

// Remove elements from a collection.
// All but clear return true if the collection changes.
c.remove("zero");       // Remove a single element
c.removeAll(e);         // Remove a collection of elements
c.retainAll(d);         // Remove all elements that are not in e
c.clear();              // Remove all elements from the collection

// Querying collection size
boolean b = c.isEmpty(); // c is now empty, so true
int s = c.size();        // Size of c is now 0.

// Restore collection from the copy we made
c.addAll(copy);

// Test membership in the collection. Membership is based on the equals
// method, not the == operator.
b = c.contains("zero");  // true
b = c.containsAll(d);    // true

// Most Collection implementations have a useful toString()  method
System.out.println(c);

// Obtain an array of collection elements.  If the iterator guarantees
// an order, this array has the same order. The array is a copy, not a
// reference to an internal data structure.
Object[] elements = c.toArray();

// If we want the elements in a String[], we must pass one in
String[] strings = c.toArray(new String[c.size()]);

// Or we can pass an empty String[] just to specify the type and
// the toArray method will allocate an array for us
strings = c.toArray(new String[0]);
```

Remember that you can use any of the methods shown here with any Set, List, or Queue. These subinterfaces may impose membership restrictions or ordering constraints on the elements of the collection but still provide the same basic methods.

Methods such as add(), remove(), clear(), and retainAll() that alter the collection were conceived of as optional parts of the API. Unfortunately, they were specified a long time ago, when the received wisdom was to indicate the absence of an optional method by throwing UnsupportedOperation Exception. Accordingly, some implementations (notably read-only forms) may throw this unchecked exception.

Collection, Map, and their subinterfaces do *not* extend the Cloneable or Serializable interfaces. All of the collection and map implementation classes provided in the Java Collections Framework, however, do implement these interfaces.

Some collection implementations place restrictions on the elements that they can contain. An implementation might prohibit null as an element, for example. And EnumSet restricts membership to the values of a specified enumerated type.

Attempting to add a prohibited element to a collection always throws an unchecked exception such as NullPointerException or ClassCastException. Checking whether a collection contains a prohibited element may also throw such an exception, or it may simply return false.

The Set Interface

A *set* is a collection of objects that does not allow duplicates: it may not contain two references to the same object, two references to null, or references to two objects a and b such that a.equals(b). Most general-purpose Set implementations impose no ordering on the elements of the set, but ordered sets are not prohibited (see SortedSet and LinkedHashSet). Sets are further distinguished from ordered collections like lists by the general expectation that they have an efficient contains method that runs in constant or logarithmic time.

Set defines no additional methods beyond those defined by Collection but places additional restrictions on those methods. The add() and addAll() methods of a Set are required to enforce the no-duplicates rules: they may not add an element to the Set if the set already contains that element. Recall that the add() and addAll() methods defined by the Collection interface return true if the call resulted in a change to the collection and false if it did not. This return value is relevant for Set objects because the no-duplicates restriction means that adding an element does not always result in a change to the set.

Table 8-1 lists the implementations of the Set interface and summarizes their internal representation, ordering characteristics, member restrictions, and the performance of the basic add(), remove(), and contains operations as well as iteration performance. You can read more about each class in the reference section. Note that CopyOnWriteArraySet is in the java.util.concurrent package; all the other implementations are part of java.util. Also note that java.util.BitSet is not a Set implementation. This legacy class is useful as a compact and efficient list of boolean values but is not part of the Java Collections Framework.

Table 8-1. Set implementations

Class	Internal representation	Since	Element order	Member restrictions	Basic operations	Iteration performance	Notes
Hash Set	Hashtable	1.2	None	None	O(1)	O(capacity)	Best general-purpose implementation.
Linked Hash Set	Linked hashtable	1.2	Insertion order	None	O(1)	O(n)	Preserves insertion order.
Enum Set	Bit fields	5.0	Enum declaration	Enum values	O(1)	O(n)	Holds non-null enum values only.
Tree Set	Red-black tree	1.2	Sorted ascending	Comparable	O(log(n))	O(n)	Comparable elements or Comparator.
CopyOn Wri teAr raySet	Array	5.0	Insertion order	None	O(n)	O(n)	Threadsafe without synchronized methods.

The TreeSet implementation uses a red-black tree data structure to maintain a set that is iterated in ascending order according to the natural ordering of Comparable objects or according to an ordering specified by a Comparator object. TreeSet actually implements the SortedSet interface, which is a subinterface of Set.

The SortedSet interface offers several interesting methods that take advantage of its sorted nature. The following code illustrates:

```
public static void testSortedSet(String[] args) {
    // Create a SortedSet
    SortedSet<String> s = new TreeSet<>(Arrays.asList(args));

    // Iterate set: elements are automatically sorted
    for (String word : s) {
        System.out.println(word);
    }

    // Special elements
    String first = s.first();  // First element
    String last = s.last();    // Last element

    // all elements but first
```

```
SortedSet<String> tail = s.tailSet(first + '\0');
System.out.println(tail);

// all elements but last
SortedSet<String> head = s.headSet(last);
System.out.println(head);

SortedSet<String> middle = s.subSet(first+'\0', last);
System.out.println(middle);
}
```

 The addition of \0 characters is needed because the tail
Set() and related methods use the *successor* of an element,
which for strings is the string value with a NULL character
(ASCII code 0) appended.

The List Interface

A List is an ordered collection of objects. Each element of a list has a position in
the list, and the List interface defines methods to query or set the element at a particular position, or *index*. In this respect, a List is like an array whose size changes
as needed to accommodate the number of elements it contains. Unlike sets, lists
allow duplicate elements.

In addition to its index-based get() and set() methods, the List interface defines
methods to add or remove an element at a particular index and also defines methods to return the index of the first or last occurrence of a particular value in the list.
The add() and remove() methods inherited from Collection are defined to
append to the list and to remove the first occurrence of the specified value from the
list. The inherited addAll() appends all elements in the specified collection to the
end of the list, and another version inserts the elements at a specified index. The
retainAll() and removeAll() methods behave as they do for any Collection,
retaining or removing multiple occurrences of the same value, if needed.

The List interface does not define methods that operate on a range of list indexes.
Instead, it defines a single subList() method that returns a List object that represents just the specified range of the original list. The sublist is backed by the parent
list, and any changes made to the sublist are immediately visible in the parent list.
Examples of subList() and the other basic List manipulation methods are shown
here:

```
// Create lists to work with
List<String> l = new ArrayList<String>(Arrays.asList(args));
List<String> words = Arrays.asList("hello", "world");

// Querying and setting elements by index
String first = l.get(0);            // First element of list
String last = l.get(l.size -1);     // Last element of list
```

```
l.set(0, last);                     // The last shall be first

// Adding and inserting elements.  add  can append or insert
l.add(first);           // Append the first word at end of list
l.add(0, first);        // Insert first at the start of the list again
l.addAll(words);        // Append a collection at the end of the list
l.addAll(1, words);     // Insert collection after first word

// Sublists: backed by the original list
List<String> sub = l.subList(1,3);    // second and third elements
sub.set(0, "hi");                     // modifies 2nd element of l
// Sublists can restrict operations to a subrange of backing list
String s = Collections.min(l.subList(0,4));
Collections.sort(l.subList(0,4));
// Independent copies of a sublist don't affect the parent list.
List<String> subcopy = new ArrayList<String>(l.subList(1,3));

// Searching lists
int p = l.indexOf(last);    // Where does the last word appear?
p = l.lastIndexOf(last);    // Search backward

// Print the index of all occurrences of last in l.  Note subList
int n = l.size();
p = 0;
do {
    // Get a view of the list that includes only the elements we
    // haven't searched yet.
    List<String> list = l.subList(p, n);
    int q = list.indexOf(last);
    if (q == -1) break;
    System.out.printf("Found '%s' at index %d%n", last, p+q);
    p += q+1;
} while(p < n);

// Removing elements from a list
l.remove(last);           // Remove first occurrence of the element
l.remove(0);              // Remove element at specified index
l.subList(0,2).clear();   // Remove a range of elements using subList
l.retainAll(words);       // Remove all but elements in words
l.removeAll(words);       // Remove all occurrences of elements in words
l.clear();                // Remove everything
```

Foreach loops and iteration

One very important way of working with collections is to process each element in
turn, an approach known as iteration. This is an older way of looking at data structures, but is still very useful (especially for small collections of data) and is easy to
understand. This approach fits naturally with the for loop, as shown in this bit of
code, and is easiest to illustrate using a List:

```
ListCollection<String> c = new ArrayList<String>();
// ... add some Strings to c
```

```
for(String word : c) {
    System.out.println(word);
}
```

The sense of the code should be clear—it takes the elements of c one at a time and uses them as a variable in the loop body. More formally, it iterates through the elements of an array or collection (or any object that implements java.lang.Iterable). On each iteration it assigns an element of the array or Iterable object to the loop variable you declare and then executes the loop body, which typically uses the loop variable to operate on the element. No loop counter or Iterator object is involved; the foreach loop performs the iteration automatically, and you need not concern yourself with correct initialization or termination of the loop.

This type of for loop is often referred to as a foreach loop. Let's see how it works. The following bit of code shows a rewritten (and equivalent) for loop, with the methods actually shown:

```
// Iteration with a for loop
for(Iterator<String> i = c.iterator(); i.hasNext();) {
    System.out.println(i.next());
}
```

The Iterator object, i, is produced from the collection, and used to step through the collection one item at a time. It can also be used with while loops:

```
//Iterate through collection elements with a while loop.
//Some implementations (such as lists) guarantee an order of iteration
//Others make no guarantees.
Iterator<String> iterator() = c.iterator();
while (iterator.hasNext()) {
    System.out.println(iterator.next());
}
```

Here are some more things you should know about the syntax of the foreach loop:

- As noted earlier, *expression* must be either an array or an object that implements the java.lang.Iterable interface. This type must be known at compile time so that the compiler can generate appropriate looping code.

- The type of the array or Iterable elements must be assignment-compatible with the type of the variable declared in the *declaration*. If you use an Iterable object that is not parameterized with an element type, the variable must be declared as an Object.

- The *declaration* usually consists of just a type and a variable name, but it may include a final modifier and any appropriate annotations (see Chapter 4). Using final prevents the loop variable from taking on any value other than the array or collection element the loop assigns it and serves to emphasize that the array or collection cannot be altered through the loop variable.

- The loop variable of the foreach loop must be declared as part of the loop, with both a type and a variable name. You cannot use a variable declared outside the loop as you can with the `for` loop.

To understand in detail how the foreach loop works with collections, we need to consider two interfaces, `java.util.Iterator` and `java.lang.Iterable`:

```java
public interface Iterator<E> {
    boolean hasNext();
    E next();
    void remove();
}
```

`Iterator` defines a way to iterate through the elements of a collection or other data structure. It works like this: while there are more elements in the collection (`has Next()` returns `true`), call `next` to obtain the next element of the collection. Ordered collections, such as lists, typically have iterators that guarantee that they'll return elements in order. Unordered collections like `Set` simply guarantee that repeated calls to `next()` return all elements of the set without omissions or duplications but do not specify an ordering.

The `next()` method of `Iterator` performs two functions—it advances through the collection and also returns the old head value of the collection. This combination of operations can cause problems when programming in an immutable style, as it fundamentally mutates the collection.

The `Iterable` interface was introduced to make the foreach loop work. A class implements this interface in order to advertise that it is able to provide an `Iterator` to anyone interested:

```java
public interface Iterable<E> {
    java.util.Iterator<E> iterator();
}
```

If an object is `Iterable<E>`, that means that that it has an `iterator()` method that returns an `Iterator<E>`, which has a `next()` method that returns an object of type E.

Note that if you use the foreach loop with an `Iterable<E>`, the loop variable must be of type E or a superclass or interface.

For example, to iterate through the elements of a `List<String>`, the variable must be declared `String` or its superclass `Object`, or one of the interfaces it implements: `CharSequence`, `Comparable`, or `Serializable`.

Random access to Lists

A general expectation of `List` implementations is that they can be efficiently iterated, typically in time proportional to the size of the list. Lists do not all provide efficient random access to the elements at any index, however. Sequential-access lists, such as the `LinkedList` class, provide efficient insertion and deletion operations at the expense of random-access performance. Implementations that provide efficient random access implement the `RandomAccess` marker interface, and you can test for this interface with `instanceof` if you need to ensure efficient list manipulations:

```
// Arbitrary list we're passed to manipulate
List<?> l = ...;

// Ensure we can do efficient random access.  If not, use a copy
// constructor to make a random-access copy of the list before
// manipulating it.
if (!(l instanceof RandomAccess)) l = new ArrayList<?>(l);
```

The `Iterator` returned by the `iterator()` method of a `List` iterates the list elements in the order that they occur in the list. `List` implements `Iterable`, and lists can be iterated with a foreach loop just as any other collection can.

To iterate just a portion of a list, you can use the `subList()` method to create a sublist view:

```
List<String> words = ...;  // Get a list to iterate

// Iterate just all elements of the list but the first
for(String word : words.subList(1, words.size ))
    System.out.println(word);
```

Table 8-2 summarizes the five general-purpose `List` implementations in the Java platform. `Vector` and `Stack` are legacy implementations and should not be used. `CopyOnWriteArrayList` is part of the `java.util.concurrent` package and is only really suitable for multithreaded use cases.

Table 8-2. List implementations

Class	Representation	Since	Random access	Notes
ArrayList	Array	1.2	Yes	Best all-around implementation.
LinkedList	Double-linked list	1.2	No	Efficient insertion and deletion.
CopyOnWriteArrayList	Array	5.0	Yes	Threadsafe; fast traversal, slow modification.
Vector	Array	1.0	Yes	Legacy class; synchronized methods. Do not use.

Class	Representation	Since	Random access	Notes
Stack	Array	1.0	Yes	Extends Vector; adds push( ), pop( ), peek( ). Legacy; use Deque instead.

The Map Interface

A *map* is a set of *key* objects and a mapping from each member of that set to a *value* object. The Map interface defines an API for defining and querying mappings. Map is part of the Java Collections Framework, but it does not extend the Collection interface, so a Map is a little-c collection, not a big-C Collection. Map is a parameterized type with two type variables. Type variable K represents the type of keys held by the map, and type variable V represents the type of the values that the keys are mapped to. A mapping from String keys to Integer values, for example, can be represented with a Map<String,Integer>.

The most important Map methods are put( ), which defines a key/value pair in the map, get( ), which queries the value associated with a specified key, and remove( ), which removes the specified key and its associated value from the map. The general performance expectation for Map implementations is that these three basic methods are quite efficient: they should usually run in constant time and certainly no worse than in logarithmic time.

An important feature of Map is its support for "collection views." A Map is not a Collection, but its keys can be viewed as a Set, its values can be viewed as a Collection, and its mappings can be viewed as a Set of Map.Entry objects. (Map.Entry is a nested interface defined within Map: it simply represents a single key/value pair.)

The following sample code shows the get( ), put( ), remove( ), and other methods of a Map and also demonstrates some common uses of the collection views of a Map:

```
// New, empty map
Map<String,Integer> m = new HashMap();

// Immutable Map containing a single key-value pair
Map<String,Integer> singleton = Collections.singletonMap("test", -1);

// Note this rarely used syntax to explicitly specify the parameter
// types of the generic emptyMap method. The returned map is immutable
Map<String,Integer> empty = Collections.<String,Integer>emptyMap();

// Populate the map using the put method to define mappings
// from array elements to the index at which each element appears
String[] words = { "this", "is", "a", "test" };
for(int i = 0; i < words.length; i++) {
    m.put(words[i], i);  // Note autoboxing of int to Integer
}
```

```java
// Each key must map to a single value. But keys may map to the
// same value
for(int i = 0; i < words.length; i++) {
    m.put(words[i].toUpperCase(), i);
}

// The putAll() method copies mappings from another Map
m.putAll(singleton);

// Query the mappings with the get() method
for(int i = 0; i < words.length; i++) {
    if (m.get(words[i]) != i) throw new AssertionError();
}

// Key and value membership testing
m.containsKey(words[0]);        // true
m.containsValue(words.length);  // false

// Map keys, values, and entries can be viewed as collections
Set<String> keys = m.keySet();
Collection<Integer> values = m.values();
Set<Map.Entry<String,Integer>> entries = m.entrySet();

// The Map and its collection views typically have useful
// toString  methods
System.out.printf("Map: %s%nKeys: %s%nValues: %s%nEntries: %s%n",
                  m, keys, values, entries);

// These collections can be iterated.
// Most maps have an undefined iteration order (but see SortedMap)
for(String key : m.keySet()) System.out.println(key);
for(Integer value: m.values()) System.out.println(value);

// The Map.Entry<K,V> type represents a single key/value pair in a map
for(Map.Entry<String,Integer> pair : m.entrySet()) {
    // Print out mappings
    System.out.printf("'%s' ==> %d%n", pair.getKey(), pair.getValue());
    // And increment the value of each Entry
    pair.setValue(pair.getValue() + 1);
}

// Removing mappings
m.put("testing", null);   // Mapping to null can "erase" a mapping:
m.get("testing");          // Returns null
m.containsKey("testing"); // Returns true: mapping still exists
m.remove("testing");       // Deletes the mapping altogether
m.get("testing");          // Still returns null
m.containsKey("testing"); // Now returns false.

// Deletions may also be made via the collection views of a map.
// Additions to the map may not be made this way, however.
m.keySet().remove(words[0]);  // Same as m.remove(words[0]);
```

```
// Removes one mapping to the value 2 - usually inefficient and of
// limited use
m.values().remove(2);
// Remove all mappings to 4
m.values().removeAll(Collections.singleton(4));
// Keep only mappings to 2 & 3
m.values().retainAll(Arrays.asList(2, 3));

// Deletions can also be done via iterators
Iterator<Map.Entry<String,Integer>> iter = m.entrySet().iterator();
while(iter.hasNext()) {
    Map.Entry<String,Integer> e = iter.next();
    if (e.getValue() == 2) iter.remove();
}

// Find values that appear in both of two maps.  In general, addAll()
// and retainAll() with keySet() and values() allow union and
// intersection
Set<Integer> v = new HashSet<Integer>(m.values());
v.retainAll(singleton.values());

// Miscellaneous methods
m.clear();              // Deletes all mappings
m.size();               // Returns number of mappings: currently 0
m.isEmpty();            // Returns true
m.equals(empty);        // true: Maps implementations override equals
```

The Map interface includes a variety of general-purpose and special-purpose implementations, which are summarized in Table 8-3. As always, complete details are in
the JDK's documentation and javadoc. All classes in Table 8-3 are in the java.util
package except ConcurrentHashMap and ConcurrentSkipListMap, which are part of
java.util.concurrent.

Table 8-3. Map implementations

Class	Representation	Since	null keys	null values	Notes
HashMap	Hashtable	1.2	Yes	Yes	General-purpose implementation.
Concurren tHashMap	Hashtable	5.0	No	No	General-purpose threadsafe implementation; see ConcurrentMap interface.
Concurrent SkipList Map	Hashtable	6.0	No	No	Specialized threadsafe implementation; see ConcurrentNavigableMap interface.
EnumMap	Array	5.0	No	Yes	Keys are instances of an enum.

Class	Representation	Since	null keys	null values	Notes
LinkedHash Map	Hashtable plus list	1.4	Yes	Yes	Preserves insertion or access order.
TreeMap	Red-black tree	1.2	No	Yes	Sorts by key value. Operations are O(log(n)). See SortedMap interface.
Identity HashMap	Hashtable	1.4	Yes	Yes	Compares with == instead of equals().
WeakHash Map	Hashtable	1.2	Yes	Yes	Doesn't prevent garbage collection of keys.
Hashtable	Hashtable	1.0	No	No	Legacy class; synchronized methods. Do not use.
Properties	Hashtable	1.0	No	No	Extends Hashtable with String methods.

The ConcurrentHashMap and ConcurrentSkipListMap classes of the java.util.con current package implement the ConcurrentMap interface of the same package. Con currentMap extends Map and defines some additional atomic operations that are important in multithreaded programming. For example, the putIfAbsent method is like put() but adds the key/value pair to the map only if the key is not already mapped.

TreeMap implements the SortedMap interface, which extends Map to add methods that take advantage of the sorted nature of the map. SortedMap is quite similar to the SortedSet interface. The firstKey() and lastKey() methods return the first and last keys in the keySet(). And headMap(), tailMap(), and subMap() return a restricted range of the original map.

The Queue and BlockingQueue Interfaces

A *queue* is an ordered collection of elements with methods for extracting elements, in order, from the *head* of the queue. Queue implementations are commonly based on insertion order as in first-in, first-out (FIFO) queues or last-in, first-out (LIFO) queues.

LIFO queues are also known as stacks, and Java provides a Stack class, but its use is strongly discouraged—instead implementations of the Deque interface should be used.

Other orderings are also possible: a *priority queue* orders its elements according to an external Comparator object, or according to the natural ordering of Comparable elements. Unlike a Set, Queue implementations typically allow duplicate elements. Unlike List, the Queue interface does not define methods for manipulating queue elements at arbitrary positions. Only the element at the head of the queue is available for examination. It is common for Queue implementations to have a fixed capacity: when a queue is full, it is not possible to add more elements. Similarly, when a queue is empty, it is not possible to remove any more elements. Because full and empty conditions are a normal part of many queue-based algorithms, the Queue interface defines methods that signal these conditions with return values rather than by throwing exceptions. Specifically, the peek() and poll() methods return null to indicate that the queue is empty. For this reason, most Queue implementations do not allow null elements.

A *blocking queue* is a type of queue that defines blocking put() and take() methods. The put() method adds an element to the queue, waiting, if necessary, until there is space in the queue for the element. And the take() method removes an element from the head of the queue, waiting, if necessary, until there is an element to remove. Blocking queues are an important part of many multithreaded algorithms, and the BlockingQueue interface (which extends Queue) is defined as part of the java.util.concurrent package.

Queues are not nearly as commonly used as sets, lists, and maps, except perhaps in certain multithreaded programming styles. In lieu of example code here, we'll try to clarify the different possible queue insertion and removal operations.

Adding elements to queues

add()
> This Collection method simply adds an element in the normal way. In bounded queues, this method may throw an exception if the queue is full.

offer()
> This Queue method is like add() but returns false instead of throwing an exception if the element cannot be added because a bounded queue is full.
>
> BlockingQueue defines a timeout version of offer() that waits up to a specified amount of time for space to become available in a full queue. Like the basic version of the method, it returns true if the element was inserted and false otherwise.

put()
> This BlockingQueue method blocks: if the element cannot be inserted because the queue is full, put() waits until some other thread removes an element from the queue, and space becomes available for the new element.

Removing elements from queues

remove()

In addition to the Collection.remove() method, which removes a specified element from the queue, the Queue interface defines a no-argument version of remove() that removes and returns the element at the head of the queue. If the queue is empty, this method throws a NoSuchElementException.

poll()

This Queue method removes and returns the element at the head of the queue, like remove() does but returns null if the queue is empty instead of throwing an exception.

BlockingQueue defines a timeout version of poll() that waits up to a specified amount of time for an element to be added to an empty queue.

take()

This BlockingQueue method removes and returns the element at the head of the queue. If the queue is empty, it blocks until some other thread adds an element to the queue.

drainTo()

This BlockingQueue method removes all available elements from the queue and adds them to a specified Collection. It does not block to wait for elements to be added to the queue. A variant of the method accepts a maximum number of elements to drain.

Querying

In this context, querying refers to examining the element at the head without removing it from the queue.

element()

This Queue method returns the element at the head of the queue but does not remove that element from the queue. If the queue is empty, it throws NoSuchE lementException.

peek()

This Queue method is like element but returns null if the queue is empty.

 When using queues, it is usually a good idea to pick one particular style of how to deal with a failure. For example, if you want operations to block until they succeed, then choose put() and take(). If you want to examine the return code of a method to see if the queue operation suceeded, then offer() and poll() are an appropriate choice.

The LinkedList class also implements Queue. It provides unbounded FIFO ordering, and insertion and removal operations require constant time. LinkedList allows null elements, although their use is discouraged when the list is being used as a queue.

There are two other Queue implementations in the java.util package. Priority Queue orders its elements according to a Comparator or orders Comparable elements according to the order defined by their compareTo() methods. The head of a Priori tyQueue is always the smallest element according to the defined ordering. Finally, ArrayDeque is a double-ended queue implementation. It is often used when a stack implementation is needed.

The java.util.concurrent package also contains a number of BlockingQueue implementations, which are designed for use in multithreaded programing style; advanced versions that can remove the need for synchronized methods are available.

Utility Methods

The java.util.Collections class is home to quite a few static utility methods designed for use with collections. One important group of these methods are the collection *wrapper* methods: they return a special-purpose collection wrapped around a collection you specify. The purpose of the wrapper collection is to wrap additional functionality around a collection that does not provide it itself. Wrappers exist to provide thread-safety, write-protection, and runtime type checking. Wrapper collections are always *backed by* the original collection, which means that the methods of the wrapper simply dispatch to the equivalent methods of the wrapped collection. This means that changes made to the collection through the wrapper are visible through the wrapped collection and vice versa.

The first set of wrapper methods provides threadsafe wrappers around collections. Except for the legacy classes Vector and Hashtable, the collection implementations in java.util do not have synchronized methods and are not protected against concurrent access by multiple threads. If you need threadsafe collections and don't mind the additional overhead of synchronization, create them with code like this:

```
List<String> list =
    Collections.synchronizedList(new ArrayList<String>());
Set<Integer> set =
    Collections.synchronizedSet(new HashSet<Integer>());
Map<String,Integer> map =
    Collections.synchronizedMap(new HashMap<String,Integer>());
```

A second set of wrapper methods provides collection objects through which the underlying collection cannot be modified. They return a read-only view of a collection: any attempt to change the content of the collection results in an Unsupported OperationException. These wrappers are useful when you must pass a collection to a method that must not be allowed to modify or mutate the content of the collection in any way:

```
List<Integer> primes = new ArrayList<Integer>();
List<Integer> readonly = Collections.unmodifiableList(primes);
// We can modify the list through primes
primes.addAll(Arrays.asList(2, 3, 5, 7, 11, 13, 17, 19));
// But we can't modify through the read-only wrapper
readonly.add(23);  // UnsupportedOperationException
```

The java.util.Collections class also defines methods to operate on collections. Some of the most notable are methods to sort and search the elements of collections:

```
Collections.sort(list);
// list must be sorted first
int pos = Collections.binarySearch(list, "key");
```

Here are some other interesting Collections methods:

```
// Copy list2 into list1, overwriting list1
Collections.copy(list1, list2);
// Fill list with Object o
Collections.fill(list, o);
// Find the largest element in Collection c
Collections.max(c);
// Find the smallest element in Collection c
Collections.min(c);

Collections.reverse(list);     // Reverse list
Collections.shuffle(list);     // Mix up list
```

It is a good idea to familiarize yourself fully with the utility methods in Collections and Arrays as they can save you from writing your own implementation of a common task.

Special-case collections

In addition to its wrapper methods, the java.util.Collections class also defines utility methods for creating immutable collection instances that contain a single element and other methods for creating empty collections. singleton(), singleton List(), and singletonMap() return immutable Set, List, and Map objects that contain a single specified object or a single key/value pair. These methods are useful when you need to pass a single object to a method that expects a collection.

The Collections class also includes methods that return empty collections. If you are writing a method that returns a collection, it is usually best to handle the no-values-to-return case by returning an empty collection instead of a special-case value like null:

```
Set<Integer> si = Collections.emptySet();
List<String> ss = Collections.emptyList();
Map<String,Integer> m = Collections.emptyMap();
```

Finally, nCopies() returns an immutable List that contains a specified number of copies of a single specified object:

```
List<Integer> tenzeros = Collections.nCopies(10, 0);
```

Arrays and Helper Methods

Arrays of objects and collections serve similar purposes. It is possible to convert from one to the other:

```
String[] a ={ "this", "is", "a", "test" };  // An array
// View array as an ungrowable list
List<String> l = Arrays.asList(a);
// Make a growable copy of the view
List<String> m = new ArrayList<String>(l);

// asList() is a varargs method so we can do this, too:
Set<Character> abc = new HashSet<Character>(Arrays.asList('a', 'b', 'c'));

// Collection defines the toArray  method.  The no-args version creates
// an Object[] array, copies collection elements to it and returns it
// Get set elements as an array
Object[] members = set.toArray();
// Get list elements as an array
Object[] items = list.toArray();
// Get map key objects as an array
Object[] keys = map.keySet().toArray();
// Get map value objects as an array
Object[] values = map.values().toArray();

// If you want the return value to be something other than Object[],
// pass in an array of the appropriate type. If the array is not
// big enough, another one of the same type will be allocated.
// If the array is too big, the collection elements copied to it
// will be null-filled
String[] c = l.toArray(new String[0]);
```

In addition, there are a number of useful helper methods for working with Java's arrays, which are included here for completeness.

The java.lang.System class defines an arraycopy() method that is useful for copying specified elements in one array to a specified position in a second array. The second array must be the same type as the first, and it can even be the same array:

```
char[] text = "Now is the time".toCharArray();
char[] copy = new char[100];
// Copy 10 characters from element 4 of text into copy,
// starting at copy[0]
System.arraycopy(text, 4, copy, 0, 10);

// Move some of the text to later elements, making room for insertions
System.arraycopy(copy, 3, copy, 6, 7);
```

There are also a number of useful static methods defined on the `Arrays` class:

```java
int[] intarray = new int[] { 10, 5, 7, -3 }; // An array of integers
Arrays.sort(intarray);                        // Sort it in place
// Value 7 is found at index 2
int pos = Arrays.binarySearch(intarray, 7);
// Not found: negative return value
pos = Arrays.binarySearch(intarray, 12);

// Arrays of objects can be sorted and searched too
String[] strarray = new String[] { "now", "is", "the", "time" };
Arrays.sort(strarray);   // sorted to: { "is", "now", "the", "time" }

// Arrays.equals  compares all elements of two arrays
String[] clone = (String[]) strarray.clone();
boolean b1 = Arrays.equals(strarray, clone);  // Yes, they're equal

// Arrays.fill  initializes array elements
// An empty array; elements set to 0
byte[] data = new byte[100];
// Set them all to -1
Arrays.fill(data, (byte) -1);
// Set elements 5, 6, 7, 8, 9 to -2
Arrays.fill(data, 5, 10, (byte) -2);
```

Arrays can be treated and manipulated as objects in Java. Given an arbitrary object
o, you can use code such as the following to find out if the object is an array and, if
so, what type of array it is:

```java
Class type = o.getClass();
if (type.isArray()) {
  Class elementType = type.getComponentType();
}
```

Lambda Expressions in the Java Collections

One of the major reasons for introducing lambda expressions in Java 8 was to facilitate the overhaul of the Collections API to allow more modern programming styles
to be used by Java developers. Until the release of Java 8, the handling of data structures in Java looked a little bit dated. Many languages now support a programming
style that allows collections to be treated as a whole, rather than requiring them to
be broken apart and iterated over.

In fact, many Java developers had taken to using alternative data structures libraries
to achieve some of the expressivity and productivity that they felt was lacking in the
Collections API. The key to upgrading the APIs was to introduce new methods that
would accept lambda expressions as parameters—to define *what* needed to be done,
rather than precisely *how*.

The desire to add new methods to existing interfaces was directly responsible for the new language feature referred to as *default methods* (see "Default Methods" on page 140 for more details). Without this new mechanism, older implementations of the Collections interfaces would fail to compile under Java 8, and would fail to link if loaded into a Java 8 runtime.

In this section, we will give a basic introduction to the use of lambda expressions in the Java Collections. For a fuller treatment, see *Java 8 Lambdas* by Richard Warburton (O'Reilly).

Functional Approaches

The approach that Java 8 wished to enable was derived from functional programming languages and styles. We met some of these key patterns in "Method References" on page 173—let's reintroduce them and look at some examples of each.

Filter

The idiom applies a piece of code (that returns either true or false) to each element in a collection, and builds up a new collection consisting of those elements that "passed the test" (i.e., the bit of code returned true when applied to the element).

For example, let's look at some code to work with a collection of cats and pick out the tigers:

```
String[] input = {"tiger", "cat", "TIGER", "Tiger", "leopard"};
List<String> cats = Arrays.asList(input);
String search = "tiger";
String tigers = cats.stream()
                    .filter(s -> s.equalsIgnoreCase(search))
                    .collect(Collectors.joining(", "));
System.out.println(tigers);
```

The key piece is the call to filter(), which takes a lambda expression. The lambda takes in a string, and returns a Boolean value. This is applied over the whole collection cats, and a new collection is created, which only contains tigers (however they were capitalized).

The filter() method takes in an instance of the Predicate interface, from the new package java.util.function. This is a functional interface, with only a single non-default method, and so is a perfect fit for a lambda expression.

Note the final call to collect(); this is an essential part of the API and is used to "gather up" the results at the end of the lambda operations. We'll discuss it in more detail in the next section.

Predicate has some other very useful default methods, such as for constructing combined predicates by using logic operations. For example, if the tigers want to admit leopards into their group, this can be represented by using the or() method:

```
Predicate<String> p = s -> s.equalsIgnoreCase(search);
Predicate<String> combined = p.or(s -> s.equals("leopard"));
String pride = cats.stream()
                   .filter(combined)
                   .collect(Collectors.joining(", "));
System.out.println(pride);
```

Note that the `Predicate<String>` object p must be explicitly created, so that the defaulted `or()` method can be called on it and the second lambda expression (which will also be automatically converted to a `Predicate<String>`) passed to it.

Map

The map idiom in Java 8 makes use of a new interface `Function<T, R>` in the package `java.util.function`. Like `Predicate<T>`, this is a functional interface, and so only has one nondefaulted method, `apply()`. The map idiom is about transforming a collection of one type in a collection of a potentially different type. This shows up in the API as the fact that `Function<T, R>` has two separate type parameters. The name of the type parameter R indicates that this represents the return type of the function.

Let's look at a code example that uses `map()`:

```
List<Integer> namesLength = cats.stream()
                   .map(String::length)
                   .collect(Collectors.toList());
System.out.println(namesLength);
```

forEach

The map and filter idioms are used to create one collection from another. In languages that are strongly functional, this would be combined with requiring that the original collection was not affected by the body of the lambda as it touched each element. In computer science terms, this means that the lambda body should be "side-effect free."

In Java, of course, we often need to deal with mutable data, so the new Collections API provides a way to mutate elements as the collection is traversed—the `for Each()` method. This takes an argument of type `Consumer<T>`, that is a functional interface that is expected to operate by side effects (although whether it actually mutates the data or not is of lesser importance). This means that the signature of lambdas that can be converted to `Consumer<T>` is `(T t) → void`. Let's look at a quick example of `forEach()`:

```
List<String> pets =
   Arrays.asList("dog", "cat", "fish", "iguana", "ferret");
pets.stream().forEach(System.out::println);
```

In this example, we are simply printing out each member of the collection. However, we're doing so by using a special kind of method reference as a lambda expression. This type of method reference is called a *bound method reference*, as it involves a specific object (in this case, the object `System.out`, which is a static public field of `System`). This is equivalent to the lambda expression:

```
s -> System.out.println(s);
```

This is of course eligible for conversion to an instance of a type that implements `Consumer<? super String>` as required by the method signature.

 Nothing prevents a `map()` or `filter()` call from mutating elements. It is only a convention that they must not, but it's one that every Java programmer should adhere to.

There's one final functional technique that we should look at before we move on. This is the practice of aggregating a collection down to a single value, and it's the subject of our next section.

Reduce

Let's look at the `reduce()` method. This implements the reduce idiom, which is really a family of similar and related operations, some referred to as fold, or aggregation operations.

In Java 8, `reduce()` takes two arguments. These are the initial value, which is often called the identity (or zero), and a function to apply step by step. This function is of type `BinaryOperator<T>`, which is another functional interface that takes in two arguments of the same type, and returns another value of that type. This second argument to `reduce()` is a two-argument lambda. `reduce()` is defined in the java doc like this:

```
T reduce(T identity, BinaryOperator<T> aggregator);
```

The easy way to think about the second argument to `reduce()` is that it creates a "running total" as it runs over the stream. It starts by combining the identity with the first element of the stream to produce the first result, then combines that result with the second element of the stream, and so on.

It can help to imagine that the implementation of `reduce()` works a bit like this:

```
public T reduce(T identity, BinaryOperator<T> aggregator) {
    T runningTotal = identity;
    for (T element : myStream) {
        runningTotal = aggregator.apply(runningTotal, element);
    }

    return result;
}
```

In practice, implementations of reduce() can be more sophisticated than these, and can even execute in parallel if the data structure and operations are amenable to this.

Let's look at a quick example of a reduce() and calculate the sum of some primes:

```
double sumPrimes = ((double)Stream.of(2, 3, 5, 7, 11, 13, 17, 19, 23)
        .reduce(0, (x, y) -> {return x + y;})));
System.out.println("Sum of some primes: " + sumPrimes);
```

In all of the examples we've met in this section, you may have noticed the presence of a stream() method call on the List instance. This is part of the evolution of the Collections—it was originally chosen partly out of necessity, but has proved to be an excellent abstraction. Let's move on to discuss the Streams API in more detail.

The Streams API

The issue that caused the library designers to introduce the Streams API was the large number of implementations of the core collections interfaces present in the wild. As these implementations predate Java 8 and lambdas, they would not have any of the methods corresponding to the new functional operations. Worse still, as method names such as map() and filter() have never been part of the interface of the Collections, implementations may already have methods with those names.

To work around this problem, a new abstraction called a Stream was introduced— the idea being that a Stream object can be generated from a collection object via the stream() method. This Stream object, being new and under the control of the library designers, is then guaranteed to be free of method name collisions. This then mitigates the risk of clash, as only implementations that contained a stream() method would be affected.

A Stream object plays a similar role to an Iterator in the new approach to collections code. The overall idea is for the developer to build up a sequence (or "pipeline") of operations (such as map, filter, or reduce) that need to be applied to the collection as a whole. The actual content of the operations will usually be expressed by using a lambda expression for each operation.

At the end of the pipeline, the results need to be gathered up, or "materialized" back into an actual collection again. This is done either by using a Collector or by finishing the pipeline with a "terminal method" such as reduce() that returns an actual value, rather than another stream. Overall, the new approach to collections looks like this:

```
             stream()   filter()   map()   collect()
Collection -> Stream -> Stream -> Stream -> Collection
```

The Stream class behaves as a sequence of elements that are accessed one at a time (although there are some types of streams that support parallel access and can be

---

used to process larger collections in a naturally multithreaded way). In a similar way to an `Iterator`, the `Stream` is used to take each item in turn.

As is usual for generic classes in Java, `Stream` is parameterized by a reference type. However, in many cases, we actually want streams of primitive types, especially ints and doubles. We cannot have `Stream<int>`, so instead in `java.util.stream` there are special (nongeneric) classes such as `IntStream` and `DoubleStream`. These are known as *primitive specializations* of the `Stream` class and have APIs that are very similar to the general `Stream` methods, except that they use primitives where appropriate.

For example, in the `reduce()` example, we're actually using primitive specialization over most of the pipeline.

Lazy evaluation

In fact, streams are more general than iterators (or even collections), as streams do not manage storage for data. In earlier versions of Java, there was always a presumption that all of the elements of a collection existed (usually in memory). It was possible to work around this in a limited way by insisting on the use of iterators everywhere, and by having the iterators construct elements on the fly. However, this was neither very convenient or that common.

By contrast, streams are an abstraction for managing data, rather than being concerned with the details of storage. This makes it possible to handle more subtle data structures than just finite collections. For example, infinite streams can easily be represented by the `Stream` interface, and can be used as a way to, for example, handle the set of all square numbers. Let's see how we could accomplish this using a `Stream`:

```
public class SquareGenerator implements IntSupplier {
    private int current = 1;

    @Override
    public synchronized int getAsInt() {
        int thisResult = current * current;
        current++;
        return thisResult;
    }
}

IntStream squares = IntStream.generate(new SquareGenerator());
PrimitiveIterator.OfInt stepThrough = squares.iterator();
for (int i = 0; i < 10; i++) {
    System.out.println(stepThrough.nextInt());
}
System.out.println("First iterator done...");

// We can go on as long as we like...
for (int i = 0; i < 10; i++) {
```

```
    System.out.println(stepThrough.nextInt());
  }
```

One significant consequence of modeling the infinite stream is that methods like collect() won't work. This is because we can't materialize the whole stream to a collection (we would run out of memory before we created the infinite amount of objects we would need). Instead, we must adopt a model in which we pull the elements out of the stream as we need them. Essentially, we need a bit of code that returns the next element as we demand it. The key technique that is used to accomplish this is *lazy evaluation*. This essentially means that values are not necessarily computed until they are needed.

 Lazy evaluation is a big change for Java, as until JDK 8 the value of an expression was always computed as soon as it was assigned to a variable (or passed into a method). This familiar model, where values are computed immediately, is called "eager evaluation" and it is the default behavior for evaluation of expressions in most mainstream programming languages.

Fortunately, lazy evaluation is largely a burden that falls on the library writer, not the developer, and for the most part when using the Streams API, Java developers don't need to think closely about lazy evaluation. Let's finish off our discussion of streams by looking at an extended code example using reduce(), and calculate the average word length in some Shakespeare quotes:

```
String[] billyQuotes = {"For Brutus is an honourable man",
  "Give me your hands if we be friends and Robin shall restore amends",
  "Misery acquaints a man with strange bedfellows"};
List<String> quotes = Arrays.asList(billyQuotes);


// Create a temporary collection for our words
List<String> words = quotes.stream()
        .flatMap(line -> Stream.of(line.split(" +")));
        .collect(Collectors.toList());
long wordCount = words.size();

// The cast to double is only needed to prevent Java from using
// integer division
double aveLength = ((double) words.stream()
        .map(String::length)
        .reduce(0, (x, y) -> {return x + y;})) / wordCount;
System.out.println("Average word length: " + aveLength);
```

In this example, we've introduced the flatMap() method. In our example, it takes in a single string, line, and returns a stream of strings, which is obtained by splitting up the line into its component words. These are then "flattened" so that all the substreams from each string are just combined into a single stream.

This has the effect of splitting up each quote into its component words, and making one superstream out of them. We count the words by creating the object words, essentially "pausing" halfway through the stream pipeline, and rematerializing into a collection to get the number of words before resuming our stream operations.

Once we've done that, we can proceed with the reduce, and add up the length of all the words, before dividing by the number of words that we have, across the quotes. Remember that streams are a lazy abstraction, so to perform an eager operation (like getting the size of a collection that backs a stream) we have to rematerialize the collection.

Streams utility default methods

Java 8 takes the opportunity to introduce a number of new methods to the Java Collections libraries. Now that the language supports default methods, it is possible to add new methods to the Collections without breaking backward compatibility.

Some of these methods are "scaffolding methods" for the Streams abstraction. These include methods such as Collection::stream, Collection::parallelStream, and Collection::spliterator (which has specialized forms List::spliterator and Set::spliterator).

Others are "missing methods," such as Map::remove and Map::replace. This also includes the List::sort method, that is defined in List like this:

```java
// Essentially just forwards to the helper method in Collections
public default void sort(Comparator<? super E> c) {
    Collections.<E>sort(this, c);
}
```

Also in the missing methods is Map::putIfAbsent, which has been adopted from the ConcurrentMap interface in java.util.concurrent.

Another missing method worth noting is Map::getOrDefault, which allows the programmer to avoid a lot of tedious null checks, by providing a value that should be returned if the key is not found.

The remaining methods provide additional functional techniques using the interfaces of java.util.function:

Collection::removeIf
: This method takes a Predicate and iterates internally over the collection, removing any elements that satisfy the predicate object.

Map::forEach
: The single argument to this method is a lambda expression that takes two arguments (one of the key's type and one of the value's type) and returns void. This is converted to an instance of BiConsumer and is applied to each key-value pair in the map.

`Map::computeIfAbsent`

Takes a key and a lambda expression that maps the key type to the value type. If the specified key (first parameter) is not present in the map, then, computes a default value by using the lambda expression and puts it in the map.

(See also `Map::computeIfPresent`, `Map::compute`, and `Map::merge`.)

Conclusion

In this chapter, we've met the Java Collections libraries, and seen how to start working with Java's implementations of fundamental and classic data structures. We've met the general `Collection` interface, as well as `List`, `Set`, and `Map`. We've seen the original, iterative way of handling collections, and also introduced the new Java 8 style, based on ideas from fundamental programming. Finally, we've met the Streams API and seen how the new approach is more general, and is able to express more subtle programming concepts than the classic approach.

Let's move on. In the next chapter, we'll continue looking at data, and common tasks like text processing, handling numeric data, and Java 8's new date and time libraries.

Handling Common
Data Formats

Most of programming is handling data in various formats. In this chapter, we will introduce Java's support for handling two big classes of data—text and numbers. The second half of the chapter will focus on handling date and time information. This is of particular interest as Java 8 ships a completely new API for handling date and time. We cover this new interface in some depth, before finishing the chapter by briefly discussing Java's original date and time API.

Many applications are still using the legacy APIs, so developers need to be aware of the old way of doing things, but the new APIs are so much better that we recommend converting as soon as possible. Before we get to those more complex formats, let's get underway by talking about textual data and strings.

Text

We have already met Java's strings on many occasions. They consist of sequences of Unicode characters, and are represented as instances of the `String` class. Strings are one of the most common types of data that Java programs process (a claim you can investigate for yourself by using the `jmap` tool that we'll meet in Chapter 13).

In this section, we'll meet the `String` class in some more depth, and understand why it is in a rather unique position within the Java language. Later in the section, we'll introduce regular expressions, a very common abstraction for searching text for patterns (and a classic tool in the programmer's arsenal).

Special Syntax for Strings

The `String` class is handled in a somewhat special way by the Java language. This is because, despite not being a primitive type, strings are so common that it makes sense for Java to have a number of special syntax features designed to make handling strings easy. Let's look at some examples of special syntax features for strings that Java provides.

String literals

As we saw in Chapter 2, Java allows a sequence of characters to be placed in double quotes to create a literal string object. Like this:

```
String pet = "Cat";
```

Without this special syntax, we would have to write acres of horrible code like this:

```
char[] pullingTeeth = {'C', 'a', 't'};
String pet = new String(pullingTeeth);
```

This would get tedious extremely quickly, so it's no surprise that Java, like all modern programming languages, provides a simple string literal syntax. The string literals are perfectly sound objects, so code like this is completely legal:

```
System.out.println("Dog".length());
```

toString()

This method is defined on Object, and is designed to allow easy conversion of any object to a string. This makes it easy to print out any object, by using the method System.out.println(). This method is actually PrintStream::println because System.out is a static field of type PrintStream. Let's see how this method is defined:

```
public void println(Object x) {
    String s = String.valueOf(x);
    synchronized (this) {
        print(s);
        newLine();
    }
}
```

This creates a new string by using the static method String::valueOf():

```
public static String valueOf(Object obj) {
    return (obj == null) ? "null" : obj.toString();
}
```

The static valueOf() method is used instead of toString() directly, to avoid a NullPointerException in the case where obj is null.

This construction means that toString() is always available for any object, and this turns out to come in very handy for another major syntax feature that Java provides —string concatenation.

String concatenation

Java has a language feature where we can create new strings by "adding" the characters from one string onto the end of another. This is called *string concatenation* and uses the operator +. It works by first creating a "working area" in the form of a StringBuilder object that contains the same sequence of characters as the original string.

The builder object is then updated and the characters from the additional string are added onto the end. Finally, toString() is called on the StringBuilder object (which now contains the characters from both strings). This gives us a new string with all the characters in it. All of this code is created automatically by javac whenever we use the + operator to concatenate strings.

The concatenation process returns a completely new String object, as we can see in this example:

```
String s1 = "AB";
String s2 = "CD";

String s3 = s1;
System.out.println(s1 == s3); // Same object?

s3 = s1 + s2;
System.out.println(s1 == s3); // Still same?
System.out.println(s1);
System.out.println(s3);
```

The concatentation example directly shows that the + operator is not altering (or *mutating*) s1 in place. This is an example of a more general principle: Java's strings are immutable. This means that once the characters that make up the string have been chosen and the String object has been created, the String cannot be changed. This is an important language principle in Java, so let's look at it in a little more depth.

String Immutability

In order to "change" a string, as we saw when we discussed string concatenation, we actually need to create an intermediate StringBuilder object to act as a temporary scratch area, and then call toString() on it, to bake it into a new instance of String. Let's see how this works in code:

```
String pet = "Cat";
StringBuilder sb = new StringBuilder(pet);
sb.append("amaran");
```

```
String boat = sb.toString();
System.out.println(boat);
```

Code like this is equivalent to what javac would generate if, instead, we had written:

```
String pet = "Cat";
String boat = pet + "amaran";
System.out.println(boat);
```

Of course, as well as being used under the hood by javac, the StringBuilder class can also be used directly in application code, as we've seen.

 Along with StringBuilder Java also has a StringBuffer class. This comes from the oldest versions of Java, and should not be used for new development—use String Builder instead, unless you really need to share the construction of a new string between multiple threads.

String immutability is an extremely useful language feature. For example, suppose the + changed a string instead of creating a new one; then whenever any thread concatenated two strings together, all other threads would also see the change. This is unlikely to be a useful behavior for most programs, and so immutability makes good sense.

Hash codes and effective immutability

We have already met the hashCode() method in Chapter 5, where we described the contract that the method must satisfy. Let's take a look at the JDK source code and see how the method String::hashCode() is defined:

```
public int hashCode() {
    int h = hash;
    if (h == 0 && value.length > 0) {
        char val[] = value;

        for (int i = 0; i < value.length; i++) {
            h = 31 * h + val[i];
        }
        hash = h;
    }
    return h;
}
```

The field hash holds the hash code of the string, and the field value is a char[] that holds the characters that actually make up the string. As we can see from the code, the hash is computed by looping over all the characters of the string. It therefore takes a number of machine instructions proportional to the number of characters in the string. For very large strings this could take a bit of time. Rather than precompute the hash value, Java only calculates it when it is needed.

When the method runs, the hash is computed by stepping through the array of characters. At the end of the array, we exit the for loop and write the computed hash back into the field hash. Now, when this method is called again, the value has already been computed, and so we can just use the cached value. So subsequent calls to hashCode() return immediately.

The computation of a string's hash code is an example of a *benign data race*. In a program with multiple threads, they could race to compute the hash code. However, they would all eventually arrive at exactly the same answer—hence the term *benign*.

All of the fields of the String class are final, except for hash. So Java's strings are not, strictly speaking, immutable. However, because the hash field is just a cache of a value that is deterministically computed from the other fields, which are all immutable, then provided String has been coded correctly, it will behave as if it was immutable. Classes that have this property are called *effectively immutable*—they are quite rare in practice, and working programmers can usually ignore the distinction between truly immutable and effectively immutable data.

Regular Expressions

Java has support for *regular expressions* (often shortened to *regex* or *regexp*). These are a representation of a search pattern used to scan and match text. A regex is a sequence of characters that we want to search for. They can be very simple—for example, abc means that we're looking for *a*, followed immediately by *b*, followed immediately by *c*, anywhere within the text we're searching through. Note that a search pattern may match an input text in zero, one, or more places.

The simplest regexs are just sequences of literal characters, like abc. However, the language of regexs can express more complex and subtle ideas than just literal sequences. For example, a regex can represent patterns to match like:

- A numeric digit
- Any letter
- Any number of letters, which must all be in the range *a* to *j* but can be upper- or lowercase
- *a* followed by any four characters, followed by *b*

The syntax we use to write regular expressions is simple, but because we can build up complex patterns, it is often possible to write an expression that does not implement precisely what we wanted. When using regexs, it is very important to always test them fully. This should include both test cases that should pass and cases that should fail.

To express these more complex patterns, regexs use *metacharacters*. These are special characters that indicate that special processing is required. This can be thought of as similar to the use of the * character in the Unix or Windows shell. In those circumstances, it is understood that the * is not to be interpreted literally but instead means "anything." If we wanted to list all the Java source files in the current directory on Unix, we would issue the command:

```
ls *.java
```

The metacharacters of regexs are similar, but there are far more of them, and they are far more flexible than the set available in shells. They also have different meanings than they do in shell scripts, so don't get confused.

Let's meet a couple of examples. Suppose we want to have a spell-checking program that is relaxed about the difference in spelling between British and American English. This means that *honor* and *honour* should both be accepted as valid spelling choices. This is easy to do with regular expressions.

Java uses a class called `Pattern` (from the package `java.util.regex`) to represent a regex. This class can't be directly instantiated, however. Instead, new instances are created by using a static factory method, `compile()`. From a pattern, we then derive a `Matcher` for a particular input string that we can use to explore the input string. For example, let's examine a bit of Shakespeare from the play *Julius Caesar*:

```
Pattern p = Pattern.compile("honou?r");

String caesarUK = "For Brutus is an honourable man";
Matcher mUK = p.matcher(caesarUK);

String caesarUS = "For Brutus is an honorable man";
Matcher mUS = p.matcher(caesarUS);

System.out.println("Matches UK spelling? " + mUK.find());
System.out.println("Matches US spelling? " + mUS.find());
```

Be careful when using `Matcher` as it has a method called `matches()`. However, this method indicates whether the pattern can cover the entire input string. It will return `false` if the pattern only starts matching in the middle of the string.

The last example introduces our first regex metacharacter ?, in the pattern honou?r. This means "the preceding character is optional"—so both honour and honor will match. Let's look at another example. Suppose we want to match both *minimize* and *minimise* (the latter spelling is more common in British English). We can use square brackets to indicate that any character from a set (but only one alternative) [ ] can be used—like this:

```
Pattern p = Pattern.compile("minimi[sz]e");
```

Table 9-1 provides an expanded list of metacharacters available for Java regexs.

Table 9-1. Regex metacharacters

Metacharacter	Meaning	Notes
?	Optional character—zero or one instance	
*	Zero or more of preceding character	
+	One or more of preceding character	
{M,N}	Between M and N instances of preceding character	
\d	A digit	
\D	A nondigit character	
\w	A word character	Digits, letters, and _
\W	A nonword character	
\s	A whitespace character	
\S	A nonwhitespace character	
\n	Newline character	
\t	Tab character	
.	Any single character	Does not include newline in Java
[ ]	Any character contained with the brackets	Called a character class
[^]	Any character not contained with the brackets	Called a negated character class
( )	Build up a group of pattern elements	Called a group (or capturing group)
		Define alternative possbilities	Implements logical OR
^	Start of string	
$	End of string	

There are a few more, but this is the basic list, and from this, we can construct more complex expressions for matching such as the examples given earlier in this section:

```
// Note that we have to use \\ because we need a literal \
// and Java uses a single \ as an escape character
String pStr = "\\d"; // A numeric digit
String text = "Apollo 13";
Pattern p = Pattern.compile(pStr);
Matcher m = p.matcher(text);
System.out.print(pStr + " matches " + text + "? " + m.find());
System.out.println(" ; match: " + m.group());


pStr = "[a..zA..Z]"; //Any letter
p = Pattern.compile(pStr);
m = p.matcher(text);
System.out.print(pStr + " matches " + text + "? " + m.find());
System.out.println(" ; match: " + m.group());

// Any number of letters, which must all be in the range 'a' to 'j'
// but can be upper- or lowercase
pStr = "([a..jA..J]*)";
p = Pattern.compile(pStr);
m = p.matcher(text);
System.out.print(pStr + " matches " + text + "? " + m.find());
System.out.println(" ; match: " + m.group());

text = "abacab";
pStr = "a....b"; // 'a' followed by any four characters, followed by 'b'
p = Pattern.compile(pStr);
m = p.matcher(text);
System.out.print(pStr + " matches " + text + "? " + m.find());
System.out.println(" ; match: " + m.group());
```

Let's conclude our quick tour of regular expressions by meeting a new method that was added to Pattern as part of Java 8: asPredicate(). This method is present to allow us to easily bridge from regular expressions to the Java Collections and their new support for lambda expressions.

For example, suppose we have a regex and a collection of strings. It's very natural to ask the question: "Which strings match against the regex?" We do this by using the filter idiom, and by converting the regex to a Predicate using the helper method, like this:

```
String pStr = "\\d"; // A numeric digit
Pattern p = Pattern.compile(pStr);

String[] inputs = {"Cat", "Dog", "Ice-9", "99 Luftballoons"};
List<String> ls = Arrays.asList(inputs);
List<String> containDigits = ls.stream()
                               .filter(p.asPredicate())
                               .collect(Collectors.toList());
System.out.println(containDigits);
```

Java's built-in support for text processing is more than adequate for the majority of text processing tasks that business applications normally require. More advanced tasks, such as the search and processing of very large data sets, or complex parsing (including formal grammars) are outside the scope of this book, but Java has a large ecosystem of helpful libraries and bindings to specialized technologies for text processing and analysis.

Numbers and Math

In this section, we will discuss Java's support for numeric types in some more detail. In particular, we'll discuss the two's complement representation of integral types that Java uses. We'll introduce floating-point representations, and touch on some of the problems they can cause. We'll work through examples that use some of Java's library functions for standard mathematical operations.

How Java Represents Integer Types

Java's integer types are all signed, as we first mentioned in "Primitive Data Types" on page 22. This means that all integer types can represent both positive and negative numbers. As computers work with binary, this means that the only really logical way to represent this is to split the possible bit patterns up and use half of them to represent negative numbers.

Let's work with Java's byte type to investigate how Java represents integers. This has 8 bits, so can represent 256 different numbers (i.e., 128 negative and 128 non-negative numbers). It's logical to use the pattern 0b0000_0000 to represent zero (recall that Java has the syntax 0b<binary digits> to represent numbers as binary), and then it's easy to figure out the bit patterns for the positive numbers:

```java
byte b = 0b0000_0001;
System.out.println(b); // 1

b = 0b0000_0010;
System.out.println(b); // 2

b = 0b0000_0011;
System.out.println(b); // 3

// ...

b = 0b0111_1111;
System.out.println(b); // 127
```

When we set the first bit of the byte, the sign should change (as we have now used up all of the bit patterns that we've set aside for non-negative numbers). So the pattern 0b1000_0000 should represent some negative number—but which one?

As a consequence of how we've defined things, in this representation we have a very simple way to identify whether a bit pattern corresponds to a negative number: if the high-end bit of a bit pattern is a 1, then the number being represented is negative.

Consider the bit pattern consisting of all set bits: `0b1111_1111`. If we add 1 to this number, then the result will overflow the 8 bits of storage that a `byte` has, resulting in `0b1_0000_0000`. If we want to constrain this to fit within the `byte` data type, then we should ignore the overflow, so this becomes `0b0000_0000` - zero. It is therefore natural to adopt the representation that "all set bits is -1." This allows for natural arithmetic behavior, like this:

```
b = (byte) 0b1111_1111; // -1
System.out.println(b);
b++;
System.out.println(b);

b = (byte) 0b1111_1110; // -2
System.out.println(b);
b++;
System.out.println(b);
```

Finally, let's look at the number that `0b1000_0000` represents. It's the most negative number that the type can represent, so for `byte`:

```
b = (byte) 0b1000_0000;
System.out.println(b); // -128
```

This representation is called *two's complement*, and is the most common representation for signed integers. To use it effectively, there are only two points that you need to remember:

- A bit pattern of all 1's is the representation for -1.
- If the high bit is set, the number is negative.

Java's other integer types (`short`, `int`, and `long`) behave in very similar ways but with more bits in their representation. The `char` datatype is different because it represents a Unicode character, but in some ways behaves as an unsigned 16-bit numeric type. It is not normally regarded as an integer type by Java programmers.

Java and Floating-Point Numbers

Computers represent numbers using binary. We've seen how Java uses the two's complement representation for integers. But what about fractions or decimals? Java, like almost all modern programming languages, represents them using *floating-point arithmetic*. Let's take a look at how this works, first in base-10 (regular decimal) and then in binary. Java defines the two most important mathematical constants, e and π as constants in `java.lang.Math` like this:

```
public static final double E = 2.7182818284590452354;
public static final double PI = 3.14159265358979323846;
```

Of course, these constants are actually *irrational numbers* and cannot be precisely expressed as a fraction, or by any finite decimal number.[1] This means that whenever we try to represent them in a computer, there is always rounding error. Let's suppose we only want to deal with eight digits of π, and we want to represent the digits as a whole number. We can use a representation like this:

$$314159265 \cdot 10^{-8}$$

This starts to suggest the basis of how floating-point numbers work. We use some of the bits to represent the significant digits (314159265, in our example) of the number and some bits to represent the *exponent* of the base (-8, in our example). The collection of significant digits is called the *significand* and the exponent describes whether we need to shift the significand up or down to get to the desired number.

Of course, in the examples we've met until now, we've been working in base-10. Computers use binary, so we need to use this as the base in our floating-point examples. This introduces some additional complications.

 The number `0.1` cannot be expressed as a finite sequence of binary digits. This means that virtually all calculations that humans care about will lose precision when performed in floating point, and rounding error is essentially inevitable.

Let's look at an example that shows the rounding problem:

```
double d = 0.3;
System.out.println(d); // Special-cased to avoid ugly representation

double d2 = 0.2;
// Should be -0.1 but prints -0.09999999999999998
System.out.println(d2 - d);
```

The standard that describes floating-point arithmetic is IEEE-754 and Java's support for floating point is based on that standard. The standard uses 24 binary digits for standard precision and 53 binary digits for double precision.

As we mentioned briefly in Chapter 2, Java can be more accurate than the standard requires, by using hardware features if they are available. In extremely rare cases, usually where very strict compatability with other (possibly older) platforms is required, this behavior can be switched off by using `strictfp` to mandate perfect compliance with the IEEE-754 standard. This is almost never necessary and the vast majority of programmers will never need to use (or even see) this keyword.

---

1 In fact, they are actually two of the known examples of *transcendental numbers*.

BigDecimal

Rounding error is a constant source of headaches for programmers who work with floating-point numbers. In response, Java has a class `java.math.BigDecimal` that provides arbitrary precision arithmetic, in a decimal representation. This works around the problem of `0.1` not having a finite representation in binary, but there are still some edge conditions when converting to or from Java's primitive types, as you can see:

```java
double d = 0.3;
System.out.println(d);

BigDecimal bd = new BigDecimal(d);
System.out.println(bd);

bd = new BigDecimal("0.3");
System.out.println(bd);
```

However, even with all arithmetic performed in base-10, there are still numbers, such as 1/3, that do not have a terminating decimal representation. Let's see what happens when we try to represent such numbers using `BigDecimal`:

```java
bd = new BigDecimal(BigInteger.ONE);
bd.divide(new BigDecimal(3.0));
System.out.println(bd); // Should be 1/3
```

As `BigDecimal` can't represent 1/3 precisely, the call to `divide()` blows up with `ArithmeticException`. When working with `BigDecimal`, it is therefore necessary to be acutely aware of exactly which operations could result in a nonterminating decimal result. To make matters worse, `ArithmeticException` is an unchecked, runtime exception and so the Java compiler does not even warn about possible exceptions of this type.

As as a final note on floating-point numbers, the paper "What Every Computer Scientist Should Know About Floating-Point Arithmetic" by David Goldberg should be considered essential further reading for all professional programmers. It is easily and freely obtainable on the Internet.

Java's Standard Library of Mathematical Functions

To conclude this look at Java's support for numeric data and math, let's take a quick tour of the standard library of functions that Java ships with. These are mostly static helper methods that are located on the class `java.lang.Math` and include functions like:

abs()
:   Returns the absolute value of a number. Has overloaded forms for various primitive types.

Trigonometric functions

Basic functions for computing the sine, cosine, tangent, etc. Java also includes hyperbolic versions and the inverse functions (such as arc sine).

max(), min()

Overloaded functions to return the greater and smaller of two arguments (both of the same numeric type).

floor()

Used to return the largest integer smaller than the argument (which is a double). ceil() returns the smallest integer larger than the argument.

pow(), exp(), log()

Functions for raising one number to the power of another, and for computing exponentials and natural logarithms. log10() provides logarithms to base-10, rather than the natural base.

Let's look at some simple examples of how to use these functions:

```
System.out.println(Math.abs(2));
System.out.println(Math.abs(-2));

double cosp3 = Math.cos(0.3);
double sinp3 = Math.sin(0.3);
System.out.println((cosp3 * cosp3 + sinp3 * sinp3)); // Always 1.0

System.out.println(Math.max(0.3, 0.7));
System.out.println(Math.max(0.3, -0.3));
System.out.println(Math.max(-0.3, -0.7));

System.out.println(Math.min(0.3, 0.7));
System.out.println(Math.min(0.3, -0.3));
System.out.println(Math.min(-0.3, -0.7));

System.out.println(Math.floor(1.3));
System.out.println(Math.ceil(1.3));
System.out.println(Math.floor(7.5));
System.out.println(Math.ceil(7.5));

System.out.println(Math.round(1.3)); // Returns long
System.out.println(Math.round(7.5)); // Returns long

System.out.println(Math.pow(2.0, 10.0));
System.out.println(Math.exp(1));
System.out.println(Math.exp(2));
System.out.println(Math.log(2.718281828459045));
System.out.println(Math.log10(100_000));
System.out.println(Math.log10(Integer.MAX_VALUE));

System.out.println(Math.random());
System.out.println("Let's toss a coin: ");
```

```
if (Math.random() > 0.5) {
    System.out.println("It's heads");
} else {
    System.out.println("It's tails");
}
```

To conclude this section, let's briefly discuss Java's random() function. When this is first called, it sets up a new instance of java.util.Random. This is a *pseudorandom number generator* (PRNG)—a deterministic piece of code that produces numbers that *look* random but are actually produced by a mathematical formula.[2] In Java's case, the formula used for the PRNG is pretty simple, for example:

```
// From java.util.Random
public double nextDouble() {
    return (((long)(next(26)) << 27) + next(27)) * DOUBLE_UNIT;
}
```

If the sequence of pseudorandom numbers always starts at the same place, then exactly the same stream of numbers will be produced. To get around this problem, the PRNG is seeded by a value that should contain as much true randomness as possible. For this source of randomness for the seed value, Java uses a CPU counter value that is normally used for high-precision timing.

 While Java's built-in pseudorandom numbers are fine for most general applications, some specialist applications (notably cryptography and some types of simulations) have much more stringent requirements. If you are working on an application of that sort, seek expert advice from programmers who are already working in the area.

Now that we've looked at text and numeric data, let's move on to look at another of the most frequently encountered kinds of data: date and time information.

Java 8 Date and Time

Almost all business software applications have some notion of date and time. When modeling real-world events or interactions, collecting a point at which the event occurred is critical for future reporting or comparison of domain objects. Java 8 brings a complete overhaul to the way that developers work with date and time. This section introduces those concepts for Java 8. In earlier versions, the only support is via classes such as java.util.Date that do not model the concepts. Code that uses the older APIs should move as soon as possible.

---

2 It is very difficult to get computers to produce true random numbers, and in the rare cases where this is done, specialized hardware is usually necessary.

Introducing the Java 8 Date and Time API

Java 8 introduces a new package `java.time`, which contains the core classes that most developers work with. It is split into four subpackages:

`java.time.chrono`
Alternative chronologies that developers using calendaring systems that do not follow the ISO standard will interact with. An example would be a Japanese calendaring system.

`java.time.format`
Contains the `DateTimeFormatter` used for converting date and time objects into a `String` and also for parsing strings into the data and time objects.

`java.time.temporal`
Contains the interfaces required by the core date and time classes and also abstractions (such as queries and adjusters) for advanced operations with dates.

`java.time.zone`
Classes used for the underlying time zone rules; most developers won't require this package.

One of the most important concepts when representing time is the idea of an instantaneous point on the timeline of some entity. While this concept is well defined within, for example, Special Relativity, representing this within a computer requires us to make some assumptions. In Java 8, we represent a single point in time as an `Instant`, which has these key assumptions:

- We cannot represent more seconds than can fit into a `long`.
- We cannot represent time more precisely than nanosecond precision.

This means that we are restricting ourselves to modeling time in a manner that is consistent with the capabilities of current computer systems. However, there is another fundamental concept that should also be introduced.

An `Instant` is about a single event in space-time. However, it is far from uncommon for programmers to have to deal with intervals between two events, and so Java 8 also introduces the `java.time.Duration` class. This class ignores calendar effects that might arise (e.g., from daylight saving time). With this basic conception of instants and durations between events, let's move on to unpack the possible ways of thinking about an instant.

The parts of a timestamp

In Figure 9-1, we show the breakdown of the different parts of a timestamp in a number of possible ways.

Common Data Formats

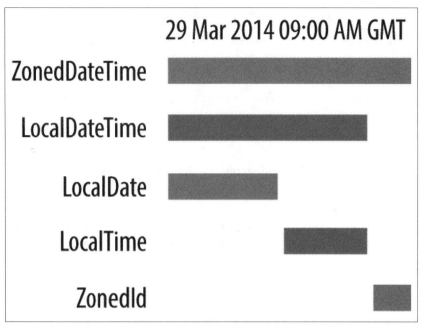

29 Mar 2014 09:00 AM GMT

ZonedDateTime

LocalDateTime

LocalDate

LocalTime

ZonedId

Figure 9-1. Breaking apart a timestamp

The key concept here is that there are a number of different abstractions that might be appropriate at different times. For example, there are applications where a `Local Date` is key to business processing, where the needed granularity is a business day. Alternatively, some applications require subsecond, or even millisecond precision. Developers should be aware of their domain and use a suitable representation within their application.

Example

The date and time API can be a lot to take in at first glance, so let's start by looking at an example, and discuss a diary class that keeps track of birthdays. If you happen to be very forgetful about birthdays, then a class like this (and especially methods like `getBirthdaysInNextMonth()`) might be very helpful:

```
public class BirthdayDiary {
    private Map<String, LocalDate> birthdays;

    public BirthdayDiary() {
        birthdays = new HashMap<>();
    }

    public LocalDate addBirthday(String name, int day, int month,
                                 int year) {
        LocalDate birthday = LocalDate.of(year, month, day);
        birthdays.put(name, birthday);
```

```java
        return birthday;
    }

    public LocalDate getBirthdayFor(String name) {
        return birthdays.get(name);
    }

    public int getAgeInYear(String name, int year) {
        Period period = Period.between(birthdays.get(name),
            birthdays.get(name).withYear(year));

        return period.getYears();
    }

    public Set<String> getFriendsOfAgeIn(int age, int year) {
        return birthdays.keySet().stream()
                .filter(p -> getAgeInYear(p, year) == age)
                .collect(Collectors.toSet());
    }

    public int getDaysUntilBirthday(String name) {
        Period period = Period.between(LocalDate.now(),
            birthdays.get(name));
        return period.getDays();
    }

    public Set<String> getBirthdaysIn(Month month) {
        return birthdays.entrySet().stream()
                .filter(p -> p.getValue().getMonth() == month)
                .map(p -> p.getKey())
                .collect(Collectors.toSet());
    }

    public Set<String> getBirthdaysInNextMonth() {
        return getBirthdaysIn(LocalDate.now().getMonth());
    }

    public int getTotalAgeInYears() {
        return birthdays.keySet().stream()
                .mapToInt(p -> getAgeInYear(p,
                    LocalDate.now().getYear()))
                .sum();
    }
}
```

This class shows how to use the low-level API to build up useful functionality. It also uses innovations such as the Java Streams API, and demonstrates how to use LocalDate as an immutable class and how dates should be treated as values.

Queries

Under a wide variety of circumstances we may find ourselves wanting to answer a question about a particular temporal object. Some example questions we may want answers to are:

- Is the date before March 1st?

- Is the date in a leap year?

- How many days is it from today until my next birthday?

This is acheived by the use of the `TemporalQuery` interface, which is defined like this:

```
public interface TemporalQuery<R> {
    R queryFrom(TemporalAccessor temporal);
}
```

The parameter to `queryFrom()` should not be null, but if the result indicates that a value was not found, null could be used as a return value.

The `Predicate` interface can be thought of as a query that can only represent answers to yes-or-no questions. Temporal queries are more general and can return a value of "How many?" or "Which?" instead of just "yes" or "no."

Let's look at an example of a query in action, by considering a query that answers the following question: "Which quarter of the year is this date in?" Java 8 does not support the concept of a quarter directly. Instead, code like this is used:

```
LocalDate today = LocalDate.now();
Month currentMonth = today.getMonth();
Month firstMonthofQuarter = currentMonth.firstMonthOfQuarter();
```

This still doesn't give quarter as a separate abstraction and instead special case code is still needed. So let's slightly extend the JDK support by defining this enum type:

```
public enum Quarter {
    FIRST, SECOND, THIRD, FOURTH;
}
```

Now, the query can be written as:

```
public class QuarterOfYearQuery implements TemporalQuery<Quarter> {
    @Override
    public Quarter queryFrom(TemporalAccessor temporal) {
        LocalDate now = LocalDate.from(temporal);

        if(now.isBefore(now.with(Month.APRIL).withDayOfMonth(1))) {
            return Quarter.FIRST;
        } else if(now.isBefore(now.with(Month.JULY)
```

```
                        .withDayOfMonth(1))) {
            return Quarter.SECOND;
        } else if(now.isBefore(now.with(Month.NOVEMBER)
                        .withDayOfMonth(1))) {
            return Quarter.THIRD;
        } else {
            return Quarter.FOURTH;
        }
    }
}
```

TemporalQuery objects can be used directly or indirectly. Let's look at an example of each:

```
QuarterOfYearQuery q = new QuarterOfYearQuery();

// Direct
Quarter quarter = q.queryFrom(LocalDate.now());
System.out.println(quarter);

// Indirect
quarter = LocalDate.now().query(q);
System.out.println(quarter);
```

Under most circumstances, it is better to use the indirect approach, where the query object is passed as a parameter to query(). This is because it is normally a lot clearer to read in code.

Adjusters

Adjusters modify date and time objects. Suppose, for example, that we want to return the first day of a quarter that contains a particular timestamp:

```
public class FirstDayOfQuarter implements TemporalAdjuster {
    @Override
    public Temporal adjustInto(Temporal temporal) {

        final int currentQuarter = YearMonth.from(temporal)
                .get(IsoFields.QUARTER_OF_YEAR);

        switch (currentQuarter) {
            case 1:
                return LocalDate.from(temporal)
                        .with(TemporalAdjusters.firstDayOfYear());
            case 2:
                return LocalDate.from(temporal)
                        .withMonth(Month.APRIL.getValue())
                        .with(TemporalAdjusters.firstDayOfMonth());
            case 3:
                return LocalDate.from(temporal)
                        .withMonth(Month.JULY.getValue())
                        .with(TemporalAdjusters.firstDayOfMonth());
            case 4:
```

```
                return LocalDate.from(temporal)
                        .withMonth(Month.OCTOBER.getValue())
                        .with(TemporalAdjusters.firstDayOfMonth());
            default:
                return null; // Will never happen
        }
    }
}
```

Let's look at an example of how to use an adjuster:

```
LocalDate now = LocalDate.now();
Temporal fdoq = now.with(new FirstDayOfQuarter());
System.out.println(fdoq);
```

The key here is the with() method, and the code should be read as taking in one Temporal object and returning another object that has been modified. This is completely usual for APIs that work with immutable objects.

Legacy Date and Time

Unfortunately, many applications are not yet converted to use the superior date and time libraries that ship with Java 8. So, for completeness, we briefly mention the legacy date and time support (which is based on java.util.Date).

The legacy date and time classes, especially java.util.Date, should *not* be used in Java 8 environments.

In older versions of Java, java.time is not available. Instead, programmers rely upon the legacy and rudimentary support provided by java.util.Date. Historically, this was the only way to represent timestamps, and although named Date this class actually consisted of both a date and a time component—and this led to a lot of confusion for many programmers.

There are many problems with the legacy support provided by Date, for example:

- The Date class is incorrectly factored. It doesn't actually refer to a date, and instead is more like a timestamp. It turns out that we need different representations for a date, versus a date and time, versus an instantaneous timestamp.

- Date is mutable. We can obtain a reference to a date, and then change when it refers to.

- The Date class doesn't actually accept ISO-8601, the universal ISO date standard, as being as valid date.

- Date has a very large number of deprecated methods.

The current JDK uses two constructors for Date—the void constructor that is intended to be the "now constructor," and a constructor that takes a number of milliseconds since epoch.

Conclusion

In this chapter, we've met several different classes of data. Textual and numeric data are the most obvious examples, but as working programmers we will meet a large number of different sorts of data. Let's move on to look at whole files of data, and new ways to work with I/O and networking. Fortunately, Java provides good support for dealing with many of these abstractions.

10

File Handling and I/O

Java has had input/output (I/O) support since the very first version. However, due to Java's strong desire for platform independence, the earlier versions of I/O functionality emphasized portability over functionality. As a result, they were not always easy to work with.

We'll see later in the chapter how the original APIs have been supplemented—they are now rich, fully featured, and very easy to develop with. Let's kick off the chapter by looking at the original, "classic" approach to Java I/O, which the more modern approaches layer on top of.

Classic Java I/O

The File class is the cornerstone of Java's original way to do file I/O. This abstraction can represent both files and directories, but in doing so is sometimes a bit cumbersome to deal with, and leads to code like this:

```
// Get a file object to represent the user's home directory
File homedir = new File(System.getProperty("user.home"));

// Create an object to represent a config file (should
// already be present in the home directory)
File f = new File(homedir, "app.conf");

// Check the file exists, really is a file & is readable
if (f.exists() && f.isFile() && f.canRead()) {

  // Create a file object for a new configuration directory
  File configdir = new File(f, ".configdir");
  // And create it
  configdir.mkdir();
```

```
    // Finally, move the config file to its new home
    f.renameTo(new File(configdir, ".config"));
}
```

This shows some of the flexibility possible with the File class, but also demonstrates some of the problems with the abstraction. It is very general, and this requires a lot of methods to interrogate a File object in order to determine what it actually represents and its capabilities.

Files

The File class has a very large number of methods on it, but some basic functionality (notably a way to read the contents of a file) is not, and never has been provided directly.

Here's a quick summary of File methods:

```
// Permissions management
boolean canX = f.canExecute();
boolean canR = f.canRead();
boolean canW = f.canWrite();

boolean ok;
ok = f.setReadOnly();
ok = f.setExecutable(true);
ok = f.setReadable(true);
ok = f.setWritable(false);

// Different views of the file's name
File absF = f.getAbsoluteFile();
File canF = f.getCanonicalFile();
String absName = f.getAbsolutePath();
String canName = f.getCanonicalPath();
String name = f.getName();
String pName = getParent();
URI fileURI = f.toURI(); // Create URI for File path

// File metadata
boolean exists = f.exists();
boolean isAbs = f.isAbsolute();
boolean isDir = f.isDirectory();
boolean isFile = f.isFile();
boolean isHidden = f.isHidden();
long modTime = f.lastModified(); // milliseconds since epoch
boolean updateOK = f.setLastModified(updateTime); // milliseconds
long fileLen = f.length();

// File management operations
boolean renamed = f.renameTo(destFile);
boolean deleted = f.delete();

// Create won't overwrite existing file
```

```
boolean createdOK = f.createNewFile();

// Temporary file handling
File tmp = File.createTempFile("my-tmp", ".tmp");
tmp.deleteOnExit();

// Directory handling
boolean createdDir = dir.mkdir();
String[] fileNames = dir.list();
File[] files = dir.listFiles();
```

The File class also has a few methods on it that aren't a perfect fit for the abstraction. They largely involve interrogating the filesystem (e.g., inquiring about available free space):

```
long free, total, usable;

free = f.getFreeSpace();
total = f.getTotalSpace();
usable = f.getUsableSpace();

File[] roots = File.listRoots(); // all available Filesystem roots
```

Streams

The I/O stream abstraction (not to be confused with the streams that are used when dealing with the Java 8 Collection APIs) was present in Java 1.0, as a way of dealing with sequential streams of bytes from disks or other sources.

The core of this API is a pair of abstract classes, InputStream and OutputStream. These are very widely used, and in fact the "standard" input and output streams, which are called System.in and System.out, are streams of this type. They are public, static fields of the System class, and are often used in even the simplest programs:

```
System.out.println("Hello World!");
```

Specific subclasses of streams, including FileInputStream, and FileOutputStream can be used to operate on individual bytes in a file—for example, by counting all the times ASCII 97 (small letter *a*) occurs in a file:

```
try (InputStream is = new FileInputStream("/Users/ben/cluster.txt")) {
  byte[] buf = new byte[4096];
  int len, count = 0;
  while ((len = is.read(buf)) > 0) {
    for (int i=0; i<len; i++)
      if (buf[i] == 97) count++;
  }
  System.out.println("'a's seen: "+ count);
} catch (IOException e) {
  e.printStackTrace();
}
```

This approach to dealing with on-disk data can lack some flexibility—most developers think in terms of characters, not bytes. To allow for this, the streams are usually combined with the higher-level `Reader` and `Writer` classes, that provide a character-stream level of interaction, rather than the low-level byte stream provided by `Input Stream` and `OutputStream` and their subclasses.

Readers and Writers

By moving to an abstraction that deals in characters, rather than bytes, developers are presented with an API that is much more familiar, and that hides many of the issues with character encoding, Unicode, and so on.

The `Reader` and `Writer` classes are intended to overlay the byte stream classes, and to remove the need for low-level handling of I/O streams. They have several subclasses that are often used to layer on top of each other, such as:

- `FileReader`
- `BufferedReader`
- `InputStreamReader`
- `FileWriter`
- `PrintWriter`
- `BufferedWriter`

To read all lines in from a file, and print them out, we use a `BufferedReader` layered on top of a `FileReader`, like this:

```
try (BufferedReader in =
  new BufferedReader(new FileReader(filename))) {
  String line;

  while((line = in.readLine()) != null) {
    System.out.println(line);
  }
} catch (IOException e) {
  // Handle FileNotFoundException, etc. here
}
```

If we need to read in lines from the console, rather than a file, we will usually use an `InputStreamReader` applied to `System.in`. Let's look at an example where we want to read in lines of input from the console, but treat input lines that start with a special character as special—commands ("metas") to be processed, rather than regular text. This is a common feature of many chat programs, including IRC. We'll use regular expressions from Chapter 9 to help us:

```
Pattern SHELL_META_START = Pattern.compile("^#(\\w+)\\s*(\\w+)?");

try (BufferedReader console =
  new BufferedReader(new InputStreamReader(System.in))) {
```

```
String line;

READ: while((line = console.readLine()) != null) {
    // Check for special commands ("metas")
    Matcher m = SHELL_META_START.matcher(line);
    if (m.find()) {
        String metaName = m.group(1);
        String arg = m.group(2);
        doMeta(metaName, arg);
        continue READ;
    }

    System.out.println(line);
    }
} catch (IOException e) {
    // Handle FileNotFoundException, etc. here
}
```

To output text to a file, we can use code like this:

```
File f = new File(System.getProperty("user.home")
 + File.separator + ".bashrc");
try (PrintWriter out
    = new PrintWriter(new BufferedWriter(new FileWriter(f)))) {
    out.println("## Automatically generated config file. DO NOT EDIT");
} catch (IOException iox) {
    // Handle exceptions
}
```

This older style of Java I/O has a lot of other functionality that is occasionally useful. For example, to deal with text files, the FilterInputStream class is quite often useful. Or for threads that want to communicate in a way similar to the classic "piped" I/O approach, PipedInputStream, PipedReader, and their write counterparts are provided.

Throughout this chapter so far, we have used the language feature known as "try-with-resources" (TWR). This syntax was briefly introduced in "The try-with-resources Statement" on page 63, but it is in conjunction with operations like I/O that it comes into its fullest potential, and it has granted a new lease on life to the older I/O style.

try-with-resources Revisited

To make the most of Java's I/O capabilities, it is important to understand how and when to use TWR. It is very easy to understand when code should use TWR—whenever it is possible to do so.

Before TWR, resources had to be closed manually, and complex interactions between resources that could fail to close led to buggy code that could leak resources.

In fact, Oracle's engineers estimate that 60% of the resource handling code in the initial JDK 6 release was incorrect. So, if even the platform authors can't reliably get manual resource handling right, then all new code should definitely be using TWR.

The key to TWR is a new interface—AutoCloseable. This is a new interface (appears in Java 7) that is a direct superinterface of Closeable. It marks a resource that must be automatically closed, and for which the compiler will insert special exception-handling code.

Inside a TWR resource clause, only declarations of objects that implement Auto Closeable objects may appear—but the developer may declare as many as required:

```
try (BufferedReader in = new BufferedReader(
                        new FileReader("profile"));
     PrintWriter out = new PrintWriter(
                        new BufferedWriter(
                          new FileWriter("profile.bak")))) {
  String line;
  while((line = in.readLine()) != null) {
    out.println(line);
  }
} catch (IOException e) {
  // Handle FileNotFoundException, etc. here
}
```

The consequences of this are that resources are automatically scoped to the try block. The resources (whether readable or writable) are automatically closed in the correct order, and the compiler inserts exception handling that takes dependencies between resources into account.

The overall effect of TWR is similar to C#'s using keyword, and the developer may regard it as "finalization done right." As noted in "Finalization" on page 206, new code should never directly use the finalization mechanism, and should always use TWR instead. Older code should be refactored to use TWR as soon as is practicable.

Problems with Classic I/O

Even with the welcome addition of try-with-resources, the File class and friends have a number of problems that make them less than ideal for extensive use when performing even standard I/O operations. For instance:

- "Missing methods" for common operations
- Does not deal with filenames consistently across platforms
- Fails to have a unified model for file attributes (e.g., modeling read/write access)
- Difficult to traverse unknown directory structures
- No platform or OS–specific features

- Nonblocking operations for filesystems not supported

To deal with these shortcomings, Java's I/O has evolved over several major releases. It was really with the release of Java 7 that this support became truly easy and effective to use.

Modern Java I/O

Java 7 brought in a brand new I/O API—usually called NIO.2—and it should be considered almost a complete replacement for the original File approach to I/O. The new classes are contained in the java.nio.file package.

The new API that was brought in with Java 7 is considerably easier to use for many use cases. It has two major parts. The first is a new abstraction called Path (which can be thought of as representing a file location, which may or may not have anything actually at that location). The second piece is lots of new convenience and utility methods to deal with files and filesystems. These are contained as static methods in the Files class.

Files

For example, when using the new Files functionality, a basic copy operation is now as simple as:

```
File inputFile = new File("input.txt");
try (InputStream in = new FileInputStream(inputFile)) {
  Files.copy(in, Paths.get("output.txt"));
} catch(IOException ex) {
  ex.printStackTrace();
}
```

Let's take a quick survey of some of the major methods in Files—the operation of most of them is pretty self-explanatory. In many cases, the methods have return types. We have omitted handling these, as they are rarely useful except for contrived examples, and for duplicating the behavior of the equivalent C code:

```
Path source, target;
Attributes attr;
Charset cs = StandardCharsets.UTF_8;

// Creating files
//
// Example of path --> /home/ben/.profile
// Example of attributes --> rw-rw-rw-
Files.createFile(target, attr);

// Deleting files
Files.delete(target);
boolean deleted = Files.deleteIfExists(target);

// Copying/Moving files
```

```
Files.copy(source, target);
Files.move(source, target);

// Utility methods to retrieve information
long size = Files.size(target);

FileTime fTime = Files.getLastModifiedTime(target);
System.out.println(fTime.to(TimeUnit.SECONDS));

Map<String, ?> attrs = Files.readAttributes(target, "*");
System.out.println(attrs);

// Methods to deal with file types
boolean isDir = Files.isDirectory(target);
boolean isSym = Files.isSymbolicLink(target);

// Methods to deal with reading and writing
List<String> lines = Files.readAllLines(target, cs);
byte[] b = Files.readAllBytes(target);

BufferedReader br = Files.newBufferedReader(target, cs);
BufferedWriter bwr = Files.newBufferedWriter(target, cs);

InputStream is = Files.newInputStream(target);
OutputStream os = Files.newOutputStream(target);
```

Some of the methods on Files provide the opportunity to pass optional arguments, to provide additional (possibly implementation-specific) behavior for the operation.

Some of the API choices here produce occasionally annoying behavior. For example, by default, a copy operation will not overwrite an existing file, so we need to specify this behavior as a copy option:

```
Files.copy(Paths.get("input.txt"), Paths.get("output.txt"),
        StandardCopyOption.REPLACE_EXISTING);
```

StandardCopyOption is an enum that implements an interface called CopyOption. This is also implemented by LinkOption. So Files.copy() can take any number of either LinkOption or StandardCopyOption arguments. LinkOption is used to specify how symbolic links should be handled (provided the underlying OS supports symlinks, of course).

Path

Path is a type that may be used to locate a file in a filesystem. It represents a path that is:

- System dependent
- Hierarchical
- Composed of a sequence of path elements

- Hypothetical (may not exist yet, or may have been deleted)

It is therefore fundamentally different to a File. In particular, the system dependency is manifested by Path being an interface, not a class. This enables different filesystem providers to each implement the Path interface, and provide for system-specific features while retaining the overall abstraction.

The elements of a Path consist of an optional root component, which identifies the filesystem hierarchy that this instance belongs to. Note that, for example, relative Path instances may not have a root component. In addition to the root, all Path instances have zero or more directory names and a name element.

The name element is the element farthest from the root of the directory hierarchy and represents the name of the file or directory. The Path can be thought of consisting of the path elements joined together by a special separator or delimiter.

Path is an abstract concept; it isn't necessarily bound to any physical file path. This allows us to talk easily about the locations of files that don't exist yet. Java ships with a Paths class that provides factory methods for creating Path instances.

Paths provides two get() methods for creating Path objects. The usual version takes a String, and uses the default filesystem provider. The URI version takes advantage of the ability of NIO.2 to plug in additional providers of bespoke filesystems. This is an advanced usage, and interested developers should consult the primary documentation:

```
Path p = Paths.get("/Users/ben/cluster.txt");
Path p = Paths.get(new URI("file:///Users/ben/cluster.txt"));
System.out.println(p2.equals(p));

File f = p.toFile();
System.out.println(f.isDirectory());
Path p3 = f.toPath();
System.out.println(p3.equals(p));
```

This example also shows the easy interoperation between Path and File objects. The addition of a toFile() method to Path and a toPath() method to File allows the developer to move effortlessly between the two APIs and allows for a straightforward approach to refactoring the internals of code based on File to use Path instead.

We can also make use of some useful "bridge" methods that the Files class also provides. These provide convenient access to the older I/O APIs—for example, by providing convenience methods to open Writer objects to specified Path locations:

```
Path logFile = Paths.get("/tmp/app.log");
try (BufferedWriter writer =
        Files.newBufferedWriter(logFile, StandardCharsets.UTF_8,
                            StandardOpenOption.WRITE)) {
    writer.write("Hello World!");
    // ...
```

```
} catch (IOException e) {
  // ...
}
```

We're making use of the StandardOpenOption enum, which provides similar capabilities to the copy options, but for the case of opening a new file instead.

In this example use case, we have used the Path API to:

- Create a Path corresponding to a new file
- Use the Files class to create that new file
- Open a Writer to that file
- Write to that file
- Automatically close it when done

In our next example, we'll build on this to manipulate a *.jar* file as a FileSystem in its own right, modifying it to add an additional file directly into the JAR. JAR files are just ZIP files, so this technique will also work for *.zip* archives:

```
Path tempJar = Paths.get("sample.jar");
try (FileSystem workingFS =
  FileSystems.newFileSystem(tempJar, null)) {
  Path pathForFile = workingFS.getPath("/hello.txt");
  List<String> ls = new ArrayList<>();
  ls.add("Hello World!");

  Files.write(pathForFile, ls, Charset.defaultCharset(),
          StandardOpenOption.WRITE, StandardOpenOption.CREATE);
}
```

This shows how we use a FileSystem to make the Path objects inside it, via the getPath() method. This enables the developer to effectively treat FileSystem objects as black boxes.

One of the criticisms of Java's original I/O APIs was the lack of support for native and high-performance I/O. A solution was initially added in Java 1.4, the Java New I/O (NIO) API, and it has been successively refined in successive Java versions.

NIO Channels and Buffers

NIO buffers are a low-level abstraction for high-performance I/O. They provide a container for a linear sequence of elements of a specific primitive type. We'll work with the ByteBuffer (the most common case) in our examples.

ByteBuffer

This is a sequence of bytes, and can conceptually be thought of as a performance-critical alternative to working with a byte[]. To get the best possible performance,

---

`ByteBuffer` provides support for dealing directly with the native capabilities of the platform the JVM is running on.

This approach is called the "direct buffers" case, and it bypasses the Java heap wherever possible. Direct buffers are allocated in native memory, not on the standard Java heap, and they are not subject to garbage collection in the same way as regular on-heap Java objects.

To obtain a direct `ByteBuffer`, call the `allocateDirect()` factory method. An on-heap version, `allocate()`, is also provided, but in practice this is not often used.

A third way to obtain a byte buffer is to wrap an existing `byte[]`—this will give an on-heap buffer that serves to provide a more object-oriented view of the underlying bytes:

```
ByteBuffer b = ByteBuffer.allocateDirect(65536);
ByteBuffer b2 = ByteBuffer.allocate(4096);

byte[] data = {1, 2, 3};
ByteBuffer b3 = ByteBuffer.wrap(data);
```

Byte buffers are all about low-level access to the bytes. This means that developers have to deal with the details manually—including the need to handle the endianness of the bytes and the signed nature of Java's integral primitives:

```
b.order(ByteOrder.BIG_ENDIAN);

int capacity = b.capacity();
int position = b.position();
int limit = b.limit();
int remaining = b.remaining();
boolean more = b.hasRemaining();
```

To get data in or out of a buffer, we have two types of operation—single value, which reads or writes a single value, and bulk, which takes a `byte[]` or `ByteBuffer` and operates on a (potentially large) number of values as a single operation. It is from the bulk operations that performance gains would expect to be realized:

```
b.put((byte)42);
b.putChar('x');
b.putInt(0xcafebabe);

b.put(data);
b.put(b2);

double d = b.getDouble();
b.get(data, 0, data.length);
```

The single value form also supports a form used for absolute positioning within the buffer:

```
b.put(0, (byte)9);
```

Buffers are an in-memory abstraction. To affect the outside world (e.g., the file or network), we need to use a Channel, from the package java.nio.channels. Channels represent connections to entities that can support read or write operations. Files and sockets are the usual examples of channels, but we could consider custom implementations used for low-latency data processing.

Channels are open when they're created, and can subsequently be closed. Once closed, they cannot be reopened. Channels are usually either readable or writable, but not both. The key to understanding channels is that:

- Reading from a channel puts bytes into a buffer
- Writing to a channel takes bytes from a buffer

For example, suppose we have a large file that we want to checksum in 16M chunks:

```
FileInputStream fis = getSomeStream();
boolean fileOK = true;

try (FileChannel fchan = fis.getChannel()) {
  ByteBuffer buffy = ByteBuffer.allocateDirect(16 * 1024 * 1024);
  while(fchan.read(buffy) != -1 || buffy.position() > 0 || fileOK) {
    fileOK = computeChecksum(buffy);
    buffy.compact();
  }
} catch (IOException e) {
  System.out.println("Exception in I/O");
}
```

This will use native I/O as far as possible, and will avoid a lot of copying of bytes on and off the Java heap. If the computeChecksum() method has been well implemented, then this could be a very performant implementation.

Mapped Byte Buffers

These are a type of direct byte buffer that contain a memory-mapped file (or a region of one). They are created from a FileChannel object, but note that the File object corresponding to the MappedByteBuffer must not be used after the memory-mapped operations, or an exception will be thrown. To mitigate this, we again use try-with-resources, to scope the objects tightly:

```
try (RandomAccessFile raf =
  new RandomAccessFile(new File("input.txt"), "rw");
    FileChannel fc = raf.getChannel();) {

  MappedByteBuffer mbf =
    fc.map(FileChannel.MapMode.READ_WRITE, 0, fc.size());
  byte[] b = new byte[(int)fc.size()];
  mbf.get(b, 0, b.length);
  for (int i=0; i<fc.size(); i++) {
    b[i] = 0; // Won't be written back to the file, we're a copy
  }
```

```
        mbf.position(0);
        mbf.put(b); // Zeros the file
    }
```

Even with buffers, there are limitations of what can be done in Java for large (e.g., transferring 10G between filesystems) I/O operations that perform synchronously on a single thread. Before Java 7, these types of operations would typically be done by writing custom multithreaded code, and managing a separate thread for performing a background copy. Let's move on to look at the new asynchronous I/O features that were added with JDK 7.

Async I/O

The key to the new asynchronous functionality are some new subclasses of `Channel` that can deal with I/O operations that need to be handed off to a background thread. The same functionality can be applied to large, long-running operations, and to several other use cases.

In this section, we'll deal exclusively with `AsynchronousFileChannel` for file I/O, but there are a couple of other asynchronous channels to be aware of. We'll deal with asynchronous sockets at the end of the chapter. We'll look at:

- `AsynchronousFileChannel` for file I/O
- `AsynchronousSocketChannel` for client socket I/O
- `AsynchronousServerSocketChannel` for asynchronous sockets that accept incoming connections

There are two different ways to interact with an asynchronous channel—`Future` style, and callback style.

Future-Based Style

We'll meet the `Future` interface in detail in Chapter 11, but for the purpose of this chapter, it can be thought of as an ongoing task that may or may not have completed yet. It has two key methods:

`isDone()`
    Returns a Boolean indicating whether the task has finished.

`get()`
    Returns the result. If finished, returns immediately. If not finished, blocks until done.

Let's look at an example of a program that reads a large file (possibly as large as 100 Mb) asynchronously:

```
    try (AsynchronousFileChannel channel =
            AsynchronousFileChannel.open(Paths.get("input.txt"))) {
        ByteBuffer buffer = ByteBuffer.allocateDirect(1024 * 1024 * 100);
```

```
Future<Integer> result = channel.read(buffer, 0);

while(!result.isDone()) {
  // Do some other useful work....
}

System.out.println("Bytes read: " + result.get());
}
```

Callback-Based Style

The callback style for asynchronous I/O is based on a `CompletionHandler`, which defines two methods, `completed()` and `failed()`, that will be called back when the operation either succeeds or fails.

This style is useful if you want immediate notification of events in asynchronous I/O—for example, if there are a large number of I/O operations in flight, but failure of any single operation is not necessarily fatal:

```
byte[] data = {2, 3, 5, 7, 11, 13, 17, 19, 23};
ByteBuffer buffy = ByteBuffer.wrap(data);

CompletionHandler<Integer,Object> h =
  new CompletionHandler() {
  public void completed(Integer written, Object o) {
    System.out.println("Bytes written: " + written);
  }

  public void failed(Throwable x, Object o) {
    System.out.println("Asynch write failed: "+ x.getMessage());
  }
};

try (AsynchronousFileChannel channel =
        AsynchronousFileChannel.open(Paths.get("primes.txt"),
          StandardOpenOption.CREATE, StandardOpenOption.WRITE)) {

  channel.write(buffy, 0, null, h);
  Thread.sleep(1000); // Needed so we don't exit too quickly
}
```

The `AsynchronousFileChannel` object is associated with a background thread pool, so that the I/O operation proceeds, while the original thread can get on with other tasks.

By default, this uses a managed thread pool that is provided by the runtime. If required, it can be created to use a thread pool that is managed by the application (via an overloaded form of `AsynchronousFileChannel.open()`), but this is not often necessary.

Finally, for completeness, let's touch upon NIO's support for multiplexed I/O. This enables a single thread to manage multiple channels and to examine those channels

---

to see which are ready for reading or writing. The classes to support this are in the java.nio.channels package and include SelectableChannel and Selector.

These nonblocking multiplexed techniques can be extremely useful when writing advanced applications that require high scalability, but a full discussion is outside the scope of this book.

Watch Services and Directory Searching

The last class of asynchronous services we will consider are those that watch a directory, or visit a directory (or a tree). The watch services operate by observing everything that happens within a directory—for example, the creation or modification of files:

```
try {
  WatchService watcher = FileSystems.getDefault().newWatchService();

  Path dir = FileSystems.getDefault().getPath("/home/ben");
  WatchKey key = dir.register(watcher,
                    StandardWatchEventKinds.ENTRY_CREATE,
                    StandardWatchEventKinds.ENTRY_MODIFY,
                    StandardWatchEventKinds.ENTRY_DELETE);

  while(!shutdown) {
    key = watcher.take();
    for (WatchEvent<?> event: key.pollEvents()) {
      Object o = event.context();
      if (o instanceof Path) {
        System.out.println("Path altered: "+ o);
      }
    }
    key.reset();
  }
}
```

By contrast, the directory streams provide a view into all files currently in a single directory. For example, to list all the Java source files and their size in bytes, we can use code like:

```
try(DirectoryStream<Path> stream =
    Files.newDirectoryStream(Paths.get("/opt/projects"), "*.java")) {
  for (Path p : stream) {
    System.out.println(p +": "+ Files.size(p));
  }
}
```

One drawback of this API is that this will only return elements that match according to glob syntax, which is sometimes insufficiently flexible. We can go further by using the new Files.find() and Files.walk() methods to address each element obtained by a recursive walk through the directory:

```
final Pattern isJava = Pattern.compile(".*\\.java$");
final Path homeDir = Paths.get("/Users/ben/projects/");
Files.find(homeDir, 255,
  (p, attrs) -> isJava.matcher(p.toString()).find())
    .forEach(q -> {System.out.println(q.normalize());});
```

It is possible to go even further, and construct advanced solutions based on the File Visitor interface in java.nio.file, but that requires the developer to implement all four methods on the interface, rather than just using a single lambda expression as done here.

In the last section of this chapter, we will discuss Java's networking support and the core JDK classes that enable it.

Networking

The Java platform provides access to a large number of standard networking protocols, and these make writing simple networked applications quite easy. The core of Java's network support lives in the package java.net, with additional extensibility provided by javax.net (and in particular, javax.net.ssl).

One of the easiest protocols to use for building applications is HyperText Transmission Protocol (HTTP), the protocol that is used as the basic communication protocol of the Web.

HTTP

HTTP is the highest-level network protocol that Java supports out of the box. It is a very simple, text-based protocol, implemented on top of the standard TCP/IP stack. It can run on any network port, but is usually found on port 80.

URL is the key class—it supports URLs of the form http://, ftp://, file://, and https:// out of the box. It is very easy to use, and the simplest example of Java HTTP support is to download a particular URL. With Java 8, this is just:

```
URL url = new URL("http://www.jclarity.com/");
try (InputStream in = url.openStream()) {
  Files.copy(in, Paths.get("output.txt"));
} catch(IOException ex) {
  ex.printStackTrace();
}
```

For more low-level control, including metadata about the request and response, we can use URLConnection to give us more control, and achieve something like:

```
try {
  URLConnection conn = url.openConnection();

  String type = conn.getContentType();
  String encoding = conn.getContentEncoding();
  Date lastModified = new Date(conn.getLastModified());
  int len = conn.getContentLength();
```

```
    InputStream in = conn.getInputStream();
} catch (IOException e) {
    // Handle exception
}
```

HTTP defines "request methods," which are the operations that a client can make on a remote resource. These methods are called:

GET, POST, HEAD, PUT, DELETE, OPTIONS, TRACE

Each has slightly different usages, for example:

- GET should only be used to retrieve a document and NEVER should perform any side effects.

- HEAD is equivalent to GET except the body is not returned—useful if a program wants to quickly check whether a URL has changed.

- POST is used when we want to send data to a server for processing.

By default, Java always uses GET, but it does provide a way to use other methods for building more complex applications; however, doing so is a bit involved. In this next example, we're using the search function provided by the BBC website to search for news articles about Java:

```
URL url = new URL("http://www.bbc.co.uk/search");

String rawData = "q=java";
String encodedData = URLEncoder.encode(rawData, "ASCII");
String contentType = "application/x-www-form-urlencoded";

HttpURLConnection conn = (HttpURLConnection) url.openConnection();
conn.setInstanceFollowRedirects(false);
conn.setRequestMethod("POST");
conn.setRequestProperty("Content-Type", contentType );
conn.setRequestProperty("Content-Length",
  String.valueOf(encodedData.length()));

conn.setDoOutput(true);
OutputStream os = conn.getOutputStream();
os.write( encodedData.getBytes() );

int response = conn.getResponseCode();
if (response == HttpURLConnection.HTTP_MOVED_PERM
    || response == HttpURLConnection.HTTP_MOVED_TEMP) {
  System.out.println("Moved to: "+ conn.getHeaderField("Location"));
} else {
  try (InputStream in = conn.getInputStream()) {
    Files.copy(in, Paths.get("bbc.txt"),
                StandardCopyOption.REPLACE_EXISTING);
  }
}
```

Notice that we needed to send our query parameters in the body of a request, and to encode them before sending. We also had to disable following of HTTP redirects, and to treat any redirection from the server manually. This is due to a limitation of the HttpURLConnection class, which does not deal well with redirection of POST requests.

In most cases, when implementing these types of more advanced HTTP applications, developers would usually use a specialist HTTP client library, such as the one provided by Apache, rather than coding the whole thing from scratch using JDK classes.

Let's move on to look at the next layer down the networking stack, the Transmission Control Protocol (TCP).

TCP

TCP is the basis of reliable network transport over the Internet. It ensures that web pages and other Internet traffic are delivered in a complete and comprehensible state. From a networking theory standpoint, the protocol properties that allow TCP to function as this "reliability layer" for Internet traffic are:

Connection based
Data belongs to a single logical stream (a connection).

Guaranteed delivery
Data packets will be resent until they arrive.

Error checked
Damage caused by network transit will be detected and fixed automatically.

TCP is a two-way (or bidirectional) communication channel, and uses a special numbering scheme (TCP Sequence numbers) for data chunks to ensure that both sides of a communication stream stay in sync. In order to support many different services on the same network host, TCP uses port numbers to identify services, and ensures that traffic intended for one port does not go to a different one.

In Java, TCP is represented by the classes Socket and ServerSocket. They are used to provide the capability to be the client and server side of the connection respectively—meaning that Java can be used both to connect to network services, and as a language for implementing new services.

As an example, let's consider reimplementing HTTP. This is a relatively simple, text-based protocol. We'll need to implement both sides of the connection, so let's start with a HTTP client on top of a TCP socket. To accomplish this, we will actually need to implement the details of the HTTP protocol, but we do have the advantage that we have complete control over the TCP socket.

We will need to both read and write from the client socket, and we'll construct the actual request line in accordance with the HTTP standard (which is known as RFC 2616). The resulting code will look something like this:

```
String hostname = "www.example.com";
int port = 80;
String filename = "/index.html";

try (Socket sock = new Socket(hostname, port);
  BufferedReader from = new BufferedReader(
      new InputStreamReader(sock.getInputStream()));
  PrintWriter to = new PrintWriter(
      new OutputStreamWriter(sock.getOutputStream())); ) {

  // The HTTP protocol
  to.print("GET " + filename +
    " HTTP/1.1\r\nHost: "+ hostname +"\r\n\r\n");
  to.flush();

  for(String l = null; (l = from.readLine()) != null; )
    System.out.println(l);

}
```

On the server side, we'll need to receive possibly multiple incoming connections. To handle this, we'll need to kick off a main server loop, then use accept() to take a new connection from the operating system. The new connection then will need to be quickly passed to a separate handler class, so that the main server loop can get back to listening for new connections. The code for this is a bit more involved than the client case:

```
// Handler class
private static class HttpHandler implements Runnable {
  private final Socket sock;
  HttpHandler(Socket client) { this.sock = client; }

  public void run() {
    try (BufferedReader in =
          new BufferedReader(
            new InputStreamReader(sock.getInputStream()));
        PrintWriter out =
          new PrintWriter(
            new OutputStreamWriter(sock.getOutputStream())); ) {
      out.print("HTTP/1.0 200\r\nContent-Type: text/plain\r\n\r\n");
      String line;
      while((line = in.readLine()) != null) {
        if (line.length() == 0) break;
        out.println(line);
      }
    } catch(Exception e) {
      // Handle exception
    }
  }
}

// Main server loop
```

```
public static void main(String[] args) {
  try {
    int port = Integer.parseInt(args[0]);

    ServerSocket ss = new ServerSocket(port);
    for(;;) {
      Socket client = ss.accept();
      HTTPHandler hndlr = new HTTPHandler(client);
      new Thread(hndlr).start();
    }
  } catch (Exception e) {
    // Handle exception
  }
}
```

When designing a protocol for applications to communicate over TCP, there's a simple and profound network architecture principle, known as Postel's Law (after Jon Postel, one of the fathers of the Internet) that should always be kept in mind. It is sometimes stated as follows: "Be strict about what you send, and liberal about what you will accept." This simple principle means that communication can remain broadly possible in a network system, even in the event of quite imperfect implementations.

Postel's Law, when combined with the general principle that the protocol should be as simple as possible (sometimes called the KISS principle), will make the developer's job of implementing TCP-based communication much easier than it otherwise would be.

Below TCP is the Internet's general-purpose haulage protocol—the Internet Protocol (IP) itself.

IP

IP is the "lowest common denominator" transport, and provides a useful abstraction over the physical network technologies that are used to actually move bytes from A to B.

Unlike TCP, delivery of an IP packet is not guaranteed, and a packet can be dropped by any overloaded system along the path. IP packets do have a destination, but usually no routing data—it's the responsiblity of the (possibly many different) physical transports along the route to actually deliver the data.

It is possible to create "datagram" services in Java that are based around single IP packets (or those with a UDP header, instead of TCP), but this is not often required except for extremely low-latency applications. Java uses the class DatagramSocket to implement this functionality, although few developers should ever need to venture this far down the network stack.

Finally, it's worth noting some changes that are currently in-flight in the addressing schemes that are used across the Internet. The current version of IP that is in use is

IPv4, which has a 32-bit space of possible network addresses. This space is now very badly squeezed, and various mitigation techniques have been deployed.

The next version of IP (IPv6) is coming but it is not widely used yet. However, in the next 10 years, IPv6 should become much more widespread, and the good news is that Java already has good support for the addressing scheme it introduces.

11

Classloading, Reflection, and Method Handles

In Chapter 3, we met Java's Class objects, as a way of representing a live type in a running Java process. In this chapter, we will build on this foundation to discuss how the Java environment loads and makes new types available. In the second half of the chapter, we will introduce Java's introspection capabilities—both the original Reflection API and the newer Method Handles capabilities.

Class Files, Class Objects, and Metadata

Class files, as we saw in Chapter 1, are the result of compiling Java source files (or, potentially, other languages) into the intermediate form used by the JVM. These are binary files that are not designed to be human readable.

The runtime representation of these class files are the class objects that contain metadata, which represents the Java type that the class file was created from.

Examples of Class Objects

You can obtain a class object in Java in several ways. The simplest is:

```
Class<?> myCl = getClass();
```

This returns the class object of the instance that it is called from. However, as we know from our survey of the public methods of Object, the getClass() method on Object is public, so we can also obtain the class of an arbitrary object o:

```
Class<?> c = o.getClass();
```

Class objects for known types can also be written as "class literals":

```
// Express a class literal as a type name followed by ".class"
c = int.class; // Same as Integer.TYPE
c = String.class; // Same as "a string".getClass()
c = byte[].class; // Type of byte arrays
```

For primitive types and void, we also have class objects that are represented as literals:

```
// Obtain a Class object for primitive types with various
// predefined constants
c = Void.TYPE; // The special "no-return-value" type
c = Byte.TYPE; // Class object that represents a byte
c = Integer.TYPE; // Class object that represents an int
c = Double.TYPE; // etc; see also Short, Character, Long, Float
```

For unknown types, we will have to use more sophisticated methods.

Class Objects and Metadata

The class objects contain metadata about the given type. This includes the methods, fields, constructors, etc. that are defined on the class in question. This metadata can be accessed by the programmer to investigate the class, even if nothing is known about the class when it is loaded.

For example, we can find all the deprecated methods in the class file (they will be marked with the @Deprecated annotation):

```
Class<?> clz = getClassFromDisk();
for (Method m : clz.getMethods()) {
  for (Annotation a : m.getAnnotations()) {
    if (a.annotationType() == Deprecated.class) {
      System.out.println(m.getName());
    }
  }
}
```

We could also find the common ancestor class of a pair of class files. This simple form will work when both classes have been loaded by the same classloader:

```
public static Class<?> commonAncestor(Class<?> cl1, Class<?> cl2) {
  if (cl1 == null || cl2 == null) return null;
  if (cl1.equals(cl2)) return cl1;
  if (cl1.isPrimitive() || cl2.isPrimitive()) return null;

  List<Class<?>> ancestors = new ArrayList<>();
  Class<?> c = cl1;
  while (!c.equals(Object.class)) {
    if (c.equals(cl2)) return c;
    ancestors.add(c);
    c = c.getSuperclass();
  }
  c = cl2;
  while (!c.equals(Object.class)) {
```

```
    for (Class<?> k : ancestors) {
      if (c.equals(k)) return c;
    }
    c = c.getSuperclass();
  }

  return Object.class;
}
```

Class files have a very specific layout that they must conform to if they are to be legal and loadable by the JVM. The sections of the class file are (in order):

- Magic number (all class files start with the four bytes `CA FE BA BE` in hexadecimal)
- Version of class file standard in use
- Constant pool for this class
- Access flags (`abstract`, `public`, etc.)
- Name of this class
- Inheritance info (e.g., name of superclass)
- Implemented Interfaces
- Fields
- Methods
- Attributes

The class file is a simple binary format, but it is not human readable. Instead, tools like `javap` (see Chapter 13) should be used to comprehend the contents.

One of the most often used sections in the classfile is the Constant Pool—this contains representations of all the methods, classes, fields and constants that the class needs to refer to (whether they are in this class, or another). It is designed so that bytecodes can simply refer to a constant pool entry by its index number—which saves space in the bytecode representation.

There are a number of different class file versions created by various Java versions. However, one of Java's backward compatibility rules is that JVMs (and tools) from newer versions can always use older class files.

Let's look at how the classloading process takes a collection of bytes on disk and turns it into a new class object.

Phases of Classloading

Classloading is the process by which a new type is added to a running JVM process. This is the only way that new code can enter the system, and the only way to turn data into code in the Java platform. There are several phases to the process of classloading, so let's examine them in turn.

Loading

The classloading process starts with a loading a byte array. This is usually read in from a filesystem, but can be read from a URL or other location (often represented as a Path object).

The Classloader::defineClass() method is responsible for turning a class file (represented as a byte array) into a class object. It is a protected method and so is not accessible without subclassing.

The first job of defineClass() is loading. This produces the skeleton of a class object, corresponding to the class you're attempting to load. By this stage, some basic checks have been performed on the class (e.g., the constants in the constant pool have been checked to ensure that they're self-consistent).

However, loading doesn't produce a complete class object by itself, and the class isn't yet usable. Instead, after loading, the class must be linked. This step breaks down into separate subphases:

- Verification
- Preparation and resolution
- Initialization

Verification

Verification confirms that the class file conforms to expectations, and that it doesn't try to violate the JVM's security model (see "Secure Programming and Classloading" on page 315 for details).

JVM bytecode is designed so that it can be (mostly) checked statically. This has the effect of slowing down the classloading process but speeding up runtime (as checks can be omitted).

The verification step is designed to prevent the JVM from executing bytecodes that might crash it or put it into an undefined and untested state where it might be vulnerable to other attacks by malicious code. Bytecode verification is a defense against malicious hand-crafted Java bytecodes and untrusted Java compilers that might output invalid bytecodes.

The default methods mechanism works via classloading. When an implementation of an interface is being loaded, the class file is examined to see if implementations for default methods are present. If they are, classloading continues normally. If some are missing, the implementation is patched to add in the default implementation of the missing methods.

Preparation and Resolution

After successful verification, the class is prepared for use. Memory is allocated and static variables in the class are readied for initialization.

At this stage, variables aren't initialized, and no bytecode from the new class has been executed. Before we run any code, the JVM checks that every type referred to by the new class file is known to the runtime. If the types aren't known, they may also need to be loaded—which can kick off the classloading process again, as the JVM loads the new types.

This process of loading and discovery can execute iteratively until a stable set of types is reached. This is called the "transitive closure" of the original type that was loaded.[1]

Let's look at a quick example, by examining the dependencies of java.lang.Object. Figure 11-1 shows a simplified dependency graph for Object. It only shows the direct dependencies of Object that are visible in the public API of Object, and the direct, API-visible dependencies of those dependencies. In addition, the dependencies of Class on the reflection subsystem, and of PrintStream and PrintWriter on the I/O subsystems, are shown in very simplified form.

In Figure 11.1 we can see part of the transitive closure of Object.

Initialization

Once resolved, the JVM can finally initialize the class. Static variables can be initialized and static initialization blocks are run.

This is the first time that the JVM is executing bytecode from the newly loaded class. When the static blocks complete, the class is fully loaded and ready to go.

Secure Programming and Classloading

Java programs can dynamically load Java classes from a variety of sources, including untrusted sources, such as websites reached across an insecure network. The ability to create and work with such dynamic sources of code is one of the great strengths and features of Java. To make it work successfully, however, Java puts great emphasis on a security architecture that allows untrusted code to run safely, without fear of damage to the host system.

Java's classloading subsystem is where a lot of safety features are implemented. The central idea of the security aspects of the classloading architecture is that there is only one way to get new executable code into the process: a class.

---

1 As in Chapter 6, we're borrowing the expression transitive closure from the branch of mathematics called graph theory.

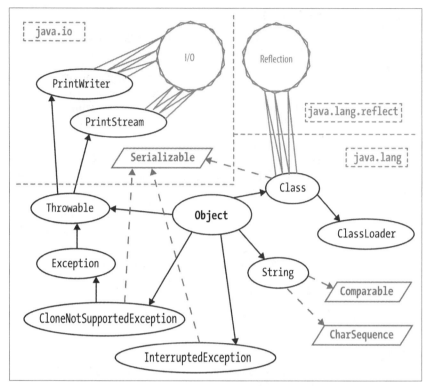

Figure 11-1. Transitive closure of types

This provides a "pinch point"—the only way to create a new class is to use the functionality provided by `Classloader` to load a class from a stream of bytes. By concentrating on making classloading secure, we can constrain the attack surface that needs to be protected.

One aspect of the JVM's design that is extremely helpful is that the JVM is a stack machine—so all operations are evaluated on a stack, rather than in registers. The stack state can be deduced at every point in a method, and this can be used to ensure that the bytecode doesn't attempt to violate the security model.

Some of the security checks that are implemented by the JVM are:

- All the bytecode of the class has valid parameters.
- All methods are called with the right number of parameters of the correct static types.
- Bytecode never tries to underflow or overflow the JVM stack.
- Local variables are not used before they are initialized.
- Variables are only assigned suitably typed values.

- Field, method, and class access control modifiers must be respected.

- No unsafe casts (e.g., attempts to convert an `int` to a pointer).

- All branch instructions are to legal points within the same method.

Of fundamental importance is the approach to memory, and pointers. In assembly and C/C++, integers and pointers are interchangeable, so an integer can be used as a memory address. We can write it in assembly like this:

```
mov eax, [STAT] ; Move 4 bytes from addr STAT into eax
```

The lowest level of the Java security architecture involves the design of the Java Virtual Machine and the bytecodes it executes. The JVM does not allow any kind of direct access to individual memory addresses of the underlying system, which prevents Java code from interfering with the native hardware and operating system. These intentional restrictions on the JVM are reflected in the Java language itself, which does not support pointers or pointer arithmetic.

Neither the language nor the JVM allow an integer to be cast to an object reference or vice versa, and there is no way whatsoever to obtain an object's address in memory. Without capabilities like these, malicious code simply cannot gain a foothold.

Recall from Chapter 2 that Java has two types of values—primitives and object references. Theses are the only things that can be put into variables. Note that "object contents" cannot be put into variables. Java has no equivalent of C's `struct` and always has pass-by-value semantics. For reference types, what is passed is a copy of the reference—which is a value.

References are represented in the JVM as pointers—but they are not directly manipulated by the bytecode. In fact, bytecode does not have opcodes for "access memory at location X."

Instead, all we can do is access fields and methods—bytecode cannot call an arbitrary memory location. This means that the JVM always knows the difference between code and data. In turn, this prevents a whole class of stack overflow and other attacks.

Applied Classloading

To apply knowledge of classloading, it's important to fully understand `java.lang.ClassLoader`.

This is an abstract class that is fully functional and has no abstract methods. The `abstract` modifier exists only to ensure that users must subclass `ClassLoader` if they want to make use of it.

In addition to the aforementioned `defineClass()` method, we can load classes via a public `loadClass()` method. This is commonly used by the `URLClassLoader` subclass, that can load classes from a URL or file path.

We can use `URLClassLoader` to load classes from the local disk like this:

```
String current = new File( "." ).getCanonicalPath();
try (URLClassLoader ulr =
  new URLClassLoader(new URL[] {new URL("file://"+ current + "/")})) {
  Class<?> clz = ulr.loadClass("com.example.DFACaller");
  System.out.println(clz.getName());
}
```

The argument to loadClass() is the binary name of the class file. Note that in order
for the URLClassLoader to find the classes correctly, they need to be in the expected
place on the filesystem. In this example, the class com.example.DFACaller would
need to be found in a file *com/example/DFACaller.class* relative to the working
directory.

Alternatively, Class provides Class.forName(), a static method that can load
classes that are present on the classpath but that haven't been referred to yet.

This method takes a fully qualified class name. For example:

```
Class<?> jdbcClz = Class.forName("oracle.jdbc.driver.OracleDriver");
```

It throws a ClassNotFoundException if class can't be found. As the example indicates, this was commonly used in older versions of JDBC to ensure that the correct
driver was loaded, while avoiding a direct import dependency on the driver classes.

With the advent of JDBC 4.0, this initialization step is no longer required.

Class.forName() has an alternative, three-argument form, which is sometimes
used in conjunction with alternative class loaders:

```
Class.forName(String name, boolean inited, Classloader classloader);
```

There are a host of subclasses of ClassLoader that deal with individual special cases
of classloading—which fit into the classloader hierarchy.

Classloader Hierarchy

The JVM has a hierarchy of classloaders—each classloader in the system (apart
from the initial, "primordial" classloader) has a parent that they can delegate to.

The convention is that a classloader will ask its parent to resolve and load a class,
and will only perform the job itself if the parent classloader is unable to comply.
Some common classloaders are shown in Figure 11.2.

Primordial classloader

This is the first classloader to appear in any JVM process, and is only used to load
the core system classes (which are contained in *rt.jar*). This classloader does no verification, and relies on the boot classpath being secure.

The boot classpath can be affected with the -Xbootclasspath switch—see Chapter 13 for details.

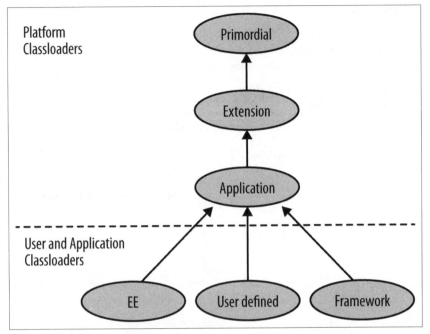

Figure 11-2. Classloader hierarchy

Extension classloader

This classloader is only used to load JDK extensions—usually from the *lib/ext* directory of the JVM installation directory.

It has the primordial classloader as its parent. It is not widely used, but does sometimes play a role in implementing debuggers and related development tools.

This is also the classloader used to load the Nashorn JavaScript environment (see Chapter 12).

Application classloader

This was historically sometimes called the system classloader, but this is a bad name, as it doesn't load the system (the primordial classloader does). Instead, it is the classloader that loads application code from the classpath. It is the most commonly encountered classloader, and has the extension classloader as its parent.

The application classloader is very widely used, but many advanced Java frameworks require functionality that the main classloaders do not supply. Instead, extensions to the standard classloaders are required. This forms the basis of "custom classloading"—which relies on implementing a new subclass of ClassLoader.

Custom classloader

When performing classloading, sooner or later we have to turn data into code. As noted earlier, the defineClass() (actually a group of related methods) is responsible for converting a byte[] into a class object.

This method is usually called from a subclass—for example, this simple custom classloader that creates a class object from a file on disk:

```
public static class DiskLoader extends ClassLoader {
  public DiskLoader() {
    super(DiskLoader.class.getClassLoader());
  }

  public Class<?> loadFromDisk(String clzName) throws IOException {
    byte[] b = Files.readAllBytes(Paths.get(clzName));

    return defineClass(null, b, 0, b.length);
  }
}
```

Notice that in the preceding example we didn't need to have the class file in the "correct" location on disk, as we did for the URLClassLoader example.

We need to provide a classloader to act as parent for any custom classloader. In this example, we provided the classloader that loaded the DiskLoader class (which would usually be the application classloader).

Custom classloading is a very common technique in Java EE and advanced SE environments, and it provides very sophisticated capabilities to the Java platform. We'll see an example of custom classloading later on in this chapter.

One drawback of dynamic classloading is that when working with a class object that we loaded dynamically, we typically have little or no information about the class. To work effectively with this class, we will therefore usually have to use a set of dynamic programming techniques known as reflection.

Reflection

Reflection is the capability of examining, operating on, and modifying objects at runtime. This includes modifying their structure and behavior—even self-modification.

Reflection is capable of working even when type and method names are not known at compile time. It uses the essential metadata provided by class objects, and can discover method or field names from the class object—and then acquire an object representing the method or field.

Instances can also be constructed reflexively (by using Class::newInstance() or another constructor). With a reflexively constructed object, and a Method object, we can then call any method on an object of a previously unknown type.

This makes reflection a very powerful technique—so it's important to understand when we should use it, and when it's overkill.

When to Use Reflection

Many, if not most Java frameworks use reflection in some capacity. Writing architectures that are flexible enough to cope with code that is unknown until runtime usually requires reflection. For example, plug-in architectures, debuggers, code browsers and REPL-like environments are usually implemented on top of reflection.

Reflection is also widely used in testing, for example by the JUnit and TestNG libraries, and for mock object creation. If you've used any kind of Java framework then you have almost certainly been using reflective code, even if you didn't realize it.

To start using the Reflection API in your own code, the most important thing to realize is that it is about accessing objects where virtually no information is known, and that the interactions can be cumbersome because of this.

Wherever possible, if some static information is known about dynamically loaded classes (e.g., that the classes loaded all implement a known interface), then this can greatly simplify the interaction with the classes and reduce the burden of operating reflectively.

It is a common mistake to try to create a reflective framework that tries to account for all possible circumstances, instead of dealing only with the cases that are immediately applicable to the problem domain.

How to Use Reflection

The first step in any reflective operation is to get a Class object representing the type to be operated on. From this, other objects, representing fields, methods, or constructors can be accessed, and applied to instances of the unknown type.

To get an instance of an unknown type, the simplest way is to use the no-arg constructor, which is made available directly via the Class object:

```
Class<?> clz = getSomeClassObject();
Object rcvr = clz.newInstance();
```

For constructors that take arguments, you will have to look up the precise constructor needed, represented as a Constructor object.

The Method objects are one of the most commonly used objects provided by Reflection. We'll discuss them in detail—the Constructor and Field objects are similar in many respects.

Method objects

A class object contains a Method object for each method on the class. These are lazily created after classloading, and so aren't immediately visible in an IDE's debugger.

Let's look at the source code from Method to see what information and metadata is held for each method:

```
private Class<?>                clazz;
private int                     slot;
// This is guaranteed to be interned by the VM in the 1.4
// reflection implementation
private String                  name;
private Class<?>                returnType;
private Class<?>[]              parameterTypes;
private Class<?>[]              exceptionTypes;
private int                     modifiers;
// Generics and annotations support
private transient String        signature;
// Generic info repository; lazily initialized
private transient MethodRepository genericInfo;
private byte[]                  annotations;
private byte[]                  parameterAnnotations;
private byte[]                  annotationDefault;
private volatile MethodAccessor methodAccessor;
```

This provides all available information, including the exceptions the method can throw, annotations (with a retention policy of RUNTIME), and even the generics information that was otherwise removed by javac.

We can explore the metadata contained on the Method object, by calling accessor methods, but by far the single biggest use case for Method is reflexive invocation.

The methods represented by these objects can be executed by reflection using the invoke() method on Method. An example of invoking hashCode() on a String object follows:

```
Object rcvr = "a";
try {
  Class<?>[] argTypes = new Class[] { };
  Object[] args = null;

  Method meth = rcvr.getClass().getMethod("hashCode", argTypes);
  Object ret = meth.invoke(rcvr, args);
  System.out.println(ret);

} catch (IllegalArgumentException | NoSuchMethodException |
        SecurityException e) {
  e.printStackTrace();
} catch (IllegalAccessException | InvocationTargetException x) {
  x.printStackTrace();
}
```

To get the Method object we want to use, we call getMethod() on the class object. This will return a reference to a Method corresponding to a public method on the class.

Note that the static type of rcvr was declared to be Object. No static type information was used during the reflective invocation. The invoke() method also returns Object, so the actual return type of hashCode() has been autoboxed to Integer.

This autoboxing is one of the aspects of Reflection where some of the slight awkwardness of the API can be seen—which is the subject of the next section.

Problems with Reflection

Java's Reflection API is often the only way to deal with dynamically loaded code, but there are a number of annoyances in the API that can make it slightly awkward to deal with:

- Heavy use of Object[] to represent call arguments and other instances.
- Also Class[] when talking about types.
- Methods can be overloaded on name, so we need an array of types to distinguish between methods.
- Representing primitive types can be problematic—we have to manually box and unbox.

void is a particular problem—there is a void.class, but it's not used consistently. Java doesn't really know whether void is a type or not, and some methods in the Reflection API use null instead.

This is cumbersome, and can be error prone—in particular, the slight verbosity of Java's array syntax can lead to errors.

One further problem is the treatment of non-public methods. Instead of using get Method(), we must use getDeclaredMethod() to get a reference to a non-public method, and then override the Java access control subsystem with setAccessible() to allow it to be executed:

```java
public class MyCache {
  private void flush() {
    // Flush the cache...
  }
}

Class<?> clz = MyCache.class;
try {
  Object rcvr = clz.newInstance();
  Class<?>[] argTypes = new Class[] { };
  Object[] args = null;

  Method meth = clz.getDeclaredMethod("flush", argTypes);
  meth.setAccessible(true);
  meth.invoke(rcvr, args);
} catch (IllegalArgumentException | NoSuchMethodException |
        InstantiationException | SecurityException e) {
```

```
          e.printStackTrace();
    } catch (IllegalAccessException | InvocationTargetException x) {
        x.printStackTrace();
    }
```

However, it should be pointed out that reflection always involves unknown information. To some degree, we just have to live with some of this verbosity as the price of dealing with reflective invocation, and the dynamic, runtime power that it gives to the developer.

As a final example in this section, let's show how to combine reflection with custom classloading to inspect a class file on disk and see if it contains any deprecated methods (these should be marked with @Deprecated):

```
public class CustomClassloadingExamples {
    public static class DiskLoader extends ClassLoader {

        public DiskLoader() {
            super(DiskLoader.class.getClassLoader());
        }

        public Class<?> loadFromDisk(String clzName)
          throws IOException {
            byte[] b = Files.readAllBytes(Paths.get(clzName));

            return defineClass(null, b, 0, b.length);
        }
    }

    public void findDeprecatedMethods(Class<?> clz) {
        for (Method m : clz.getMethods()) {
            for (Annotation a : m.getAnnotations()) {
                if (a.annotationType() == Deprecated.class) {
                    System.out.println(m.getName());
                }
            }
        }
    }

    public static void main(String[] args)
      throws IOException, ClassNotFoundException {
        CustomClassloadingExamples rfx =
          new CustomClassloadingExamples();

        if (args.length > 0) {
            DiskLoader dlr = new DiskLoader();
            Class<?> clzToTest = dlr.loadFromDisk(args[0]);
            rfx.findDeprecatedMethods(clzToTest);
        }
    }
}
```

Dynamic Proxies

One last piece of the Java Reflection story is the creation of dynamic proxies. These are classes (which extend `java.lang.reflect.Proxy`) that implement a number of interfaces. The implementing class is constructed dynamically at runtime, and forwards all calls to an invocation handler object:

```java
InvocationHandler h = new InvocationHandler() {
  @Override
  public Object invoke(Object proxy, Method method, Object[] args)
                                        throws Throwable {
    String name = method.getName();
    System.out.println("Called as: "+ name);
    switch (name) {
      case "isOpen":
        return false;
      case "close":
        return null;
    }

    return null;
  }
};

Channel c =
  (Channel) Proxy.newProxyInstance(Channel.class.getClassLoader(),
                          new Class[] { Channel.class }, h);
c.isOpen();
c.close();
```

Proxies can be used as stand-in objects for testing (especially in test mocking approaches).

Another use case is to provide partial implementations of interfaces, or to decorate or otherwise control some aspect of delegation:

```java
public class RememberingList implements InvocationHandler {
  private final List<String> proxied = new ArrayList<>();

  @Override
  public Object invoke(Object proxy, Method method, Object[] args)
                      throws Throwable {
    String name = method.getName();
    switch (name) {
      case "clear":
        return null;
      case "remove":
      case "removeAll":
        return false;
    }

    return method.invoke(proxied, args);
```

```
    }
  }

RememberingList hList = new RememberingList();

List<String> l =
  (List<String>) Proxy.newProxyInstance(List.class.getClassLoader(),
                                        new Class[] { List.class },
                                        hList);
l.add("cat");
l.add("bunny");
l.clear();
System.out.println(l);
```

Proxies are an extremely powerful and flexible capability that are used within many Java frameworks.

Method Handles

In Java 7, a brand new mechanism for introspection and method access was introduced. This was originally designed for use with dynamic languages, which may need to participate in method dispatch decisions at runtime. To support this at the JVM level, the new invokedynamic bytecode was introduced. This bytecode was not used by Java 7 itself, but with the advent of Java 8, it was extensively used in both lambda expressions and the Nashorn JavaScript implementation.

Even without invokedynamic, the new Method Handles API is comparable in power to many aspects of the Reflection API—and can be cleaner and conceptually simpler to use, even standalone. It can be thought of as Reflection done in a safer, more modern way.

MethodType

In Reflection, method signatures are represented as Class[]. This is quite cumbersome. By contrast, method handles rely on MethodType objects. These are a typesafe and object-orientated way to represent the type signature of a method.

They include the return type and argument types, but not the receiver type or name of the method. The name is not present as this allows any method of the correct signature to be bound to any name (as per the functional interface behavior of lambda expressions).

A type signature for a method is represented as an immutable instance of Method Type, as acquired from the factory method MethodType.methodType(). For example:

```
MethodType m2Str = MethodType.methodType(String.class); // toString()

// Integer.parseInt()
MethodType mtParseInt =
  MethodType.methodType(Integer.class, String.class);
```

```
// defineClass() from ClassLoader
MethodType mtdefClz = MethodType.methodType(Class.class, String.class,
                                            byte[].class, int.class,
                                            int.class);
```

This single piece of the puzzle provides significant gains over Reflection, as it makes method signatures significantly easier to represent and discuss. The next step is to acquire a handle on a method. This is achieved by a lookup process.

Method Lookup

Method lookup queries are performed on the class where a method is defined, and are dependent on the context that they are executed from. In this example, we can see that when we attempt to lookup the protected `Class::defineClass()` method from a general look up context, we fail to resolve it with an `IllegalAccessException`, as the protected method is not accessible:

```
public static void lookupDefineClass(Lookup l) {
  MethodType mt = MethodType.methodType(Class.class, String.class,
                                        byte[].class, int.class,
                                        int.class);

  try {
    MethodHandle mh =
      l.findVirtual(ClassLoader.class, "defineClass", mt);
    System.out.println(mh);
  } catch (NoSuchMethodException | IllegalAccessException e) {
    e.printStackTrace();
  }
}

Lookup l = MethodHandles.lookup();
lookupDefineClass(l);
```

We always need to call `MethodHandles.lookup()`—this gives us a lookup context object based on the currently executing method.

Lookup objects have several methods (which all start with `find`) declared on them for method resolution. These include `findVirtual()`, `findConstructor()`, and `findStatic()`.

One big difference between the Reflection and Method Handles APIs is access control. A `Lookup` object will only return methods that are accessible to the context where the lookup was created—and there is no way to subvert this (no equivalent of Reflection's `setAccessible()` hack).

Method handles therefore always comply with the security manager, even when the equivalent reflective code does not. They are access-checked at the point where the lookup context is constructed—the lookup object will not return handles to any methods to which it does not have proper access.

The lookup object, or method handles derived from it, can be returned to other contexts, including ones where access to the method would no longer be possible. Under those circumstances, the handle is still executable—access control is checked at lookup time, as we can see in this example:

```
public class SneakyLoader extends ClassLoader {
  public SneakyLoader() {
    super(SneakyLoader.class.getClassLoader());
  }

  public Lookup getLookup() {
    return MethodHandles.lookup();
  }
}

SneakyLoader snLdr = new SneakyLoader();
l = snLdr.getLookup();
lookupDefineClass(l);
```

With a Lookup object, we're able to produce method handles to any method we have access to. We can also produce a way of accessing fields that may not have a method that gives access. The findGetter() and findSetter() methods on Lookup produce method handles that can read or update fields as needed.

Invoking Method Handles

A method handle represents the ability to call a method. They are strongly typed and as typesafe as possible. Instances are all of some subclass of java.lang.invoke.MethodHandle, which is a class that needs special treatment from the JVM.

There are two ways to invoke a method handle—invoke() and invokeExact(). Both of these take the receiver and call arguments as parameters. invokeExact() tries to call the method handle directly as is, whereas invoke() will massage call arguments if needed.

In general, invoke() performs an asType() conversion if necessary—this converts arguments according to these rules:

- A primitive argument will be boxed if required.
- A boxed primitive will be unboxed if required.
- Primitives will be widened is necessary.
- A void return type will be massaged to 0 or null, depending on whether the expected return was primitive or of reference type.
- null values are passed through, regardless of static type.

With these potential conversions in place, invocation looks like this:

```
Object rcvr = "a";
try {
  MethodType mt = MethodType.methodType(int.class);
  MethodHandles.Lookup l = MethodHandles.lookup();
  MethodHandle mh = l.findVirtual(rcvr.getClass(), "hashCode", mt);

  int ret;
  try {
    ret = (int)mh.invoke(rcvr);
    System.out.println(ret);
  } catch (Throwable t) {
    t.printStackTrace();
  }
} catch (IllegalArgumentException |
  NoSuchMethodException | SecurityException e) {
  e.printStackTrace();
} catch (IllegalAccessException x) {
  x.printStackTrace();
}
```

Method handles provide a clearer and more coherent way to access the same dynamic programming capabilities as Reflection. In addition, they are designed to work well with the low-level execution model of the JVM and thus hold out the promise of much better performance than Reflection can provide.

12

Nashorn

With Java 8, Oracle has included Nashorn, a new JavaScript implementation that runs on the JVM. Nashorn is designed to replace the original JavaScript-on-the-JVM project—which was called Rhino (Nashorn is the German word for "rhino").

Nashorn is a completely rewritten implementation and strives for easy interoperability with Java, high performance, and precise conformance to the JavaScript ECMA specifications. Nashorn was the first implementation of JavaScript to hit a perfect 100% on spec compliance and is already at least 20 times faster than Rhino on most workloads.

Introduction to Nashorn

In this chapter, we will assume some basic understanding of JavaScript. If you aren't already familiar with basic JavaScript concepts, then *Head First JavaScript* by Michael Morrison (O'Reilly) is a good place to start.

If you recall the differences between Java and JavaScript outlined in "Java Compared to JavaScript" on page 12, you know that we can see that the two languages are very different. It may, therefore, seem surprising that JavaScript should be able to run on top of the same virtual machine as Java.

Non-Java Languages on the JVM

In fact, there are a very large number of non-Java languages that run on the JVM—and some of them are a lot more unlike Java than JavaScript is. This is made possible by the fact that the Java language and JVM are only very loosely coupled, and only really interact via the definition of the class file format. This can be accomplished in two different ways:

- The source language has an interpreter that has been implemented in Java.

The interpreter runs on the JVM and executes programs written in the source language.

- The source language ships with a compiler that produces class files from units of source language code.

The resulting compiled class files are then directly executed on the JVM, usually with some additional language-specific runtime support.

Nashorn takes the second approach—but with the added refinement that the compiler is inside the runtime, so that JavaScript source code is never compiled before program execution begins. This means that JavaScript that was not specifically written for Nashorn can still be easily deployed on the platform.

Nashorn is unlike many other JVM languages (such as JRuby) in that it does not implement any form of interpreter. Nashorn always compiles JavaScript to JVM bytecode and executes the bytecode directly.

This is interesting, from a technical perspective, but many developers are curious as to what role Nashorn is intended to play in the mature and well-established Java ecosystem. Let's look at that role next.

Motivation

Nashorn serves several purposes within the Java and JVM ecosystem. Firstly, it provides a viable environment for JavaScript developers to discover the power of the JVM. Second, it enables companies to continue to leverage their existing investment in Java technologies while additionally adopting JavaScript as a development language. Last, it provides a great engineering showcase for the advanced virtual machine technology present in the HotSpot Java Virtual Machine.

With the continued growth and adoption of JavaScript, broadening out from its traditional home in the browser to more general-purpose computing and the server side, Nashorn represents a great bridge between the existing rock-solid Java ecosystem and a promising wave of new technologies.

For now, let's move on to discuss the mechanics of how Nashorn works, and how to get started with the platform. There are several different ways in which JavaScript code can be executed on Nashorn, and in the next section we'll look at two of the most commonly used.

Executing JavaScript with Nashorn

In this section, we'll be introducing the Nashorn environment, and discuss two different ways of executing JavaScript (both of which are present in the *bin* subdirectory of *$JAVA_HOME*):

`jrunscript`

A simple script runner for executing JavaScript as *.js* files.

`jjs`

A more full-featured shell—suitable for both running scripts and use as an interactive, read-eval-print-loop (REPL) environment for exploring Nashorn and its features.

Let's start by looking at the basic runner, which is suitable for the majority of simple JavaScript applications.

Running from the Command Line

To run a JavaScript file called *my_script.js* with Nashorn, just use the `jrunscript` command:

```
jrunscript my_script.js
```

`jrunscript` can also be used with different script engines than Nashorn (see "Nashorn and javax.script" on page 340 for more details on script engines) and it provides a `-l` switch to specify them if needed:

```
jrunscript -l nashorn my_script.js
```

With this switch, `jrunscript` can even run scripts in languages other than JavaScript, provided a suitable script engine is available.

The basic runner is perfectly suitable for simple use cases but it has limitations and so for serious use we need a more capable execution environment. This is provided by `jjs`, the Nashorn shell.

Using the Nashorn Shell

The Nashorn shell command is `jjs`. This can be used either interactively, or non-interactively, as a drop-in replacement for `jrunscript`.

The simplest JavaScript example is, of course, the classic "Hello World," so let's look at how we would achieve this in the interactive shell:

```
$ jjs
jjs> print("Hello World!");
Hello World!
jjs>
```

Nashorn interoperability with Java can be easily handled from the shell. We'll discuss this in full detail in "Calling Java from Nashorn" on page 342, but to give a first example, we can directly access Java classes and methods from JavaScript by using the fully qualified class name. As a concrete example, let's access Java's builtin regular expression support:

```
jjs> var pattern = java.util.regex.Pattern.compile("\\d+");
jjs> var myNums = pattern.split("a1b2c3d4e5f6");

jjs> print(myNums);
[Ljava.lang.String;@10b48321

jjs> print(myNums[0]);
a
```

When we used the REPL to print out the JavaScript variable myNums, we got the result [Ljava.lang.String;@10b48321— this is a tell-tale sign that despite being represented in a JavaScript variable, myNums is really a Java array of strings.

We'll have a great deal more to say about interoperation between Nashorn and Java later on, but first let's discuss some of the additional features of jjs. The general form of the jjs command is:

```
jjs [<options>] <files> [-- <arguments>]
```

There are a number of options that can be passed to jjs—some of the most common are:

- -cp or -classpath indicates where additional Java classes can be found (to be used via the Java.type mechanism, as we'll see later).

- -doe or -dump-on-error will produce a full error dump if Nashorn is forced to exit.

- -J is used to pass options to the JVM. For example, if we want to increase the maximum memory available to the JVM:

```
$ jjs -J-Xmx4g
jjs> java.lang.Runtime.getRuntime().maxMemory()
3817799680
```

- -strict causes all script and functions to be run in JavaScript strict mode. This is a feature of JavaScript that was introduced with ECMAScript version 5, and is intended to reduce bugs and errors. Strict mode is recommended for all new development in JavaScript, and if you're not familiar with it you should read up on it.

- -D allows the developer to pass key-value pairs to Nashorn as system properties, in the usual way for the JVM. For example:

```
$ jjs -DmyKey=myValue
jjs> java.lang.System.getProperty("myKey");
myValue
```

- `-v` or `-version` is the standard Nashorn version string.
- `-fv` or `-fullversion` prints the full Nashorn version string.
- `-fx` is used to execute a script as a JavaFX GUI application. This allows a JavaFX programmer to write a lot less boilerplate by making use of Nashorn.[1]
- `-h` is the standard help switch.
- `-scripting` can be used to enable Nashorn-specific scripting extensions. This is the subject of the next subsection.

Scripting with jjs

The `jjs` shell can be a good way to test out some basic JavaScript, or to work interactively with an unfamiliar JavaScript package (e.g., when learning it). However, it is slightly hampered by lacking multiline input and other more advanced features that are often expected when developing with languages that make heavy use of a REPL.

Instead, `jjs` is very suitable for noninteractive use, such as bringing up a daemon process written in JavaScript. For use cases like this, we invoke `jjs` like this:

```
$ jjs -scripting my_script.js
```

This enables us to make use of the enhanced features of `jjs`. These include some useful extensions, many of which make using Nashorn slightly more familiar to the script programmer.

Scripting comments

In traditional Unix scripting, the `#` character is used to indicate a comment that runs until the end of the line. JavaScript, of course, uses C/C++ style comments that include `//` to indicate a comment that runs to the end of the line. Nashorn conforms to this as well, but in scripting mode also accepts the Unix scripting style, so that this code is perfectly legal:

```
#!/usr/bin/jjs

# A perfectly legal comment in scripting mode

print("After the comment");
```

---

1 JavaFX is a standard Java technology used for making GUIs—but it is outside the scope of this book.

Inline command execution

This feature is usually referred to as "backticks" by seasoned Unix programmers. So, just as we could write this bit of bash to download content from Google by using the Unix curl command:

```
echo "Google says: " `curl http://www.google.co.uk`
```

we can also use the ` backtick quotes to enclose a Unix shell command that we want to run from within a Nashorn script. Like this:

```
print("Google says: "+ `curl http://www.google.co.uk`);
```

String interpolation

String interpolation is a special bit of syntax that allows the programmer to directly include the contents of a variable without using string concatenation. In Nashorn scripting, we can use the syntax ${<variable name>} to interpolate variables within strings. For example, the previous example of downloading a web page can be rewritten using interpolation like this:

```
var url = "www.google.co.uk";
var pageContents = `curl http://${url}`;

print("Google says: ${pageContents}");
```

Special variables

Nashorn also provides several special global variables and functions that are specifically helpful for scripting and are not normally available in JavaScript. For example, the arguments to a script can be accessed via the variable $ARG. The arguments must be passed using the -- convention, like this:

```
jjs test1.jjs -- aa bbb cccc
```

Then the arguments can be accessed as shown in this example:

```
print($ARG);

for(var i=0; i < $ARG.length; i++) {
    print("${i}: "+ $ARG[i]);
}
```

> The variable $ARG is a JavaScript array (as we can see from how it behaves when it's passed to print()) and needs to be treated as one. This syntax may be a little confusing for programmers coming from other languages, where the $ symbol often indicates a scalar variable.

The next special global variable that we'll meet is $ENV, that provides an interface to the current environment variables. For example, to print out the current user's home directory:

```
print("HOME = "+ $ENV.HOME); # Prints /home/ben for me
```

Nashorn also provides access to a special global function called $EXEC(). This works like the backticks we met just now, as this example shows:

```
var execOutput = $EXEC("echo Print this on stdout");
print(execOutput);
```

You may have noticed that when we use the backtick or $EXEC() then the output of the executed command is not printed—but instead ends up as the return value of the function. This is to prevent the printed output of executed commands from corrupting the output of the main script.

Nashorn provides two other special variables that can help the programmer to work with the output of commands that are executed from within a script: $OUT and $ERR. These are used to capture the output and any error messages from a command that is executed from within a script. For example:

```
$EXEC("echo Print this on stdout");

// Code that doesn't change stdout

var saveOut = $OUT;
print("- - - - - - -");
print(saveOut);
```

The contents of $OUT and $ERR persist until they are overwritten by subsequent code in the main script that can also affect the values held there (such as another command execution).

Inline documents

JavaScript, like Java, does not support strings where the opening quote is on one line and the closing quote on another (known as *multiline strings*). However, Nashorn in scripting mode supports this as an extension. This feature is also known as an inline document or a *heredoc* and is a common feature of scripting languages.

To use a heredoc, use the syntax <<END_TOKEN to indicate that the heredoc starts on the next line. Then, everything until the end token (which can be any string, but is usually all capitals—strings like END, END_DOC, END_STR, EOF, and EOSTR are all quite common) is part of the multiline string. After the end token, the script resumes as normal. Let's look at an example:

```
var hw = "Hello World!";
var output = <<EOSTR;

This is a multiline string
```

```
It can interpolate too - ${hw}
EOSTR
print(output);
```

Nashorn helper functions

Nashorn also provides some helper functions to make it easier for developers to accomplish common tasks that shell scripts often want to perform:

`print()` / `echo()`
> We've been using `print()` throughout many of our examples, and these functions behave exactly as expected. They print the string they've been passed, followed by a newline character.

`quit()` / `exit()`
> These two functions are completely equivalent—they both cause the script to exit. They can take an integer parameter that will be used as the return code of the script's process. If no argument is supplied, they will default to using 0, as is customary for Unix processes.

`readLine()`
> Reads a single line of input from standard input (usually the keyboard). By default, it will print the line out on standard output, but if the return value of `readLine()` is assigned to a variable, the entered data will end up there instead, as in this example:

```
print("Please enter your name: ");
var name = readLine();
print("Please enter your age: ");
var age = readLine();

print(<<EOREC);
Student Record
-+-+-+-+-+-+-+-
Name: ${name}
Age:  ${age}
EOREC
```

`readFully()`
> Instead of reading from standard input, `readFully()` loads the entire contents of a file. As with `readLine()`, the contents are either printed to standard output, or assigned to a variable:

```
var contents = readFully("input.txt");
```

`load()`
> This function is used to load and evaluate (via JavaScript's `eval`) a script. The script can be located by a local path, or a URL. Alternatively, it may be defined as a string using JavaScript's *script object* notation.

When using load() to evaluate other scripts, unexpected errors may occur. JavaScript supports a form of exception handling using try-catch blocks, so you should use it when loading code.

Here's a quick example of how to load the D3 graphics visualization library from Nashorn:

```
try {
    load("http://d3js.org/d3.v3.min.js");
} catch (e) {
    print("Something went wrong, probably that we're not a web browser");
}
```

loadWithNewGlobal()

When we use load(), it evaluates the script based on the current JavaScript context. Sometimes we want to put the script into its own, clean context. In these cases, use loadWithNewGlobal() instead, as this starts off the script with a fresh, global context.

Shebang syntax

All the features in this section help to make jjs a good alternative language that can easily be used to write shell scripts as bash, Perl, or other scripting languages. One final feature helps to round out this support—the availability of the "shebang" syntax for starting up scripts written in Nashorn.

If the first line of an executable script starts with #! followed by a path to an executable, then a Unix operating system will assume the path points at an interpreter that is able to handle this type of script. If the script is executed, the OS will execute the interpreter and pass it the script file to be handled.

In the case of Nashorn, it is good practice to symlink (possibly needing sudo access) so that there is a link from */usr/bin/jjs* (or */usr/local/bin/jjs*) to the actual location of the jjs binary (usually *$JAVA_HOME/bin/jjs*). The Nashorn shell scripts can then be written like this:

```
#!/usr/bin/jjs

# ... rest of script
```

For more advanced use cases (e.g., long-running daemons) Nashorn can even provide compatibility with Node.js. This is achieved by the Avatar.js portion of Project Avatar, that is discussed in "Project Avatar" on page 347.

The tools we've seen in this section easily enable JavaScript code to be run directly from the command line, but in many cases we will want to go the other way. That is, we will want to call out to Nashorn and execute JavaScript code from within a Java program. The API that enables us to do this is contained in the Java package javax.script, so let's move on to examine that package next, and discuss how Java interacts with engines for interpreting scripting languages.

Nashorn and javax.script

Nashorn is not the first scripting language to ship with the Java platform. The story starts with the inclusion of javax.script in Java 6, which provided a general interface for engines for scripting languages to interoperate with Java.

This general interface included concepts fundamental to scripting languages, such as execution and compilation of scripting code (whether a full script or just a single scripting statement in an already existing context). In addition, a notion of binding between scripting entities and Java was introduced, as well as script engine discovery. Finally, javax.script provides optional support for invocation (distinct from execution, as it allows intermediate code to be exported from a scripting language's runtime and used by the JVM runtime).

The example language provided was Rhino, but many other scripting languages were created to take advantage of the support provided. With Java 8, Rhino has been removed, and Nashorn is now the default scripting language supplied with the Java platform.

Introducing javax.script with Nashorn

Let's look at a very simple example of how to use Nashorn to run JavaScript from Java:

```java
import javax.script.*;

ScriptEngineManager m = new ScriptEngineManager();
ScriptEngine e = m.getEngineByName("nashorn");

try {
  e.eval("print('Hello World!');");
} catch (final ScriptException se) {
  // ...
}
```

The key concept here is ScriptEngine, which is obtained from a ScriptEngineManager. This provides an empty scripting environment, to which we can add code via the eval() method.

The Nashorn engine provides a single global JavaScript object, so all calls to eval() will execute on the same environment. This means that we can make a series of eval() calls and build up JavaScript state in the script engine. For example:

```java
e.eval("i = 27;");
e.put("j", 15);
e.eval("var z = i + j;");

System.out.println(((Number) e.get("z")).intValue()); // prints 42
```

Note that one of the problems with interacting with a scripting engine directly from Java is that we don't normally have any information about what the types of values are.

Nashorn has a fairly close binding to much of the Java type system, so we need to be somewhat careful, however. When dealing with the JavaScript equivalents of primitive types, these will typically be converted to the appropriate (boxed) types when they are made visible to Java. For example, if we add the following line to our previous example:

```
System.out.println(e.get("z").getClass());
```

we can easily see that the value returned by e.get("z") is of type java.lang.Integer. If we change the code very slightly, like this:

```
e.eval("i = 27.1;");
e.put("j", 15);
e.eval("var z = i + j;");

System.out.println(e.get("z").getClass());
```

then this is sufficient to alter the type of the return value of e.get("z") to type java.lang.Double, which marks out the distinction between the two type systems. In other implementations of JavaScript, these would both be treated as the numeric type (as JavaScript does not define integer types). Nashorn, however, is more aware of the actual type of the data.

When dealing wih JavaScript that the Java programmer must be consciously aware of the difference between Java's static typing and the dynamic nature of JavaScript types. Bugs can easily creep in if this awareness is lost.

In our examples, we have made use of the get() and put() methods on the Script Engine. These allow us to directly get and set objects within the global scope of the script being executed by a Nashorn engine, without having to write or eval JavaScript code directly.

The javax.script API

Let's round out this section with a brief description of some key classes and interfaces in the javax.script API. This is a fairly small API (six interfaces, five classes, and one exception) that has not changed since its introduction in Java 6.

ScriptEngineManager

The entry point into the scripting support. It maintains a list of available scripting implementations in this process. This is achieved via Java's *service provider* mechanism, which is a very general way of managing extensions to the platform that may have wildly different implementations. By default, the only scripting extension available is Nashorn, although other scripting environments (such as Groovy or JRuby) can also be made available.

`ScriptEngine`

This class represents the script engine responsible for maintaining the environment in which our scripts will be interpreted.

`Bindings`

This interface extends `Map` and provides a mapping between strings (the names of variables or other symbols) and scripting objects. Nashorn uses this to implement the `ScriptObjectMirror` mechanism for interoperability.

In practice, most applications will deal with the relatively opaque interface offered by methods on `ScriptEngine` such as `eval()`, `get()`, and `put()`, but it's useful to understand the basics of how this interface plugs in to the overall scripting API.

Advanced Nashorn

Nashorn is a sophisticated programming environment, which has been engineered to be a robust platform for deploying applications, and to have great interoperability with Java. Let's look at some more advanced use cases for JavaScript to Java integration, and examine how this is achieved by looking inside Nashorn at some implementation details.

Calling Java from Nashorn

As each JavaScript object is compiled into an instance of a Java class, it's perhaps not surprising that Nashorn has seamless integration with Java—despite the major difference in type systems and language features. However, there are still mechanisms that need to be in place to get the most out of this integration.

We've already seen that we can directly access Java classes and methods from Nashorn, for example:

```
$ jjs -Dkey=value
jjs> print(java.lang.System.getProperty("key"));
value
```

Let's take a closer look at the syntax and see how to achieve this support in Nashorn.

JavaClass and JavaPackage

From a Java perspective, the expression `java.lang.System.getProperty("key")` reads as fully qualified access to the static method `getProperty()` on `java.lang.System`. However, as JavaScript syntax, this reads like a chain of property accesses, starting from the symbol `java`—so let's investigate how this symbol behaves in the `jjs` shell:

```
jjs> print(java);
[JavaPackage java]
```

```
jjs> print(java.lang.System);
[JavaClass java.lang.System]
```

So java is a special Nashorn object that gives access to the Java system packages, which are given the JavaScript type JavaPackage, and Java classes are represented by the JavaScript type JavaClass. Any top-level package can be directly used as a package navigation object, and subpackages can be assigned to a JavaScript object. This allows syntax that gives concise access to Java classes:

```
jjs> var juc = java.util.concurrent;
jjs> var chm = new juc.ConcurrentHashMap;
```

In addition to navigation by package objects, there is another object, called Java, which has a number of useful methods on it. One of the most important is the Java.type() method. This allows the user to query the Java type system, and get access to Java classes. For example:

```
jjs> var clz = Java.type("java.lang.System");
jjs> print(clz);
[JavaClass java.lang.System]
```

If the class is not present on the classpath (e.g., specified using the -cp option to jjs), then a ClassNotFoundException is thrown (jjs will wrap this in a Java Runti meException):

```
jjs> var klz = Java.type("Java.lang.Zystem");
java.lang.RuntimeException: java.lang.ClassNotFoundException:
    Java.lang.Zystem
```

The JavaScript JavaClass objects can be used like Java class objects in most cases (they are a slightly different type—but just think of them as the Nashorn-level mirror of a class object). For example, we can use a JavaClass to create a new Java object directly from Nashorn:

```
jjs> var clz = Java.type("java.lang.Object");
jjs> var obj = new clz;
jjs> print(obj);
java.lang.Object@73d4cc9e

jjs> print(obj.hashCode());
1943325854

// Note that this syntax does not work
jjs> var obj = clz.new;
jjs> print(obj);
undefined
```

However, you should be slightly careful. The jjs environment automatically prints out the results of expressions—which can lead to some unexpected behavior:

```
jjs> var clz = Java.type("java.lang.System");
jjs> clz.out.println("Baz!");
```

```
Baz!
null
```

The point here is that `java.lang.System.out.println()` has a return type of void (i.e., it does not return a value). However, `jjs` expects expressions to have a value and, in the absence of a variable assignment, it will print it out. So the nonexistent return value of `println()` is mapped to the JavaScript value `null`, and printed out.

 Java programmers who are not familiar with JavaScript should be aware that the handling of `null` and missing values in Java-Script is subtle, and in particular that `null != undefined`.

JavaScript functions and Java lambda expressions

The interoperability between JavaScript and Java goes to a very deep level. We can even use JavaScript functions as anonymous implementations of Java interfaces (or as lambda expressions). For example, let's use a JavaScript function as an instance of the `Callable` interface (which represents a block of code to be called later). This has only a single method, `call()`, which takes no parameters and returns void. In Nashorn, we can use a JavaScript function as a lambda expression instead:

```
jjs> var clz = Java.type("java.util.concurrent.Callable");
jjs> print(clz);
[JavaClass java.util.concurrent.Callable]
jjs> var obj = new clz(function () { print("Foo"); } );
jjs> obj.call();
Foo
```

The basic fact that is being demonstrated is that, in Nashorn, there is no distinction between a JavaScript function and a Java lambda expression. Just as we saw in Java, the function is being automatically converted to an object of the appropriate type. Let's look at how we might use a Java `ExecutorService` to execute some Nashorn JavaScript on a Java thread pool:

```
jjs> var juc = java.util.concurrent;
jjs> var exc = juc.Executors.newSingleThreadExecutor();
jjs> var clbl = new juc.Callable(function (){
  \java.lang.Thread.sleep(10000); return 1; });
jjs> var fut = exc.submit(clbl);
jjs> fut.isDone();
false
jjs> fut.isDone();
true
```

The reduction in boilerplate compared to the equivalent Java code (even with Java 8 lambdas) is quite staggering. However, there are some limitations caused by the manner in which lambdas have been implemented. For example:

```
jjs> var fut=exc.submit(function (){\
java.lang.Thread.sleep(10000); return 1;});
java.lang.RuntimeException: java.lang.NoSuchMethodException: Can't
unambiguously select between fixed arity signatures
[(java.lang.Runnable), (java.util.concurrent.Callable)] of the method
java.util.concurrent.Executors.FinalizableDelegatedExecutorService↵
.submit for argument types
[jdk.nashorn.internal.objects.ScriptFunctionImpl]
```

The problem here is that the thread pool has an overloaded submit() method. One
version will accept a Callable and the other will accept a Runnable. Unfortunately,
the JavaScript function is eligible (as a lambda expression) for conversion to both
types. This is where the error message about not being able to "unambiguously
select" comes from. The runtime could choose either, and can't choose between
them.

Nashorn's JavaScript Language Extensions

As we've discussed, Nashorn is a completely conformant implementation of ECMA-
Script 5.1 (as JavaScript is known to the standards body). In addition, however, Nashorn also implements a number of JavaScript language syntax extensions, to make
life easier for the developer. These extensions should be familiar to developers used
to working with JavaScript, and quite a few of them duplicate extensions present in
the Mozilla dialect of JavaScript. Let's take a look at a few of the most common, and
useful, extensions.

Foreach loops

Standard JavaScript does not have an equivalent of Java's foreach loop, but Nashorn
implements the Mozilla syntax for *for each in* loops, like this:

```
var jsEngs = [ "Nashorn", "Rhino", "V8", "IonMonkey", "Nitro" ];
for each (js in jsEngs) {
    print(js);
}
```

Single expression functions

Nashorn also supports another small syntax enhancement, designed to make one-
line functions that comprise a single expression easier to read. If a function (named
or anonymous) comprises just a single expression, then the braces and return statements can be omitted. In the example that follows, cube() and cube2() are completely equivalent functions, but cube() is not normally legal JavaScript syntax:

```
function cube(x) x*x*x;

function cube2(x) {
    return x*x*x;
}
```

```
print(cube(3));
print(cube2(3));
```

Multiple catch clauses

JavaScript supports try, catch, and throw in a similar way to Java.

 JavaScript has no support for checked exceptions—all Java-
Script exceptions are unchecked.

However, standard JavaScript only allows a single catch clause following a try block.
There is no support for different catch clauses handling different types of exception. Fortunately, there is already an existing Mozilla syntax extension to offer this
feature, and Nashorn implements it as well, as shown in this example:

```
function fnThatMightThrow() {
    if (Math.random() < 0.5) {
        throw new TypeError();
    } else {
        throw new Error();
    }
}

try {
    fnThatMightThrow();
} catch (e if e instanceof TypeError) {
    print("Caught TypeError");
} catch (e) {
    print("Caught some other error");
}
```

Nashorn implements a few other nonstandard syntax extensions (and when we met
scripting mode for jjs we saw some other useful syntax innovations), but these are
likely to be the most familiar and widely used.

Under the Hood

As we have previously discussed, Nashorn works by compiling JavaScript programs
directly to JVM bytecode, and then runs them just like any other class. It is this
functionality that enables, for example, the straightforward representation of Java-
Script functions as lambda expressions and their easy interoperability.

Let's take a closer look at an earlier example, and see how we're able to use a function as an anonymous implementation of a Java interface:

```
jjs> var clz = Java.type("java.util.concurrent.Callable");
jjs> var obj = new clz(function () { print("Foo"); } );
```

```
jjs> print(obj);
jdk.nashorn.javaadapters.java.util.concurrent.Callable@290dbf45
```

This means that the actual type of the JavaScript object implementing Callable is jdk.nashorn.javaadapters.java.util.concurrent.Callable. This class is not shipped with Nashorn, of course. Instead, Nashorn spins up dynamic bytecode to implement whatever interface is required and just maintains the original name as part of the package structure for readability.

 Remember that dynamic code generation is an essential part of Nashorn, and that all JavaScript code is compiled by Nashorn in Java bytecode and never interpreted.

One final note is that Nashorn's insistence on 100% compliance with the spec does sometimes restrict the capabilities of the implementation. For example, consider printing out an object, like this:

```
jjs> var obj = {foo:"bar",cat:2};
jjs> print(obj);
[object Object]
```

The ECMAScript specification requires the output to be [object Object]—conformant implementations are not allowed to give more useful detail (such as a complete list of the properties and values contained in obj).

Conclusion

In this chapter, we've met Nashorn, the JavaScript implementation on top of the JVM that ships with Oracle's Java 8. We've seen how to use it to execute scripts and even replace bash and Perl scripts with enhanced JavaScript scripts that can leverage the full power of Java and the JVM. We've met the JavaScript engine API and seen how the bridge between Java and scripting languages is implemented.

We've seen the tight integration between JavaScript and Java that Nashorn provides, and some of the small language syntax extensions that Nashorn provides to make programming a little bit easier. Finally, we've had a brief peek under the hood at how Nashorn implements all of this functionality. To conclude, let's take a quick look into the future and meet Project Avatar, which could be the future of Java/JavaScript web applications.

Project Avatar

One of the most successful movements in the JavaScript community in recent years has been Node.js. This is a simple server-side JavaScript implementation developed by Ryan Dahl and now curated by Joyent. Node.js provides a programming model that is heavily asynchronous—designed around callbacks, nonblocking I/O, and a simple, single-threaded event loop model.

While it is not suitable for developing complex enterprise applications (due to limitations of the callback model in larger codebases), Node.js (often referred to simply as Node) has nonetheless become an interesting option for developing prototypes, simple "glue" servers, and single-purpose HTTP and TCP server applications of low to moderate complexity.

The Node ecosystem has also prospered by promoting reusable units of code, known as Node packages. Similar to the Maven archives (and to earlier systems, such as the Perl CPAN), Node packages allow the easy creation and redistribution of code, although they suffer from the relative immaturity of JavaScript, which is missing many modularity and deployment features.

The original implementation of Node is composed of several basic components—a JavaScript execution engine (the V8 engine developed by Google for their Chrome browser), a thin abstraction layer, and a standard library (of mostly JavaScript code).

In September 2013, Oracle announced Project Avatar. This is an effort by Oracle to produce a future-state architecture for web applications and to marry JavaScript (and Node) to the mature ecosystem that already exists for Java web apps.

As part of Project Avatar, Oracle open sourced their implementation of the Node API, which runs on top of Nashorn and the JVM. This implementation, known as Avatar.js, is a faithful implementation of most of the Node API. It is currently (April 2014) capable of running a large number of Node modules—essentially anything that does not depend on native code.

The future is, of course, unknown, but Avatar points the way towards a possible world where the JVM is the foundation of a new generation of web applications that combine JavaScript with Java and hopefully provide the best of both worlds.

13

Platform Tools and Profiles

This chapter discusses the tools that ship with the Oracle and OpenJDK version of the Java platform. The tools covered mostly comprise command-line tools, but we also discuss the GUI tool `jvisualvm`. If you are using a different version of Java, you may find similar but different tools as part of your distribution instead.

Later in the chapter, we also discuss Java 8 profiles, which are cut-down installations of Java that nevertheless satisfy the language and virtual machine specifications.

Command-Line Tools

The command-line tools we cover are the most commonly used tools, and those of greatest utility—they are not a complete description of every tool that is available. In particular, tools concerned with CORBA and the server portion of RMI are not covered in detail.

In some cases, we need to discuss switches that take filesystem paths. As elsewhere in the book, we use Unix conventions for such cases.

The tools we discuss are:

- javac
- java
- jar
- javadoc

- jdeps
- jps
- jstat
- jstatd
- jinfo
- jstack
- jmap
- javap

javac

Basic usage

```
javac some/package/MyClass.java
```

Description

javac is the Java source code compiler—it produces bytecode (in the form of *.class* files) from *.java* source files.

For modern Java projects, javac is not often used directly, as it is rather low-level and unwieldy, especially for larger codebases. Instead, modern integrated development environments (IDEs) either drive javac automatically for the developer or have built-in compilers for use while code is being written. For deployment, most projects will make use of a separate build tool, such as Maven, Ant, or Gradle. Discussion of these tools is outside the scope of this book.

Nevertheless, it is useful for developers to understand how to use javac as there are cases when compiling small codebases by hand is preferable to having to install and manage a production-grade build tool such as Maven.

Common switches

-classpath
> Supplies classes we need for compilation.

-d some/dir
> Tells javac where to output class files.

@project.list
> Load options and source files from the file *project.list*.

-help
> Help on options.

-X
> Help on nonstandard options.

-source <version>

Control the Java version that *javac* will accept.

-target <version>

Control the version of class files that *javac* will output.

-profile <profile>

Control the profile that `javac` will use when compiling the application. See later in this chapter for more detail on Compact Profiles.

-Xlint

Enable detail about warnings.

-Xstdout

Redirect output of compilation run to a file.

-g

Add debug information to class files.

Notes

`javac` has traditionally accepted switches (`-source` and `-target`) that control the version of the source language that the compiler would accept, and the version of the class file format that was used for the outputted class files.

This facility introduces additional compiler complexity (as multiple language syntaxes must be supported internally) for some small developer benefit. In Java 8, this capability has begun to be slightly tidied up and placed on a more formal basis.

From JDK 8 onward, `javac` will only accept source and target options from three versions back. That is, only the formats from JDK 5, 6, 7, and 8 will be accepted by `javac`. This does not affect the `java` interpreter—any class file from any Java version will still work on the JVM shipped with Java 8.

C and C++ developers may find that the -g switch is less helpful to them than it is in those other languages. This is largely due to the widespread use of IDEs in the Java ecosystem—integrated debugging is simply a lot more useful, and easier to use, than additional debug symbols in class files.

The use of the lint capability remains somewhat controversial among developers. Many Java developers produce code that triggers a large number of compilation warnings, which they then simply ignore. However, experience on larger codebases (especially on the JDK codebase itself) suggests that in a substantial percentage of cases, code that triggers warnings is code in which subtle bugs may lurk. Use of the lint feature, or static analysis tools (such as FindBugs), is strongly recommended.

java

Basic usage

`java some.package.MyClass java -jar my-packaged.jar`

Description

java is the executable that starts up a Java virtual machine. The initial entry point into the program is the `main()` method that exists on the named class, and that has the signature:

`public static void main(String[] args);`

This method is run on the single application thread that is created by the JVM startup. The JVM process will exit once this method returns (and any additional nondaemon application threads that were started have terminated).

If the form takes a JAR file rather than a class (the executable jar form), the JAR file must contain a piece of metadata that tells the JVM which class to start from.

This bit of metadata is the `Main-Class:` attribute, and it is contained in the *MANI-FEST.MF* file in the *META-INF/* directory. See the description of the `jar` tool for more details.

Common switches

-cp <classpath>
Define the classpath to read from.

-X, -?, -help
Provide help about the `java` executable and its switches.

-D<property=value>
Sets a Java system property that can be retrieved by the Java program. Any number of such properties can be specified this way.

-jar
Run an executable JAR (see the entry for jar).

-Xbootclasspath(/a or /p)
Run with an alternative system classpath (very rarely used).

-client, -server
Select a HotSpot JIT compiler (see "Notes" for this entry).

-Xint, -Xcomp, -Xmixed
Control JIT compilation (very rarely used).

-Xms<size>
Set the minimum committed heap size for the JVM.

-Xmx<size>
> Set the maximum committed heap size for the JVM.

-agentlib:<agent>, -agentpath:<path to agent>
> Specify a JVM Tooling Interface (JVMTI) agent to attach to the process being started. Agents are typically used for instrumentation or monitoring.

-verbose
> Generate additional output, sometimes useful for debugging.

Notes

The HotSpot VM contains two separate JIT compilers—known as the client (or C1) compiler and the server (or C2) compiler. These were designed for different purposes, with the client compiler offering more predictable performance and quicker startup, at the expense of not performing aggressive code optimization.

Traditionally, the JIT compiler that a Java process used was chosen at process startup via the -client or -server switch. However, as hardware advances have made compilation ever cheaper, a new possibility has become available—to use the client compiler early on, while the Java process is warming up, and then to switch to the high-performance optimizations available in the server compiler when they are available. This scheme is called Tiered Compilation, and it is the default in Java 8. Most processes will no longer need explicit -client or -server switches.

On the Windows platform, a slightly different version of the java executable is often used—javaw. This version starts up a Java Virtual Machine, without forcing a Windows console window to appear.

In older Java versions, a number of different legacy interpreters and virtual machine modes were supported. These have now mostly been removed, and any remaining should be regarded as vestigial.

Switches that start with -X were intended to be nonstandard switches. However, the trend has been to standardize a number of these switches (particularly -Xms and -Xmx). In parallel, Java versions have introduced an increasing number of -XX: switches. These were intended to be experimental and not for production use. However, as the implementations have stabilized, some of these switches are now suitable for some advanced users (even in production deployments).

In general, a full discussion of switches is outside the scope of this book. Configuration of the JVM for production use is a specialist subject, and developers are urged to take care, especially when modifying any switches related to the garbage collection subsystem.

jar

Basic usage

```
jar cvf my.jar someDir/
```

Description

The jar utility is used to manipulate Java Archive (*.jar*) files. These are ZIP format files that contain Java classes, additional resources, and (usually) metadata. The tool has five major modes of operation—Create, Update, Index, List, and Extract—on a *.jar* file.

These are controlled by passing a command option character (not a switch) to jar. Only one command character can be specified, but optional modifier characters can also be used.

Command options

c
> Create a new archive

u
> Update archive

i
> Index an archive

t
> List an archive

x
> Extract an archive

Modifiers

v
> Verbose mode

f
> Operate on a named file, rather than standard input

0
> Store, but do not compress, files added to the archive

m
> Add the contents of the specified file to the jar metadata manifest

e
> Make this jar executable, with the specified class as the entry point

---

Notes

The syntax of the jar command is intentionally very similar to that of the Unix tar command. This similarity is the reason why jar uses command options, rather than switches (as the other Java platform commands do).

When creating a *.jar* file, the jar tool will automatically add a directory called *META-INF* that contains a file called *MANIFEST.MF*—this is metadata in the form of headers paired with values. By default, *MANIFEST.MF* contains just two headers:

```
Manifest-Version: 1.0
Created-By: 1.8.0 (Oracle Corporation)
```

By using the m option, additional metadata can be added into *MANIFEST.MF* at JAR creation time. One frequently added piece is the Main-Class: attribute, which indicates the entry point into the application contained in the JAR. A JAR with a specified Main-Class: can be directly executed by the JVM, via java -jar.

The addition of the Main-Class: attribute is so common that jar has the e option to create it directly in *MANIFEST.MF*, rather than having to create a separate text file for this purpose.

javadoc

Basic usage

```
javadoc some.package
```

Description

javadoc produces documentation from Java source files. It does so by reading a special comment format (known as Javadoc comments) and parsing it into a standard documentation format, which can then be output into a variety of document formats (although HTML is by far the most common).

For a full description of Javadoc syntax, refer to Chapter 7.

Common switches

-cp <classpath>
    Define the classpath to use

-D <directory>
    Tell javadoc where to output the generated docs

-quiet
    Suppress output except for errors and warnings

Notes

The platform API docs are all written in Javadoc.

javadoc is built on top of the same classes as javac, and uses some of the source compiler infrastructure to implement Javadoc features.

The typical way to use javadoc is to run it against a whole package, rather than just a class.

javadoc has a very large number of switches and options that can control many aspects of its behavior. Detailed discussion of all the options is outside the scope of this book.

jdeps

The jdeps tool is a static analysis tool for analyzing the dependencies of packages or classes. The tool has a number of usages, from identifying developer code that makes calls into the internal, undocumented JDK APIs (such as the sun.misc classes), to helping trace transitive dependencies.

jdeps can also be used to confirm whether a JAR file can run under a Compact Profile (see later in the chapter for more details on Compact Profiles).

Basic usage

```
jdeps com.me.MyClass
```

Description

jdeps reports dependency information for the classes it is asked to analyze. The classes can be specified as any class on the classpath, a file path, a directory, or a JAR file.

Common switches

-s, -summary
> Prints dependency summary only.

-v, -verbose
> Prints all class-level dependencies.

-verbose:package
> Prints package-level dependencies, excluding dependencies within the same archive.

-verbose:class
> Prints class-level dependencies, excluding dependencies within the same archive.

-p <pkg name>, -package <pkg name>
> Finds dependencies in the specified package. You can specify this option multiple times for different packages. The -p and -e options are mutually exclusive.

-e <regex>, -regex <regex>

Finds dependencies in packages matching the specified regular expression pattern. The -p and -e options are mutually exclusive.

-include <regex>

Restricts analysis to classes matching pattern. This option filters the list of classes to be analyzed. It can be used together with -p and -e.

-jdkinternals

Finds class-level dependences in JDK internal APIs (which may change or disappear in even minor platform releases).

-apionly

Restricts analysis to APIs—for example, dependencies from the signature of public and protected members of public classes including field type, method parameter types, returned type, and checked exception types.

-R, -recursive

Recursively traverses all dependencies.

-h, -?, -help

Prints help message for jdeps.

Notes

While Project Jigsaw did not ship as part of Java 8, jdeps is a first step toward making developers aware of their dependencies on the JRE not as a monolithic environment, but as something more modular.

jps

Basic usage

jps jps <remote URL>

Description

jps provides a list of all active JVM processes on the local machine (or a remote machine, if a suitable instance of jstatd is running on the remote side).

Common switches

-m

Output the arguments passed to the main method

-l

Output the full package name for the application's main class (or the full path name to the application's JAR file)

-v

Output the arguments passed to the JVM

Notes

This command is not strictly necessary as the standard Unix ps command could suffice. However, it does not use the standard Unix mechanism for interrogating the process, so there are circumstances where a Java process stops responding (and looks dead to jps) but is still listed as alive by the operating system.

jstat

Basic usage

jstat <pid>

Description

This command displays some basic statistics about a given Java process. This is usually a local process, but can be located on a remote machine, provided the remote side is running a suitable jstatd process.

Common switches

-options
> Reports a list of report types that jstat can produce

-class
> Report on classloading activity to date

-compiler
> JIT compilation of the process so far

-gcutil
> Detailed GC report

-printcompilation
> More detail on compilation

Notes

The general syntax jstat uses to identify a process (which may be remote) is:

```
[<protocol>://]<vmid>[@hostname][:port][/servername]
```

The general syntax is used to specify a remote process (which is usually connected to via JMX over RMI), but in practice, the local syntax is far more common, which simply uses the VM ID, which is the operating system process ID on mainstream platforms (such as Linux, Windows, Unix, Mac, etc.).

jstatd

Basic usage

jstatd <options>

Description

jstatd provides a way of making information about local JVMs available over the network. It achieves this using RMI, and can make these otherwise-local capabilities accessible to JMX clients. This requires special security settings, which differ from the JVM defaults. To start jstatd, first we need to create the following file and name it *jstatd.policy*:

```
grant codebase "file:${java.home}../lib/tools.jar {
    permission java.security.AllPermission
}
```

This policy file grants all security permissions to any class loaded from the JDK's *tools.jar* file.

To launch jstatd with this policy, use this command line:

```
jstatd -J-Djava.security.policy=<path to jstat.policy>
```

Common switches

-p <port>
   Look for an existing RMI registry on that port, and create one if not found

Notes

It is recommended that jstatd is always switched on in production environments, but not over the public Internet. For most corporate and enterprise environments, this is nontrivial to achieve and will require the cooperation of Operations and Network Engineering staff. However, the benefits of having telemetry data from production JVMs, especially during outages, are difficult to overstate.

A full discussion of JMX and monitoring techniques is outside the scope of this book.

jinfo

Basic usage

jinfo <process ID> jinfo <core file>

Description

This tool displays the system properties and JVM options for a running Java process (or a core file).

Common switches

-flags
> Display JVM flags only

-sysprops
> Display system properties only

Notes

In practice, this is very rarely used—although it can occasionally be useful as a sanity check that the expected program is actually what is executing.

jstack

Basic usage

```
jstack <process ID>
```

Description

The `jstack` utility produces a stack trace for each Java thread in the process.

Common switches

-F
> Force a thread dump

-l
> Long mode (contains additional information about locks)

Notes

Producing the stack trace does not stop or terminate the Java process. The files that `jstack` produces can be very large, and some post-processing of the file is usually necessary.

jmap

Basic usage

```
jmap <process>
```

Description

`jmap` provides a view of memory allocation for a running Java process.

Common switches

-histo
> Produces a histogram of the current state of allocated memory.

-histo:live
> This version of the histogram only displays information for live objects.

-heap

Produces a heap dump from the running process.

Notes

The histogram forms walk the JVMs allocation list. This includes both live and dead (but not yet collected) objects. The histogram is organized by the type of objects using memory, and is ordered from greatest to least number of bytes used by a particular type. The standard form does not pause the JVM.

The live form ensures that it is accurate, by performing a full, stop-the-world (STW) garbage collection before executing. As a result, it should not be used on a production system at a time when a full GC would appreciably impact users.

For the -heap form, note that the production of a heap dump can be a time-consuming process, and is STW. Note that for many processes, the resulting file may be extremely large.

javap

Basic usage

```
javap <classname>
```

Description

javap is the Java class disassembler—effectively a tool for peeking inside class files. It can show the bytecode that Java methods have been compiled into, as well as the "constant pool" information (which contains information similar to that of the symbol table of Unix processes).

By default, javap shows signatures of public, protected, and default methods. The -p switch will also show private methods.

Common switches

-c

Decompile bytecode

-v

Verbose mode (include constant pool information)

-p

Include private methods

Notes

The javap tool will work with any class file, provided javap is from a JDK version the same as (or later) than the one that produced the file.

Some Java language features may have surprising implementations in bytecode. For example, as we saw in Chapter 9, Java's String class has effectively immutable instances and the JVM implements the string concatenation operator + by instantiating a new StringBuilder object from the orginal string, mutating it and finally calling toString() on the resulting (new) instance. This is clearly visible in the disassembled bytecode shown by javap.

VisualVM

JVisualVM (often referred to as VisualVM) is a graphical tool, based on the Netbeans platform. It is used for monitoring JVMs and essentially acts as an equivalent, graphical aggregate of many of the tools featured in "Command-Line Tools" on page 349.

jvisualvm is a replacement for the jconsole tool common in earlier Java versions. The compatability plug-in available for visualvm obsoletes jconsole; all installations using jconsole should migrate.

VisualVM was introduced with Java 6, and is contained in the Java distribution package. However, generally, the standalone version of VisualVM is more up to date and a better choice for serious work. You can download the latest version from *http://visualvm.java.net/*.

After downloading, ensure that the visualvm binary is added to your PATH or you'll get the JRE default binary.

The first time you run VisualVM, it will calibrate your machine, so make sure that you aren't running any other applications while calibration is being performed. After calibration, VisualVM will open to a screen like that shown in Figure 13.1.

To attach VisualVM to a running process, there are slightly different approaches depending on whether the process is local or remote.

Local processes are listed down the left-hand side of the screen. Double-click on one of the local processes and it will appear as a new tab on the right-hand pane.

For a remote process, enter the hostname and a display name that will be used on the tab. The default port to connect to is 1099, but this can be changed.

In order to connect to a remote process, jstatd must be running on the remote host (see the entry for jstatd in "Command-Line Tools" on page 349 for more details). If you are connecting to an application server, you may find that the app server vendor provides an equivalent capability to jstatd directly in the server, and that jstatd is unnecessary.

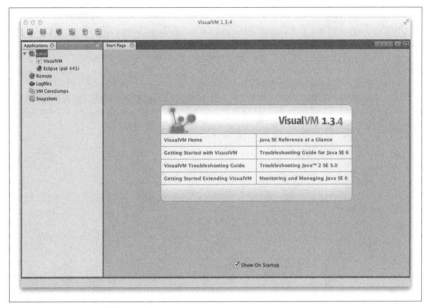

Figure 13-1. VisualVM welcome screen

The Overview tab (see Figure 13-2) provides a summary of information about your Java process. This includes the flags and system properties that were passed in, and the exact Java version being executed.

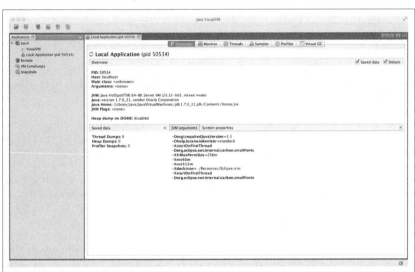

Figure 13-2. Overview tab

In the Monitor tab, as shown in Figure 13-3, graphs and data about the active parts of the JVM system are displayed. This is essentially high-level telemetry data for the JVM—including CPU usage and how much CPU is being used for GC.

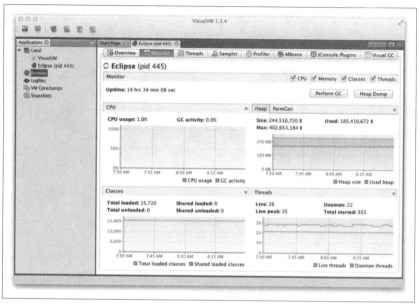

Figure 13-3. Monitor tab

Other information displayed includes the number of classes loaded and unloaded, basic heap memory information, and an overview of the numbers of threads running.

From this tab, it is also possible to ask the JVM to produce a heap dump, or to perform a full GC—although in normal production operation, neither are recommended.

Figure 13-4 shows the Threads tab, which displays data on actively running threads in the JVM. This is displayed as a continuous timeline, with the ability to inspect individual thread details and perform thread dumps for deeper analysis.

This presents a similar view to `jstack`, but with better abilities to diagnose deadlocks and thread starvation. Note that the difference between `synchronized` locks (i.e., operating system monitors) and the user-space lock objects of `java.util.con current` can be clearly seen here.

Threads that are contending on locks backed by operating system monitors (i.e., synchronized blocks) will be placed into the BLOCKED state. This shows up as red in VisualVM.

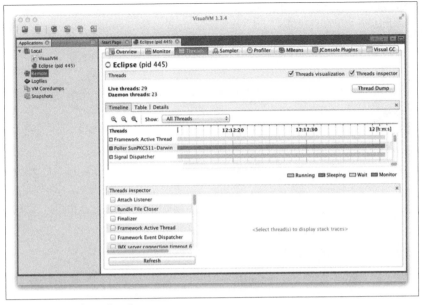

Figure 13-4. Threads tab

Locked `java.util.concurrent` lock objects place their threads into WAITING (yellow in VisualVM). This is because the implementation provided by `java.util.concurrent` is purely user space and does not involve the operating system.

The Sampler tab, as shown in Figure 13-5, samples either memory or CPU. In the memory mode, it samples object creation—either overall, or JVM only, or even on a per-thread basis.

This enables the developer to see what the most common objects are—in terms of bytes and instances (in a manner similar to `jmap -histo`).

The objects displayed on the Metaspace submode are typically core Java/JVM constructs.[1] Normally, we need to look deeper into other parts of the system, such as classloading to see the code responsible for creating these objects.

`jvisualvm` has a plug-in system, which can be used to extend the functionality of the framework by downloading and installing extra plug-ins. We recommend always installing the MBeans plugin (shown in Figure 13-6) and the VisualGC plugin (discussed next, and shown in Figure 13-7), and usually the JConsole compatibility plugin, just in case.

---

[1] Before Java 8, a construct called PermGen was used instead of Metaspace.

The MBeans tab allows the operator to interact with Java management servies (essentially MBeans). JMX is a great way to provide runtime control of your Java/JVM applications, but a full discussion is outside the scope of this book.

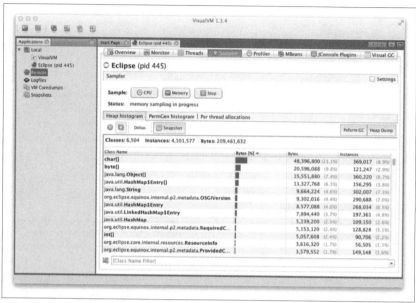

Figure 13-5. Sampler tab

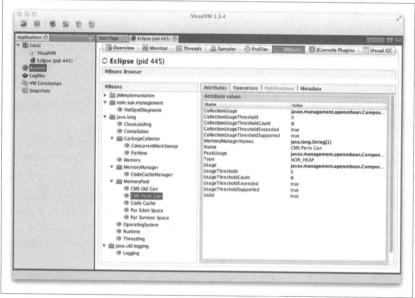

Figure 13-6. MBeans plug-in

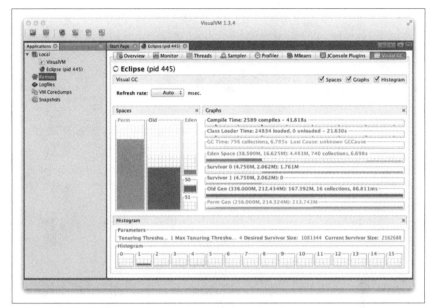

Figure 13-7. VisualGC plug-in

The VisualGC plug-in, shown in Figure 13-7, is one of the simplest and best initial GC debugging tools available. As mentioned in Chapter 6, for serious analysis, GC logs are to be preferred to the JMX-based view that VisualGC provides. Having said that, VisualGC can be a good way to start to understand the GC behavior of an application, and to inform deeper investigations. It provides a near real-time view of the memory pools inside HotSpot, and allows the developer to see how GC causes objects to flow from space to space over the course of GC cycles.

Java 8 Profiles

The original roadmap for Java 8 included Project Jigsaw, a full-featured modularity solution that included a modularization of the platform itself and a move away from a single, monolithic *rt.jar*.

However, the constraints of the Java 8 release cycle meant that this work could not be completed in time for the intended launch date. Rather than delay the release of Java 8, the project team opted to put off the modularization of the platform until Java 9.

Motivation

Instead of full modularity, Java 8 was updated to include Profiles. These are reduced versions of Java SE, which must satisfy these requirements:

- They must completely implement the JVM specification.

- They must completely implement the Java language specification.

- Profiles are lists of packages. Profiles should usually be identical to the package of the same name in the full Java SE platform, and any exceptions (which should be very rare) must be explicitly called out.

- A Profile may declare that it is larger than another package. In this case, it must be a strict superset of that Profile.

As a consequence of the second requirement, all Profiles must include all classes and packages that are explicitly mentioned in the Java language specification.

The general purpose of Profiles is to reduce the size of *rt.jar*. This is helpful for reduced capability platforms, which may not need the full features of Java SE (such as the Swing/AWT graphical toolkits).

Profiles can be seen, in this light, as a step toward modernizing the Java ME platform and harmonizing (or even unifying) it with Java SE. However, it is also possible to conceive of using a Profile as the basis for a server application or other environment, where deploying unnecessary capability is seen as undesirable.

Finally, it is worth noting that a large number of Java's security vulnerabilities in recent years have been connected to Java's graphical client features, as implemented in Swing and AWT. By not deploying the packages that implement such features, a modest amount of additional security for server applications is achieved.

Let's move on to discuss each of the three standard profiles (the Compact Profiles) that Java 8 ships with.

Compact Profiles

Compact 1 is the smallest set of packages that it is feasible to deploy an application on. It contains the packages:

- java.io
- java.lang
- java.lang.annotation
- java.lang.invoke
- java.lang.ref
- java.lang.reflect
- java.math
- java.net
- java.nio
- java.nio.channels
- java.nio.channels.spi
- java.nio.charset

- java.nio.charset.spi
- java.nio.file
- java.nio.file.attribute
- java.nio.file.spi
- java.security
- java.security.cert
- java.security.interfaces
- java.security.spec
- java.text
- java.text.spi
- java.time
- java.time.chrono
- java.time.format
- java.time.temporal
- java.time.zone
- java.util
- java.util.concurrent
- java.util.concurrent.atomic
- java.util.concurrent.locks
- java.util.function
- java.util.jar
- java.util.logging
- java.util.regex
- java.util.spi
- java.util.stream
- java.util.zip
- javax.crypto
- javax.crypto.interfaces
- javax.crypto.spec
- javax.net
- javax.net.ssl
- javax.script
- javax.security.auth

- javax.security.auth.callback
- javax.security.auth.login
- javax.security.auth.spi
- javax.security.auth.x500
- javax.security.cert

 It is important to understand that *any* profile must at least ship the transitive closure of types referred to by `Object`. Figure 11-1 shows a partial piece of this graph, and Compact 1 is as close to this minimum bootstrap set as is realistic.

Compact 2 comprises all of Compact 1 plus these additional packages:

- java.rmi
- java.rmi.activation
- java.rmi.dgc
- java.rmi.registry
- java.rmi.server
- java.sql
- javax.rmi.ssl
- javax.sql
- javax.transaction
- javax.transaction.xa
- javax.xml
- javax.xml.datatype
- javax.xml.namespace
- javax.xml.parsers
- javax.xml.stream
- javax.xml.stream.events
- javax.xml.stream.util
- javax.xml.transform
- javax.xml.transform.dom
- javax.xml.transform.sax
- javax.xml.transform.stax

- javax.xml.transform.stream
- javax.xml.validation
- javax.xml.xpath
- org.w3c.dom
- org.w3c.dom.bootstrap
- org.w3c.dom.events
- org.w3c.dom.ls
- org.xml.sax
- org.xml.sax.ext
- org.xml.sax.helpers
- javax.xml.crypto.dsig
- javax.xml.crypto.dsig.dom
- javax.xml.crypto.dsig.keyinfo
- javax.xml.crypto.dsig.spec
- org.ietf.jgss

Compact 3 is the most comprehensive of the Profiles that ships with Java 8. It comprises all of Compact 2 plus these additional packages:

- java.lang.instrument
- java.lang.management
- java.security.acl
- java.util.prefs
- javax.annotation.processing
- javax.lang.model
- javax.lang.model.element
- javax.lang.model.type
- javax.lang.model.util
- javax.management
- javax.management.loading
- javax.management.modelmbean
- javax.management.monitor
- javax.management.openmbean
- javax.management.relation
- javax.management.remote

- javax.management.remote.rmi
- javax.management.timer
- javax.naming
- javax.naming.directory
- javax.naming.event
- javax.naming.ldap
- javax.naming.spi
- javax.security.auth.kerberos
- javax.security.sasl
- javax.sql.rowset
- javax.sql.rowset.serial
- javax.sql.rowset.spi
- javax.tools
- javax.xml.crypto
- javax.xml.crypto.dom

Despite not being the complete modularity solution we might have wished for, Profiles are a significant step towards our future goals—both for capability-restricted devices and for server-side developers.

Having Profiles actively deployed as part of Java 8 will help inform the conversation around modularity and provide feedback into the development process of Java 9.

Conclusion

Java has changed a huge amount over the last 15+ years, and yet, the platform and community remain vibrant. To have achieved this, while retaining a recognizable language and platform, is no small accomplishment.

Ultimately, the continued existence and viability of Java depends upon the individual developer. On that basis, the future looks bright, and we look forward to the next wave, Java's 25th birthday, and beyond.

Index

Symbols

! (exclamation point)
    != (not equal to) operator, 32, 39
    boolean NOT operator, 32, 40
" (quotes, double)
    enclosing string literals, 25
    escaping in char literals, 24
    in string literals, 75
    literals in, 21
(pound sign)
    #!, shebang syntax, 339
    indicating comments, 335
$ (dollar sign), 225
% (percent sign)
    %= (modulo assignment) operator, 32, 43
    modulo operator, 32, 36
& (ampersand)
    && (conditional AND) operator, 32, 35, 39
    &= (bitwise AND assignment) operator, 32, 43
    bitwise AND operator, 32, 41
    boolean AND operator, 32, 40
' (quotes, single)
    enclosing character literals, 23
    escaping in char literals, 24
    in char literals, 75
    in string literals, 25
    literals in, 21
( ) (parentheses)
    cast operator, 32, 46

    enclosing expressions in if statements, 50
    enclosing method parameter list, 68
    method invocation operator, 32, 35, 45
    overriding operator precedence, 31
    separators (tokens), 22
* (asterisk)
    *= (multiply assignment) operator, 32, 43
    in doc comments, 228
    in multiline comments, 20
    in Unix or Windows shell, 272
    multiplication operator, 32, 36
+ (plus sign)
    ++ (increment) operator, 32, 35, 37, 54
    += (add assignment) operator, 32, 37, 43
    addition operator, 32, 36
    string concatenation operator, 32, 37, 75, 269
    unary plus operator, 32
, (comma) separators (tokens), 22
- (minus sign)
    -- (decrement) operator, 32, 38
    -= (subtract assignment) operator, 32, 43
    subtraction operator, 32, 34, 36
    unary minus operator, 32, 34, 37
. (dot)
    object member access operator, 32, 45
    separators (tokens), 22
... (elipses)
    separators (tokens), 22
/ (slash)

/* */ in multiline comments, 19
/** */ in doc comments, 20, 226
// in single-line comments, 19
//, denoting JavaScript comments, 335
/= (divide assignment) operator, 32, 43
division operator, 32, 36
0 (zero)
    division by zero, 36
    negative and positive zero, 27
    represented by float and double types, 27
    represented by integral types, 275
: (colon), :: separators (tokens), 22
; (semicolon)
    for empty statements, 48
    in abstract methods, 69
    in break statements, 58
    in for loops, 56
    separators (tokens), 22
    terminating do loops, 55
< > (angle brackets)
    < (less than) operator, 32, 39
    << (signed left shift) operator, 32, 42
    <<= (left shift assignment) operator, 32, 43
    <<END_TOKEN syntax for heredocs, 337
    <= (less than or equal to) operator, 32, 39
    <> (diamond syntax), 145
    > (greater than) operator, 32, 39
    >= (greater than or equal to) operator, 32, 39
    >> (signed right shift) operator, 32, 42
    >>= (right shift assignment) operator, 32, 43
    >>> (unsigned right shift) operator, 32, 42
    >>>= (unsigned right shift assignment) operator, 32, 43
    enclosing payload type in generic types, 143
= (equals sign)
    = (assignment) operator, confusion with == (equal to) operator, 43
    == (equal to) operator, 32, 38, 181
        comparing objects, 87
    assignment operator, 32, 43
? (question mark)

<?> wildcard for unknown types, 146
? : (conditional) operator, 32, 34, 35, 44
regular expression metacharacter, 272
@ (at sign)
    in doc-comment tags, 228
    separators (tokens), 22
[ ] (brackets)
    accessing array elements, 45, 80
    after array element type, 77
    array access operator, 32
\ (backslash)
    in escape sequences, 23
    \\ escape sequence in char literals, 24
^ (caret)
    bitwise XOR operator, 32, 42
    boolean XOR operator, 32, 40, 42
    ^= (bitwise XOR assignment) operator, 32, 43
` ` (backticks), 336
{ } (curly braces)
    enclosing class members, 99
    in nested if/else statements, 51
    in switch statements, 52
    in try/catch/finally statements, 61
    separators (tokens), 22
| (vertical bar)
    bitwise OR operator, 32, 41
    boolean OR operator, 32, 40
    |= (bitwise OR assignment) operator, 32, 43
    || (conditional OR) operator, 32, 35, 40
~ (tilde), bitwise complement operator, 32, 41
… (ellipses)
    in variable-length argument lists, 71
→ (lambda arrow) operator, 32, 46

A

a tag (HTML), 233
abs(), 278
abstract classes, 68, 99
    interfaces versus, 184
abstract methods, 68
abstract modifier
    abstract classes and methods, 128-132
    abstract methods of interfaces, 137
    classes implementing an interface, 138

summary of use, 133
AbstractList class, 184
access control, 122-126
    access to members, 122
    and inheritance, 125
    local classes, 164
    member access summary, 125
    member classes, 160
    Reflection API versus Method Handles API, 327
access modifiers
    anonymous classes, 168
    class members, 98
    for classes, 99
    for fields, 101
    for methods, 69
    interface members and, 137
    member access, 122
    static member types, 158
    top-level types and, 158
accessor methods, 127
    field inheritance and, 189
addition operator (+), 36
    (see also + (plus sign), in Symbols section)
adjusters, modifying date and time objects, 285
aggregation operations, 261
allocateDirect(), ByteBuffer class, 299
allocation table, 199
AND operator (see & (ampersand), in Symbols section)
annotations, 99, 152
    basic, in java.lang, 153
    custom, defining, 153
    special properties of, 153
    static member types nested in, 158
    type, 155
anonymous classes, 156, 167
    defining and creating an instance, 168
    enumerator implemented as, 167
    implementation, 170
    lambda expressions versus, 172
    naming conventions for, 170
    restrictions on, 168
Apache Commons project, 90
application classloader, 319
apply() method, Function interface, 260
$ARG variable (Nashorn), 336

arithmetic operators, 36
ArithmeticException, 26, 278
array covariance, 78, 149
arrayCopy(), System class, 82, 257
ArrayDeque class, 255
ArrayIndexOutOfBoundsException, 81
ArrayList class, 184, 248
arrays, 77-84, 99
    accessing array elements, 45, 80
    array bounds, 81
    array types, 77
        widening conversions, 77
    Arrays class, static methods, 258
    as operand type, 38, 44
    comparing for equality, 87
    conversions, 132
    copying, 81
    creating and initializing, 79
        array initializers, 79
    creation with new operator, 46
    helper methods for working with, 257
    iterating, 81
    iterating through using foreach statement, 57
    multidimensional, 82
    of collections, 257
    utility methods for working with, 82
Arrays class, 82
ArrayStoreException, 78
ASCII
    7-bit character set, 18
    escape sequences representing nonprinting characters, 23
assert statements, 64
AssertionError, 64
assertions, 64
    enabling, 65
assignment operators, 43
    associativity, 31
    combined with arithmetic , bitwise, and shift operators, 43
associativity, operator, 31
async I/O, 301
    callback-based style, 302
    Future-based style, 301
AsynchronousServerSocketChannel, 301
AsynchronousSocketChannel, 301
@author doc-comment tag, 228
autoboxing, 88

in reflection, 323
AutoCloseable interface, 294
automatic imports, 90

B

\b (escape sequence for backspace), 24
backticks (`), 336
backwards compatibility, 7
    generic types and type erasure, 145
    of interfaces, 140
benign data race, 271
BigDecimal class, 278
binary operators, 34
BinaryOperator interface, 261
Bindings interface, 342
bitwise operators, 41
blocking queue, defined, 253
BlockingQueue interface, 253
    implementations, 255
    methods to add elements to queues,
        253
    methods to remove elements from
        queues, 254
body of a class, 98
body of a method, 66
Boolean operators, 39
boolean type, 23
    Boolean class, 50
    get() accessor methods and, 128
    no conversions to other primitive
        types, 28
    operator return values, 35, 38
    using +=, -=, &= , and |= to work with
        boolean flags, 43
bound method reference, 260
bounded wildcards, 148
boxing and unboxing conversions, 88
    primitive types to JavaScript equiva-
        lents, 341
break statements, 58, 63
    labels, use of, 48
    specifying end of case clauses in switch
        statements, 53
    stopping switch statements, 53
BufferedReader class, 292
buffers, NIO, 298
    getting data out of, 299
    mapped byte buffers, 300

build tools, 350
byte type, 25, 35, 275
    Byte class, 26
    conversions to other primitive types,
        28
ByteBuffer class, 298
bytecode
    defined, 9
    frequently asked questions about, 10
byte[], 298, 299

C

C#, using keyword, 294
C/C++
    comma operator (,) in C, 149
    comparison of Java to C, 12
    comparison of Java to C++, 12
    compatibility syntax in variable decla-
        rations, 78
    constant integers in C++, 151
    memory management, 197
    native methods, using to interface Java
        code to C/C++ libraries, 69
    object contents in variables, 177
    operator precedence, 31
    pointers or memory addresses, refer-
        ences as, 85
    structs in C, 317
    switch statement, 52
    variable declarations, 49
    virtual method lookup, 119
Callable interface, 344
callback style for async I/O, 302
case labels (switch statements), 53
    restrictions on, 53
case sensitivity in Java, 19
casts, 29
    ( ) (cast) operator, 46
    of primitive types, 29
catch clause (try/catch/finally), 62
catch clauses (multiple) in Nashorn Java-
    Script, 346
ceil(), 279
channels, 300
    async I/O, subclasses of Channel, 301
    asynchronous, 301
        callback-based interactions with,
            302

Future-based interactions with, 301
multiplexed I/O, 303
char type, 23, 35
  Character class, static method, 24
  conversion to and from integer and
    floating-point types, 28
  conversion to other primitive types, 24
  escape characters in char literals, 24
  surrogate pair, Unicode supplemen-
    tary characters, 25
character sets, 18
characters in identifiers, 225
checked exceptions, 70, 193
  in throws clause of method signature,
    68
  working with, 71
Class class, 75
  forName(), 318
  newInstance(), 320
class files, 5, 9, 311
  Constant Pool section, 313
  creation of, 10
  inspecting for deprecated methods,
    using custom classloading and
    reflection, 324
  required layout, 313
  verification of, 314
class hierarchy, 113, 131
class methods
  choosing between class and instance
    methods, 185
  static modifier, 69
Class object, 321
class objects, 311
  metdata in, 312
classes, 72-73, 97
  abstract, 128-132
  access to, 122
  access to, from Nashorn, 343
  anonymous, 156, 167-168
  constructors, 106
  core classes of Java platform, 88
  data hiding and encapsulation, 121
  defining, 73
  definition syntax, 99
  effectively immutable, 271
  fields and methods, 100
    class fields, 102, 108
    class methods, 103, 105

field declaration syntax, 101
implementing interfaces, 136, 138
  inheritance and, 137
instance initializers, 110
local, 156, 162-167
modifiers, 133
name collisions, preventing, 89
names, simple and fully qualified, 89
naming conventions for, 224
nonstatic member classes, 156,
  159-162
overview, 97
  basic object-oriented definitions,
    98
  other reference types, 99
serialization, 230
static initializers for class fields, 109
subclasses and inheritance, 110-120
  access control and inheritance, 125
  constructor chaining and default
    constructor, 114
  extending a class, 111
  hiding superclass fields, 115
  superclasses, Object, and the class
    hierarchy, 112
undocumented, 235
ClassLoader class, 317
  defineClass(), 314
  subclasses and classloader hierarchy,
    318
classloader hierarchy, 318
  application classloader, 319
  custom classloader, 320
  extension classloader, 319
  primordial classloader, 318
classloading, 311
  applied, 317
    classloader hierarchy, 318
  custom classloading, combining with
    reflection, 324
  defined, 313
  initialization phase, 315
  loading phase, 314
  preparation and resolution phase, 315
  secure programming and, 315
  verification phase, 314
ClassNotFoundException, 318
clone()
  arrays, 77, 81

Object class, 182
Cloneable interface, 77, 81, 182
    Collections interfaces and, 242
CloneNotSupportedException, 77
closures, 167
@code doc-comment tag, 232
collect(), Predicate interface, 259
Collection interface, 239
    operations on Collection objects, 240
    removeIf method, 265
    Streams utility default methods, 265
collections, 239-266
    arrays and helper methods, 257
    autoboxing and, 88
    Collection interface, 240
        operations on Collection objects,
        240
    Collections class
        special-case collections, 256
        utility methods, 256
        wrapper methods, 255
    Collections classes and inheritance,
    239
    iterating over with foreach loops, 57
    iteration over, 245
    lambda expressions in, 258
        regular expressions and, 274
        Streams API, 262
    List interface, 244
    Map interface, 249
    Queue and BlockingQueue interfaces,
    252
    restrictions on elements in, 242
    Set interface, 242
Collector interface, 262
command-line tools, 349
    commonly used, list of, 349
    jar, 353
    java, 351
    javac, 350
    javadoc, 355
    javap, 361
    jdeps, 356
    jinfo, 359
    jmap, 360
    jps, 357
    jstack, 360
    jstat, 358
    jstatd, 359

comments, 19
    doc comments, 226
    scripting in jjs, 335
Compact Profiles, 368
    Compact 2, additional packages, 370
    Compact 3, additional packages, 371
Comparable interface, 179
    compareTo(), 182
    parameterized, or generic version,
        implementing, 179
comparison operators, 38
compilation, 10
    in Nashorn, 332
compilation units, 18
compile time typing, 150
compilers
    javac and, 10
    JIT compilers, 353
CompletionHandler interface, 302
composition versus inheritance, 187
compound statements, 48
concurrency
    Java support for, 208
    safety of multithreaded programs, 212
        exclusion and protecting state, 212
        Thread class, useful methods of, 215
        thread lifecycle, 209
        volatile keyword, 215
        working with threads, 218
concurrent collectors, 204
Concurrent Mark and Sweep (CMS), 205
ConcurrentHashMap class, 251
concurrently safe code, 212
ConcurrentMap interface, 252
    putIfAbsent() method, 265
ConcurrentSkipListMap class, 251
conditional AND operator (&&), 39
conditional operator (? :), 44
constants, 183
    importing into code, 92
constructors, 18, 46, 67, 106
    chaining, and the default constructor,
        114
    Constructor object, 321
    default, 106
    defining a constructor, 106
    defining multiple constructors, 107
    invoking one constructor from
        another, 107

subclass, 113
superclass, calling from subclass constructor, 114
Consumer interface, 260
containment hierarchy, 162
continue statements, 58, 63
labels, use of, 48
copy constructors, 182
CopyOnWriteArrayList class, 248
CopyOnWriteArraySet class, 242
CopyOption interface, 296
corporate nature of Java, criticisms of, 15
counters for loops, incrementing, 54
countStackFrames(), Thread class, 217
covariant return, 117
critical section (of code), 213
cross-references in doc comments, 233
currency symbols in identifiers, 21
custom classloader, 320
combining custom classloading with reflection, 324

D

daemon threads, 216
data encapsulation, 98
data formats (common), handling, 267-287
mathematical functions, 278-280
numbers and math, 275-280
text, 267-275
data types
array index expressions, 81
array types, 77
expressions in switch statements, 53
field type, 101
in class method declarations, 103
instanceof operator, 44
interfaces as, 139
Java type system, characteristics of, 174
JavaScript versus Java, 341
Nashorn and, 341
numeric, 275-278
of array elements, 77
of operands, 34
primitive, 22
boolean type, 23
char type, 23

conversions, 28
floating-point types, 26
integer types, 25
raw types, 145
reference, 84-88
boxing and unboxing conversions, 87
conversions, 131
transitive closure in classloading process, 315
type conversion or casting with ( ), 46
type safety, 195
DatagramSocket class, 308
date and time, 280
Java 8 API, 281-286
adjusters, 285
example of use, 282
temporal queries, 284
timestamp, parts of, 281
legacy, 286
Date class, 286
debugging, using assertions, 64
decorator pattern, 188
decrement operator (--), 38
(see also - (minus sign), in Symbols section)
default constructors, 115
default modifier, 133
default methods in interfaces, 136, 140
and choice between interfaces and abstract classes, 184
implementation of, 141
Streams API utility default methods, 265
working via classloading, 314
default: label, 53
defineClass(), Classloader, 314
delegation, 187
use of proxies, 325
dependencies, analysis with jdeps tool, 356
@Deprecated annotation, 153, 312
@deprecated doc-comment tag, 230
design patterns, 177
(see also object-oriented design)
destroy(), Thread class, 218
diamond syntax, 145
directories
searching, 303

watch services for, 303
division operator, 36
   (see also / (slash), in Symbols section)
do statements, 54
   continue statement in, 59
doc comments, 20, 226
   cross-references in, 233
   for packages, 234
   structure of, 227
doc-comment tags, 228
   inline, 231
@docRoot doc-comment tag, 232
documentation (doc comments), 226-235
@Documented meta-annotation, 155
domain names in package names, 90
double type, 26
   conversions, 28
   Double class, 28
   return type for operators, 35
DoubleStream class, 263
Duration class, 281
dynamic proxies, 325

E

eager evaluation, 264
effectively immutable classes, 271
ElementType enum, 154
   TYPE_PARAMETER and TYPE_USE
     values, 155
else clause (if/else statements), 50
   in nested if/else statements, 50
else if clause (if/else statements), 51
empty collections, Collections class methods for, 256
empty statements, 48
encapsulation, 121-128
   access control, 122-126
   data accessor methods, 126
   data hiding and, 121
   nested types and, 155
endianness, 10
<<END_TOKEN syntax for heredocs, 337
enumerated types (see enums)
EnumMap class, 251
enums, 99, 151
   special characteristics of, 152
EnumSet class, 242
$ENV variable (Nashorn), 337

equality operator (==), 28, 38
   (see also = (equals sign), in Symbols
     section)
   comparing reference types, 87
equality operators, 38
equals()
   Arrays class, 87
   Object class, 181
   testing two nonidentical objects for
     equality, 87
$ERR variable (Nashorn), 337
Error class, 70, 193
error messages, 193
escape sequences
   in char literals, 24
   in string literals, 25, 75
   Unicode characters, 19
evacuating collectors, 202
evacuation, 202
eval(), 340
evaluation of expressions
   lazy evaluation, 263
   shortcutting, 39
@exception doc-comment tag, 229
Exception class, 193
   constructors, implementation of, 194
exception handlers, 60
exception handling, antipatterns to avoid,
  194
exceptions, 193
   advantages/disadvantages of using,
    193
   checked, 68
   checked and unchecked, 70
     working with checked exceptions,
      71
   designing, guidelines for, 194
   Exception class, 70
   JavaScript, 346
   subclasses of Error, 193
   sublcasses of Exception, 193
   thread exiting by throwing, 217
   throwing, 60
exclusion, 212
$EXEC() function (Nashorn), 337
exec() method, Runtime class, 235
ExecutorService, 344
exp(), 279
exponential notation, 27

expression statements, 48
expressions, 30
    array creation, 79
    following return statements, 59
    in assert statements, 64
    in for loops, 55
    in if statements, 50
    in switch statements, 52
    in synchronize statements, 60
    in throw statements, 60
    in while statements, 54
    initialization expressions for class fields, 109
    operators and, 30-46
    statements versus, 46
extending interfaces, 137
extends clause
    in interface definitions, 137
    superclass specified in, 112
extends keyword, 99, 111
    expressing type covariance, 148
    for container types acting as producers of types, 148
    in bounded wildcards, 148
extensions
    extension classloader, 319
    standard, to the Java platform, 89, 236

F

\f (form feed) escape sequence, 24
false reserved word, 21
fields, 18, 100
    access control and inheritance, 125
    accessible to a local class, 165
    accessing and manipulating with method handles, 328
    class, 102
        initialization, 109
    declaration syntax, 101
    default values and initializers, 108
    inheritance of, 112
    instance, 103
    interface, 137
    modifiers, 133
    naming conventions for, 224
    subclass, initialization of, 113
    superclass, hiding, 115
File class, 90, 289
    interaction between Path and File objects, 297
    methods, summary of, 290
file handling and I/O
    async I/O
        AsynchronousFileChannel, 301
        callback-based style, 302
        Future-based style, 301
        watch services and directory searching, 303
    classic Java I/O, 289
        File class methods, 290
        problems with, 294
        readers and writers, 292
        streams, 291
    modern Java I/O, 295
        Files class methods, 295
        NIO API in Java 7, 295
        Path interface, 296
    networking, 304-309
    NIO channels and buffers, 298
        ByteBuffer, 298
        channels, 300
        mapped byte buffers, 300
    try-with-resources, 293
FileChannel class, 300
FileInputStream class, 291
filenames, hardcoded, 236
FileOutputStream class, 291
FileReader class, 292
files, 289
    (see also file handling and I/O)
    Java file structure, 93
Files class, 295
    bridge methods to older I/O APIs, 297
    find() method, 303
    walk() method, 303
FileSystem class, 298
FileVisitor interface, 304
filter(), 174
    Predicate interface, 259
FilterInputStream class, 293
final modifier, 211
    and local classes, 164
    class fields, 102
    classes, 100, 112
    fields, 101
    in variable declaration statements, 49
    interface fields, 137

methods, 69
  summary of use, 133
finalization, 206
finalizer method, 206
finally clause (try/catch/finally), 63
first-in, first-out (FIFO) queues, 252
flatMap(), 264
floating-point numbers, 276-278
  BigDecimal class, 278
floating-point types, 26
  conversions, 28
    using casts, 29
  division by zero, 36
  Double class, 28
  double type, 26
    return type for operators, 35
  Float class, 28
  float type, 26
    return type for operators, 35
  floating-point arithmetic, 28, 36
  floating-point literals, 27
  strictfp modifier for methods, 69
  testing if value is Nan, 38
  wrapper classes, 28
floor(), 279
flow-control statements, 46
fold operations, 261
for each in loops, 345
for statements, 55
  break statement in, 58
  comparison operators in, 38
  continue statement in, 59
  initialize, test, and update expressions
    in, 55
  interating arrays, 81
  iterating lists, 246
foreach statements, 56
  iterating arrays, 81
  iterating lists, 245
  limitations of, 57
  syntax, 246
forEach(), 260
format()
  Formatter class, 237
  String class, 71
Formatter class, 237
frequently asked questions about Java, 9
function types, Java and, 174
functional programming, 173, 259

Java support for slightly functional
  programming, 174
functional programming languages, 76
@FunctionalInterface annotation, 153,
  173
functions
  compose() method of Function class,
    185
  JavaScript
    and lambda expressions, 344
    strict mode, 334
    Nashorn helper functions, 338
Future interface, interactions with asynchronous channels, 301

G

G1 (Garbage First) collector, 205
garbage collection, 197
  evacuation and evacuating collectors,
    202
  mark and sweep algorithm, 199
  of objects in the heap, 204
  optimization by the JVM, 201
garbage collectors, 204
  (see also garbage collection; HotSpot
    JVM)
  Concurrent Mark and Sweep (CMS),
    205
  other than HotSpot, 204
Garbage First collector (G1), 205
generational garbage collector, 202
generations, 201
generic methods, 66, 149
generic types, 142-151
  and type parameters, 144
  creating an instance of, using diamond
    syntax, 145
  declaring, 143
  type erasure, 145
  using and designing, 150
    compile and runtime typing, 150
  wildcards for unknown type, 146
get and set methods, 127
GET method (HTTP), 305
get(), Future interface, 301
getClass(), Object class, 311
getId(), Thread class, 215

getName() and setName(), Thread class, 216

getPriority() and setPriority(), Thread class, 215

getState(), Thread class, 216

global methods or functions, class methods as, 103

global variables
in Nashorn, 336
public static fields as, 102

Graceful Completion pattern, 215

greater than operator (>), 39
(see also < > (angle brackets), in Symbols section)

greater than or equal to operator (>=), 39

H

handling common data formats (see data formats (common), handling)

hash tables, memory leaks from, 198

hashCode()
Object class, 181
String class, 270

HashMap class, 251

HashSet class, 242

Hashtable class, 252

hasNext(), Interator, 247

HEAD method (HTTP), 305

heap
HotSpot JVM, 203
sharing by application threads, 210

heredocs, 337

HotSpot JVM, 198
collecting the old generation, 204
heap, 203
JIT compilers, 353
optimization of garbage collection, 202

HTTP, 304
implementing a client on a TCP socket, 306
implementing on server side, 307
redirects, 306
request methods, 305

HttpURLConnection class, 306

I

I/O (input/output), 289-304
async I/O, 301
callback-based style, 302
Future-based interactions with async channels, 301
watch services and directory searching, 303
classic Java I/O, 289
File class methods, 290
problems with, 294
readers and writers, 292
streams, 291
try-with-resources, 293
interruptable, 216
modern Java I/O, 295
Files class, methods of, 295
Path interface, 296
networking, 304-309
NIO channels and buffers, 298
ByteBuffer, 298
channels, 300
mapped byte buffers, 300

identifiers, 21
characters allowed in, 225
method names, 67

IdentityHashMap class, 252

IEEE-754 floating-point arithmetic standard, 277

if statements, 50

if/else statements, 50
conditional operator (? :) as version of, 44
else clause, 50
else if clause, 51
nested, 50

immutability of strings, 269
hash codes and effective immutability, 270

implementation-specific code, 236

implements clause, 138

implements keyword, 99

import declarations, 18, 90
causing naming conflicts and shadowing, 91
importing static member types, 158
on-demand imports, 91
single type imports, 90

import static declarations, 92
   static member imports and overloaded
     methods, 93
increment operator (++), 37
   (see also + (plus sign), in Symbols sec-
     tion)
   side effect of, 35
indexes
   array, 77
     too small or too large, 81
   list, 244
infinite loops
   creating with syntax while(true), 54
   writing with for(;;), 56
infinite streams, 263
infinity
   modulo operator (%) and, 37
   positive and negative, 27
   positive infinity, division by zero in
     floating-point arithmetic, 36
inheritance, 110, 131
   (see also subclasses and inheritance)
   access control and, 125
   between container types and their pay-
     load types, 148
   composition versus, 187
   field inheritance and accessors, 189
   interfaces, 137
   nonstatic member classes, 162
@inheritDoc doc-comment tag, 232
@Inherited meta-annotation, 155
initialization, 315
initialize expressions (for loops), 55
initializers
   array, 79
   defining a constructor, 106
   defining multiple constructors, 107
   field, 101
   field defaults and, 108
   in variable declarations, 49
   instance initializers, 110
   invoking one constructor from
     another, 107
   static initializer, 109
   subclass constructors, 113
inline command execution (jjs), 336
inline doc-comment tags, 231
inner classes, 155
   (see also nested types)

representation of functions via, 173
InputStream class, 291
InputStreamReader class, 292
instance fields, 103
   class methods and, 103
   default values, 108
instance initializers, 110
instance methods, 104
   choosing between class methods and,
     185
   class methods and, 103
   overridden, 118
   this reference, how it works, 105
instanceof operator, 32, 44, 181
   testing for RamdomAccess, 248
instances
   constructed reflexively, 320
   finalizers acting on, 208
Instant class, 281
int type, 25, 276
   32-bit int values, 26
   conversions to other primitive types,
     28
   Integer class, 26
   return type for operators, 35
integer types, 25, 275
   conversions, 28
   integer arithmetic, 26, 36
   integer literals, 25
   wrapper classes, 26
interface keyword, 136
interfaces, 97, 136-142
   @FunctionalInterface annotation, 153
   constants in definitions, 183
   conversion of lambda expressions to,
     172
   default methods, 140
     implementation of, 141
   defined, 99
   defining, 136
   extending, 137
   following implements keyword in class
     definitions, 99
   implementing an interface, 138
   implementing multiple interfaces, 139
   marker, 141
   modifiers, 133
   naming conventions for, 224

Nashorn JavaScript implementation of, 346
partial implementations, with proxies, 325
static member interface, defining and using, 157
static member types nested in, 158
versus abstract classes, 184
interpreted languages, Java and, 10
interpreters
implementation for other languages in Java, 11
JVM and, 10
interrupt(), Thread class, 216
IntStream class, 263
invokedynamic bytecode, 326
IOException objects, 71
IP (Internet Protocol), 308
IPv4 and IPv6, 308
irrational numbers, 277
isAlive(), Thread class, 216
isDone(), Future interface, 301
isJavaIdentifierPart(): Character, 21
isJavaIdentifierStart(): Character, 21
isNan()
Double class, 38
Float class, 38
Iterable interface, 240, 246, 247
iteration, 245
Iterator interface, 240, 247
implementation as a member class, 159
Iterator object, 246
foreach loop and, 57
iterator(), List, 248

J

JAR (Java archive) files, 95
manipulating as a FileSystem, 298
jar utility, 353
Java
brief history of, 7
calling from Nashorn, 342
comparing to other languages, 11
criticisms of, 13
overly corporate, 15
performance problems, 14
security, 15
slowness to change, 14
verbosity of Java, 13
security (see security)
Java 7
async I/O, 301
Method Handles API, 326
NIO.2 API, 295
Java 8, 11
@FunctionalInterface annotation, 153
Collections libraries, new methods for, 265
Date and Time API, 280-286
adjusters, 285
example of use, 282
java.time package and subpackages, 281
temporal queries, 284
timestamps, 281
default methods in interfaces, 140
lamdba expressions, 76, 171-174
Nashorn, 331-348
optional methods in interfaces, 136
profiles, 367-372
radical changes in, 5
security problems, 11
Streams API, 262-266
Java bytecode, 5
java command, 94, 351
-client or -server switch, 353
common switches, 352
Java ecosystem, 7
Java interpreter, 94
(see also java command)
running, 94
Java language, 4
syntax, 17-95
arrays, 77-84
case sensitivity and whitespace, 19
classes and objects, 72, 77
comments, 19
defining and running Java programs, 94
expressions and operators, 30-46
identifiers, 21
Java file structure, 93
literals, 21
methods, 66-72
packages and the Java namespace, 88, 93

primitive data types, 22-28
primitive type conversions, 28
punctuation, 22
reserved words, 20
statements, 46-65
Unicode character set, 18
Java Language Specification (JLS), 5
java object, 342
Java platform
backwards compatibility, 140
command-line tools, 349-362
graphical tool, VisualVM, 362-367
Java programming
conventions for portable programs, 235
documentation comments, 226-235
naming and capitalization conventions, 223-226
Java programming environment, 3-15
Java language, 4
JVM (Java Virtual Machine), 5
Java programs
contents of, 18
defining and running, 94
lexical structure, 18
lifecycle of, 9
Java SE, 367
java., package names beginning with, 88
java.awt.List, 91
java.awt.peer package, 236
java.io.IOException objects, 71
java.io.ObjectInputStream class, 74
java.io.ObjectStreamConstants, 183
java.io.PrintStream, 187
java.lang package, 90
annotations in, 153
java.lang.annotation.Annotation, 153
java.lang.Cloneable, 182
(see also Cloneable interface)
java.lang.Comparable (see Comparable interface)
java.lang.Enum, 152
java.lang.Error, 193
java.lang.Exception, 193
java.lang.Iterable, 247
java.lang.Object class, 77, 112
(see also Object class)
java.lang.reflect, 71
java.lang.Throwable, 193

java.lang.UnsupportedOperationException, 185
java.net package, 304
java.nio.channels package, 300
java.nio.file package, 295, 304
java.time package, 281
java.time.chrono package, 281
java.time.format package, 281
java.time.temporal package, 281
java.time.zone package, 281
Java.type(), 343
java.util package
Map interface implementations, 251
Set implementations, 242
java.util.AbstractList, 184
java.util.Arrays class, 82
java.util.concurrent, 209, 242
Map implementations, 251
java.util.Formatter, 237
java.util.function package, 259
interfaces, 265
java.util.function.Function, 185
java.util.Iterator, 247
java.util.Iterator interface, 159
java.util.List, 91, 184
java.util.RandomAccess, 142
java.util.regex package, 272
java.util.stream package, 263
javac, 9, 350
-g switch, 351
-source and -target options, 351
and @deprecated doc-comment tag, 230
class initialization method, generation of, 109
code generated for a constructor, 108
common switches, 350
compilation and, 10
compile-time typing, 150
constructor chaining and the default constructor, 114
creation of bytecode that uses virtual method lookup, 119
field initialization code, generation of, 108
lint capability, 351
nested types, treatment of, 169
JavaClass object, 343
javadoc, 20, 355

common switches, 355
doc-comment tags recognized by, 228
inline doc-comment tags, 231
version information in its documentation, 229
javap disassembler, 169, 361
JavaPackage object, 343
JavaScript, 331
  (see also Nashorn)
  Java compared to, 12
javaw command, 353
javax., package names beginning with, 89
javax.net package, 304
javax.script, 340-342
  key classes and interfaces, 341
  with Nashorn, 340
jdeps tool, 356
jinfo tool, 359
JIT compilation, 10
JIT compilers
  HotSpot JVM, 353
jjs (Nashorn shell), 333
  executing JavaScript, 333
  jjs command and options, 334
  scripting with, 335
    comments, 335
    inline command execution, 336
    inline documents, 337
    shebang syntax for starting scripts, 339
    special variables, 336
    string interpolation, 336
JLS (Java Language Specification), 5
jmap tool, 360
join()
  Thread class, 216
jps tool, 357
jrunscript, 333
jstack tool, 360
jstat tool, 358
jstatd tool, 358
JVisualVM (see VisualVM)
JVMs (Java Virtual Machines), 3
  as interpreters, 10
  defined, 5
  non-Java languages on, 331
  other languages running on, 11
  restrictions on, 317
  runtime typing, 150

security checks implemented by, 316

K

Kanjii character (in Java identifier), 21
KISS principle, 308

L

labeled statements, 48
  following break statement, 58
lambda expressions, 46, 67, 76, 171-174
  conversion by javac to interface type, 172
  defined, 76
  functional programming with, 173
  in Java Collections, 258-266
    filters, 259
    forEach, 260
    maps, 260
    reduce, 261
    regular expressions and, 274
    Streams API, 262, 266
  JavaScript functions and, 344
  method references, 173
last in, first-out (LIFO) queues, 252
Latin-1 character set, 19
  escaping in char literals, 24
lazy evaluation, 264
left shift operator (<<), 42
length of arrays, 77, 79
  length field, 77
less than operator (<), 39
less than or equal to operator (<=), 39
lexical scoping, 165
  (see also scope)
lexical structure of Java programs, 18
libraries, third-party, 7
life expectancy of objects (generations), 201
line separators, 237
@link doc-comment tag, 228, 231, 233
linked lists, iterating through, using for loop, 56
LinkedHashMap class, 252
LinkedHashSet class, 242
LinkedList class, 184, 248
  implementing Queue, 255
LinkOption class, 296

@linkplain doc-comment tag, 232, 233
List interface, 240, 244
    foreach loops and iteration, 245
    general-purpose implementations, 248
    methods, 244
lists
    generic, List<E> type, 144
    iterating through using foreach loop, 57
    java.util.List and java.awt.List classes, 89, 91
    java.util.List and java.util.AbstractList, 184
    random access to, 248
    storing primitive values in, 88
@literal doc-comment tag, 232
literals, 21
    in expressions, 30
live objects, 199
loadClass(), 317
local classes, 156, 162-167
    defining and using, 163
    features of, 164
    implementation, 170
    lexical scoping and local variables, 166
    naming convention for, 170
    restrictions on, 164
    scope of, 164
local variable declaration statements, 48
local variables, 48
    (see also variables)
    lexical scoping and, 165
    naming conventions for, 225
LocalDate class, 282, 283
locks, 214
    basic facts about, 218
log(), 279
log10(), 279
logical operators, 39
long type, 25, 53, 276
    64-bit long values, 26
    conversions between char values and, 29
    Long class, 26
    return type for operators, 35
Lookup object, 327
looping
    for statements, 55
    while statement, 54

low-pause applications, 205

M

main(), 61, 94
MalformedURLException, 71
Map interface, 239, 249
    computeIfAbsent() method, 266
    forEach() method, 265
    getOrDefault() method, 265
    implementations, 251
    remove(), replace() and putIfAbsent() methods, 265
    support for collection views, 249
map(), 173, 260
map, defined, 249
Map.Entry interface, 249
MappedByteBuffer class, 300
maps
    Bindings interface, 342
    Function interface, 260
mark and sweep algorithm for garbage collection, 199
    Concurrent Mark and Sweep (CMS) collector, 205
    HotSpot JVM, 204
marker interfaces, 141
Matcher class, 272
Math class, 278-280
    on-demand static import, 92
    static methods for rounding, 29
mathematical functions, 278-280
max(), 279
MAX_VALUE constant
    Float and Double classes, 28
    integer type wrapper classes, 26
member classes (see nonstatic member classes)
members, 98
    access to, 122-126
    common kinds of, 98
    fields and methods, 100
        class fields, 102
        class methods, 103
        field declarations, 101
        instance fields, 103
        instance methods, 104
    interface, restrictions on, 137
    nested types as, 155

nonstatic member classes, 159
static member types, 156-159
memory
    approach to, in Java, 317
    required by primitive and reference types, 85
memory and concurrency, 197-220
    finalization, 206
    HotSpot JVM, heap, 203
    Java support for concurrency, 208
    JVM's optimization of garbage collection, 201
    mark and sweep garbage collection, 199
    memory leaks in Java, 198
    memory management, basic concepts, 197
    safety of multithreaded programs, 212
    visibility and mutability of Java objects, 210
meta-annotations, 154
    (see also annotations)
metacharacters in regular expressions, 272
    summary of, 273
method body, 66
method handles, 326-329
    invoking, 328
    method lookup queries, 327
    MethodHandle class and subclasses, 328
    MethodType class, 326
method invocation operator (( )), 35, 45
Method object, 321
    reflexive invocation with, 322
method overloading, 67
    static member imports and, 93
method references, 173
    as lamdba expressions, 260
method signature, 66
MethodHandles.lookup(), 327
methods, 18, 66-72
    abstract, 128-132
    access control and inheritance, 125
    annotations, 153
    arguments passed to, primitive and reference types, 86
    checked and unchecked exceptions, 70

working with checked exceptions, 71
class, 103, 105
    use of class fields and methods, 103
class initialization, 109
class versus instance methods, 185
default, 140-141
defining, 66
generic, 149
implementation by classes implementing interfaces, 138
inheritance through subclassing, 112
instance, 104
    this reference, how it works, 105
interface, 136
    static methods, 137
modifiers, 68, 133
naming conventions for, 224
native, 235
non-public, treatment in reflection, 323
overriding, 117-120
    hiding versus overriding, 118
    invoking an overridden method, 119
    virtual method lookup, 119
parameter list, 68
synchronized, 60, 213
variable-length argument lists, 71
void, 59
min(), 279
MIN_VALUE constant
    Float and Double classes, 28
    integer type wrapper classes, 26
modifiers
    access, 69
    anonymous classes, 168
    class, 99
    field, 101
    local classes, 164
    method, 67, 68
    summary of, 132
modulo operator (%), 36
    (see also % (percent sign), in Symbols section)
monitors, 214
    basic facts about, 218
multidimensional arrays, 82
multiline strings, 337

multiplexed I/O, 302
multiplication operator (*), 36
    (see also * (asterisk), in Symbols section)
multithreaded programming
    Java support for, 208
    safety of programs, 212
    synchronize statement, 59
mutability, 174
    of objects, 177, 211

N

\n (newlines, escaping), 24
names
    characters used in, 225
    guidelines for choosing good names, 225
    of class fields, 102
    of methods, 67
    of static member types, 158
    of threads, 216
    package-naming rules, 89
namespaces, 88-93
    globally unique package names, 89
    importing static members, 92
    importing types, 90
    static member types nested in, 156
naming conflicts, 91
naming conventions, 223
    for four kinds of nested types, 169
NaN (Not-a-number), 27
    equality tests of, 38
    floating-point calculations, division by zero, 36
    modulo operator (%) and, 37
narrowing conversions, 28
Nashorn, 331-348
    and javax.script, 340-342
        running JavaScript from Java, 340
    calling Java from, 342
        JavaClass and JavaPackage, 342
        JavaScript functions and Java lambda expressions, 344
    executing JavaScript with, 332
        running from the command line, 333
        scripting with jjs, 335-340
        using the Nashorn shell, 333

        function as anonymous implementation of Java interface, 346
    JavaScript language extensions, 345
        foreach loops, 345
        multiple catch clauses, 346
        single expression functions, 345
    on the JVM, 332
    purposes within Java and JVM ecosystem, 332
native methods, 69, 235
native modifier, 133
negative infinity, 27
negative zero, 27
NEGATIVE_INFINITY constant, Float and Double classes, 28
nested types, 155
    anonymous classes, 167-168
    how they work, 169
        local and anonymous class implementation, 170
        nonstatic member class implementation, 170
    local classes, 162-167
    nonstatic member classes, 159-162
    static member types, 156-159
networking, 304-309
    HTTP, 304
    TCP, 306
New I/O (NIO) API (see NIO API)
new operator, 32, 35, 46
    creating arrays, 79, 83
    creating new objects, 74, 106
next(), Iterator, 247
NIO (New I/O) API, 298
nominal typing, 142
nonstatic member classes, 159
    features of, 160
    implementation, 170
    naming convention for, 169
    restrictions on, 161
    scope versus inheritance, 162
    syntax for, 161
not equals operator (!=), 39
    (see also ! (exclamation point), in Symbols section)
NOT operator
    bitwise NOT (~), 41
    boolean NOT (!), 40
Not-a-number (see NaN)

notify(), 218
notifyAll(), 219
@NotNull annotation, 155
null references, 76
    instanceof operator and, 181
null reserved word, 21
null values (in JavaScript), 344
numbers, 275-278
    floating-point, 276
    integer types, 275

O

Object class, 77, 112, 131
    constructor chaining and, 114
    dependencies of, 315
    getClass(), 311
    important methods, 178-183
        class that overrides, 179
        clone(), 182
        hashCode(), 181
        toString(), 180
    notify(), 218
    wait(), 218
object literals, 74
object member access operator (.), 45
object references, 317
object-oriented design, 177-196
    composition versus inheritance, 187
    constants, 183
    exceptions and exception handling,
        193
    field inheritance and accessors, 189
    important   methods   of
        java.lang.Object, 178-183
    instance methods or class methods,
        choosing, 185
    interfaces versus abstract classes, 184
    safe programming in Java, 195
    singleton pattern, 191
object-oriented programming, 97-134
    abstract classes and methods, 128-132
    classes, 97-100
    creating and initializing objects,
        106-110
    different meanings in different lan-
        guages, 97
    fields and methods, 100-105
    modifiers, summary of, 132

subclasses and inheritance, 110-120
ObjectInputStream class, 74, 183
ObjectOutputStream class, 183
objects
    arrays as, 77, 258
    as operand type, 38, 44
    comparing, 87
    contents of versus references to, 178
    conversions between reference types,
        131
    creating, 73
    creating and initializing, 106-110
        defining a constructor, 106
        defining multiple constructors, 107
        field defaults and initializers, 108
        invoking one constructor from
            another, 107
    creating Java object from Nashorn, 343
    creation with new operator, 46
    defined, 98
    in the heap, 204
    longer-lived garbage collection by
        HotSpot JVM, 204
    manipulating objects and reference
        copies, 85
    members of both a class type and
        interface type, 138
    memory requirements for storing, 85
    using, 74
        object literals, 74
    visibility and mutability, 211
ObjectStreamsConstants interface, 183
OpenJDK, 15
operating systems
    removing threads from a CPU, 212
    scheduler, 208
operators, 22, 30-46
    arithmetic, 36
    assignment, 43
    associativity, 31
    bitwise and shift, 41
    Boolean (or logical) operators, 39
    comparison, 38
    conditional operator, 44
    in statements, 46
    increment and decrement, 37
    instanceof, 44
    operand number and type, 34
    order of evaluation, 35

precedence of, 31
return type, 35
side effects of, 35
special (language constructs), 45
summary of Java operators, 32
optimization of garbage collection (JVM), 201
OPTIONS method (HTTP), 305
or(), Predicate interface, 259
Oracle Corporation, 4
  control of package names beginning with java, javax, and sun, 89
$OUT variable (Nashorn), 337
OutputStream class, 291
overloading methods
  static member imports and, 93
@Override annotation, 152, 179
overriding methods, 117-120
  inherited methods, 98
  invoking an overridden method, 119
  overriding is not hiding, 118
  virtual method lookup, 119

P

package access, 122, 126
package declarations, 18
package keyword, 89
packages, 88-93
  access to, 122
  access to, from Nashorn, 343
  declarations, 89
  doc comments for, 234
  globally unique names, 89
  importing static members, 92
  importing types, 90
  naming conventions for, 223
parallel collectors, 204
@param doc-comment tag, 229
parameterized types, 144
  (see also generic types)
parameters, naming conventions for, 224
pass by reference, 178
pass-by-value semantics in Java, 317
Path interface, 296
Paths class, 297
Pattern class, 272
  asPredicate() method, 274
pauses for GC

CMS collector, 205
G1 collector, 205
  stop-the-world (STW) pause, 201
per-thread allocation, 203
performance
  criticisms of Java performance, 14
  garbage collection and, 205
PHP, 10
  comparison to Java, 12
PipedInputStream class, 293
PipedReader class, 293
pointers
  in C/C++ and assembly, 317
  references represented in JVM as, 317
portable programs, 235
positive infinity, 27, 36
positive zero, 27
POSITIVE_INFINITY constant, Float and Double classes, 28
POST method (HTTP), 305
post-decrement operator (--), 38
  (see also - (minus sign), in Symbols section)
post-increment operator (++), 37
  (see also + (plus sign), in Symbols section)
Postel's Law, 308
pow(), 279
pre-decrement operator (--), 38
  (see also - (minus sign), in Symbols section)
pre-increment operator (++), 37
  (see also + (plus sign), in Symbols section)
precedence, operator, 31
Predicate interface, 259
  converting regex to a Predicate, 274
primary expressions, 30
primitive specializations of the Stream class, 263
primitive types, 22
  arrays of, 132
  boolean, 23
  boxing and unboxing conversions, 88
  char, 23
  class objects for, 312
  conversion of arguments by method handles, 328
  conversions, 28

summary of, 29
conversions to strings, 37
equals operator (==), testing operand values, 38
floating-point types, 26
integer types, 25
JavaScript equivalents of, 341
reference types versus, 84, 86
streams of, 263
wrapper classes, 87
primitive values, 317
references versus, 177
primordial classloader, 318
printf(), 71
%n format string, 237
println(), 67, 187, 268
line separators and, 237
out.println() instead of System.out.println(), 92
PrintStream class, 187
priority queues, 253
PriorityQueue class, 255
private modifier, 133
constructors for classes that should never be instantiated, 115
declaring top-level types as private, 158
fields, 101
member access and, 123
member access summary, 125
methods, 69
no inheritance of private fields and methods, 125
private members, static member type access to, 158
rules of thumb for using, 126
processes
listing active JVM processes with jps, 357
threads and, 208
Producer Extends, Consumer Super (PECS) principle, 149
profiles, 367-372
Compact Profiles, 368
Compact 2, additional packages, 370
Compact 3, additional packages, 371
purpose of, 368

requirements for, 367
Properties class, 252
protected modifier, 133
and inheritance of state, 191
declaring top-level types as protected, 158
fields, 101
inheritance of protected fields and methods, 125
member access and, 123
member access summary, 125
methods, 69
rules of thumb for using, 126
proxies, dynamic, 325
use cases, 325
pseudorandom number generator (PRNG), 280
public modifier, 133
classes, constructors and, 115
fields, 101
inheritance of public instance fields and methods, 125
interface members and, 137
member access and, 123
member access summary, 125
methods, 69
rules of thumb for using, 126
punctuation characters as tokens, 22
PUT method (HTTP), 305

Q

queries, temporal, 284
Queue interface, 240
queues
adding elements to, 253
defined, 252
failure of operations on, dealing with, 254
insertion order, 252
querying, 254
Queue and BlockingQueue interfaces, 252
adding elements, methods for, 253
implementations, 255
removing elements, methods for, 254
safe for multithreaded use, 219

R

\r (carriage return) escape sequence, 24
Random class, 280
RandomAccess interface, 142, 248
raw types, 145
reachable objects, 199
read-only collections, 255
Reader and Writer classes, 292
rectangular arrays, 84
reduce idiom, 261
reduce(), 174, 261
    example of use, 264
reentrant locks, 218
reference types, 18, 84-88
    array types, 77
    as operand type, 44
    boxing and unboxing conversions, 87
    classes, 98
    comparing objects, 87
    conversions, 131
    generic type parameters, 144
    interfaces, 99, 135-142
    manipulating objects and reference
        copies, 85
    naming conventions, 224
    null, 76
    operands of, testing with == operator,
        38
    primitive types versus, 84
    versus pointers in C/C++, 85
references versus object contents, 178
reflection, 320
    combining with custom classloading
        to inspect a class file, 324
    creation of dynamic proxies, 325
    how to use, 321
        Method object, 321
    Method Handles API versus Reflection
        API, 327
    problems with Reflection API, 323
    when to use, 321
Reflection API, 71
regular expressions, 271-275, 292
    accessing Java's builtin support of
        from jjs, 334
    classes for, 272
    metacharacters, 272
relational operators, 38

summary of, 39
reserved words, 20
resume(), Thread class, 218
@Retention meta-annotation, 154
RetentionPolicy enum, 154
@return doc-comment tag, 229
return statements, 59, 63, 67
    stopping switch statements, 53
return types
    class methods, 103
    for operators, 35
    of overriding methods, 117
    specified by type in method signature,
        67
right shift operators, 42
rounding numbers, 277
    floating-point values when converting
        to integers, 29
run(), Thread class, 216
run-until-shutdown pattern, 215
runtime environment (see JVMs (Java
    Virtual Machines))
runtime typing, 150
runtime, implementation for other lan-
    guages in Java, 11
runtime-managed concurrency, 208
Runtime.exec(), 235
Runtime::addShutdownHook, 208
RuntimeException, 70, 230

S

safe Java programming, 195
    safety of multithreaded programs, 212
@SafeVarargs annotation, 153
scheduler (operating system), 208
scientific notation, 27
scope
    containment hierarchy for nonstatic
        member classes, 162
    lexical scoping and local variables, 165
    of a local class, 164
    of local variables, 49
ScriptEngine, 340
    get() and put() methods, 341
ScriptEngine class, 342
ScriptEngineManager, 340, 341
ScriptObjectMirror, 342
security, 11

criticisms of Java security, 15
secure programming and classloading, 315
vulnerabiities connected to Java graphical clients, 368
@see doc-comment tag, 230, 233
SelectableChannel class, 303
Selector class, 303
separators, 22
@serial doc-comment tag, 230
@serialData doc-comment tag, 231
@serialField doc-comment tag, 231
Serializable interface, 77
   as a marker interface, 142
   Collections interfaces and, 242
ServerSocket class, 306
Set interface, 240, 242
   implementations, summary of, 242
   methods, 242
set, defined, 242
setDaemon(), Thread class, 216
setUncaughtExceptionHandler(), Thread class, 217
shebang syntax, 339
shift operators, 42
short type, 25, 35, 276
   conversions to other primitive types, 28
   Short class, 26
shutdown(), 215
side effects
   expressions having, 47
   of operators, 35
signature of a class, 98
signature of a method, 66
@since doc-comment tag, 230
single abstract method (SAM) type, 172
single expression functions, 345
singleton pattern, 191
singletons, Collections class methods for, 256
sleep() method, Thread class, 210
slowness of Java to change, 14
Socket class, 306
sockets, asynchronous, 301
sort()
   as a default method, 141
   static member imports and, 93
SortedMap interface, 252

SortedSet interface, 243
special operators (language constructs), 45
Stack class, 248
stacks, 252
StandardCopyOption enum, 296
StandardOpenOption enum, 298
standards bodies, packages named for, 89
start(), Thread class, 216
statements, 18, 46-65
   assert, 64
   break, 58
   compound, 48
   continue, 58
   defined by Java, summary of, 46
   do/while, 54
   empty, 48
   expression statements, 47
   for, 55
   foreach, 56
   if/else, 50
   labeled, 48
   local variable declaration, 48
   return, 59
   switch, 52
   synchronized, 60
   throw, 60
   try-with-resources, 63
   try/catch/finally, 61-63
   versus expressions, 46
   while, 54
statements section, synchronize statement, 60
static methods, 69
static modifier, 134
   class fields, 102
   class methods, 103
   fields, 101
   final modifier and, 101
   instance fields, 103
   interface fields, 137
   interface methods, 137
   members of local classes and, 164
   members of nonstatic member classes and, 161
   methods, 186
   static initializers, 109
   static member types, 155, 169
      basic properties of, 156

defining and using, 157
features of, 158
stop(), Thread class, 217
stop-the-world (STW) pause for garbage
collection, 201
CMS collector and, 205
stream(), 262
generation of Stream object from collections, 262
streams, 291
Reader and Writer classes for, 292
Streams API, 262, 283
Stream class, 262
lazy evaluation, 263
primitive specializations of, 263
utility default methods, 265
strict mode (JavaScript), 334
strictfp modifier, 69, 100, 134, 277
String class
hashCode() method, 270
valueOf() method, 268
string concatenation operator (+), 37, 75,
269
(see also + (plus sign), in Symbols section)
string interpolation (in jjs), 336
string literals, 75
StringBuffer class, 270
StringBuilder class, 269
strings, 25, 267-271
conversions for all primitive types, 37
converting to integer values, 26
immutability, 269
multiline, 337
Object.toString() method, 180
special syntax for, 267
string concatenation, 269
string literals, 268
toString(), 268
String class, 25, 75, 89
final class, 112
subclasses and inheritance, 110-120
access control and inheritance, 125
constructor chaining and default constructor, 114
extending a class, 111
hiding superclass fields, 115
overriding   superclass   methods,
117-120

superclasses, Object, and the class
hierarchy, 112
subclass constructors, 113
subList(), List interface, 244, 248
subtraction operator (-), 36
(see also - (minus sign), in Symbols
section)
subtyping relationships between generic
types, unknown type and, 147
sun.misc.Unsafe class, 235
super keyword, 114
expressing type contravariance, 148
for container types purely as consumers of instances of a type, 148
using to invoke overridden methods,
119
using to refer to superclass fields, 116
super(), 114
called by javac compiler, 114
superclasses, 112, 131
(see also subclasses and inheritance)
hiding superclass fields, 115
superinterfaces, 137
@SuppressWarnings annotation, 153
surrogate pairs (Unicode supplementary
characters), 25
survivor space, 203
suspend(), Thread class, 217
switch statements, 52
case labels, 53
data type of expression in, 52
default: label, 53
restrictions on, 53
switches for command-line tools, 349
symbolic links (symlinks), 296
synchronization
of collections, 255
of threads, 218
synchronized keyword, 60, 134, 213
synchronized methods, 69
collection implementations in java.util
and, 255
synchronized statements, 59
system classes, 236
System.arraycopy(), 82, 257
System.exit(), 63
System.getenv(), 235
System.identityHashCode(), 181
System.in, 291

InputStreamReader class applied to, 292

System.out, 291

System.out.printf(), 71

System.out.println(), 67, 92, 187
in a lambda expression, 260

T

\t (tab), 24

\<T\> (type parameters), 144

@Target meta-annotation, 154

TCP, 306
HTTP client on a TCP socket, 306
Java classes for, 306
Postel's Law for communications over, 308

Temporal class, 285

TemporalAdjuster interface, 285

TemporalQuery interface, 284
direct or indirect use of Temporal-Query object, 285

tenuring threshold, 203

ternary operator (see ? : (conditional) operator, in Symbols section)

test expressions (for loops), 55

testing, use of reflection in, 321

text, 267-275
pattern matching with regular expressions, 271-275
strings, 267-271
immutability of, 269
String class, 267
string concatenation, 269
string literals, 268
toString(), 268

third-party libraries and components, 7

this keyword
explicitly referring to the container of the this object, 161
how the reference works, 105
reference to object through which instance methods are invoked, 104
referring to hidden fields, 116
using in invoking one constructor from another, 107

Thread class
deprecated methods, 217
useful methods, 215

thread pool, executing Nashorn JavaScript on, 344

thread-local allocation buffer, 203

Thread.sleep method, 210

Thread.State enum, 209, 216

threads
creating, 208
defined, 208
in synchronized blocks or methods, 214
lifecycle of, 209
monitors and locks, basic facts about, 218

throw statements, 60, 63
methods using to throw checked exceptions, 68
stopping switch statements, 53

Throwable class, 62, 193

Throwable objects, 70

@throws doc-comment tag, 230

throws clause (method signature), 68, 71

Tiered Compilation, 353

timestamps, parts of, 281

toFile(), Path interface, 297

top-level types, 155

toPath(), File class, 297

toString(), 37, 268
Object class, 180
using in string concatenation, 269

TRACE method (HTTP), 305

transient modifier, 134
fields, 102

transient objects, 201

transitive closure of types, 315, 370

Transmission Control Protocol (see TCP)

TreeMap class, 252

TreeSet class, 243

trigonometric functions, 279

true reserved word, 21

try-with-resources statements, 63, 293
AutoCloseable interface, 294
using instead of finalization, 206

try/catch/finally statements, 61-63
catch clause, 62
finally clause, 63
try block syntax, 61
try clause, 62
try/finally, 63

two's complement, 276

TWR statements (see try-with-resources statements)
type annotations, 155
type contravariance, 148
type conversion or casting operator (( )), 46
type covariance, 148
    array convariance, 149
type erasure, 145, 174
type inference, 76
type literals, 75
type parameter constraints, 148
type parameters (<T>), 144
type safety, 195
    of multithreaded code, 212
type signature of a method, 326
type variance, 148

U

unary operators, 34
    associativity, 31
    unary minus (-) operator, 37
unboxing conversions, 88
unchecked exceptions, 70
Unicode, 18
    escaping in char literals, 24
    supplementary characters, 24
unknown type, 146
Unsafe class, 235
UnsupportedOperationException, 185
update expressions (for loops), 55
URIs, 297
URL class, 71, 304
URLClassLoader, loadClass(), 317
URLConnection class, 304
user threads, 216
UTF-8 identifier, 21

V

@value doc-comment tag, 232
    cross-references in, 233
values, 177
    pass by value, 178
    primitives and object references, 177
varargs methods, 71
    @SafeVarargs annotation, 153
variables

accessible to a local class, 165
declaring, 48
    compatibility syntax for C/C++, 78
    initialization of static variables, 315
    local variable declaration statements, 48
    local, lexical scoping and, 165
    naming conventions for, 225
    special variables in Nashorn, 336
    types of values in, 317
Vector class, 248
verbosity of Java, 13
@version doc-comment tag, 229
visibility (of objects), 211
VisualVM, 362-367
void keyword, 59, 67
    problem in reflection, 323
volatile modifier, 134, 215
    fields, 102

W

wait(), 218
watch services, 303
weak generational hypothesis (WGH), 201
WeakHashMap class, 252
while statements, 54
    comparison operators in, 38
    continue statement in, 58
    data type of expression in, 54
    do statements versus, 54
    Iterator object used with, 246
whitespace in Java code, 19
widening conversions, 28, 29
    array types, 77
wildcard types, 146
    bounded wildcards, 148
working set of a program, 201
wrapper collections, 255

X

XOR operator
    bitwise XOR (^), 42
    boolean XOR (^), 40

Z

zero (0)
    division by zero, 36
    positive and negative zero, 27

    represented by float and double types,
        27
    represented by integral types, 275
zero extension, 42

About the Authors

Benjamin J. Evans is the cofounder of jClarity, a startup that delivers performance tools to help development and ops teams. He is an organizer for the LJC (London's JUG) and a member of the JCP Executive Committee, helping define standards for the Java ecosystem. He is a Java Champion; JavaOne Rockstar; coauthor of *The Well-Grounded Java Developer*; and a regular public speaker on the Java platform, performance, concurrency, and related topics. Ben holds a masters degree in mathematics from the University of Cambridge.

David Flanagan is a computer programmer who spends most of his time writing about JavaScript and Java. His books with O'Reilly include *Java in a Nutshell*, *Java Examples in a Nutshell*, *Java Foundation Classes in a Nutshell*, *JavaScript: The Definitive Guide*, and *JavaScript Pocket Reference*. David has a degree in computer science and engineering from the Massachusetts Institute of Technology. He lives with his wife and children in the Pacific Northwest between the cities of Seattle, Washington and Vancouver, British Columbia. David has a blog at *davidflanagan.com*.

Colophon

The animal on the cover of *Java in a Nutshell, Sixth Edition*, is a Javan tiger (*Panthera tigris sondaica*), a subspecies unique to the island of Java. Although this tiger's genetic isolation once presented an unrivaled opportunity to biologists and other researchers, the subspecies has all but disappeared in the wake of human encroachment on its habitat: in a worst-case scenario for the tiger, Java developed into the most densely populated island on Earth, and awareness of the Javan tiger's precarious position apparently came too late to secure the animal's survival even in captivity.

The last confirmed sighting of the tiger occurred in 1976, and it was declared extinct by the World Wildlife Fund in 1994. However, reports of sightings around Meru Betiri National Park in East Java and in the Muria mountain range persist. Camera traps have been used as recently as 2012 in efforts to verify the Javan tiger's continued existence.

Many of the animals on O'Reilly covers are endangered; all of them are important to the world. To learn more about how you can help, go to animals.oreilly.com.

The cover image is a 19th-century engraving from the *Dover Pictorial* Archive. The cover fonts are URW Typewriter and Guardian Sans. The text font is Adobe Minion Pro; the heading font is Adobe Myriad Condensed; and the code font is Dalton Maag's Ubuntu Mono.

Get even more for your money.

Join the O'Reilly Community, and register the O'Reilly books you own. It's free, and you'll get:

- $4.99 ebook upgrade offer
- 40% upgrade offer on O'Reilly print books
- Membership discounts on books and events
- Free lifetime updates to ebooks and videos
- Multiple ebook formats, DRM FREE
- Participation in the O'Reilly community
- Newsletters
- Account management
- 100% Satisfaction Guarantee

Signing up is easy:

1. Go to: oreilly.com/go/register
2. Create an O'Reilly login.
3. Provide your address.
4. Register your books.

Note: English-language books only

To order books online:
oreilly.com/store

For questions about products or an order:
orders@oreilly.com

To sign up to get topic-specific email announcements and/or news about upcoming books, conferences, special offers, and new technologies:
elists@oreilly.com

For technical questions about book content:
booktech@oreilly.com

To submit new book proposals to our editors:
proposals@oreilly.com

O'Reilly books are available in multiple DRM-free ebook formats. For more information:
oreilly.com/ebooks